Naval
Operations
Analysis

Naval Operations Analysis

SECOND EDITION

Prepared by the Operations Analysis Study Group
United States Naval Academy
Annapolis, Maryland

NAVAL INSTITUTE PRESS
Annapolis, Maryland

Dedicated
to the
blending of
mathematical analysis,
military technology,
operational experience,
wisdom and
courage

Preface

This book is written principally for naval officers and prospective naval officers. It addresses the elements of two essential functions required of a commander—making decisions and conducting naval operations. In making important decisions, a commander must rely heavily upon the *experience, judgment* and *technical competence* of himself and his subordinates. He should be aware of the most effective techniques that can be used to provide him with a sound basis for weighing the consequences of his possible courses of action. He should be aware, as well, of the limitations of those on his staff and of the methods used by them to produce answers to questions when uncertainties are present.

In all decision problems, an officer can benefit from a logical approach, not an approach that supersedes sound judgment or automatically guarantees the correct solution, but one that stimulates creative thought processes, leads him to ask the right questions and points toward possible methods of finding the answers. In many problems judgment and experience can be supplemented by a quantitative analysis to provide the best possible basis for decision. This quantitative approach, to analyze problems that are susceptible to such an approach, is termed *Operations Analysis*. It brings the fundamental principles of the scientific method to bear on operational problems and thus brings objectivity into the realm of military decisions.

The original edition was an outgrowth of a two-semester course in Naval Operations Analysis which had been taught to prospective naval officers at the United States Naval Academy since 1959. The material was adapted from many sources, particularly reports of the Operations Evaluation Group (OEG) which pioneered in the Navy's effort to analyze operations. The most widely used was OEG Report Number 56 on *Search and Screening* by Bernard O. Koopman, which provided a basis for much of the material in Chapters five, six, seven, eight and ten.

Through the addition of 14 new sections, this second edition extends several of the tactical models and analyses into areas not previously addressed. Moreover, the experiences from administering this course to approximately 200 midshipmen each of the past several years have generated numerous improvements throughout the text.

The material has been kept on an undergraduate level, requiring only that the reader be familiar with the fundamentals of *calculus, set theory* and *probability*. Appendix I is included to provide a ready reference to those fundamentals of set theory and probability used in the text.

This revision has been accomplished through coordinated efforts within the *Operations Analysis Study Group* of the U. S. Naval Academy. This group is composed of the following military and civilian faculty members who administer a total of eight different courses in Operations Analysis, including the one for which this book is the assigned text: Commander J. L. Bagby, Lieutenant Commander R. T. E. Bowler III, Professor T. D. Burnett, Lieutenant Commander G. M. Marlowe, Professor W. C. Mylander, Lieutenant Commander J. F. Sigler and Major E. A. Smyth. The Study Group is grateful for the excellent manuscript-typings accomplished by Delores Craig and Mary Tomanio and for the superb copy-editing by Constance MacDonald.

A complete list of all persons who have made contributions over the years in developing either the first or this second edition would be impossible. Contributions by the following persons, however, have indeed been *conspicuous:* F. A. Andrews, J. G. Burton, L. B. Greene, G. B. Hannah, M. J. Healy, R. Herrmann, R. T. Isaacson, R. R. McArthur, P. G. Schenk and P. M. Tullier, Jr., while at the *U. S. Naval Academy,* Annapolis, Maryland, and R. N. Forrest and J. K. Hartman of the *Naval Postgraduate School,* Monterey, California.

Contents

Naval
Operations
Analysis

1 Operations Analysis: A Scientific Approach to the Resolution of Operational Problems

A naval officer is a leader. His primary mission is to conduct successful operations of the Navy both in war and in peace. His primary functions are to organize, plan and supervise such tasks necessary to accomplish the mission given him. His single most needed attribute is the ability to make wise decisions which are paramount in determining the success of an operation.

The executive who effectively trains himself in all aspects of decision-making is in demand in any organization. But what are these aspects, and which of them can be learned at all? Certainly experience is an essential element, and perhaps the single most effective guide in making a decision. Yet no naval officer or any other executive can hope to reach the point where he has experienced all the situations in which he might have to make a decision. In the procurement of a new weapons system, the decision as to which system is *best* must be made in a situation which is different from any encountered before.

In protecting a task force against enemy submarines, the decision as to the *best* screen placement may have to be based on estimates of submarine capabilities not encountered before. Furthermore, in many cases it is impossible to determine, even after the action has been taken, whether the choice was optimum, or whether a better one might have been made. In such cases, little experience is gained which will help to make a future decision, even if the situation is identical.

A decision then, can seldom be made merely by referring to past experience alone. Rather, the crucial element in making a decision becomes one of how to *apply* the experience and knowledge gained in the past to the present problem in order to optimize the results. This requires sound reasoning, clear thinking and good logic. It requires an approach which guides one to correct conclusions and prevents the overlooking of any essential elements. It requires sufficient knowledge about fields

1

related to the problem to enable one to make reasonable assumptions and to separate the details from the essential elements in the problem.

There have been many methods devised for guiding an executive to the *correct* solution of a problem. In the Navy, for example, the established planning process includes the *Estimate of the Situation* which guides an officer in making the decision as to how best to carry out his mission. This is an efficient and effective guide, tested and tried as it has developed over the years. The objective is studied, courses of action are developed and weighed in terms of enemy capabilities, and a decision is reached as to which course of action is best. In many cases the combined judgment and experience of a commander and his staff are sufficient to accurately predict the outcome for each course of action and weigh its relative merits. In other situations the factors involved are either so numerous or so complicated that additional techniques and computations, beyond the capability of most naval officers, are required. Herein lies the role of Operations Analysis in the Navy—to provide the techniques for measuring the effectiveness of different courses of action, in order that the decision-maker may be able to make a more intelligent choice between them.

101 OPERATIONS ANALYSIS

In recent years several related fields have emerged, each concerned with the role of the executive in decision-making. These include the fields of *Operations Analysis, Operations Research, Systems Analysis,* as well as those of Industrial Engineering, Industrial Administration, Market Research and others. The difference between these disciplines is not so much in their objectives, their approach, or their methods, as in the types of decision problems to which each is orientated and applied.

The dividing line between analysis and research is obviously very thin; yet, it is important to make this distinction in order to maintain a functional division between the responsibilities of the practitioners, in this case the naval officer (operations analyst) in charge and responsible for preparing alternate proposals for decision-making, and the researcher and student of operations analysis and research. Both the analyst and the researcher are interested in the analysis of specific outcomes of a fleet exercise, the analyst-practitioner in how to plan for future operations basing solutions on a set of given data, the researcher in the interplay of cause and effect, possibly experimenting laboratory style with different sets of data which may be either factual or hypothetical. Breaking a problem up into its elements war game style* is the task for the operations researcher using all methods and techniques of operations research to find solutions to real and hypothetical problems.

As the interest of the Navy Department in operations analysis and research is bound to intensify, it is appropriate here to emphasize the value of these tools in the hands of planners and decision-makers who have gradually progressed to the point of understanding the newly developed concepts in practical, complex and sophisticated implementation of long term plans. With weapons systems capabilities improving without let-up, now and in the foreseeable future, in submerged, surface and above

---

*War gaming refers to methods of analysis which are available for the study of military problems. These methods range from the complete realism of war or battle situations to the pure abstractions of a mathematical nature (equations). These methods may include among others direct observations of real situations, field maneuvers, map exercises, simulated situations and the mathematical representation of military situations.

surface operations, developments are in a constant flux. The fact is that the world around us is more than ever before concerned with all three areas of operations.

*SO*und *N*avigation *A*nd *R*anging (SONAR) systems are used in a modern navy for *communication, navigation,* and *the detection, classification and localization of submarine targets.*

Submarine and sonar operations are of particular interest to the operations analyst as an area in which great progress has undoubtedly been made in the years since World War II. However, in spite of great technological advances in submarine construction, in sonar operating techniques, as well as in understanding the behavior of sound waves in different environments, much room is still left for improvement.

Sonar systems employing the propagation of acoustic energy in water have moved into the foreground of naval concern because of the important part they play in search for and detection of enemy targets. The operations analyst as well as the operations researcher are both interested in the subject, but in different ways. While the operations analyst is concerned with the development and evaluation of specific action plans based on the optimal utilization of sonar sensors, the operations researcher studies the cause and effect relationships in hypothetical cases of naval warfare, checking not only the interrelationships of factors influencing sonar performance but also how different tactics or other weapons systems may possibly influence the search effectiveness under varying environmental conditions. Some of the variables may be controllable, such as the speed of the searching ship; others, such as sound conditions, may be beyond present-day control but with more and intensified research may some day be understood and become controllable due to the effort of the operations researcher. In this connection the operations researcher's approach to the problem may be closely related to the teaching effort which, equally, is in some degree restricted to imparting knowledge and know-how to the student of the subject. However, the purpose of this text is not to examine the differences in these fields but to study some of the ways in which they are similar.

Decision-making fields are linked together by the common objective of providing a decision-maker with a basis for making an intelligent choice as to which alternative is best. The approach of each involves the use of the scientific method which brings objectivity to the results, and makes verification possible. The methods are quantitative, using the techniques of mathematics to deal with the quantifiable aspects of a problem.

In this text, the term *Operations Analysis* (OA) will be used in its broadest sense as representative of each of these previously mentioned disciplines. A classical definition of OA is:

> A scientific method of providing executive departments with a quantitative basis for decisions regarding the operations under their control.*

This sufficed as a working definition of OA. It served to emphasize some of the essential aspects of OA and those characteristics which caused it to be recognized as an applied science in its own right. These aspects will be pointed out in detail in the following pages. It should be noted, however, that although OA is here defined in its broadest sense, and applicable in many fields, the examples and applications in following chapters are drawn specifically from the area of naval operations. This will give a naval officer both an insight into the science of Operations Analysis and also

---

*Morse and Kimball, *Methods of Operations Research,* MIT Press, 1951.

some knowledge of the principles underlying certain operational tactics such as search, patrol and screening.

It is to be emphasized strongly at the outset, and again and again throughout this text, that the function of OA is not to present ready-made decisions to the military commander or civilian executive. Rather, the proper function of OA rests in laying out for the decision-maker the essential factors of the real problem, in proper relationship and expressed in terms of a meaningful common reference—the objective aspects of the problem situation. It remains the prerogative—and responsibility—of the military commander to integrate these objective considerations with the qualitative and intangible factors in the problem according to the dictates of his experience and professional judgment in arriving at a final decision. Regarding the choice of an optimal weapon delivery tactic, the military commander concerned may perceive on the basis of his experience that the tactic ranked best in terms of effectiveness will prove undesirable because of weather conditions at the target, and therefore is to be rejected for another less accurate but more operationally feasible maneuver. OA has presented him with a quantitative basis for his decision; nonetheless, he knows what compromises his decision will entail. Ideally, the analysis has considered such factors as weather, and includes a breakdown according to the different possible general conditions at the target. The assumptions made in an analysis are usually at least as valuable information to the commander as are the analyst's conclusions.

Symbolically, the relationship of OA and the decision-maker's judgment may be represented as follows:

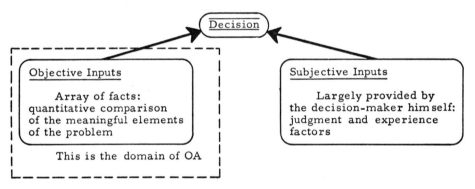

Figure 1-1.

Often it is both necessary and feasible for the managers to provide their own operations analysis. Given the scientific knowledge and proper analytic methodology, it might not be necessary to procure additional consultation or research. Time might not be available. Additional time could be used up by the consultant becoming acquainted with the particular situation, or higher command might deem the problem to be not as significant as other current problems and assign it a low priority awaiting an analyst. In view of the probability of the operator executive-analyst, this more thorough modern definition is sometimes preferred:

> Operations analysis is the application of scientific knowledge toward the solution of problems which occur in operational activities (in their real environment). Its special technique is to invent a strategy of control by measuring, comparing, and predicting possible behavior through a scientific model of a situation or activity.

102 HISTORICAL BACKGROUND IN THE MILITARY

Discussions of the beginnings of OA relate how the military turned to civilian scientists, in Great Britain and the United States, for assistance in the resolution of operational problems under the exigencies of a world war grown more complex than any heretofore in human experience. The contributions made by these scientists—who came to be called *operations analysts*—were exceptional. Perhaps their greatest and most lasting contribution, however, lay in the *idea* of applying the established methods of science to the resolution of military *operational* problems—problems which at first examination would appear hardly amenable to that kind of treatment. The concept of that application was well established, if not widely known, at the end of World War II.

This resort to civilian assistance, in what had historically been the exclusive province of the military, does not imply that the military officers concerned were incapable of thinking for themselves. In the United States Navy, for example, experienced officers were busy organizing a rapidly expanding service and fighting a war in two oceans. They were not afforded the luxury of time to educate themselves to this task so they turned to those who already had the scientific competence to cope—in analytical terms—with a burgeoning military technology producing new weapons and equipment under wartime pressure, at a rate far more rapid than had ever prevailed before.

It may be asked why, if the scientific method were to prove so effective in analysis of military problems, it had not been applied long before. To a very limited extent, it had been. There are examples of OA to be found throughout history. In 1906, Admiral Bradley Fiske, U. S. Navy, published a little-heralded paper which anticipated by 10 years the analytical methods of Frederick Lanchester, in the latter's milestone mathematical analysis of air combat in World War I. Thomas Edison is known to have done investigations in antisubmarine warfare during World War I. But these were scattered and occasional and by no means represent a general awareness of OA. Certainly in the U. S. Navy between the two world wars there were detailed statistical analyses conducted of naval gunfirings, for instance, and of the results of a variety of other competitive evolutions. But none of these were true scientific analyses. It may be safe to say that the scientific method was not adopted sooner by the military because its effectiveness was not recognized.

Speculation will provide several probable reasons why the scientist did not venture forth sooner from his laboratory to take part in military problem solving. For one thing, he was not invited. Military operational problems were simpler between the wars; there was no wartime pressure for their solution, and military thinking produced answers which were, presumably, adequate unto the time. Furthermore, weapons and weapons systems changed slowly, and in both the United States and Great Britain, the military establishment was not popular and budgetary support was meager. Even had such an invitation been tendered, it is doubtful that it would have generated much of a response in the civilian academic community prior to the imminence of war in the late 1930s.

The world today is vastly different. Scientific analysis is an accepted feature of creative problem solving in the military, by professional officers as well as civilians, for reasons which will be elicited.

103   OPERATIONS ANALYSIS IN THE NAVY

Before beginning a detailed consideration of the nature of Operations Analysis and of its significance to the naval officer, it will be useful to place Operations Analysis in a present-day perspective in terms of the Navy.

The OA organization developed in the Navy during World War II was retained after the end of hostilities allowing many of the pioneers in its establishment to continue their wartime endeavors. In the years immediately following the war, however, it became apparent that there were shortcomings in the notion of operations research on naval operational problems by civilians alone. Capable as were the scientists, they lacked one characteristic vital to an appreciation of the subtleties of many military problems: an understanding of the operational environment such as one may achieve only through the experience of having been an OOD, a fighter pilot, or a destroyer commanding officer. An interface was discerned to exist between the naval officer, knowing the problem but not having the scientific depth to attack it analytically or to explain it in terms completely meaningful to the civilian, and the civilian scientist having the competence but not the deep-seated appreciation for the problem. The realization arose, accordingly, of a need for U. S. Navy and Marine officers of broad operational experience, schooled in Operations Analysis, to perform analyses themselves, or to guide the civilian analysts in problem areas which demanded both operational insight and the competence of the scientifically trained analyst. To meet this need, the Navy in 1951 established the Operations Analysis curriculum at the Naval Postgraduate School, Monterey, California. (The Navy, incidentally, was first among the services to recognize this need, and remains today foremost in the number of officers educated in OA, and in the strength of its internal OA organization.)

The growth in the realization of the potential of the OA discipline by the Navy, and in the breadth and depth of its application, is epitomized by the number of officers enrolled, over the years, in the OA curriculum at the Naval Postgraduate School. The number of billets throughout the Navy prescribed for officers with a subspecialty in Operations Analysis has doubled in recent years.

Naval officers today are applying the methods and concepts of OA to challenging problems across the whole spectrum of naval operations:

a. In research and development at such activities as the Navy Missile Center, the Naval Air Development Center and the Naval Ordnance Test Station.
b. In operational evaluation of equipment, and development of tactics, in Air Development Squadrons (VX) One, Four, and Five, Submarine Development Group Two, the Destroyer Development Groups, Atlantic and Pacific, and the Staff of Commander, Operational Test and Evaluation Forces.
c. In design and analysis of fleet exercises and analysis of fleet combat readiness, by the staffs of the numbered fleets, Fleet Commanders-in-Chief and Force Commanders.
d. In determination of Navy force requirements for the immediate, near future and long-range needs of the Navy—considering such problems as the optimum composition of an attack carrier air wing and the composition of the Navy for 1985—in the office of the Chief of Naval Operations.
e. In determination of command and control requirements of the Navy, in the Navy Command Systems Support Activity.

The number of civilian scientists integrated into the Navy organization for OA has grown apace with the growth of OA applications. Under the Center for Naval Analysis

(CNA) these analysts work very often as members of military-civilian teams in the commands, and on the problems just cited. Certain additional OA projects are pursued by private research organizations working under contract to the Navy; such groups as the Applied Physics Laboratory of Johns Hopkins University (APL-JHU), and the Stanford Research Institute (SRI), are well known in the field. The Navy, however, has developed over the years a broadly based and well-staffed internal organization for OA and, consequently, needs less often than the Army and Air Force to turn to private research for solutions to its problems (though the resources of the private OA community are of great value, and their contributions unique in certain areas).

Growing awareness of the value of education in the fundamentals of Operations Analysis for professional naval officers led to the incorporation at the U. S. Naval Academy of a major field of study in Naval Operations Analysis.

In summary, there is a wide application of OA throughout the Navy today. There is every indication that application will continue to grow in the years to come as weapons systems become still more complex (and expensive); as the cost of wrong decisions in operational matters continues to grow exponentially; and as a burgeoning technology presents new concepts and techniques of warfare untested in combat to replace earlier generations of concepts and systems, themselves never tested under fire.

104 OPERATIONS ANALYSIS AND THE NAVAL OFFICER

Knowledge of basic methodology of Operations Analysis and competence in the application of fundamental techniques is important to the naval officer. Here are some of the reasons why this is so:

a. For what it conduces toward objective, analytic thought processes in general, sound reasoning and a logical approach to problems.
b. For the greater insight afforded into the essential features of naval operations.
c. As preparation for a later subspecialty in the field.
d. For what it contributes to an understanding of technical studies being done for and in the Navy.

Objective, analytic thought processes have always been important to the naval officer but never more than at the present. History records the glories of the military leaders who, down through the centuries, have thrown caution to the winds and elected to follow their intuition rather than reason and met with great success. Their contemporaries who followed the same decision criteria and failed tend to be forgotten in ignominy, although one suspects there were at least as many of the latter as the former and they were quite as competent. They were simply not as lucky. It is the business of OA to *put luck on our side*. Opinion, preconceived notion, personal bias, whatever term chosen to employ for the subjective predilections with which one approaches a decision, are insidious and pervasive and it is a rare human being who can avoid their pitfalls without having made a conscious effort to train his mind. An important benefit to be gained from the OA approach to problem solving is an ability to think through, in a logical and ordered manner, the everyday dilemmas of a junior naval officer. Analytic techniques may not be applicable, but logical thinking in the vein of the OA method brings solutions much faster than trial and error.

Insight into the fundamentals of an operational situation—an appreciation of the fundamental processes operating behind the *black box,* the tabulated search and attack plans, the operation order—is a quality not always gained with experience. Experience alone is a slow and expensive teaching device, and one which may destroy the student before he finishes the course. The naval officer who comes by this insight naturally is a gifted one indeed, and rather the exception than the rule. Operations Analysis, with its attention to the essential features vice the externals of operational problems, and its consideration of the probabilistic nature of the events which can take place, is of particular value in the development of this insight.

Operations Analysis is of considerable interest to the junior naval officer as a possible subspecialty. It is a stated goal of the Navy that at least 50 percent of regular officers shall have had significant postgraduate education in a subspecialty area. The nature of the OA subspecialty has already been stated. For the unrestricted line officer, in particular, Operations Analysis bears as directly upon the essence of his profession as any other field of study in the military sciences. OA-educated officers are very much in demand.

Many officers who do not become associated with Operations Analysis as a subspecialty, nevertheless will often have access to studies which analyze naval problems of interest to them. The ability to understand or evaluate these studies is greatly enhanced by some insight into the approach and methods of OA.

105   THE OA METHOD

It has been asserted above that Operations Analysis is essentially the application of the *scientific method* to the resolution of operational problems. Without digressing for a discussion of what constitutes the scientific method, it is reasonable to state that examination of successful applications of OA reveals a consistent pattern, a general form. That general approach is termed the *OA method*. It is by no means a gouge or a problem-solving algorithm but most if not all of its features are to be found in varying degrees of development in all cases of creative problem solving through OA. The OA method may be described in the following terms:

a. Formulation of the problem, through:
    (1) Determination of the objectives of the operation involved.
    (2) Enumeration of all alternative courses of action.
    (3) Defining a measure of effectiveness by which to compare alternatives.
    (4) Determination and enumeration of the variables to be considered.
b. Problem Solution. Any one or a combination of the following:
    (1) Theoretical analyses.
    (2) Statistical analyses of empirical data (data on operations already conducted).
    (3) Controlled trials or exercises.
    (4) Simulation (experimental investigation using physical, analog or digital models of the operational situation).
c. Communication of results.

Each of these factors will be discussed in turn in the succeeding chapter.

2 The Formulation and Solution of a Problem

In Chapter one the OA method was outlined as a guide in problem solving. The problems with which OA deals are not those in which a solution can be reached and labeled *answer* as in a typical mathematics problem. The general question asked by the decision-maker is: *What course of action will best accomplish my objective?* This chapter discusses some of the important elements in an OA approach to such problems.

201 FORMULATION OF THE PROBLEM

An unlimited number and variety of decision-problems require an answer to the introductory question. No matter how complicated or difficult these problems are, the following specific questions must be considered before any intelligent course of action can be chosen:

a. What objective is to be achieved?
b. What different courses of action (alternatives) are available?
c. What factors (variables) will contribute to the success or failure of each possible course of action in achieving the objective?
d. What yardstick can be used to measure and compare the effectiveness of the different alternatives?

The formulation of the problem consists, essentially, of answering these basic questions. However, they are usually much less trivial than they seem at first glance. Their answers frequently seem to defy expression or, when expressed, are subject to disagreement. In major problems they merit not just a superficial concern but deep and searching consideration, after which the solution to the problem may sometimes require only a few computations or the collection of sufficient data.

Note: Bracketed numbers in text refer to bibliographic entries at end of chapter.

202   THE OBJECTIVE OF THE OPERATION

Finding the *real* problem is often one of the most difficult features of operational problems, as exemplified in the following case. Early in World War II a great number of British merchant vessels were being sunk or seriously damaged by Axis aircraft attack in the Mediterranean. The obvious answer was to equip these ships with antiaircraft guns and gun crews. This was done at great expense of men and equipment badly needed elsewhere. Questions concerning the soundness of this allocation of scarce resources were raised when reports showed that the gun crews were shooting down only about 4 percent of all attacking aircraft. This was a poor showing and seemed to indicate that the AA guns and crews were not worth the cost of installation. On more careful consideration, it was realized that the guns were not there primarily to shoot down German or Italian aircraft, but their objective was to protect the merchant vessels. And, in fact, as figures were accumulated, it became apparent that the AA guns and crews were doing the job rather well; of the ships attacked, 25 percent of those without protection had been sunk, while only 10 percent of the ships with protection were lost in the same period. [1]

The objective being considered here is that of the person who has the ultimate responsibility for making the decision. A commanding officer's objective may often be determined by studying the mission given him by his superior. A business executive's objective is largely determined by, or at least consistent with, the purpose and goals of his organization.

In a typical problem involving a major decision, the analysis would be conducted for the decision-maker by members of his staff or by an independent research firm. In either case the analyst must determine exactly what the objective is. It may be very vague and elusive at first, but the analysis cannot proceed far until it is clearly defined. Even then, as the analysis proceeds, it may be determined that the objective as stated is not specific enough and further clarification is necessary. Suppose, in a problem involving excess shipping losses, the stated objective is *to minimize the number of merchant vessels sunk*. One way of accomplishing it would be to keep all merchant vessels in port. In a wartime shipping situation, this would hardly be a reasonable solution; hence, the objective as stated must not be the real one.

The objective is sometimes confused with the action taken to accomplish it. The person considering the purchase of life insurance may state his objective as *to determine how much and what kind of life insurance to buy*. The purchase of life insurance, however, is an action taken to accomplish some real objective such as providing security for his dependents.

The aim of the analyst should be to provide the decision-maker with an accurate and unbiased basis for decision. The objective under consideration is that of the decision-maker in conducting the operation. This objective always exists, however difficult it may be to define or express. The first step in the OA method is to find and clearly state it.

203   THE ALTERNATIVE COURSES OF ACTION

While the objective is usually determined first, the steps in formulating a problem do not always follow in any definite sequence. Rather, the analyst must consider each step in terms of the others, going from one to another and back again.* The first questions raised when trying to list reasonable alternatives are: *How limited are my choices and may I consider alternatives involving an increase in men, material, or equipment; or am I limited to different tactics and methods of operation using the resources at hand?*

Such questions become easier to answer after some consideration of the variables which will be discussed in Section 204. Very often the immediacy of the problem will not only limit the alternatives to those which can be put into use quickly, but also limit the time which can be spent on the analysis itself. Most of the problems treated by OA during World War II were undertaken under circumstances that required doing *the best you can with what you've got*. In most organizations, moral and social considerations rule out alternatives which involve dishonest or unlawful practices, or which violate accepted standards or customs.

One approach would be to list every conceivable course of action which could reasonably be expected to accomplish the objective, reserving further judgment until later. This approach would tend to decrease the possibility of overlooking the best alternative merely because it didn't occur to the analyst. Sometimes an individual closely associated with an operation finds it difficult to think of any alternatives except those tried previously, where some other individual with identical knowledge and experience, but viewing the situation from a distance, would see other possible courses of action. There is no set procedure for discovering good alternatives, although the ingenuity, experience and vantage point of the individual surely contribute.

An obvious difficulty arises when the number of alternatives is so large that listing them becomes tedious or impossible. It may be that each can be put in one of several categories. For example, in protecting a task force from aircraft attack with airborne Combat Air Patrol (CAP), an infinite number of alternatives would be included in the category of *stationing x aircraft at altitude h_1 spaced equidistantly on a circle of radius r_1 from formation center, and y aircraft at altitude h_2 spaced equidistantly at radius r_2.*

One test for a valid alternative is that it must, by itself, provide a complete means of accomplishing the objective. If the alternative provides only part of the means then it is not complete. For example, if the objective is to protect the task force against submarines, an alternative which provides a means for detection only is not complete in itself, and hence not valid.

204   THE VARIABLES

A listing of variables in the approach to a problem can accomplish several purposes:

a. Serve as a guide to the data that must be gathered before the problem can be solved.
b. Indicate the complexity of the problem and help to determine the method or methods to be used in the analysis.
c. Help in preventing any important elements in the problem from being overlooked.
d. Provide a guide to listing alternatives.
e. Include those quantities which will be useful in computing the measuré of effectiveness.

---

*See [2], pages 155–160, for amplification of this iterative process of problem formulation.

Variables may be placed in one of several categories. Some variables can be controlled or at least influenced to some degree by the decision-maker. For example, the number, x_1, of destroyers assigned to an ASW screen is a variable controlled by the Officer in Tactical Command (OTC) at least to the extent that he has destroyers available.

Other variables which influence the outcome of an operation may be completely uncontrollable. Some of these have values which are known or can be determined. Others have values which are not known but can be estimated or assumed. As examples, the number, x_2, of destroyers assigned to a task force is known but cannot generally be controlled by the OTC; hence, it establishes some restrictions on the alternatives at his disposal. The isothermal surface layer depth, x_3, a variable which influences the possibility of detecting a submarine with sonar, is uncontrollable yet measurable. The number, x_4, of enemy submarines operating in a given area cannot be controlled by the OTC nor can it usually be determined by measurement, but may be estimated from intelligence reports, etc. A list of such variables will provide a guide to needed data.

Finally, there are those uncontrollable variables whose values cannot be determined because of their random nature. The time, x_5, that a sonar installation will operate before failure, and the range, x_6, at which a target will be detected, are variables whose values vary widely even for a given situation because of the numerous unknown factors upon which they depend. Such quantities are called *random variables,* and the uncertain events associated with them can be treated effectively only by using probability theory.

In a general sense, the outcome of an operation may be thought of as a function of the many variables which are involved. Symbolically,

$$\text{Outcome} = f(x_1, x_2, x_3, \cdots, x_n).$$

It is of fundamental importance that these variables be defined explicitly. Some of them may then be eliminated from further consideration if it can be seen they have little significant effect on the outcome. In that way the problem can be reduced to its essentials.

In solving a problem, a *sensitivity analysis* should be made in order to determine the variables to which the outcome is most sensitive. Particular care must be taken to insure that the values assigned to these variables are determined or estimated as accurately as possible.

An alternative course of action may be thought of as a specific assignment of values to the different controllable variables. Therefore, identifying these controllable variables is a necessary first step to gain insight into the various alternatives which are available.

All of the variables discussed so far have been those whose values could be described by numbers. There are certainly other variables whose nature makes it difficult if not impossible to describe their values in such a quantitative way. Such variables as morale, training, political climate, health, intelligence and education are difficult to treat quantitatively. Yet, scales have been devised which quantitatively describe, more or less accurately, the value of some of these. Other scales and methods are sure to be devised so that more and more of these factors can be treated quantitatively in the future. Since Operations Analysis is to provide a decision-maker with a *quantitative* basis for decision, it must leave those factors which cannot be so treated to the judgment and experience of the decision-maker himself.

205 THE MEASURE OF EFFECTIVENESS

A basis for decision consists essentially of predicting and describing the expected results of each possible course of action. The decision-maker's choice can then be based on a comparison of these results. If the expected results are described in qualitative terms, it may be possible to rank, but only in a general way, each course of action as to desirability. The question still unanswered would be: *How much better is one course of action than the next?* To answer this, a quantitative approach is necessary with the expected results expressed in quantitative terms, i.e., with numbers.

It is seldom easy to predict the outcome of an operation and even more difficult to find a quantitative way of expressing the results. The quantitative measure used to compare the effectiveness of the alternatives in achieving the objective is called the Measure of Effectiveness (MOE).

In a problem where the objective is to detect a target, a possible measure of effectiveness would be *probability of detection* or *expected time to detection*. In an operation involving the movement of supplies by truck to a forward area, the measure of effectiveness might be *tons delivered per truck day*. In cases where economic considerations are important, as in developing a new weapons system, the measure used to compare different systems should include both cost and effectiveness, such as *cost of providing a 90 percent chance of kill* or *probability of kill for a given cost*.

A measure of effectiveness, then, must be closely related to the objective of the operation. The *number of submarines sunk per month* may be a satisfactory MOE if the objective is to destroy submarines; whereas if the real objective is to protect shipping, the best course of action may be one which sinks fewer submarines. An example in which a wrong MOE was considered was given earlier concerning merchant vessel armament against air attack.

Another requirement of the MOE is that it be measurable. There must be the possibility of gathering sufficient data and making the necessary calculations to determine its value for each course of action. Furthermore, since the object is to provide a basis for decision as to the best course of action, these computations must be completed before the decision is made or operation conducted. These values of the MOE, determined for each course of action, are of necessity predicted values. Once the decision is made and a particular course of action taken, it may be possible to assess its effectiveness, but this information would in no way contribute to the original decision, however important it may be to a future one.

In summary then, a measure of effectiveness must:

a. **Be measurable,**
b. **Be quantifiable** and
c. **Measure** to what degree the (real) objective is achieved.

Often this MOE is in the form of a ratio expressing the expected output versus input, thus predicting the efficiency of the operation. Any probability, for example, can be thought of as a ratio of number of successes to number of trials.

The following example is taken from World War II and will serve to illustrate the importance of using the correct measure of effectiveness in equipment evaluation.

Early in the U-boat war in the Atlantic an attempt was made to save merchant vessels by equipping them with antitorpedo nets which were swung out by booms. These nets were capable of stopping some 85 percent of the German electric torpedoes (G7E) but only 20 percent of the German air-propelled torpedoes (G7A). Taking the armament of U-boats as about 60 percent G7E and 40 percent G7A gave an average protection against these torpedoes of 59 percent. Since the nets covered only about 75 percent of the ship, the *net* protection was 44 percent.

This appears to be a strong argument in favor of equipping all merchant vessels with nets. But the cost was extremely high and the nets slowed down the ships, making an additional cost for fuel and time lost. Against some opposition, about 600 ships were fitted with nets before enough operational experience had been obtained to make a reappraisal possible. This reappraisal was quite broad in scope, as it involved: (1) cost in dollars as against the cost of ships saved by the net, (2) cost in time and in cargo space, (3) cost in manpower to build and maintain the nets. The research on the cost in dollars found that the net program did not pay for itself. The operational data on the 25 ships which were torpedoed and which were fitted with nets are shown here:

	Sunk	*Damaged*	*Undamaged*
12 ships, nets not in use at time of attack	9	3	0
10 ships, nets in use	4	3	3
3 ships, use of nets unknown	3	0	0
	16	6	3

If the 10 ships with nets streamed had not had their nets in use, we should expect $7\frac{1}{2}$ to have been sunk and $2\frac{1}{2}$ damaged. The nets had thus saved the equivalent of $3\frac{1}{2}$ ships and cargoes. But a total of almost 600 ships had been fitted with nets at an initial cost equal to about twice that of $3\frac{1}{2}$ ships and cargo, not to mention costs of maintenance, etc. Thus the program had not paid for itself, and the report of the findings recommended that no further ships be equipped with nets. [1]

It frequently proves useful if the MOE is factorable so that the "weak link" can be readily established, as in the following example:

An MOE used to evaluate the performance of a submarine stationed in a barrier to oppose enemy submarines (an SSK mission) is the probability that an enemy submarine passing through (penetrating) the barrier would be killed by the SSK $= P_K$. This MOE can be factored into the following conditional probabilities:

$$P_K = P_D \times P_C \times P_A \times P_{AA} \times P_H,$$

where:

P_K = P [kill]
P_D = P [SSK detects transitor | given transitor enters barrier]
P_C = P [SSK correctly classifies transitor | given detection]
P_A = P [SSK attacks | given correctly classifies]
P_{AA} = P [SSK attack is accurate | given SSK attacks]
P_H = P [Weapon hits | given attack made]

The MOE $= P_K$ is a useful MOE because:
1. It is quantifiable, i.e., $0 \leq P_K \leq 1$.
2. It is measurable, i.e., P_K can be measured by conducting at-sea exercises and taking data such as:

$$P_D = \frac{\#\ \text{transitors detected}}{\#\ \text{transitors going through}}$$

$$P_C = \frac{\text{\# transitors correctly classified}}{\text{\# transitors detected}}$$

$$P_A = \frac{\text{\# transitors attacked}}{\text{\# transitors correctly classified}}$$

$$P_{AA} = \frac{\text{\# accurate attacks}}{\text{\# transitors attacked}}$$

P_H can be estimated from torpedo test firings $= \dfrac{\text{\# torpedo hits}}{\text{\# torpedos fired accurately}}$

Some of the *variables* which must be considered in the above are:
1. SSK class/performance (known).
2. Enemy transiting submarine characteristics (unknown but can be estimated).
3. Sea state and other environmental conditions (can be measured).
4. Transitor path (track) through barrier (can be considered random).

206   COST-EFFECTIVENESS AS AN MOE

Much of this text will be devoted to examples of other measures of effectiveness which are used in certain naval operations together with the development of techniques for determining the value of these measures. Before discussing some of these techniques, it is worthwhile to cover in somewhat greater detail a general measure of effectiveness most used in the development of future weapons systems. In this area economic factors are important variables. The alternative courses of action are the different systems which may be developed, and the type of measure of effectiveness used is termed cost-effectiveness.

> Military decisions, whether they specifically involve budgetary allocations or not, are in one of their important aspects economic decisions; and . . . unless the right questions are asked, the appropriate alternatives selected for comparison, and an economic criterion used for choosing the most efficient, military power—and national security—will suffer. [3]

The situation currently facing military planners is considerably different from what it had been historically up to World War II. The years since 1939 have marked revolutionary growth in military technology. A serious miscalculation by the planners in this environment could prove critical to our national security for years to come. Among the primary by-products of this revolution are the greatly increased costs of modern weapons systems and an increased time lag between conception of the system and operational production. [4] The potentially grave consequences of all this becomes apparent when viewed in light of the rapidity with which an enemy could now deal a crushing blow to the United States.

A major change [5] in the procurement of weapons systems has been initiated to deal with this problem. First, the structure of the U. S. Armed Forces is no longer derived on the basis of priorities of individual services, but has become major-mission-oriented in the following categories:

I. Strategic Forces
II. General Purpose Forces
III. Specialized Activities
IV. Airlift and Sealift
V. Reserve and Guard Forces

> VI. Research and Development
> VII. Logistics
> VIII. Personnel Support
> IX. Administration

This is intended to result in a best mix of forces of all the services taken together. Strategic retaliatory forces, for example, could be composed of manned bombers (both land and carrier based), and missiles (both land and submarine based).

Second, budgetary planning is now carried out on a five-year (vice annual) basis. The planning provides for both financial and nonfinancial estimates of the resource inputs required to obtain time-phased military outputs. It permits the decision-maker to view, in the long run, the situation several years hence as pertains to resource/monetary constraints. This is most important since the quantity of national resources is limited, in the long run. In the final analysis, this limitation rests upon the nation's capability to produce, as measured by the gross national product.

The third change requires that planning must develop both physical and financial data in forms suitable for making cost-effective studies of alternative force structures.

What exactly, does cost-effectiveness mean? *Cost-effectiveness* is a term often misconstrued, misjudged and misused. To many, cost-effectiveness is an odious word when applied to national defense. To this school of thought, cost-effectiveness implies economy—and to economize implies inferior quality or quantity. Therefore, it is necessary to begin with definitions of important terms.

Economizing, in a strict sense, implies efficiency; that is, making the most efficient use of available resources. Consider the following situation: given that certain targets are to be destroyed with a fixed set of weapons, a military commander will attempt to maximize the attainment of his objectives, i.e., he will strive to use his resources most efficiently. Should the commander have a specified fixed target to destroy with certain weapons, he will try to minimize the number of weapons utilized in accomplishing the mission, i.e., he will attempt to economize on the use of resources. These are logically equivalent problems, the solution to which may be stated as follows:*

> For any level of either budget or objective, the choices that maximize the attainment of an objective for a given budget are the same choices that minimize the cost of attaining that objective. [3]

The second definition of interest is cost-effectiveness itself. It is well to stress at this point that cost-effectiveness is not a methodology unto itself. To understand the implications of cost-effectiveness, it is first necessary to have some understanding of systems analysis. Systems analysis can be thought of as an inquiry to aid a decision-maker's choice of a course of action by systematically investigating his proper objectives, comparing quantitatively where possible, the cost, effectiveness and risks associated with alternative policies; and formulating additional alternatives if those examined are found wanting. [3] In short, systems analysis is a methodology by which decisions concerning future systems are made in the face of uncertainty. Such an economic analysis is a many-faceted problem, and one which must take place early in the planning of a new weapons system. The major elements of this type of analysis are as follows:

---

*The solution to these equivalent problems is similar to the solution of a matrix game introduced in Chapter three.

a. An objective or objectives. What is to be accomplished with the forces, equipment, systems, etc. which are being compared? The choice of an objective is critical and fundamental; for the right answer to the wrong question is of no help.

b. Alternatives. By what alternative forces may the objective be accomplished? These alternatives are frequently referred to as a system. This system may be similar, such as various attack type aircraft; or may be entirely different concepts, such as manned bombers versus missiles. The important aspect here is that all good alternatives are at least considered; then the feasible ones used in the analysis.

c. Costs or resources used. To each alternative there must be an associated *real cost*. The real costs may be in terms of scarce materials used, time, manpower, etc. Generally the real costs are equated to some dollar cost due to the need for reference to a common base in the performance of the analysis.

d. Model or models. A model is some abstract representation of the real world. In the case of systems analysis it is usually a mathematical expression. The quantifiable parameters, constants and variables of each alternative are run through the model in an attempt to reduce the information to some *number* that is significant *relative* to the other alternatives. A model for both cost and effectiveness is used.

e. Criterion. A criterion is the test by which one system or alternative is chosen over another. The criterion should weigh the positive factors of each alternative's *effectiveness*, versus the negative factors of the alternative's *cost*.

Prior to any consideration of why a *cost-effectiveness* criterion is used, a note of caution is necessary. Systems analysis is a method used to give the decision-maker an organized statement of certain relevant data which may serve as an aid in the decision-making process. It is not a substitute for sound experience or military judgment. Furthermore, cost-effectiveness is not simply a ratio of total cost to some set level of effectiveness. The feasibility, suitability and acceptability of the alternatives must be weighed, and marginal cost-effectiveness must be computed. [3] The term *marginal cost-effectiveness* asks the question, *What is the incremental change in effectiveness for some incremental change in cost?* It may develop that the improvement in effectiveness of only 10 percent may double or triple the cost.

The question, *Why is cost-effectiveness used?*, may best be answered by considering three questions which often arise.

First: *Why use some dollar restriction on defense spending? Why not just buy what is required?* The answer to this is quite simple—limitation of resources. This ultimate limitation appears as a *real cost;* perhaps tons of steel, pounds of uranium or acres of trees. Once these resources are used up in one project, they may not be used in another project. They must be properly allocated in order to optimize the return. This is the philosophy behind systems analysis and cost-effectiveness.

Second: *How do you place a dollar sign on men's lives?* Answer: the analyst doesn't. Loss of lives is one of the incommensurable terms which must be weighed by the final decision-maker as a *qualitative* judgment. This is not to say, however, that an analysis should not contain estimates on the number of lives which may be lost, for it may be of great aid to the decision-maker.

Finally: *Do you expect the military commander in the field to perform cost-effectiveness analyses?* This question is not easily answered. As a matter of fact, most military commanders do utilize cost-effectiveness thinking in the battlefield whenever they ask: *Is it worth the loss?* However, the field commander will seldom utilize dollar costs since these rapidly fluctuate as the battle proceeds. In his case, it is more appropriate to use *real costs,* i.e., loss of equipment, time, ground or lives.

Perhaps the most fitting summary is a statement by Mr. Charles J. Hitch:

> It should always be our policy to spend whatever is necessary for defense, but to spend whatever is spent in such a way as to achieve the greatest military capability—not to buy quality when the same amount spent on quantity will purchase greater effectiveness, and vice versa. [6]

207   THE PROBLEM SOLUTION

It has already been pointed out that the *solution* to an OA problem does not mean exactly what the term usually implies. No answer to the problem is necessarily found nor does the decision automatically follow. Rather the solution consists of taking the measure of effectiveness and determining, i.e., predicting, its value for each alternative.

Suppose for the objective of detecting a target, the MOE selected is the probability of detection, and the possible alternatives have been reduced to four search plans which seem most feasible. The solution to this problem would then consist of predicting the probability of detection for each of the four search plans. The end result might then be tabulated as follows:

Alternatives	MOE (*Probability of Detection*)
Search plan one:	.9
Search plan two:	.7
Search plan three:	.8
Search plan four:	.5

The methods used to make these predictions are discussed in the following section. The problem of making the decision as to which alternative is best is included in the next chapter.

Three questions which should immediately arise when the result is considered are: *How reliable are the numbers? By what methods were these numbers computed?* and *Which alternative is best?*

The numbers themselves are subject to several kinds of errors. Variables may be omitted which are really significant, variables may be given assumed or estimated values, or errors of judgment or logic may be made as when statistical independence is unjustifiably assumed. Obviously, a good analysis must guard against letting any of these assumptions or errors invalidate the results. A sensitivity analysis will determine those variables to which the results are most sensitive. In the preceding example, suppose a sensitivity analysis revealed that the probability of detection for some search plans varied widely for different sea states. Perhaps the sea state was assumed to be one or less in determining the probabilities. Since the sea state is a variable that is impossible to predict for a future operation, its actual value cannot be determined. One approach, however, would be to calculate the probability of detection for each combination of search plans and sea states which may occur. The results might then be reproduced in the following table (often referred to as a *payoff matrix*):

Alternatives	Sea state 0 *or* 1	Sea state 2 *or* 3	Sea state 4 *or more*
Search plan one:	.9	.4	.1
Search plan two:	.7	.5	.4
Search plan three:	.8	.7	.2
Search plan four:	.5	.5	.5

This additional information would give the decision-maker a basis for a more intelligent decision, but also a more difficult decision to make. His approach to such a decision will be covered in the next chapter.

A somewhat different aspect will now be considered. Suppose that instead of the critical variable being the sea state, it is the tactic of the enemy. If the original computations were based on the assumption that his tactic would be to snorkel at night and remain submerged during the day, what would happen if he had the capability to use a second tactic of remaining submerged throughout the operation? The consideration of this additional possibility may lead to the following payoff matrix:

Alternatives	Enemy tactic one	Enemy tactic two
Search plan one:	.9	.5
Search plan two:	.7	.6
Search plan three:	.8	.3
Search plan four:	.5	.4

The significant difference between this and the previous matrix is that an enemy can be expected to choose his own tactic with some regard for frustrating the attainment of the commander's objective, while the weather hopefully has no such malevolent intent.

208 METHODS OF SOLUTION

The solution involves an analysis to predict the effectiveness of each alternative in achieving the objective, and expresses this outcome or payoff in terms of the measure of effectiveness. The methods used in making these predictions can be placed in four categories: *theoretical analysis, statistical analysis of empirical data, controlled trials or exercises* and *simulation.*

Usually the solution will require the use of a combination of two or more of these methods. Even an analysis which is essentially theoretical must in the end make use of parameters whose values are measured or determined from empirical data. Which of the methods are to be used in a particular problem depends on many factors including the size and complexity of the problem, the amount of data and experience gained from similar problems in the past, and the time and talent available for the solution.

All of the methods rely heavily on the use of mathematical disciplines. In any quantitative approach, the classical mathematics of algebra, trigonometry, geometry, calculus, differential equations, etc., are required. In addition, when uncertainties are present, as they typically are in an operational situation, the use of probability theory is indispensable. Other areas of mathematics—some developed very recently—find application in the solution of specific classes of problems. These include such diverse areas as statistics, linear programming, queueing theory, war gaming and other simulation models, reliability theory, econometrics, cybernetics, models of production, inventory, allocation and transportation and many others. The problem of making a decision using a quantitative basis is considered in such mathematical topics as decision criteria, decision theory, games of strategy, utility theory and others.

While mathematics provides the basic framework and tools for a quantitative approach, it is by no means a sufficient prerequisite for the solution of operational problems. In problems involving the detection of underwater targets, for example, a knowledge of the physics of underwater sound propagation is essential. In developing a new weapons system, economic factors play an important part. In all problems, knowledge of related fields is essential to an understanding of the problem itself. Thus the analysis of an important problem may properly involve mathematicians, physicists, economists, psychologists, engineers, etc.—a *mixed-team* approach.

In general, the solution to a problem involves the development of a *mathematical model* which represents or simulates a physical operation. This model building technique is by no means peculiar to Operations Analysis. It is used widely in all scientific fields. The expression $y = xz$ is simply an equation relating the quantities x, y and z. It cannot properly be called a model since it represents no particular physical phenomenon. However, if the same equation is written as $F = ma$, it is recognized as a model in mechanics which represents the relationship between the mass, acceleration and resultant force on a physical body. It may be safely stated that until this model was formulated and verified, these concepts could not be well understood. Similarly in a decision problem, if a mathematical model can be discovered which expresses the relationship between the variables involved, then predictions can be made about the results and the problem itself can be better understood. Many of the expressions derived and studied in the following chapters are mathematical models which represent or describe a particular naval operation.

209 COMMUNICATING THE RESULTS

A problem solution is not complete until the results have been communicated to the military commander or civilian executive who is to make the final decision concerning the operations in question, *in a manner that will aid him in making that decision.* Many hours of tedious analysis and the most brilliant aspects of mathematical wizardry may be completely wasted if the results are not comprehensible to anyone but the analysts themselves. The requirement is aptly set forth in Commander, Operational Test and Evaluation Force (COMOPTEVFOR) project instructions (COMOPTEVFORINST P3930.1 series). COMOPTEVFOR reports are read by a wide audience composed of individuals with diverse backgrounds and different points of interest. Some members of this audience require an extensive amount of technical detail while others do not. An agency responsible for the correction of equipment deficiencies will require a detailed technical description of the project equipment, while a decision-maker or fleet user may require only a functional description of the equipment. Forcing the readers into a maze of technical detail beyond their needs can be just as harmful as omitting pertinent facts. In either extreme, the objectives of the report may be compromised. The solution to this conflict lies in the proper organization of the material within the report and the discreet use of technical language.

BIBLIOGRAPHY

[1] Morse and Kimball, *Methods of Operations Research,* MIT Press, 1951.
[2] E. S. Quade (ed.), *Analysis for Military Decisions,* The RAND Corporation, Santa Monica, November 1964.
[3] Charles J. Hitch and Roland N. McKean, *The Economics of Defense in the Nuclear Age,* The RAND Corporation, Santa Monica, March 1960.
[4] J. P. Large (ed.), *Concepts and Procedures of Cost Analysis,* The RAND Corporation, Santa Monica, June 1963.
[5] The reader is also referred to OPNAVINST 5000.19 series and NAVEXOS P-2457 (Department of the Navy RDT&E Management Guide, Volume I, dated 1 July 1964).
[6] Gaither Memorial Lectures, University of California, April 5–9, 1965, *Decision-Making in the Defense Department,* Part III, Cost Effectiveness.

PROBLEMS

1. Assume you are the decision-maker concerned with each of these problems. State what your real objective would be in each case.

   a. A midshipman first class about to graduate considering the best automobile to buy.
   b. A commanding officer considering the best action to take concerning Seaman Jones' return from liberty two hours late.
   c. The decision-maker faced with excess shipping losses referred to in Section 202.
   d. A married Lieutenant junior grade with one child considering the buying of life insurance.

2. In Section 203, how many ways are there of assigning CAP as described by the example if the following conditions exist:
   - $x \geq 1, y \geq 1, x + y \leq 6$, x and y integer valued, and
   - $h_1 < h_2$, where h_1 and h_2 have as possible values 5,000 feet, 10,000 feet, ..., 30,000 feet, and
   - r_1 and r_2 have as possible values $10, 20, ..., 50$ miles.

3. For one of the situations in Problem one list several reasonable alternative courses of action.

4. A decision-maker is considering the problem of detecting a target. Determine for each of the listed variables,

   (1) the amount of money available for procuring new detection equipment
   (2) the size of the enemy target
   (3) the target aspect angle during the search
   (4) the search time necessary for detection
   (5) the speed of the search unit
   (6) the speed of the target
   (7) the radar operator's current state of training
   (8) the distance between adjacent search units

   whether it is essentially:

   a. controllable.
   b. uncontrollable, but one whose value is known or can be measured.
   c. random.
   d. one whose value must be estimated or assumed.

5. For the situation you used in Problem three:

   a. List as many variables as you can which will significantly influence the outcome.
   b. For each of your variables indicate which of the categories (listed in Problem four) applies.
   c. Of these variables, which have values which can be represented quantitatively, i.e., by a number?
   d. Can any of your nonquantitative variables be changed or rephrased to make them quantitative?

6. For the antitorpedo net example in Section 205, assume the MOE is the difference between *number of ships saved because they carried nets* and *numbers of ships (with cargo) equivalent to costs associated with fitting nets*. If

   n = number of ships fitted with nets
   n_c = number of ships equivalent to cost of fitting nets, i.e., if cost associated with fitting nets was 10 million dollars and a ship with cargo was worth 2.5 million dollars then n_c would be four
   k_1 = fraction of ships fitted with nets which are attacked
   k_2 = fraction of ships which have nets in use when attacked
   s_1 = fraction of ships sunk when attacked (if nets not in use)
   s_2 = fraction of ships sunk when attacked (if nets were in use)

   a. Find an expression for the MOE in terms of the variables as defined.
   b. Compute the value of this MOE using data collected during the operation (tabulated in Section 205). Disregard the data on ships whose use of nets was unknown.
   c. If before the original decision was made to install nets, it was known or assumed that:
      • cost of fitting each ship = one percent of value of ship and cargo,
      • nets would be in use 50 percent of the time,
      • 5 percent of ships would be attacked,
      • 80 percent of ships attacked would be sunk if nets were not in use, and
      • 44 percent reduction in sinkings would occur if nets were in use, i.e., 80 percent minus .44(80 percent) = 45 percent of ships using nets would be sunk if attacked,
      what would be the value of the MOE for equipping no ships with nets? for 600 ships?
   d. If you were to make a decision between these two alternatives, $n = 0$ and $n = 600$, what additional factors would you want to consider?
   e. How much would usage of the nets have to increase, i.e., above 50 percent, in order for the value of the MOE in part c to be positive?
   f. Are any significant variables omitted from the previous problem?

7. How could a payoff matrix be set up to depict the results if *both* sea state and enemy tactics were critical in the text example in Section 207?

3 The Decision

This chapter deals primarily with the OA method and its application to naval operations. The method is used to provide a decision-maker with a quantitative basis for making decisions, taking into account as many factors as possible. But in no way does the OA method relieve the commander of the responsibility for making the decision. Instead it allows him to weigh more precisely the relative worth of each alternative including in the balance *both* quantitative and subjective aspects. In this text the terms *decision-maker* and *commander* are used interchangeably to denote that individual whose responsibility it is to make the decision and direct the conduct of the operation.

The advantage of providing a quantitative basis to a decision-maker is *not* that it makes his decision easier, for in many cases it may actually make his choice more difficult. The advantage is that he knows better what the consequences of his decision will be. In Chapter two solutions to decision problems were seen to exist in which the commander had no single best alternative, even if he disregarded any subjective factors involved. This chapter will present different types of payoff matrices which a decision-maker may face, and includes some of the criteria which can be used to determine which alternative is best. For the most part subjective factors will be disregarded, keeping in mind that the analyst should identify these factors and that the decision-maker must take them into account before reaching his final decision.

301 DEGREES OF RISK

Decisions must be made with varying degrees of knowledge about the conditions under which an operation or action will take place. Consider again the payoff matrix which appeared in Chapter two:

Alternatives	N1: Sea state 0 *or* 1	N2: Sea state 2 *or* 3	N3: Sea state 4 *or more*
S1: Search plan one:	.9	.4	.1
S2: Search plan two:	.7	.5	.4
S3: Search plan three:	.8	.7	.2
S4: Search plan four:	.5	.5	.5

Here, $S1$, $S2$, $S3$ and $S4$ represent the *strategies* or courses of action available to the commander; $N1$, $N2$ and $N3$ represent possible *states of nature* at the time the action is to take place; and the numbers in the matrix represent the measures of effectiveness or *payoffs* for each possible combination of strategies and states of nature. The strategies are different search plans, the states of nature are different sea states and the payoffs are the probabilities of detecting the object being searched for. It should be clear that the amount of risk involved in picking the single best course of action is determined by the uncertainty as to the state of nature which will occur.

Four possible cases are of interest. The first and simplest case arises when it is known with certainty the state of nature which will occur. The matrix reduces to a single column, and there is then *no risk* involved in determining the course of action with the best payoff. This is the case of *decision-making under certainty*. If it were known that a state of nature, say $N1$, would occur, then the payoff matrix would reduce to:

	N1
S1:	.9
S2:	.7
S3:	.8
S4:	.5

and the first strategy clearly yields the highest payoff (though it is not necessarily the best decision). Therefore the criterion for comparing alternatives in the case of decision-making under certainty is the *best payoff*.

The second case arises when it is not known which state of nature will occur, but where the *chance* that each will occur is known (or can be reasonably estimated). In this case there is some risk in choosing a best course of action and this situation is termed *decision-making under risk*. Suppose the chance that the states of nature, $N1$, $N2$ and $N3$, occur is .4, .5 and .1, respectively. If the first strategy were chosen, the payoff would be .9 with probability .4, .4 with probability .5 and .1 with probability .1. The *expected payoff* would then be the weighted average: $.9(.4) + .4(.5) + .1(.1) = .57$. If expected payoffs for each course of action are similarly computed, the results can be tabulated as follows:

	N1 (.4)	N2 (.5)	N3 (.1)	Expected payoff
S1:	.9	.4	.1	$.9(.4) + .4(.5) + .1(.1) = .57$
S2:	.7	.5	.4	$.7(.4) + .5(.5) + .4(.1) = .57$
S3:	.8	.7	.2	$.8(.4) + .7(.5) + .2(.1) = .69$
S4:	.5	.5	.5	$.5(.4) + .5(.5) + .5(.1) = .50$

In decision-making under risk, one should choose the strategy which *optimizes the expected value* of the measure of effectiveness. For the given payoff matrix it can be seen that the strategy $S3$ optimizes (in this case maximizes) the expected payoff.

A third case arises when the decision-maker does not know the probabilities of occurrence for the various states of nature. This circumstance is called *decision-making under uncertainty* for which several criteria have been suggested by various authors in order to choose the best course of action. Four of these criteria will be discussed in the next section.

The foregoing three cases of decision-making—under *certainty*, under *risk* and under *uncertainty*—apply to decision situations where the states of nature occur *without* regard to their effect on the decision-maker's payoff. The techniques of mathematics and statistics applied in such cases are collectively called *statistical decision theory*.

The fourth case of decision-making arises when the states of nature are controlled by a rational opponent, who may be expected to act, i.e., choose the state of nature, in such a way as to frustrate the decision-maker's objective. A situation of this kind was referred to in Chapter two and the payoff matrix is repeated.

Alternatives	*N*1: Enemy tactic one	*N*2: Enemy tactic two
*S*1: Search plan one:	.9	.5
*S*2: Search plan two:	.7	.6
*S*3: Search plan three:	.8	.3
*S*4: Search plan four:	.5	.4

Decision problems of this type are referred to as *games of strategy* and are the subject of a highly developed branch of mathematics called the *theory of games*. A brief introduction to the solution of simple games commences in Section 303. In this game, the opponent (enemy) can do his best by using his second tactic, against which search plan two should be chosen by the decision-maker.

The term *game*, used to describe the decision situation against an active opponent, suggests the commonly used term *game against nature* to describe the first three cases of decision-making.

302   CRITERIA FOR DECISION-MAKING UNDER UNCERTAINTY [1]

Suppose a commander was faced with the earlier payoff matrix but had *no* knowledge concerning the probable state of nature.

	*N*1	*N*2	*N*3
*S*1:	.9	.4	.1
*S*2:	.7	.5	.4
*S*3:	.8	.7	.2
*S*4:	.5	.5	.5

How can he determine *which course of action is best?* It will be seen presently that the word *best* takes on meaning only when considered in conjunction with a *particular* criterion. In this matrix, *S*1 is best if the state of nature is *N*1, likewise *S*3 is best for *N*2 and *S*4 is best for *N*3. Also, *S*1 offers the highest possible payoff, *S*3 the highest average payoff and *S*4 the highest guaranteed payoff. In addition, it will be shown that *S*2 is the strategy which will guarantee a decision-maker the *least regret*. As the following four different criteria for decision-making under uncertainty are discussed, it should be kept in mind that the question of *which criterion is best* cannot be answered in general. Only for a particular decision-maker facing a particular problem does a best criterion exist.

A conservative approach would be to look for the course of action which offers the *best guaranteed payoff*. The decision-maker can easily determine the guaranteed payoffs by asking, for each course of action: *What is the worst that can happen if I use this strategy?* The resulting guarantees for the previous matrix would be as follows:

	N1	N2	N3	Guaranteed payoff
S1:	.9	.4	.1	.1
S2:	.7	.5	.4	.4
S3:	.8	.7	.2	.2
S4:	.5	.5	.5	.5

The course of action which yields the highest guaranteed payoff is then $S4$. The decision-maker who chooses this course of action can do so knowing the payoff will be *at least .5 no matter what state of nature occurs*. This *criterion of pessimism* or *Wald criterion*, named for Abraham Wald who suggested it, minimizes the risk involved in making a decision. It is also referred to as the *maximin criterion* since the minimum payoff for each course of action is first found and then the course chosen which yields the maximum value of these minimum guaranteed payoffs.

The second criterion, while similar to the first, rejects the idea of being completely pessimistic. In the previous matrix, a complete optimist would be tempted, by the prospect of getting a payoff of .9, to pick the first course of action despite the possibility of getting its less desirable payoffs. This *maximax* choice is equivalent to assuming that nature is benevolent and thus will cause that state of nature to occur which is best for the decision-maker no matter which decision is made. A more rational use for maximax thinking is its identification of the best payoff possible for each decision available.

The third criterion is based on the tendency of some decision-makers to look back on their decision after the action is completed to see how much better they could have done by predicting the correct state of nature. This gives rise to the possibility of *minimizing regret* as a criterion for decision-making. Suppose the decision-maker computes the regret he could experience and constructs a *regret matrix* from the payoff matrix as follows:

	Payoff Matrix				*Regret Matrix*		
	N1	N2	N3		N1	N2	N3
S1:	.9	.4	.1		.9 − .9	.7 − .4	.5 − .1
S2:	.7	.5	.4		.9 − .7	.7 − .5	.5 − .4
S3:	.8	.7	.2		.9 − .8	.7 − .7	.5 − .2
S4:	.5	.5	.5		.9 − .5	.7 − .5	.5 − .5

Here the decision-maker would have no regret if he chose the first course of action and the state of nature, $N1$, occurred, since he could not have done better. If $N2$ were to occur however, his regret would be .3 since he could have done that much better by using strategy 3 (i.e., .7 minus .4), etc. This criterion, which was proposed by Leonard Savage, suggests that the Wald criterion be applied to the regret matrix in order to determine the strategy which *guarantees the least regret*. The first strategy guarantees a regret of not more than .4, the second a regret of not more than .2, etc., as tabulated:

Regret Matrix

	N1	N2	N3	Maximum regret
S1:	0	.3	.4	.4
S2:	.2	.2	.1	.2
S3:	.1	0	.3	.3
S4:	.4	.2	0	.4

The second strategy thus yields the least regret.

The final criterion to be presented, called the *criterion of rationality,* is attributed to Laplace. He argued that complete uncertainty about the probable state of nature is equivalent to assuming each state of nature equally probable. That is, if any state is assumed more likely than another, it is because more information is known and the decision-maker is not faced with complete uncertainty. The validity and implications of this argument have been debated for decades past and will most likely continue to be debated in the future. However, to use this criterion the expected payoff for each course of action can be computed as in *decision-making under risk* where each payoff is now weighted equally.

	N1 (1/3)	N2 (1/3)	N3 (1/3)	Expected payoff
S1:	.9	.4	.1	.467
S2:	.7	.5	.4	.533
S3:	.8	.7	.2	.567
S4:	.5	.5	.5	.500

The third course of action then, is best under the criterion of rationality.

In discussing these four criteria for decision-making under uncertainty, it was shown that for the payoff matrix used, four different courses of action resulted as best This is not generally the case, but it is by no means unique and points to the importance the *decision criterion* plays in choosing the best course of action.

The results of the preceding discussion are summarized for easy reference in the following table:

Decision under:	Criteria:
Certainty	Highest payoff
Risk	Largest expected payoff
Uncertainty	Pessimism or Maximin Optimism or Maximax Least regret Rationality

303 THE THEORY OF GAMES

Military decisions are usually made in *conflict situations.* That is, one side has goals and desires opposed to those of the other side. These conflicts exist in politics, business, parlor games and many other activities. Students have been examining such situations for years with the objective of trying to determine what each side can expect to gain in view of the opposing interests.

In 1944, these speculations were studied and codified for the first time in the publication *Theory of Games and Economic Behavior* [2], by von Neumann and Morgenstern. In that volume some of the simpler conflict situations are subjected to rigorous mathematical analysis and proof of the theorems which predict the results. Since that time, numerous other scholars have built on the same foundation. Practical application of the theory has been made in tactical situations, weapons system analysis, logistics and economics. More important to the military planner, the implications of the theory can be brought to bear on situations more complicated and less precise than those to which it was originally applied. However, many of these applications are tentative and limited in scope and much work remains to be done in applying the theory of games to military decisions. The time is here when a naval officer should have a knowledge of the way in which game theory can assist in decision-making. It is the purpose of this section to give a simplified explanation of what game theory is, how it can be applied in its pure form to various conflict situations, and how the logic employed in game theory may aid in arriving at sound military decisions.

It is emphasized at the outset that a magic formula is not being sought to solve difficult planning situations. Such a result, if it can be expected at all, is far in the future. Neither does game theory offer hope of simplifying the decision process. If anything, considering an estimate from the game theory point of view requires a higher degree of analysis and logical thought than does the present standard planning doctrine. It is submitted that an understanding of what game theory is and the type of reasoning behind it will aid the commander in maximizing his chances of success when faced with a difficult planning and decision situation.

Game theory has been described as a mathematical theory of decision-making in a conflict situation. There are several restrictions, however, on the types of conflicts which are discussed in this text* and are amenable to analysis by game theory.

a. The conflict must be focused on some central issue. This means that the participants must have opposing interests in the same objective.
b. Participants must make simultaneous or concurrent decisions as to which of a set of alternative courses of action to employ, and these decisions cannot be subject to revision during the conflict.
c. Each participant must be able to bring some influence to bear on the situation, but must not be able to exert complete control over the situation by himself.
d. Each of the participants must measure the worth of all possible outcomes on the same scale.

Consider the conflict which arises in the following situation:

Ensigns Baker and Rogers have equal investments in a car they jointly purchased at the beginning of their tour. Their new orders are sending them to different stations and they decide that the one who is willing to pay the other the most for his interest will become the sole owner. They agree the car is worth 1,000 dollars. Baker has 600 dollars and Rogers 400 dollars in cash, and they agree to submit bids in whole hundred dollar amounts. This conflict situation lends itself to analysis by game theory. The restrictions previously mentioned are met as follows:

*The more complex elements of the theory of games of strategy are covered in [2], [3], [4] and [5].

a. The conflict is focused on a central issue, i.e., the car. The interests are definitely opposed.

b. Each participant must select one of several alternative courses of action, i.e., bids of zero to 600 dollars for Baker and zero to 400 dollars for Rogers.

c. Each participant is able to influence, but not control, the outcome.

d. Each is assumed to measure the possible outcomes on the same scale inasmuch as they each have a similar investment in the car.

Game theory provides a method by which each participant can make a decision as to which alternative to employ.

In general, restriction **d** is the most difficult to meet in real world conflict situations. It is rare to find two people who value a given sum of money equally. Furthermore, it is seldom the case that 200 dollars is worth exactly twice as much as 100 dollars. This type of consideration is treated by *utility theory,* which concerns itself with measuring the true worth of things. The problem is fraught with difficulties for many reasons. First, there is no common denominator for true worth. Second, even when measured, worth does not remain constant. Which is really worth more, a dime or a dollar? It depends on the situation. In most common situations, a dollar would have the greater value, but at night, on a freeway in a stalled car, next to a phone booth, the dime may be worth more. In any event, the possible outcomes must be worth the same to all participants. Otherwise a game theoretic approach may produce unexpected results.

Before a decision can be made regarding which of a set of alternatives to employ, the decision-maker must choose a criterion, several of which have already been discussed. For example, the decision-maker might be conservative or he might be in a speculative mood. The proper criterion depends on the expected outcomes. It may be appropriate to make speculative decisions when dealing with relatively small amounts. On the other hand, if possible losses are large, a conservative decision may be in order.

In general, a military commander makes conservative decisions. He desires to gain as much as possible, safely, in the face of a skillful opponent whose objective is diametrically opposed. This is essentially the Wald criterion, which is the reasonable criterion to use in a conflict situation involving a rational opponent. In a game situation, the Wald criterion will lead each player to a strategy which insures that the least amount he can expect to win will be as large as possible.

There are certain terms which must be defined at this point. It will be helpful if the reader recognizes these terms as technical words with special meanings for game theory.

a. Person: One of the opposing interests or players.

b. Game: The set of rules that define what can and cannot be done, the size of bets or penalties and payoff methods. The rules must be complete, must not change during the game and must be known to the participants.

c. Zero-sum game: One in which the total winnings equal the total losses.

d. Play of the game: The choosing of a particular alternative or course of action by each player, along with the exchange of the payoff which results.

e. Strategy: A player's plan of action that is complete and ready to use before the commencement of the game.

f. Optimal strategy: A strategy which guarantees a player the best he can expect regardless of what the other player does.

g. Value of the game: The expected payoff when each player is using his optimal strategy.

h. Solution: An optimal strategy for each player and a real number which is called the value of the game.

Although game theory includes many possible situations, the only ones discussed here will be *two-person, zero-sum* games. By convention, these games are portrayed in terms of matrices. The player who is attempting to maximize the payoff is conventionally known as *Blue;* his set of alternative courses of action consists of the rows of the matrix. He must choose, at any play of the game, one of the rows. The other player is known as *Red.* He attempts to minimize the payoff, and chooses one of the columns in any play of the game. The numbers in the matrix, also by convention, represent the payoffs *from Red to Blue.* Thus, if a particular play of the game dictates a payoff from *Blue to Red,* a negative number appears in the matrix.

Once a conflict situation has been formulated as a game, the next step is the procedure for solving the game.

304   SADDLE-POINT GAMES

Consider again the car problem. If Baker bids 300 dollars and Rogers bids 200 dollars, Baker gets the car and pays Rogers 300 dollars for a net gain of 200 dollars on his investment. On the other hand if Baker's 300 dollars is met by a 400 dollar bid from Rogers, then Rogers gets the car in exchange for 400 dollars and Baker suffers a net loss of 100 dollars. There are other ways of arriving at reasonable payoffs but, however done, they must be consistent. In this case, we choose to compute Baker's *net payoff* for all the combinations of bids which may appear. Suppose, however, that the bids are equal. In such a case, Baker and Rogers agree to flip a coin to see which of them gets the car in exchange for his bid. If both bid 300 dollars, for example, Baker's net gain is 200 dollars if he gets the car and -200 dollars if he receives instead the 300 dollars. Either outcome is equally probable and his net expected gain is then zero. The reader should similarly verify the other payoffs in the following matrix (in hundreds of dollars):

| | | Red (Rogers) | | | | |
		R1 Bid 0	R2 Bid 1	R3 Bid 2	R4 Bid 3	R5 Bid 4
Blue (Baker)						
B1:	Bid 0	0	-4	-3	-2	-1
B2:	Bid 1	4	0	-3	-2	-1
B3:	Bid 2	3	3	0	-2	-1
B4:	Bid 3	2	2	2	0	-1
B5:	Bid 4	1	1	1	1	0
B6:	Bid 5	0	0	0	0	0
B7:	Bid 6	-1	-1	-1	-1	-1

Baker, when faced with this payoff matrix, can immediately see that a bid of zero may result in as much as a 400 dollar loss while other bids seem to offer less risk. Using the Wald criterion he asks himself what is the worst he can do for each of his alternatives. His findings are shown in the following matrix and the zero is starred to represent the highest guarantee he has available—in this case by bidding either 400 or 500 dollars.

		R1 Bid 0	R2 Bid 1	R3 Bid 2	R4 Bid 3	R5 Bid 4	Blue Guarantee (minimum in each row)
B1:	Bid 0	0	-4	-3	-2	-1	-4
B2:	Bid 1	4	0	-3	-2	-1	-3
B3:	Bid 2	3	3	0	-2	-1	-2
B4:	Bid 3	2	2	2	0	-1	-1
B5:	Bid 4	1	1	1	1	0	0*
B6:	Bid 5	0	0	0	0	0	0*
B7:	Bid 6	-1	-1	-1	-1	-1	-1

Red (Rogers) — Blue (Baker)

maximum of row minima or maximin

But Rogers can also exert some influence on the results by the proper choice of his strategies. Being also rational he asks himself the same question, *What is the worst possible outcome?*, for each of his alternatives (realizing that Baker's gains are his losses). If he bids 100 dollars, for example, Baker's payoff may be as high as 300 dollars, whereas by a proper choice he can insure that Baker does no better than break even. The starred result in the next matrix indicates his best guarantee. In all such games,

Red (Rogers)

		R1 Bid 0	R2 Bid 1	R3 Bid 2	R4 Bid 3	R5 Bid 4
B1:	Bid 0	0	-4	-3	-2	-1
B2:	Bid 1	4	0	-3	-2	-1
B3:	Bid 2	3	3	0	-2	-1
B4:	Bid 3	2	2	2	0	-1
B5:	Bid 4	1	1	1	1	0
B6:	Bid 5	0	0	0	0	0
B7:	Bid 6	-1	-1	-1	-1	-1
Red Guarantee: (maximum in each column)		4	3	2	1	0*

Blue (Baker)

saddle-point

(minimum of column maxima or minimax)

the *minimax* is greater than or equal to the *maximin*. In this situation, something of a coincidence appears; the two are *equal* and Blue's best guarantee is equal to Red's best guarantee. When this is the case, a *saddle-point* is said to exist and the optimal strategies for both players are those which yield the saddle-point. In this example, two saddle-points exist as Baker may bid either 400 or 500 dollars while Rogers should bid 400 dollars. The reader may verify that a saddle-point must be both the minimum value in its row and the maximum value in its column. If either player varies from the saddle-point strategies, he loses his guarantee. The value of this game is zero, the expected payoff when both players use their optimal strategies. Actually, Baker may prefer to bid 400 dollars rather than 500 dollars since he would gain more if Rogers bids unwisely.

When approaching a game, the first step in finding the solution is always to check for a saddle-point. If one does exist, the solution is immediate as the optimal strategies for the Blue and Red are evident and the value of the game is the saddle-point value. If a saddle-point exists but is not found, the solution methods discussed hereafter may fail.

Although the solution came easily in the foregoing example, do not assume that the same is true of games in general. On the contrary—the solution in a large game may be extremely difficult to find.

305   DOMINANCE

Large games can often be reduced in size by inspecting the payoff matrix to discover strategies which a player should never use. Such poor strategies are said to be *dominated* by other better strategies. A strategy may be eliminated from consideration in solving a game if there is another strategy which is *as good or better* against *every* strategy the opponent may use.

Such strategies are evident in the game between Baker and Rogers. For example, compare Baker's first two strategies which are repeated. Here Baker's strategy $B2$ is as

Red

	R1	R2	R3	R4	R5
Blue B1:	0	-4	-3	-2	-1
B2:	4	0	-3	-2	-1

good or better than $B1$ no matter what Rogers does, i.e., four is better than zero, zero is better than minus four, minus three is as good as minus three, minus two is as good as minus two and minus one is as good as minus one. Hence, the strategy $B1$ may be eliminated in searching for a solution to the game. In like manner, Baker's sixth and seventh strategies may be eliminated by dominance. The reduced matrix is then:

	Red (Rogers)				
Blue (Baker)	R1	R2	R3	R4	R5
B2	4	0	-3	-2	-1
B3	3	3	0	-2	-1
B4	2	2	2	0	-1
B5	1	1	1	1	0

It can be reduced even further because Rogers also has dominated strategies. His strategy $R2$ is as good or better than strategy $R1$ no matter which of the four strategies Baker may now use (remember that large payoffs are good for Baker, poor for Rogers). Hence $R1$ can be eliminated. Also, $R2$ is worse for Rogers than any of his remaining strategies and the game can now be reduced to:

	Red (Rogers)		
Blue (Baker)	R3	R4	R5
B2	-3	-2	-1
B3	0	-2	-1
B4	2	0	-1
B5	1	1	0

Further dominance can be found by alternating between Blue and Red strategies. This matrix would finally be reduced to the single strategies $B5$ and $R5$ with payoff *zero*, a previously found solution to the game.

All games with saddle-points cannot be so reduced by dominance, however, as the following matrix shows:

	Red				
Blue	R1	R2	R3	R4	
B1	2	3	3	4	2*
B2	1	0	4	3	0
B3	1	4	0	2	0
B4	1	2	3	1	1
	2*	4	4	4	

Here a saddle-point is found at the intersection of Blue's first and Red's first strategies. Hence, the solution is $B1$, $R1$ and the game value is two. If, however, dominance is considered, only $B4$ and $R4$ can be eliminated.

In games where a saddle-point does *not* exist, the matrix should be reduced as far as possible, discarding poor strategies by dominance. Dominance could in fact have been applied to the choices of strategies in the statistical decision cases considered in *Sections 301 and 302,* although the computational effort involved might not have been worthwhile. However, *those* decision cases are made against *future states of nature*, so dominance there would *only* be applied *to the rows* and *not to the columns*. A future, indifferent state of nature will not rationalize dominance, as will a logical opponent who controls the column choices with deliberate objectives.

306   MIXED STRATEGIES

Next consider a matrix without a saddle-point in which each player has only two good strategies, i.e., a 2 × 2 (called *two by two*) matrix. This matrix may appear after reducing a larger game by dominance or it may be an original 2 × 2 game. As an example consider the following operation which may be repeated many times.

A bomb is to be delivered to a target by one of two identical bombers, the other bomber being used to decoy or to ward off enemy fighters. The lead bomber has a probability of .6 of surviving a single attack by an enemy fighter while the rear bomber has a probability of .3 of surviving a similar attack, being in a less protected position. If a single attack against the bombers occurs before reaching the target, in which bomber should the bomb be placed to maximize its chances of reaching the target? The fighter, of course, will choose to attack a particular bomber with the object of destroying the bomb.

There are several ways of setting up the payoff matrix in order to consider this situation as a game. For example, let the payoff be the *probability the bomb reaches the target*. Then the opponent with the bomb is the maximizing player, thus called Blue and shown at the left side of the payoff matrix as follows:

Red

	R1 (attack lead bomber)	R2 (attack rear bomber)
Blue B1: (place bomb in lead bomber)	.6	1.0
B2: (place bomb in rear bomber)	1.0	.3

If Blue places the bomb in the lead bomber, the chance of the bomb getting through if Red attacks the lead bomber is .6, and is 1.0 if the rear bomber is attacked. If Blue places the bomb in the rear bomber, its chance of getting through if the rear bomber is attacked is .3, and is 1.0 otherwise.

In checking for a saddle-point, guarantees are found for Blue and Red as before.

Red

	R1	R2	Blue's guarantees:
Blue B1	.6	1.0	.6*
B2	1.0	.3	.3
Red's guarantees:	1.0*	1.0*	

Blue can assure himself a payoff of at least .6 by choosing strategy *B*1. With either of Red's strategies, the bomb may get through unopposed, i.e., with probability 1.0, although he may be tempted to use his first strategy since $B1$ is Blue's best strategy. There is considerable difference in magnitude between the *maximin* and the *minimax* in this matrix. In such a case either player could benefit greatly by knowing what strategy the other player is using. Hence each player must take care that the opponent does not discover his strategy ahead of time.

Without knowledge of his opponent's strategy, Blue's best choice would be to put the bombs in the lead bomber and guarantee a payoff of at least .6. Is there any way for Blue to increase this guarantee without undue risk? Suppose this game were repeated several times and Blue put the bomb in the rear plane occasionally just to keep his opponent off guard—in the hopes of increasing his *average* payoff. He might, for example, use the *mixed strategy* of putting the bomb in the lead 8/10 of the time and in the rear 2/10 of the time. What would be the expected outcome using this mixed strategy?

If Red always attacked the lead bomber, Blue's payoff would be .6 on 8/10 of the plays and 1.0 on 2/10 of the plays for an expected (average) payoff of $.6(8/10) + 1.0(2/10) = .68$. If, however, Red always attacked the rear bomber, Blue's expected payoff would be $1.0(8/10) + .3(2/10) = .86$. Then by using this mixed strategy, Blue would have an expected payoff of at least .68 no matter what Red's strategy might be. This minimum expected payoff of .68 is certainly higher than the payoff of .6 that Blue can guarantee by always playing $B1$.

Red

		R1	R2
Blue			
B1:	(8/10)	.6	1.0
B2:	(2/10)	1.0	.3

Blue's expected payoff: .68*   .86

Notice that if Red knew what Blue's mixed strategy was (without knowing the location of the bomb on a particular play), he would prefer to attack the lead bomber $R1$ and make Blue's expectation only .68 rather than .86.

Blue may now try mixing his strategies $B1$, $B2$, in the ratio 6/10 to 4/10. Against $R1$, this mixed strategy would yield $.6(6/10) + 1.0(4/10) = .76$, and against $R2$, Blue's expected payoff would be $1.0(6/10) + .3(4/10) = .72$. The minimum expected payoff would now be .72 which is again better than before, but Red would now do better by attacking the rear bomber.

Red

		R1	R2
Blue			
B1:	(6/10)	.6	1.0
B2:	(4/10)	1.0	.3

Blue's expected payoff: .76   .72*

A method will now be given for computing the best or *optimal mixed strategy*, i.e., which will make Blue's minimum expected payoff the highest value possible. This value will be the *value of the game* (denoted by V) and will be the expected payoff against *both* of Red's strategies. The value of the game, when players use mixed strategies, will always be found to lie between the minimax and maximin values which the players would have received if they had employed their optimal pure strategies.

Let x_1 be the fraction of time that Blue should use his first strategy, and x_2 the fraction of time he should use his second in order to insure his highest minimum expected payoff. Note that $x_2 = 1 - x_1$.

Then $.6x_1 + 1.0x_2$ is the expected payoff against Red's first strategy and $1.0x_1 + .3x_2$ is the expected payoff against Red's second strategy.

	Red	
	R1	R2
Blue B1: (x_1)	.6	1.0
B2: (x_2)	1.0	.3

Blue's expected payoff:

$$.6x_1 + 1.0x_2$$

$$1.0x_1 + .3x_2$$

Since both of these expected payoffs equal the value of the game:

$$.6x_1 + x_2 = V,$$
$$x_1 + .3x_2 = V,$$

and

$$x_1 + x_2 = 1.$$

These can easily be solved for x_1 and x_2 by setting the first two equations equal to each other and substituting for x_2 the quantity $1 - x_1$, i.e.,

$$.6x_1 + x_1 = x_1 + .3x_2$$

or

$$.6x_1 + (1 - x_1) = x_1 + .3(1 - x_1).$$

Solving for x_1 then gives

$$x_1 = 7/11,$$

and

$$x_2 = 1 - x_1 = 4/11,$$

thus

$$V = .6x_1 + x_2$$
$$= .6(7/11) + 4/11$$
$$= .745.$$

Thus Blue has a way of mixing his strategies so that his expected payoff is at least .745 no matter what strategy Red chooses to use.

Red

		R1	R2
Blue			
B1:	$(x_1 = 7/11)$	.6	1.0
B2:	$(x_2 = 4/11)$	1.0	.3

Blue's expected payoff: .745   .745

Now that Blue's optimal mixed strategy has been found, is there also an optimal way for Red to mix his strategies in order to insure himself as favorable an outcome as possible? There is, and as a matter of fact the solution to a game requires that Red's optimal mixed strategy also be found. But first consider a specific example. Suppose Red uses R1 half of the time and R2 half of the time. Then against Blue's first strategy, Red would yield to Blue an expected payoff of $.6(1/2) + 1.0(1/2) = .8$, and against Blue's second strategy a payoff of $1.0(1/2) + .3(1/2) = .65$. Thus using this mixed strategy, Red would yield to Blue an expected payoff no greater than .80 no matter what strategy Blue chooses. For Red, an expected payoff of no more than .8 is better than yielding as much as 1.0 using a single strategy.

	Red		Red's expected
	R1 (1/2)	R2 (1/2)	payoff to Blue
Blue			
B1	.6	1.0	.80*
B2	1.0	.3	.65

Red's object now is to find the mixed strategy which will make the highest of these expected payoffs as low as possible. Again this will occur when both expected payoffs are equal.

Let y_1 be the fraction of time Red should use R1 and y_2 the fraction of time he uses R2, where again $y_2 = 1 - y_1$; then

	Red		Red's expected
	R1 (y_1)	R2 (y_2)	payoff to Blue
Blue			
B1	.6	1.0	$.6y_1 + 1.0y_2 = V$
B2	1.0	.3	$1.0y_1 + .3y_2 = V$

Setting these expected payoffs equal gives

$$.6y_1 + y_2 = y_1 + .3y_2$$

and substituting $y_2 = 1 - y_1$,

$$.6y_1 + (1 - y_1) = y_1 + .3(1 - y_1),$$

or

$$1.1y_1 = .7,$$

so that

$$y_1 = 7/11,$$

and

$$y_2 = 1 - y_1 = 4/11.$$

Then

$$V = .6y_2 + y_2$$
$$= .6(7/11) + 4/11$$
$$= .745.$$

Blue has a mixed strategy which guarantees him an expected payoff of at least .745 and Red has mixed strategy which yields to Blue an expected payoff of not more than .745. When both use their optimal mixed strategies, the expected payoff of .745 is the value of the game. That these two guarantees are equal is not merely coincidence. For any matrix game there exist good strategies for Red and Blue which produce this result.*

The solution to this game is: Blue should mix his first and second strategies respectively $(7/11, 4/11)$, Red should mix his first and second strategies $(7/11, 4/11)$, and the value of the game is $V = .745$. In this game Blue's and Red's strategies are the same because of symmetry in the payoff matrix, an occurrence which is not generally the case.

In order to clarify terms which are often used in games, the following additional definitions are given: A player's use of a single course of action for all plays of the game is a *pure strategy*. A *mixed strategy* is a way of using two or more courses of action on different plays of the game. The *optimal pure strategy* is the pure strategy which gives a player his best guarantee, i.e., the maximin for Blue and the minimax for Red. The *optimal strategy* called for in the solution to a game is the *optimal pure strategy* in a game with a saddle-point, and is an *optimal mixed strategy* otherwise.

When an optimal mixed strategy is used, an opponent cannot benefit from knowing what that strategy is, provided he does not know what course of action will be used on a specific play. In using a mixed strategy, then, a player can insure secrecy and prevent an opponent from out-guessing him by using some random device immediately before each play to select the particular course of action for that play. For example, if Blue wants to use the mixed strategy, $(x_1 = 7/11, x_2 = 4/11)$, he could mark a spinner into 11 equal sectors, seven marked $B1$ and four marked $B2$. He could even allow Red to see the completed spinner without affecting his success. But before each play he must spin the spinner and take the resulting course of action without Red finding it out.

307   CHECKING THE SOLUTION

What if a game does not have a saddle-point and cannot be reduced by dominance to a 2×2? Finding the solution to such games becomes more involved although several methods are readily available for use. The significant difference lies in the fact that 2×2 games either have saddle-points, in which a pure strategy is optimal, or they belong to the class of *all strategies active* games where *all* courses of action are used in an optimal mixed strategy.

---

*That this is true is a consequence of the *minimax theorem* in the game theory. For further treatment or proof see [2], [3] or [4] in the bibliography at the end of the chapter. For an excellent and interesting treatment of game theory on an elementary level see [5].

A larger game presents other possibilities. Even when a saddle-point does *not* exist the game may not have all strategies active, i.e., the optimal mixed strategy may use only part of the available pure strategies.

In the following 3×3 game, no saddle-point exists.

Red

	R1 (y_1)	R2 (y_2)	R3 (y_3)
Blue			
B1: (x_1)	3	12	8
B2: (x_2)	6	6	5
B3: (x_3)	9	4	6

Let x_1, x_2 and x_3 be the fractions of time that Blue should play B1, B2 and B3, respectively, using his optimal mixed strategy. Let y_1, y_2 and y_3 be similarly defined for Red's three strategies. Then $x_1 + x_2 + x_3 = 1$ and $y_1 + y_2 + y_3 = 1$, and some of these values may be zero for either player.

If Blue uses this mixed strategy, (x_1, x_2, x_3), the expected payoff would be:

$$3x_1 + 6x_2 + 9x_3, \quad \text{if Red uses } R1,$$
$$12x_1 + 6x_2 + 4x_3, \quad \text{if Red uses } R2 \text{ and}$$
$$8x_1 + 5x_2 + 6x_3, \quad \text{if Red uses } R3.$$

For this to be Blue's optimal mixed strategy, each of these expected payoffs must be *greater than* or *equal to* the value of the game.

Also, if Red uses the mixed strategy, (y_1, y_2, y_3), the expected payoff yielded to Blue would be:

$$3y_1 + 12y_2 + 8y_3, \quad \text{if Blue uses } B1,$$
$$6y_1 + 6y_2 + 5y_3, \quad \text{if Blue uses } B2 \text{ and}$$
$$9y_1 + 4y_2 + 6y_3, \quad \text{if Blue uses } B3.$$

For this to be Red's optimal mixed strategy, each of these expected payoffs must be *less than* or *equal to* the value of the game.

Hence the solution to this game consists of finding values for $x_1, x_2, x_3, y_1, y_2, y_3$ and V so that all of the following relationships hold:

$$3x_1 + 6x_2 + 9x_3 \geq V,$$
$$12x_1 + 6x_2 + 4x_3 \geq V,$$
$$8x_1 + 5x_2 + 6x_3 \geq V,$$
$$3y_1 + 12y_2 + 8y_3 \leq V,$$
$$6y_1 + 6y_2 + 5y_3 \leq V,$$
$$9y_1 + 4y_2 + 6y_3 \leq V,$$

$$x_1 + x_2 + x_3 = 1, \quad \text{where each } x_1 \text{ is nonnegative and}$$
$$y_1 + y_2 + y_3 = 1, \quad \text{where each } y_1 \text{ is nonnegative.}$$

Completely specific methods will not be presented in this text for solving games larger than 2×2. The preceding expressions can easily be used to verify or reject *possible* solutions.

Is it optimal, for example, for both Blue and Red to use each of their strategies 1/3 of the time, i.e., Blue: (1/3, 1/3, 1/3) and Red: (1/3, 1/3, 1/3)?

The same expressions must be tested—does a value V exist such that,

for Blue:

$$3(1/3) + 6(1/3) + 9(1/3) = 6 \geq V,$$
$$12(1/3) + 6(1/3) + 4(1/3) = 7\ 1/3 \geq V,$$
$$8(1/3) + 5(1/3) + 6(1/3) = 6\ 1/3 \geq V,$$

and for Red:

$$3(1/3) + 12(1/3) + 8(1/3) = 7\ 2/3 \leq V,$$
$$6(1/3) + 6(1/3) + 5(1/3) = 5\ 2/3 \leq V,$$
$$9(1/3) + 4(1/3) + 6(1/3) = 6\ 1/3 \leq V?$$

There is no number V which satisfies all these expressions; hence, these strategies are not optimal. With these strategies, Blue's minimum expected payoff is six and Red's maximum expected payoff (to Blue) is 7 2/3. If these strategies were optimal, Blue's minimum and Red's maximum expected payoffs would be equal (to each other and to the value of the game) and the solution would be found.

308 MILITARY DECISIONS AND GAME THEORY

A player's decision to attempt to increase his gain above that guaranteed by the optimal pure strategy always involves a certain risk. Recall that the solution in mixed strategies yields an expected payoff equal to the value of the game. The theory hinges on the word *expected*. As the number of repetitions of the game increases, the probability of actually realizing this expected payoff tends toward certainty. But for any one play of the game, the player may realize more or less than the value of the game.

Before a player chooses to use a mixed strategy solution, he must consider the number of times the game is likely to be played and what the numbers in the payoff matrix represent. There is a large difference between aircraft carriers and rifle platoons. One is less inclined to accept as much risk where the possible loss of an aircraft carrier is involved, as he would if he stood to lose a rifle platoon. Consider the following game matrix:

Red

	R1	R2
Blue B1	–2	6
B2	3	1

The optimal mixed strategy for Blue is to play $B1$ with probability 1/5 and $B2$ with probability 4/5. This may be acceptable if the numbers represent rifle platoons. That is, one might risk the loss of two platoons in order to gain six platoons. If, however, the numbers represent aircraft carriers, it is hard to imagine such a choice. The question which must always be answered in the mind of the decision-maker is whether the *expected gain* using a mixed strategy is worth the *risk* of getting an occasional payoff worse than that guaranteed by the optimal pure strategy.

Even though there is risk involved in choosing a mixed strategy solution over the more conservative pure strategy solution, there is some support for such a choice even in the case of games played only once. The first argument is that no intelligence regarding a player's past actions can aid his opponent in making his choice of alternatives. The second argument is that one expects to engage in a large number of single-play games during a lifetime. Playing a series of different single-play games is equivalent, in a sense, to playing the same game many times. A player who uses optimal mixed strategies expects to gain more than his guarantee on some games, and less than his guarantee on others.

In naval planning [6], the *estimate of the situation* is essentially a formulation of a matrix game. The commander arrays his own courses of action against enemy capabilities. All possible interactions are studied to determine expected outcomes. These outcomes then become the elements in the game matrix. It is not necessary that the outcomes be expressed as numbers, but it *is* necessary that the outcomes be ordered by worth to the commander. The problem of the commander is to select the best course of action. Established doctrine dictates the selection of that course of action which promises to be most successful in the accomplishment of the mission, *regardless of what the enemy chooses to do in opposition.*

In the following example, Blue's mission is to capture an objective defended by Red. Blue lists enemy capabilities and his own courses of action, and calculates the interactions. His description of the payoffs are shown in this matrix:

Red capabilities

		R1	R2	R3
	B1	Fail	Succeed	Succeed
Blue courses of action	B2	Draw	Succeed	Draw
	B3	Succeed	Fail	Fail

Blue's proper choice is *B*2, because at worst the result is a *draw*. This corresponds in game theory to choosing the optimal pure strategy.

Knowledge of the opponent's plan can be valuable if there is no saddle-point in the game matrix. This *intelligence* allows a player to maximize against a single enemy course of action rather than against his whole spectrum of capabilities. If it happens that the intelligence is not sufficiently complete to identify a single enemy course of action, but *does* eliminate certain of the enemy's strategies, these latter courses of action may be treated as dominated and discarded from the matrix. The use of intelligence is equivalent to listing enemy *intentions* instead of enemy *capabilities.* The *value* of intelligence is related to the difference between the *minimax* and the *maximin*—the smaller this difference, the less the intelligence is worth.

Generally, the opposing interests do not have the same scale of values. This means that the numbers put in the matrix are not regarded equally by both players. Nonetheless, a commander who uses enemy capabilities and makes a decision in terms of pure strategies does not have to worry about the enemy's value scale. If the enemy deviates from his correct strategy, he will only increase the payoff to the commander. An opponent's action in such a case may be regarded as irrational behavior. It may be that one (or both) opponents at the end of the game consider they have received a payoff greater than their guaranteed minimum. In conflict situations, therefore, one participant's gain is not necessarily another's loss. War itself is manifestation of such *non–zero sum* games.

In the preceding discussion of mixed strategies it was noted that the result is assured only after sufficient repetition to bring statistical probability into play. Successive actions in military affairs will not, in general, exactly reproduce the circumstances of the first play of the game. It would appear that this is a stumbling block to using the concept of mixed strategies.

It is interesting to note that von Neumann and Morgenstern, in deducing their theories [2] on mixed strategy, solved the problem specifically for games played only once. They showed that the course of action in the mixed strategy situation played once should be selected by a random choice in the same manner as was indicated for repeated plays of the game. In fact a mathematical purist can object that the theory is proven for the single play only. It has not been extended to include games played many times. Williams, in *The Compleat Strategyst* [5], devotes considerable attention to this point. He cites as part of his discussion the following situation:

> Consider a nonrepeatable game which is terribly important to you, and in which your opponent has excellent human intelligence of all kinds. Also assume that it will be murderous if your opponent *knows* which strategy you will adopt. Your only hope is to select a strategy by a chance device which the enemy's intelligence cannot master—he may be lucky of course and anticipate your choice anyway but you have to accept some risk. Game theory simply tells you the characteristics your chance device should have.
>
> You may also adopt the viewpoint that you will play many one-shot games between the cradle and the grave, not all of them being lethal games, and that the use of mixed strategies will improve your batting average over this set of games.

There are several reasons why a military commander, faced with a mixed strategy picture in his matrix, in a single play situation would be under pressure to follow the conservative course—play the *maximin* game on an estimate of enemy capabilities. In the first place, present doctrine favors this course: the training to which he has been subjected leads to this conclusion except in clearly exceptional circumstances. The usual pattern of superiors is to give the subordinate enough forces to accomplish the objective and then hold him strictly accountable for the results. Defeat can have a shattering effect on a leader's career. Conservatism is thus reinforced. In addition, the American tradition frowns on sacrificing men and material to set up a situation of success in the future. All of these things reinforce the tendency to conservatism, of proceeding by massing superior forces and grinding out a victory. It has been successful in the past.

It should be evident by now that such a doctrine is not sufficient for situations of equal or inferior strength. And there is grave doubt that it accomplishes the result desired at minimum cost and time even when the force *is* superior. How can we change our doctrine to take advantage of the gains of mixed strategy?

Colonel Haywood makes several sound suggestions in his thesis [7] on this matter. In the first place, it is not meant to press the superiority of mixed strategy unduly. The *fog of war* will have some effect in randomizing our (and the enemy's) strategies. He suggests, in lieu of a fully determined mixed strategy, that superiors in control of a number of subordinate units direct, in a random fashion, that these subordinates base their actions on capabilities for a certain period and intentions for another.

The purpose of Sections 303 through 307 has been to present a simplified explanation of game theory in the hope that the reader will become interested enough to pursue the subject further. Game theory gives a different point of view on the subject of military decision-making. Commanders who become familiar with it may aid their thinking by injecting a new and fresh insight. This is the most valuable contribution that game theory can make at the present time. For, except in a limited range of problems, it is not available for actual solutions of military planning dilemmas. Despite limitations in using the theory in military problems, however, there are certain conclusions which appear to be warranted at the present time.

a. The use of the matrix form for representing the interaction of strategies is superior to that recommended in the *Naval Planning Manual*. [6] It should be used as the commander's summary and visual aid.

b. Familiarity with the concepts of *maximin, minimax, pure* strategy and *mixed* strategy will enable the commander to use his matrix as a check of his *estimate of the situation*. It is *not* recommended as *the* estimate. Nevertheless, it is believed that Colonel Haywood's maxim holds good:

> If the commander is not prepared to make a matrix of the opposing strategies for the situation, he is not prepared to make a decision. [7]

c. If mathematical expressions of the worth of each outcome are available for inclusion in a matrix, the theory will give the proper strategy to follow or indicate the range of choice. Due to the lack of a scale of values to describe military payoffs, a mixed strategy can seldom be used. However, by using a qualitative scale satisfactory to himself, the commander can gain indications from the matrix relations of the proper strategy subject to the range of uncertainty contained in his scale. These relations can be useful as a check against the body of the estimate. If they do not correspond, he has a clear warning to stop and reconsider.

d. The matrix can provide, subject to the range of uncertainty of the scale of values, a measure of the worth of intelligence effort and the difference in payoff between basing an estimate on enemy capabilities and enemy intentions.

e. Game theory clearly points up the essential conservatism of present military doctrine, of basing estimates on enemy capabilities. Unlike such a doctrine, it indicates a course of action if forces are equal to or inferior to those of the enemy.

f. Since the scale of values is the crux of the matter, game theory indicates in certain circumstances the importance of *knowing your enemy*. It thus reinforces that military maxim.

BIBLIOGRAPHY

[1] David W. Miller and Martin K. Starr, *Executive Decisions and Operations Research,* Prentice Hall, Inc., Englewood Cliffs, N.J., 1960.

[2] John von Neumann and Oskar Morgenstern, *Theory of Games and Economic Behavior,* Princeton University Press, Princeton, 1944.

[3] Melvin Dresher, *Games of Strategy: Theory and Applications,* The RAND Corporation, Santa Monica, 1961.

[4] R. Duncan Luce and Howard Raiffa, *Games and Decisions,* Introduction and Critical Survey, John Wiley and Sons, Inc., New York, 1957.

[5] J. D. Williams, *The Compleat Strategyst,* McGraw-Hill, New York, 1964.
[6] *Naval Planning Manual,* Naval War College, Newport, R.I., Rev. 1966.
[7] Col. O. G. Haywood, Jr., *Military Decision and the Mathematical Theory of Games,* Air University Q., Rev 4 (1950).

PROBLEMS

1. Immediately after take-off on an important mission an *F*-4 pilot notices his oil pressure low and fluctuating. Should he continue the mission or not? It may be only the gauge; on the other hand it could be loss of oil, which could lead to disaster. His primary consideration is the completion of the mission, yet the safety of himself and the aircraft are also important.

   Suppose he had anticipated such a situation at a more leisurely time and set up the following payoff matrix:

		N1 Gauge bad	N2 Loss of oil
S1:	Continue	10	−20
S2:	Turn-back	−5	0

   a. What is the conservative choice?
   b. Which choice guarantees the least regret?
   c. The criterion of rationality would lead to which choice?

2. During an automobile trip, Ensign Brown notices that his gas gauge reads zero and doesn't know whether he can make it to his destination before running out of fuel. He judges his chances of making it to be about 80 percent. He could use the extra gallon of gas in the trunk but a heavy rain is falling and he'd rather not get wet. If he runs out and *then* puts the extra gas in the tank, his car (with a weak battery) may not start again. All things considered, he finds the following payoffs reasonable in estimating the various outcomes.

		N1 Enough gas to make it	N2 Will run out
S1:	Put in gas now	−5	−5
S2:	Take a chance	0	−15

   a. Is his decision to be made under certainty, risk or uncertainty?
   b. What should his decision be?

3. For the following payoff matrix:

	N1	N2	N3	N4
S1:	5	1	5	2
S2:	3	2	3	3
S3:	4	6	0	5

Which is the best strategy:

a. Using the Wald criterion?
b. Using the criterion of least regret?
c. Using the Laplace criterion?

4. Blue now holds two military positions which are subject to attack. He values installation A at one unit and installation B at three units. He is capable of successfully defending either installation, but not both. His opponent, Red, is capable of attacking either unit, but not both. Blue desires to analyze the situation from the viewpoint of game theory.

a. Set up the game matrix representing this situation.
b. State the measure of effectiveness you used.
c. What strategy guarantees Blue at least the maximin payoff?

5. Consider this game: Player A has three possible strategies; X, Y, Z. Player B has two possible strategies; W, V.

Agreed payments to be made according to the choice of strategies are:

X, W: A pays B seven dollars.
X, V: A pays B two dollars.
Y, W: A pays B one dollar.
Y, V: B pays A one dollar.
Z, W: B pays A three dollars.
Z, V: B pays A six dollars.

Find:
a. (1) Optimal pure strategy for A. (2) Optimal pure strategy for B.
b. The value of the game.

6. Solve the following games by finding the optimal strategy for each player and the value of the game:

(a)

3	0	3
-3	-2	2
2	-2	-1

(b)

0	-4	-5
-2	-3	-2
-5	-4	0
-1	-4	-1

(c)

2	5	3	0	1
5	0	1	1	2
3	4	5	3	4
4	1	2	0	3
0	2	0	2	1

7. Solve the following games by finding the optimal mixed strategy for each player and the value of the game:

(a)

4	2
2	3

(b)

0	7	7
10	4	5

(c)

6	3	1	2	6	5
5	3	2	2	7	5
6	5	6	5	4	4
4	6	5	7	5	4
5	7	6	7	4	4

(d)

4	-5
-3	5

(e)

-1/3	1/4
1/2	0

8. In Problem four:
   a. What is Blue's optimal pure strategy?
   b. What is Blue's optimal mixed strategy?
   c. How would Blue execute this optimal mixed strategy if the game were repeated many times?

9. Colonel Blotto (Blue) is defending two positions with three battalions. The enemy (Red), with two battalions, is expected to attack one or both positions. Blotto is trying to decide the optimum allocation of battalions between the two positions. He makes the following judgments about the situation.

   (1) Each battalion has a value of one.
   (2) Position A is equal in worth to one battalion, if captured.
   (3) Position B is equal in worth to two battalions, if captured.
   (4) The capture of any enemy battalion is worth the value of one.

(5) The side whose force is superior retains or captures the position, and also captures the opposing battalions.

(6) Where forces are equal, nothing is gained or lost.

   a. Set up a matrix whose numbers represent Colonel Blotto's net gain (or loss).

   b. With Blotto's optimal pure strategy, what payoff can he guarantee?

   c. With Red's optimal pure strategy, what can he guarantee?

   d. What do you know about the value of the game?

10. In the foregoing problem, finding the optimal mixed strategy solution is beyond the scope of this text. Without trying to solve the problem:

   a. Guess at a good mixed strategy for Blotto and compute the expected payoff against each of Red's possible courses of action. What would Blotto's *guarantee* be using this mixed strategy? (The value of this game must be no less than this *guarantee*.)

   b. Guess at a good mixed strategy for Red and compute the expected payoff against each of Blotto's possible courses of action. What would Red's *guarantee* be using this mixed strategy? (The value of the game must be no greater than this *guarantee*.)

   c. What do you know now about the value of the game?

11. In Problem nine, test to see if the following are optimal mixed strategies, and if so, find the value of the game.

For Blotto:
   Place three battalions at A and zero at B, 6/24 of the time.
   Place two battalions at A and one at B, 5/24 of the time.
   Place one battalion at A and two at B, never.
   Place zero battalions at A and three at B, 13/24 of the time.

For Red:
   Attack A with two battalions and B with zero battalions, 9/24 of the time.
   Attack A with one battalion and B with one battalion, 11/24 of the time.
   Attack A with zero battalions and B with two battalions, 4/24 of the time.

12. Show whether or not the strategies Blue (3/8, 0, 5/8) and Red (1/4, 0, 3/4) are optimal in the following game.

Red

3	12	8
6	6	5
9	4	6

Blue

13. In the bomber/fighter problem used in this chapter, it was assumed that only one attack occurs. If two independent attacks occur:

   a. How many courses of action are available to Red?

   b. Compute the payoffs for the resulting matrix.

14. Prove that the proposed strategies for Red and Blue in the following games are (or are not) optimal.

(a)

Red

	R1 (1/2)	R2 (0)	R3 (0)	R4 (0)	R5 (1/2)
Blue B1: (3/10)	4	3	2	1	0
B2: (1/10)	3	4	3	2	1
B3: (2/10)	2	3	4	3	2
B4: (1/10)	1	2	3	4	3
B5: (3/10)	0	1	2	3	4

(b)

Red

	R1 (1/2)	R2 (0)	R3 (0)	R4 (0)	R5 (1/2)
Blue B1: (3/10)	4	3	2	1	0
B2: (1/10)	3	4	3	2	1
B3: (2/10)	2	3	0	3	2
B4: (1/10)	1	2	3	4	3
B5: (3/10)	0	1	2	3	4

15. A matrix appeared in this chapter with subjective descriptions of the payoffs as follows:

Blue	Red R1	R2	R3
B1	Fail	Succeed	Succeed
B2	Draw	Succeed	Draw
B3	Succeed	Fail	Fail

    a. Does the matrix have a saddle-point?
    b. Can it be reduced by dominance?
    c. If the commander were satisfied to assign values to the payoffs as follows: fail $= -10$, draw $=$ zero, succeed $=$ five, would the following strategies be optimal: Blue: (1/2, 0, 1/2), Red: (1/2, 0, 1/2)?

16. In the following repeated game, suppose Blue intends to use his optimal *pure* strategy for the next play unless he can get reliable intelligence as to Red's intentions.

Blue	Red R1	R2
B1	.6	.9
B2	1.0	.3

How much would this intelligence increase his (expected) payoff above his payoff with no intelligence, if:

    a. Red intends to use $R1$?
    b. Red intends to use $R2$ (his best pure strategy)?
    c. Red is using his optimal mixed strategy?
    d. What is Blue's guaranteed payoff with correct intelligence no matter what Red does?

4 Detection Theory

Naval operations have become as complex and sophisticated as the equipment itself. Mariners once relied entirely on the seaworthiness of their ships, the efficiency of the crew and state of the sea. The celestial constellations were their guide and the horizon marked the limit of their observations. They were unable to detect what was hidden beyond the horizon.

In the modern naval generation, detecting the enemy has become not only one of the most important functions of any naval operation but has acquired the stature of a science with which the student of naval warfare must be familiar. Any action against an enemy must be preceded by knowledge of his presence and position. The problem of detection is dependent on three major aspects:

a. The physical characteristics of the instrument of detection and of the target, along with the physics of wave propagation and other phenomena which cause information to be transmitted between the two.

b. The path and location of the searching unit (also called the observer) relative to the presumed position and motion of the target (the object of the search).

c. The direction and deployment of naval forces in accordance with requirements to meet the challenge and threat effectively, i.e., to achieve the greatest effect with the forces available.

The science of detection, as a branch of naval tactics, seeks solutions to problems of contacting and tracking hostile forces or forces presumed to be nonfriendly. This branch of tactics achieves its end through the application of engineering, physics, mathematics and statistics. Its conclusions are stated in terms of probability—the probability of detection.

This chapter provides the general definitions as well as the mathematical methodology needed for an understanding of the problem of detection. The principles discussed here, and the reasoning behind these principles, are essential to a comprehension of this vital area of naval operations. Considerable attention will be given to the process of detection in general in order to develop the concepts needed later for a study of radar and sonar detection systems.

An understanding of the essentials of target detection will make possible the development of efficient searches, patrols and screens used in many types of naval operations. The measures of effectiveness for detection can be used in conjunction with cost, reliability and other factors to compare the effectiveness of different detection systems and to determine how to use these systems most efficiently.

401 GENERALITIES CONCERNING DETECTION

The detection or discovery of a target is constituted by becoming aware of its presence and possibly its position. Note that this definition rules out the discovery of objects which are of no concern to the searcher. Emphasis is placed on the word discovery since detection can only take place once. Acquisition of any subsequent information regarding the location of the target is regarded as tracking.

If one is to acquire information concerning the absence or presence of an object, enemy or otherwise, a transfer of energy must take place from the object being searched for to the searcher. There is simply no means in nature, other than energy transfer, by which information may be acquired across a distance. It is for this reason that any discussion of detection, be it by radar, sonar or visual means, must involve a consideration of energy transfer.

In general, detection can be thought of as having taken place when an energetic *signal*, such as the audible sound pattern of a submarine's machinery noise, is recognized by an intelligent listener. The signal may, on the other hand, be the visual image of a white snorkel wake against the dark background of the sea or the blip of a returning echo on a radar scope.

Two basic facts underlie every type of detection:

a. Certain physical requirements must be met before a detection can occur, and they, if met, will in fact make detection possible. Thus, targets must not be too far away and their view from the observer must not be completely obstructed. To be visually seen there must be some contrast between the target and its background. Radar will not reveal targets if the atmospheric conditions or background echoes are adverse, and sonar detection requires that the sound path not be completely bent away from the observer by refraction.

b. Even when the physical conditions make detection possible, it will by no means inevitably occur. Detection is an event which under the proper conditions has a positive probability, the numerical value of which may be zero or unity or anything in between. Thus, when the target just barely fulfills the physical conditions for possible detection, the probability of detection will be close to zero (at least when the time for observation is limited). As the conditions improve, the chance of detection increases, and it may become practically certain. However, experiences in everyday life show that an object in plain sight may be looked for and not found. Reconnaissance aircraft flying observational missions on clear sunny days have passed close over large ships and yet failed to detect them. It must be constantly realized that every instrument of detection is based in the last analysis on a human being, and its success is accordingly influenced by his training, alertness and fatigue. Furthermore, even under physical conditions which are as fixed and constant as it is practicable to make them, innumerable rapid fluctuations are still apt to occur (a radar target changes its aspect from moment to moment with the continual rolling and pitching of the ship, sonar ranges experience short-term oscillations about their mean, etc.). As a result, a target which may not be detected at one instant may be detected, if sought, a moment later.

Almost invariably the recognition of the signal presented by a target and hence the probability of detection depends on:

a. The signal's characteristic pattern being known to the observer.
b. The intensity of the signal presented to the observer.
c. The intensity of other competing signals, known as noise.

An observer who is *looking* for the target—trying to detect it by some means such as, visual, radar, sonar, etc.—will be using one of two basic procedures. First the observer may be making a succession of brief *separated glimpses,* a typical case being the echo-ranging procedure in which each sweep or scan affords one glimpse, successive ones occurring at specified intervals. The second case arises when the observer is *looking continuously,* as when fixing his eyes steadily in an area where the target may be located. The case of radar is intermediate. Because it scans, it would belong to the first case, but if the scanning is very fast, and there is a persistency of the image on the scope, it may be treated as continuous looking. Likewise, visual detection by a slow scan through a large angle belongs to the first rather than the second case. Very often classification of the method of detection depends simply on which affords the closest or most convenient approximation.

402 SEPARATED GLIMPSES

Consider a search being conducted to detect a particular target using a succession of brief glimpses, such as depicted in Figure 4-1. This section will be devoted to developing models to represent such quantities as: the probability that detection occurs *in a given number of glimpses;* the probability that detection occurs *on a specified glimpse;* and the *expected number of glimpses required to detect the target.*

The parameter which will be used here is the *glimpse probability,* g_i, which gives the chance of seeing the target on a particular glimpse. This probability, for which a more precise definition follows, generally varies from glimpse to glimpse as some physical conditions such as range, speed, illumination, weather, etc., change. The subscript i denotes the particular glimpse of interest. It will be assumed here that the value of each

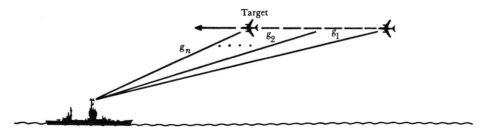

Figure 4-1.

g_i, for $i = 1, 2, 3, \ldots$, is known or has been estimated. In the next chapter a way of determining these values for a radar is discussed.

Suppose each successive glimpse is numbered from the beginning of the search. Let the *random variable, N,* denote *the glimpse on which the target is detected,* i.e., is seen for the first time. N is then a *discrete* integer-valued random variable. Expressions for the following quantities are desired:

a. $p(n) = P(N = n)$: the probability the target is detected on the nth glimpse.

b. $F(n) = P(N \leq n)$: the probability the target is detected on or before the nth glimpse, i.e., the probability that detection occurs in the first n glimpses.

c. $E(N)$: the expected number of glimpses required to detect the target.

The parameter, g_i, is now defined as *the probability of detecting the target on the ith glimpse, assuming (given) it has not been detected previously.*

For any particular value of i, this *glimpse probability* can be defined in symbols as

Equation 4-1 $$g_i = P(N = i | N > i - 1).$$

Expressions for $p(n)$, $F(n)$ and $E(N)$ can be derived after first finding the probability, $P(N > n)$, that the target is *not* detected in the first n glimpses. Let D_i be the event the target is seen on the ith glimpse. Then

$$P(N > n) = P \text{ (detection fails to occur on each of the 1}^{\text{st}} \ n \text{ glimpses)}$$
$$= P(\bar{D}_1 \cap \bar{D}_2 \cap \cdots \cap \bar{D}_n)$$
$$= P(\bar{D}_1)P(\bar{D}_2|\bar{D}_1)P(\bar{D}_3|\bar{D}_1 \cap \bar{D}_2) \cdots$$
$$P(\bar{D}_n|\bar{D}_1 \cap \bar{D}_2 \cap \cdots \cap \bar{D}_{n-1}), \text{ (from}$$

Appendix I, Equation I-6).
But

$$g_1 = P(D_1),$$
$$g_2 = P(D_2|\bar{D}_1),$$
$$g_3 = P(D_3|\bar{D}_1 \cap \bar{D}_2),$$
$$\vdots \qquad \vdots$$
$$g_n = P(D_n|\bar{D}_1 \cap \bar{D}_2 \cap \cdots \cap \bar{D}_{n-1}),$$

hence

$$1 - g_1 = P(\bar{D}_1),$$
$$1 - g_2 = P(\bar{D}_2|\bar{D}_1),$$
$$1 - g_3 = P(\bar{D}_3|\bar{D}_1 \cap \bar{D}_2), \text{ and}$$
$$\vdots \qquad \vdots$$
$$1 - g_n = P(\bar{D}_n|\bar{D}_1 \cap \bar{D}_2 \cap \cdots \cap \bar{D}_{n-1}).$$

Therefore

$$P(N > n) = (1 - g_1)(1 - g_2)(1 - g_3) \cdots (1 - g_n)$$

or written in terms of the symbol, II, for product, it becomes

Equation 4-2 $$P(N > n) = \prod_{i=1}^{n} (1 - g_i).$$

The probability, $F(n)$, of detecting the target *in the first n glimpses* can now be found easily, by

$$F(n) = P(N \leq n)$$
$$= 1 - P(N > n)$$

which, using Equation 4-2, becomes

Equation 4-3
$$F(n) = 1 - \prod_{i=1}^{n} (1 - g_i).$$

To find $p(n)$, which represents the probability of first detecting the target *on the nth glimpse,* note that

$p(n) = P(N = n)$, and since $(N = n) \subset (N > n - 1)$,

$$= P \begin{bmatrix} \text{failing to detect the target} \\ \text{on the 1}^{st} n - 1 \text{ glimpses} \end{bmatrix} \cap \begin{matrix} \text{first detecting the target on} \\ \text{the } n^{th} \text{ glimpse} \end{matrix} \end{bmatrix}$$

$$= P[(N > n - 1) \cap (N = n)]$$
$$= P[N > n - 1] \cdot P[(N = n)|(N > n - 1)], \text{ which from Equation 4-1,}$$
$$= P[N > n - 1] \cdot g_n, \text{ and from Equation 4-2,}$$

$$= \prod_{i=1}^{n-1} (1 - g_i) \cdot g_n.$$

Therefore,

Equation 4-4
$$p(n) = g_n \cdot \prod_{i=1}^{n-1} (1 - g_i).$$

It is of value to note the usual relationship between $p(n)$ and $F(n)$:

$$F(n) = P(N \leq n)$$
$$= P(N = 1) + P(N = 2) + \cdots + P(N = n)$$
$$= p(1) + p(2) + \cdots + p(n)$$

$$= \sum_{i=1}^{n} p(i).$$

The quantities $p(n)$ and $F(n)$ fulfill the requirements for a *probability function* and a *cumulative distribution function,* respectively, provided $F(\infty) = 1$. Whether or not this is true will be determined by the nature of the detection problem and in particular by the g_i's themselves. If, in a particular case, $F(\infty) = 1$, the expected number of glimpses required for detection may be found by computing the expected value of N, i.e.,

$$E(N) = \sum_{\text{All } n} n \cdot p(n).$$

The objective when searching for a target is usually to make the probability of detection as large as possible. In other cases, detection in the fewest number of glimpses may be more important. Therefore either $F(n)$ or $E(N)$ may serve as a good measure of effectiveness depending on the particular objective.

As an example, suppose as the observer approaches a target, the values of g_i are given by:

$i =$	1	2	3	4	5
$g_i =$	1/5	2/5	3/5	4/5	5/5

Then the probability of detection by the nth glimpse for the values of n can be computed from Equation 4-3 to be:

$n =$	1	2	3	4	5
$F(n) =$	1/5	13/25	101/125	601/625	1

In order to find the average number of glimpses required for detection, the probability that initial detection occurs on the nth glimpse, $p(n)$, must first be found from Equation 4-4:

$n =$	1	2	3	4	5
$p(n) =$	1/5	8/25	36/125	96/625	24/625

In this case, $p(n)$ and $F(n)$ meet the requirements for a *probability function* and *cumulative distribution function*, respectively. Hence $E(N)$ can be found by:

$$E(N) = \sum_{\text{All } n} n \cdot p(n)$$

$$= \sum_{n=1}^{5} n \cdot p(n)$$

$$= 1(1/5) + 2(8/25) + 3(36/125) + 4(96/625) + 5(24/625)$$

$$= 2.51.$$

403 SEPARATED GLIMPSES IN AN UNCHANGING ENVIRONMENT

In the special case where conditons do *not* change during the search, each glimpse probability, g_i, has the same value and hence may be denoted by g without a subscript.

The probability of detection *in the first n glimpses,* from Equation 4-3, then becomes

$$F(n) = 1 - \prod_{i=1}^{n} (1 - g)$$

$$= 1 - (1 - g)^n,$$

and the probability of detection *on the nth glimpse,* from Equation 4-4, becomes

$$p(n) = g \prod_{i=1}^{n-1} (1 - g)$$

$$= g(1 - g)^{n-1}.$$

It can be seen that $F(\infty) = 1$, if g is non-zero, so that $p(n)$ and $F(n)$ are the *probability function* and *cumulative distribution function* respectively. $p(n)$ is of the same form as the probability function for the *geometric distribution* included in Appendix I, Section I-20. The expected number of glimpses required for detection is therefore:

$$E(N) = 1/g.$$

In this case of unchanging conditions the probability of detection, $F(n)$, can be made as large as desired by increasing the number of glimpses. This is true no matter how small the glimpse probability, g, provided it is greater than zero.

404 CONTINUOUS LOOKING

In looking for a target using a detector of a continuous nature, information is being received continuously and detection is possible at any instant of time. When this is the case, the probability that detection occurs *at* a given instant must be zero and thus not very useful in describing how the chance of detection varies during the search. Let the random variable T be used to denote *the time required to detect a target,* where detection again means *initial* contact. T is a continuous random variable whose value could be any real number from zero to ∞, and $P(T = t) = 0$, as in any continuous distribution. What then can be used to describe the detector's ability to detect a target as a function of time?

The parameter which will be used is called the *instantaneous detection rate* and denoted by the symbol $\gamma(t)$. If several targets are present then the detection rate, expressed as number of targets detected per unit time, has some intuitive meaning. It is more difficult to say what is meant by the detection rate in regard to a *single* target, although this is the case of interest at this point. An equivalent concept will be encountered in a later chapter on reliability when the failure rate for a single component, such as a transistor, is defined. Accordingly $\lambda(t)$ is referred to as the *instantaneous failure rate* because its value, which may be continuously changing, can only be stated for a given instant of time. In a like manner, the speed of an aircraft is its *instantaneous mile rate,* the number of miles traveled per unit time at a given instant.

In order to measure the ability of a continuous detector to detect a target, the following two quantities will be addressed.

a. $F(t) = P(T \leq t)$: the probability that a target is detected in a search lasting time t.
b. $E(T)$: the expected time required for detection.

Let X be a random variable representing the number of detections in a time interval of length t. Where this type of situation can be approximated by the assumptions of the Poisson probability distribution (see Appendix I, Section I-18), the *probability function* for X is

$$p(x) = P(X = x) = \frac{\mu^x e^{-\mu}}{x!}$$

Here μ is the expected number of detections in some fixed time t. The product of average detection rate $\bar{\gamma}$ and time t, $\bar{\gamma} \cdot t$, would yield the value of μ. Since the event that the first detection does not occur until *after* time t, $(T > t)$, is equivalent to the event that *no detections* occur in time t, $(X = 0)$, then

$$P(T > t) = P(X = 0)$$
$$= p(0)$$

$$= \frac{\mu^0 e^{-\mu}}{0!}$$

$$= e^{-\mu},$$

and
$$F(t) = P(T \le t)$$
$$= 1 - P(T > t)$$
$$= 1 - e^{-\mu}.$$

To find μ, use for an example Figure 4-2, where $\gamma(t)$ is plotted against time.

This curve gives, at any instant of time, a value representing the detection rate at that time. The average detection rate $\bar{\gamma}$ in the first hour is approximately six detections per hour, in the second hour approximately seven detections per hour and in the third hour approximately five detections per hour. The expected number of detections in three hours is approximately 18. If the time intervals chosen were smaller, the approximation would be more accurate and in the limit:

$$\bar{\gamma} = \frac{\int_0^t \gamma(t)\,dt}{t}, \text{ and } \mu = \bar{\gamma} \cdot t = \int_0^t \gamma(t)\,dt.$$

Then

Equation 4-5
$$F(t) = 1 - e^{-\int_0^t \gamma(t)\,dt}.$$

$F(t)$ gives the probability of detecting a target in a search of time t. It is a *cumulative distribution function* provided $F(\infty) = 1$, i.e., provided the exponent:

$$\int_0^t \gamma(t)\,dt$$

approaches ∞ as t approaches ∞. This may or may not be the case depending on $\gamma(t)$. If it *is* the case, then the average time to detection, $E(T)$, can be found using the *probability density function*, $f(t)$, and the general relationship:

$$E(T) = \int t \cdot f(t)\,dt.$$
$$\text{All}$$
$$\text{values of } t$$

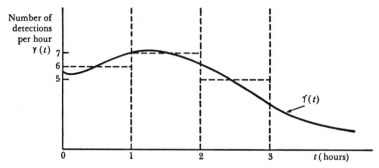

Figure 4-2.

An expression for $f(t)$ can be found by taking the derivative of the cumulative distribution function and can be written as

Equation 4-6
$$f(t) = \gamma(t)e^{-\int_0^t \gamma(t)\,dt}.$$

An expression for $E(T)$ would then be

Equation 4-7
$$E(T) = \int_0^\infty t\gamma(t)e^{-\int_0^t \gamma(t)\,dt}\,dt,$$

which may be evaluated if $\gamma(t)$ is known.

Again it should be emphasized that the measure of effectiveness for detection must depend upon the objective of the mission. Two quantities, $F(t)$ and $E(T)$, have been derived for continuous looking to measure the probability of detection and the expected time to detection.

In some operations, other measures may be important, such as the probability of detecting the target *before* being detected by it.

As an example, suppose $\gamma(t) = t/100$. Then from Equation 4-5 the probability of detection by time t would be

$$F(t) = 1 - e^{-\int_0^t \frac{t}{100}\,dt}$$
$$= 1 - e^{-t^2/200}.$$

This is a cumulative distribution function since $F(\infty)$ is seen to be one.

Therefore

$$f(t) = \frac{dF(t)}{dt}$$
$$= \frac{te^{-t^2/200}}{100},$$

and

$$E(T) = \int_0^\infty \frac{t^2 e^{-t^2/200}}{100}\,dt,$$

which when evaluated becomes

$$E(T) = \sqrt{50\pi}.$$

405 CONTINUOUS LOOKING IN AN UNCHANGING ENVIRONMENT

In the special case where $\gamma(t)$ does not change with time but displays a constant value, γ, Equation 4-5 becomes

$$F(t) = 1 - e^{-\gamma t},$$

a cumulative distribution function for all $\gamma > 0$. The associated probability density function, $f(t)$, is $\gamma e^{-\gamma t}$, the familiar exponential distribution in Appendix I, Section I-22. The expected time to detection is

$$E(T) = \int_0^\infty t\gamma e^{-\gamma t}\,dt = \frac{1}{\gamma},$$

using integration by parts to evaluate the integral.

406   DETECTION AS A FUNCTION OF RANGE

The quantities g_i and $\gamma(t)$ depend, as indicated earlier, on the sum total of physical conditions. The value of $\gamma(t)$, for example, usually varies as the search progresses because of changes in these physical conditions. In visual search, the range to the target, illumination, haze, the contrast of the target with its background, and other physical conditions all affect detection rate, $\gamma(t)$. One of the conditions which affects the ability of *any* sensor to detect is that of range to the target. It is also one of the conditions most likely to vary frequently during the search. In many cases, range may be primarily responsible for a change in detection rate and γ can be considered as a function of range alone. Where this is the case, the instantaneous detection rate will be denoted by $\gamma(r)$, representing the number of detections per unit time when range to the target is r. It will be legitimate to use this approach either when all conditions except range remain practically unchanged during the operation considered, or when other conditions have been shown not to influence the results to a degree of approximation that is unacceptable.

In general the instantaneous detection rate and glimpse probabilities tend to be small when the range is large and to increase as the range decreases. The graph of $\gamma(r)$ will be like one of the cases shown in Figure 4-3.

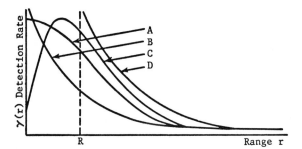

Types of instantaneous detection rate curves.

Figure 4-3.

Case A occurs when the instantaneous detection rate reaches a finite maximum at zero range. In case B, this maximum is infinite. Case C may indicate that sea return on radar diminishes the chance of detection as the target closes on the detector. In case D, the instantaneous detection rate becomes infinite at some range, R, greater than zero.

If case D holds, it can be seen that whenever a target comes within range, R, the detection rate becomes infinite and hence, the exponent in Equation 4-5 becomes infinite and the probability of detection is one. Case D frequently *approximates* an operational situation. As a further approximation, it is sometimes assumed that $\gamma(t)$ is zero for ranges greater than R. Case D, along with this *assumption,* is referred to as the *definite range law* of detection and offers a useful simplification in some detection problems. The definite range law will be referred to and amplified in later chapters.

407   INVERSE CUBE LAW OF DETECTION

An example can be used to show the evaluation of the function $\gamma(r)$ in the case when the following assumptions are reasonable:

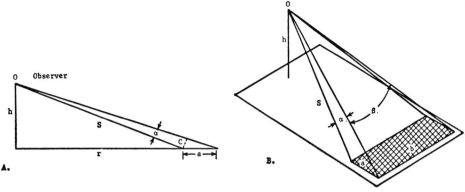

Solid angle subtended by wake.

Figure 4-4.

a. The observer is at height h above the ocean on which the target is cruising.
b. The observer detects the target by seeing its wake. (For an airborne observer the wake of a moving target is usually more readily sighted than the target itself.)
c. The instantaneous detection rate, γ, is proportional to the solid angle subtended at the point of observation by the wake.

The solid angle, shown in Figure 4-4, can be calculated for an area of ocean which has a rectangle of length a toward the observer and width b perpendicular to the direction of observation (perpendicular to the page in Figure 4-4A). The infinitesimal solid angle is the product of the angle α subtended by a, and the angle β subtended by b. The radian measure of α is C/S. By similar triangles, $C/a \cong h/S$ and hence $\alpha = ah/S^2$ and the radian measure of β is b/S. Hence the solid angle, $\alpha\beta = abh/S^3 =$ area of the rectangle times h/S^3. The actual area, A, of the target's wake is not rectangular, but can be regarded as being made up of large numbers of rectangles as in Figure 4-4B, the total solid angle being the sum of the corresponding solid angles. Hence, when the dimensions of A are small in comparison with h, r and S,

Equation 4-8
$$\alpha\beta = \frac{Ah}{S^3} = \frac{Ah}{(h^2 + r^2)^{3/2}}.$$

Since γ is assumed to be proportional to the solid angle,

Equation 4-9
$$\gamma(r) = \frac{kh}{S^3} = \frac{kh}{(h^2 + r^2)^{3/2}},$$

where the constant k depends on all the factors which are regarded as fixed and not introduced explicitly, such as contrast of wake against ocean, number of lookouts and their facilities, meteorological conditions, etc.; and of course k contains A as a factor. Dimensionally, $k =$ area per unit time. In the majority of cases r is much larger than h and Equation 4-9 can be replaced by the satisfactory approximation

Equation 4-10
$$\gamma(r) = \frac{kh}{r^3}, \quad \text{for } r \gg h.$$

Equations 4-9 and 4-10 lead to cases A and B respectively of Figure 4-3. The property of detection which they express is called the *inverse cube law* of sighting. In a detailed study of visual sightings, it has been found that many changes in this law have to be made to obtain a high degree of approximation under the various conditions of practice. Nevertheless, the inverse cube law leads to a remarkably useful model for predicting the probability of detection as will be seen in Chapter seven.

The following example indicates how the probability of detection may be found when γ is a function of range using principles developed earlier in this chapter.

Suppose that at time $t = 0$, a radar site reports an enemy missile 500 N.mi. away and closing on an anti-missile site at a speed of 10,000 knots. In order to counter the attack, acquisition must be accomplished by the site's fire control radar before the range closes to 200 N.mi. If the detection rate for the fire control radar follows the inverse cube law with $kh = 10^9$, then

$$\gamma(r) = 10^9/r^3 \text{ (in detections per hour at range } r\text{)}.$$

What is the probability of acquiring the missile in time to counter the attack?

As a function of time, the range can be given by $r = 500-10,000t$, where t is in hours, and γ can be expressed as a function of t,

$$\gamma(t) = \frac{10^9}{(500 - 10,000t)^3},$$

and the probability of acquisition by range 200 N.mi. is equivalent to the probability of acquisition by time .03 hour.

This probability can be calculated from Equation 4-5 as follows:

$$F(.03 \text{ hr}) = 1 - e^{-\int_0^{.03} \frac{10^9}{(500 - 10,000t)^3} dt}$$

$$= 1 - e^{-1.05}$$
$$= .650.$$

408 ANALOGY

This section presents the analogy between three different situations:

a. Tossing a single fair die repeatedly with the object of getting an ace.
b. Discrete glimpsing where g is constant.
c. Continuously looking for a target where γ is constant.

Fair Die (Discrete)

Random Variable: N,	*Probability Function: $p(n)$,*	*Cumulative Distribution Function: $F(n)$,*
the number of tosses required for first ace.	the probability of *first* appearance of an ace *on* the nth roll = probability ace does *not* appear on $(n - 1)$ rolls times the probability ace appears on n^{th} roll.	the probability of first appearance of an ace *by* the nth roll = 1 − probability ace does not appear in n rolls.
Basic Parameter: p,		
the probability of an ace on any roll:		

$$p = \tfrac{1}{6}$$

$$
\begin{aligned}
p(n) &= P(N = n) \\
&= (1 - p)^{n-1}p \\
&= (\tfrac{5}{6})^{n-1}(\tfrac{1}{6})
\end{aligned}
$$

$$
\begin{aligned}
F(n) &= P(N \le n) \\
&= 1 - (1 - p)^n \\
&= 1 - (\tfrac{5}{6})^n
\end{aligned}
$$

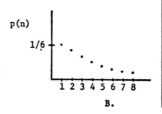

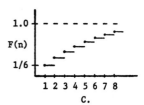

A.   B.   C.

Separated Glimpses (Discrete)

	Probability Function: $p(n)$,	*Cumulative Distribution Function: $F(n)$*,
Random Variable: N, the number of glimpses required for detection.	the probability of detection *on* the nth glimpse = probability of not detecting on $(n - 1)$ glimpses times probability of detecting on the nth glimpse.	the probability of detection *by* the nth glimpse = probability of detection on first glimpse or second glimpse or … n^{th} glimpse = 1 − probability of not detecting *in n* glimpses.

Basic Parameter: g, the probability of detection on any single glimpse.

$$g = \text{constant}$$

$$
\begin{aligned}
p(n) &= P(N = n) \\
&= (1 - g)^{n-1}(g)
\end{aligned}
$$

$$
\begin{aligned}
F(n) &= P(N \le n) \\
&= 1 - (1 - g)^n
\end{aligned}
$$

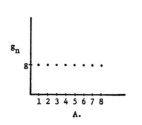

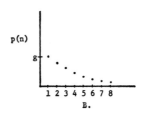

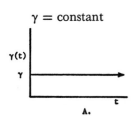

A.   B.   C.

Continuous Looking

	Probability Density Function: $f(t)$,	*Cumulative Distribution Function: $F(t)$*,
Random Variable: T, the time to detection of target.	a function such that $$P(a < T < b) = \int_a^b f(t)\,dt.$$ $$f(t) = \gamma e^{-\gamma t}$$	probability of detection *by* time $t = 1 −$ Probability of no detection in time t.

Basic Parameter: γ, the instantaneous detection rate.

$$\gamma = \text{constant}$$

$$
\begin{aligned}
F(t) &= P(T \le t) \\
&= 1 - e^{-\gamma t}
\end{aligned}
$$

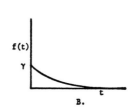

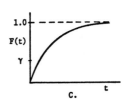

A.   B.   C.

409 HUMAN BEHAVIORAL EFFECTS ON VIGILANCE TASK OPERATIONS

Much of the mathematical modeling in introductory operations analysis utilizes expected values or similar *constant* parameters as inputs to represent the human variables from the personnel who are involved in the operation. Some intermediate models have given consideration to the distribution of performance characteristics between different operators, and to the possible variety in response by the same individual. As an application of science to operational activities, operations analysis may include human engineering aspects relevant to the systems, with a view toward applications which achieve the optima of the personnel inputs.

Differences in task performance by the same person are *not simple* functions. Relevant factors that can account for these differences are listed here in two main categories:

> *Factors Mainly Inherent in the Task*
> Task duration; required attention span
> Sufficiency of rest and sleep periods
> Energy utilization; immobility duration requirements
> Boredom, from trivia or from monotony
> Frequency of emergencies or false alarms
> Success pressures
> Time pressures
> Lack of cooperation
> Ambiguity of procedures
> > *External, Environmental Conditions*
> *Extremes, or rapid changes, in:*
> Temperature and humidity
> Glare or blackout
> Noise
> Vibration
> Living environment

This discussion of human factors is mostly confined to their effects on "Vigilance Task" operations, e.g., *watch operations* at sonar, radar, visual lookouts, and so on. Within this scope, some, but *not all* of the results could be generalized to similar effects on "Redundancy Tasks," such as some of the duty performed in communications, or enginerooms, or to "Decision Making" or other "Complex Mental Tasks," as often performed in operational planning. Emphasis is placed on items according to the extent to which they might be controlled by ideal administration, such as in the scheduling of watches.

The first two factors listed above have been found to be interrelated and are also among the factors which are *most unique* in their results upon vigilance tasks as opposed to their results on other tasks.

410 TASK-RELATED FACTORS

Duration Effects

Performance decrements occur in vigilance tasks of relatively simple nature, such as monitoring a PPI scope. The deterioration of monitoring efficiency can occur *within the first half hour* of a session when humans perform such relatively simple tasks.

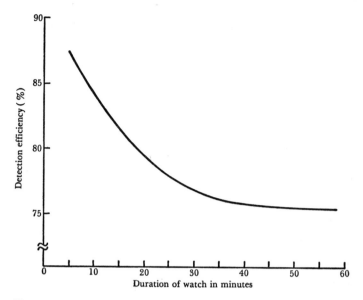

Figure 4-5. Predicted event detection efficiency of group of radar operators in terms of alerted performance as a function of watch duration.

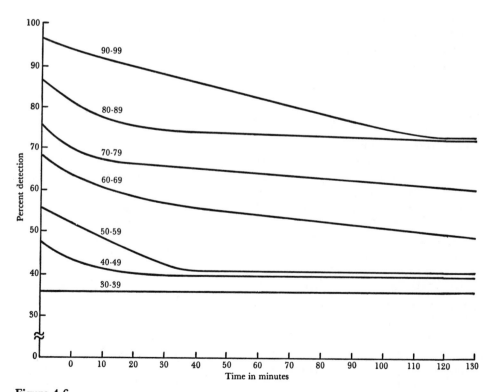

Figure 4-6.

A typical beginning operator efficiency of approximately 87 percent while monitoring an air surveillance PPI scope is shown in Figure 4-5 to drop off during the first half hour, then almost plateau near 75 percent.

Data compiled by Teichner [1] in Figure 4-6 show similar effects for seven different groups of radar target circumstances. They are grouped by the ideal (pre-test) probabilities of detection. Nearly all these increments of radar environment conditions show a decrease in performance of the vigilance task for the first 30 minutes. Then the detection percentages often level out for a long time, or at least tend toward leveling.

Response to *auditory* signals has also been studied, with seamen monitoring signals for five repeated, lengthy sessions. No significant change resulted *from session to session*, but response became increasingly latent *during the sessions*.

This effect does *not* generalize from passive tasks, such as those involving monitoring or vigilance, to active tasks. Passive tasks have been found to be much more sensitive to decrements than tasks that require an active participation by the operator.

Work-Rest Schedules [2]

Man can maintain performance level in *some* tasks despite demanding and unfamiliar work-rest schedules, at least for short intervals of time. Experiments have compared different one to one work-rest ratios; such as eight hours on duty with eight off, six on with six off, four on with four off and two on with two off. Under test situations (simulated crew compartment, not confined to compartment during off-duty periods), the schedules *did not result* in significant differences in performance on any of the tasks, which included mental arithmetic, pattern discrimination, monitoring and vigilance. However, individuals in the two on with two off, and four on with four off, groups reported themselves happier with their schedules. So performance might deteriorate particularly for the longer schedules over an extended period.

The 4:4 schedule was compared with a schedule of four hours work and two hours rest. Operators working 12 hours per day with a 4:4 schedule give a higher level of performance than operators working 16 hours per day on a 4:2 schedule. However, the *individual motivation* of the operator is very significant. A highly motivated, though fatigued, operator at any time could perform *as well as* a refreshed operator. With proper selection and motivation factors, crews can work effectively for periods at least as long as 15 days on a 4:2 schedule, but crews can work even more effectively for periods of at least a month using a 4:4 schedule; the latter schedule also requires less demanding controls of selection and motivational factors.

Both man's performance and his physiological processes are functions of his adaptation to a 24-hour day. Readjusting to different work-rest schedules takes a transition period. Individuals differ greatly both in their ability to adapt and also in the time required for adjusting. For a work-rest schedule of 4:4, heart and respiratory rate do not adapt during a 7-day confinement period. Besides the physiological and motivational problems associated with transition from the typical 24-hour schedule, a person may also suffer from sleep loss. The performance decrement due to sleep loss with a 4:2 schedule will be larger than that with a 4:4 schedule on *tasks which require sustained attention*, even if attention must be sustained for only relatively short periods of time. These factors should be considered in planning schedules of work and rest, although it has been shown that no significant change results in auditory acuity, depth perception, or deck adaptation as a function of sleep loss over brief periods of time. Likewise, for *some performance tasks*, there does not appear to be significant variation as a function of the work-rest cycle, provided the work-rest and sleep-wakefulness ratios are held constant.

An *exception* to those general rules is a decrement in the performance of *vigilance* tasks, or certain watchstanding tasks. [3,4] Passive tasks such as those involving monitoring or vigilance are more sensitive to sleep and rest losses than are tasks which require *active* participation by the operator. For instance, an operator who has been subjected to a strenuous series of watches sometimes shows a *continuous* degradation of performance over an entire watch rather than the usual 30-minute deterioration and leveling off characteristic of most vigilance work. The results of experiments involving up to 60 hours of sleep deprivation suggest two features of a task which determine whether its performance will be impaired by loss of sleep. A task will be vulnerable to sleep deprivation if it is complex or if it is lacking in interest, incentive and reward. Of the two factors, that of incentive appears to be the more influential, i.e., a highly complex task may be little affected by sleep deprivation if it is complex in an interesting or rewarding way.

Short *rest pauses* also affect vigilance tasks. [5] Experiments with two groups of naval personnel showed that when work was continuous for a period of one hour, efficiency for that group was considerably lower in the second half-hour than for the other group which had a five-minute break between the two half-hours.

When using the aforementioned findings to set up an optimum seagoing work-rest schedule, one must consider the environmental factors specific to *shipboard operations*. Personnel in Naval Task Operations are frequently subjected to extreme physiological conditions by the ocean. Excessive ship pitch and roll will not stop at the end of a watch, but will continue below deck; so little sleep (or other rest) might be obtained over a long time. Shipboard operations are thereby very different from systems wherein off-duty time can be spent away from the operational vehicle's environmental factors (for example, many airborne warfare systems). Perhaps a four-hour work to eight-hour rest schedule should be used to counterbalance such operational environment effects as fatigue caused by ship movement.

Immobility and Physical Expenditure Effects [6]

Evidence has been presented that a break in the task or a variation of the task significantly reduces the amount of decrease in vigilance. Rest periods of four to ten minutes, in which watchstanders are required either to make *postural changes* or to have *conversation*, improves vigilance efficiency to a level close to the starting level. Comparisons between using the break from passive tasks for exercise and using the break for more passive activity have shown a greater resurgence of vigilance from *exercise* breaks.

In the environment of rough weather, not only is the performance of most routine tasks more difficult, but movement of personnel may become hazardous. The following are general rough-weather guidelines:

Seated operators can perform better in rough weather than standing operators. The operators should be secure in their operating positions, by belts or straps if necessary.
Work stations should be arranged to minimize the amount of movement between stations.
Guardrails, handrails, etc., should be provided with the worst situations in mind.

Monotony Effects [7]

No correlation has been found between performance in *vigilance tasks* and performance in *other monotonous tasks*. Therefore, the vigilance task probably contains factors not found in other monotonous work. One method that arrests the drop in performance during lengthy monitoring for rare and sudden signals is providing "false" signals which appear as real signals and to which an operator must respond. This increases the signal occurrence *frequency* to a level that keeps the operator more attentive. *Artificial signals* even help maintain a high detection rate of real signals when the operator is not required to respond to the synthetic signals. The vigilance decrement is not reduced as much as when the real response is called for, but the second method is usually more feasible to implement.

Systems having *more complex displays* and *multiple stimulus sources* induce lesser decreases of vigilance. An artificial means of reducing vigilance decrement may be feasible, i.e., introducing *some novel stimulus situation*. For example, a telephone message during a monitoring session can increase the monitoring efficiency. Vigilance decrement has been decreased in a *visual vigilance* task by *auditory stimulation* like music. Similarly, auditory vigilance has sometimes been improved by adding visual stimulation. *Adding a little complexity* to the response of the task, such as choosing among buttons to be pressed, serves to lower vigilance decrement. In this event, there is some accompanying increase in reaction time.

Success Pressures

Another factor that can produce vigilance decrement by inducing boredom, other than the "monotony" inherent in a vigilance task, is the "triviality" which an operator may assign to his task. It has been mentioned that the *cumulative effect* of stress is to produce *fatigue* and thereby a vigilance *decrement*. However, the *immediate effect* of transition to an increased-stress situation is at least a *temporary increase* in vigilance. The increased-stress situation from a higher degree of enemy threat or from higher traffic density might serve as an arousal mechanism similar to those mechanisms already mentioned for reducing vigilance decrement. Such a result of immediate gain incurring a possible trade-off of long-term decrement is like the effect of using certain stimulant drugs, such as benzedrine.

The seriousness of the operational situation has been found to effect sonar operators' reporting of contacts. [8] The signal "threshold level," above which a sonar operator reports contacts, often varies for an operator according to how he *perceives the consequences* of missed contacts and of false alarms. Fleet sonar operators also differ widely from each other in their opinions of the consequences of false contact.

The effect of sleep loss was pointed out to be greatest for vigilance tasks with low incentive. [9] Further sonar detection experimentation has objectively measured the influence on performance played by "command attention"; a high *level of command attention* betters sonar contact detection performance. A suggested method for halting vigilance decrement would be to *often tell* the operator *the results* of his performance.

Time Pressures

The effects of speed stress upon an operator's decision-making capability are of interest. Decision time *decreases* as the payoff difference between the alternatives is *increased*. In other words, decision time is lessened as the apparent worth of one alternative, such as a missed target, increases relative to the other, such as a false alarm.

When the payoffs are held constant, error rate increases as decision time allotted decreases, but with a relatively minor effect on vigilance-type tasks.

411 ENVIRONMENT-ASSOCIATED FACTORS

Some of the elements of the operational environment have already been discussed, where there was direct concern with task-inherent factors. For example, rough-weather considerations required different procedures from those used to counteract immobility. It is also apparent that *time zone changes* will produce some disruption on the optimal personnel work-rest schedules.

It is noteworthy that human engineering systems usually proceed on the assumption that optimal human performance occurs at points of physical comfort. Accordingly, the following discussions are oriented toward this mean.

Heat Exchange Comfort [10]

Five variables are significant in the heat exchange process:

Temperature changes primarily by the process of convection. If the air temperature is below body temperature, then the body is cooled; if it is above body temperature, the result is body warming.

Circulation of air increases heat exchange by exposing the body to more air.

Temperature of objects in the environment (walls, machinery, and so on) affects body heat exchange through *radiation*. A net heat gain or a net loss occurs, depending on the relative temperatures of the objects to the exposed body surface.

Humidity is not important to heat exchange at normal temperatures, but it is at both low and high temperatures. High humidity reduces the possible heat exchange, thereby increasing discomfort.

Time rate of exchange could determine either a gradual acclimatization, or a detrimental prolonged exposure.

While it is not feasible to include all these factors in a single index, there are a few indices that take into account certain combinations of the factors. For our purposes, the most relevant is *effective temperature,* an index developed by subjects rating their comfort in varying conditions of temperature, humidity, and air movement. The ET scale of Figure 4-7 shows these relationships for air movement of 15 to 25 feet/minute. The vertical wet-bulb temperature scale is, in effect, a combination of dry-bulb temperature and 100 percent relative humidity.

To place the chart in perspective for application, the following measurements of general performance versus temperature are listed:

Temperature	General Performance
120°F	Tolerable for about one hour, but far above acceptable physical or mental activity range
85°	Mental activity slows, errors begin
75°	Physical fatigue appears
75°–65°	Summer comfort zone for sedentary
71°–63°	Winter comfort zone for sedentary
65°	Optimum for physically active
50°	Physical stiffness of extremities begins

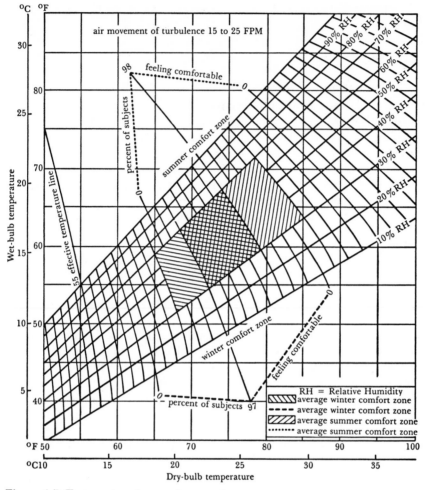

Figure 4-7. Temperature for comfort requirements.

Humidities between 30 and 70 percent are considered comfortable by most people.

When it is possible, extreme environmental conditions should be at least modified to bring them within the bounds recommended by Table 4-1.

Suggested methods of dealing with environmental extremes include:

Screening for personnel with tolerance to the conditions, perhaps by several days of tryout.

Permitting people gradually to become acclimatized.

Using insulating clothing in cold environments; in the hot environments, clothing needs to be light and loose to permit evaporation and convection heat loss, and to minimize radiant energy absorption.

Establishing work and rest schedules appropriate to the environment.

Modifying the work, reducing energy requirements.

Seeing that people drink enough water to replace that lost (thirst is not an adequate indicator of water requirements).

Table 4-1. Heating, ventilation and air conditioning recommendations

	Mobile personnel enclosures occupied extended time	Permanent and semipermanent facilities
HEATING (maintain dry-bulb temperature)	Above 50°F	Approx. 68°F
TEMPERATURE uniformity. Floor-to-head level temperature difference	10°F maximum	10°F maximum
AIR CONDITIONING	Maintain effective temperature below 85°F	Maintain dry-bulb temperature of approximately 68°F
VENTILATION	30 cfm/man minimum	30 cfm/man minimum, of which ⅔ should be outside air
AIRSPEED past man	100 ft/min, 65 if possible	100 ft/min, 65 if possible
HUMIDITY	Approx. 45% at 70°F; decreasing with rising temperature; minimum = 15%	Approx. 45%

Glare and Low-Level Illumination

Glare, or "dazzle," is a real problem when the displays are monitored in lighted spaces. It not only *reduces the visibility* of objects, but it also can cause *visual fatigue* which will degrade the operator's vision. [11]

There are two types of glare, direct and indirect. Direct glare is caused by lights placed in the operator's field of view. Indirect glare comes from reflection off surfaces.

The effect of light on *dark adaptation* is relevant to most vigilance systems. Dark adaptation refers to the fact that the eyes adjust to seeing in very low illumination levels (night light) and that higher-level light exposure impedes this adjustment. Adaptation to dark viewing takes 25 to 30 minutes; however, complete dark adaptation may require one to two hours. Low-level illumination is required in radar monitoring areas and in watch areas such as the bridge and lookout stations in order to preserve dark adaptation for nighttime operation. The fact that brief exposures to white and red light require considerable time for readaptation is an important concern. Red light reduces night adaptation much less than white light and is used for this reason. When red light is used in radar monitoring areas, no white light should be visible within the compartment, and there should be no light leakage from adjacent areas such as the chart room, etc. To maintain dark adaptation, white light from areas in view of the bridge and lookout stations should be shielded from these areas. It is recommended that no white light source be used in night bridge operations (not even to make log entries) and that exposure to red light be as brief and of as low intensity as possible. Color coding of controls or displays is not effective in low-level red light.

Light adaptation is the reverse of dark adaptation but requires only two to three minutes and thus does not constitute a problem.

Noise [12]

It was mentioned that music has been found beneficial to visual vigilance tasks. This does not generalize to all sounds to include noise; nor is there a parallel beneficial effect to be gained by such stimulus as music for an *auditory* vigilance task. There is an adverse effect from sharing in the case of auditory inputs; something has to give when two or more inputs occur simultaneously or nearly simultaneously. Moreover, this adverse effect occurs even when they are very different inputs, and only one is relevant and needs to be listened to. The adverse effect is greatest when the irrelevant message is relatively similar to the relevant one.

Noise may be considered as an auditory stimulus with no information relevant to the immediate task. It includes sounds inherent in the task but informationally useless plus sounds that are not inherent in the task.

An important possible effect of noise is hearing loss; it results from prolonged and/or extreme levels of exposure to high intensities of noise.

Aside from this damage, initial exposure (especially sudden exposure) induces other physiological reactions, although such responses usually settle down after a period of time. However, noise *adversely* affects *vigilance* tasks. Decrements in performance of vigilance tasks due to noise conditions take effect in approximately 90 minutes. For short periods of performance, no decrements would likely result from noise. But extended performance would be affected, particularly if the task were not intrinsically challenging. Under these conditions, noise might change the emotional balance or the motivational level.

Moreover, the combination of noise sources in some operational environments cannot be passed off simply as "annoying"; they probably approach the level of a health hazard because of possible effects in disturbing essential relaxation and sleep. There is a degree of adjustment to the annoying aspects of noise. However, some deafness appears before a person becomes impervious, for example, to the combined sounds of launching catapults and arresting gear machinery and operations.

Vibration

Vibrations of *nonaudible frequencies* (below 100 Hz) affect the body adversely according to their frequency. The parts of the body do not vibrate in unison and cause discomfort and loss of vigilance. Transmission of vibration to the body is affected by body position

Table 4-2. Typical vibrations with decremental effects on human performance

Performance factor degraded	Frequency (Hz)
Respiration control	3.5 to 8.0
Aiming	15.0
	25.0
	35.0
Hand coordination	2.5 to 3.5
Foot pressure consistency	2.5 to 3.5
Visual acuity	1.0 to 24.0
	35.0
	40.0
	70.0
	2.5 to 3.5
Tracking	1.0 to 50.0
Attention	2.5 to 3.5
	30.0 to 300.0

and media in use. Vibration affects one less when one is standing because the legs act as shock absorbers. Specific vigilance tasks and the frequencies that degrade them are listed in Table 4-2.

Other Relevant Conditions

The preceding factors are by no means a complete compilation of the inputs determining the variety of performance shown by an individual on a vigilance task. Other factors are listed below rather than discussed, because they are primarily functions of personal values rather than generalized values. Also they show no particular trends for vigilance tasks effects, any more or less than they affect other tasks, and are therefore outside the scope of this discussion.

Aesthetic surroundings
Atmospheric contamination
Culture, entertainment and recreation
Emotional health
Family-life interruptions
Financial problems
Mobility, convenience or efficiency
Personal safety and health
Social contact and interchange
Space adequacy

BIBLIOGRAPHY

[1] W. H. Teichner, *A Preliminary Theory of the Effects of Task and Environmental Factors on Human Performance,* Human Factors 19(4), 1971.
[2] O. S. Adams and W. D. Chiles, *Human Performance as a Function of the Work-Rest Cycle,* Wright-Patterson AFB, 1960–1961.
[3] H. L. Williams et al., *Signal Uncertainty and Sleep Loss,* Journal of Experimental Psychology 4, 1965.
[4] H. L. Williams et al., *Impaired Performance with Acute Sleep Loss,* American Psychological Association, 1959.
[5] W. P. Colquhoun, *The Effect of a Short Rest-Pause on Inspection Efficiency,* Ergonomics 3, 1959.
[6] W. B. Webb and R. Wherry, Jr., *Vigilance in Prolonged and Repeated Sessions,* U. S. Naval School of Aviation Medicine, 1961.
[7] R. A. Baker and J. R. Ware, *The Relationship between Vigilance and Monotonous Work,* Ergonomics 9, 1966.
[8] C. D. Wylie and R. R. Mackie, *Active Sonar Detection and Reporting,* Human Factors Research, Inc., 1972.
[9] D. B. Lindsley et al., *Human Factors in Undersea Warfare,* Office of Naval Research, 1949.
[10] E. J. McCormick, *Human Factors Engineering,* McGraw-Hill, New York, 1970.
[11] S. R. Mohler, *Fatigue in Aviation Activities,* FAA Office of Aviation Medicine, 1965.

PROBLEMS

1. The glimpse probability varies from glimpse to glimpse as given by the table at the top of page 72:

   a. Complete the table.
   b. If the search continues indefinitely, what is the probability the target will eventually be detected? Assume $g_n = 0$ for all $n \geq 7$.
   c. Is F(n) a cumulative distribution function?

n	g_n	p(n)	F(n)
1	.1		
2	.2		
3	.5		
4	.4		
5	.3		
6	.2		
7	0		

2. If the glimpse probability is given by

$$g_n = \frac{n}{10 - n}, \quad n = 1, 2, \ldots, 5.$$

a. What is $p(n)$, for $n = 1, 2, \ldots, 5$?
b. What is $F(n)$ for $n = 1, 2, \ldots, 5$?
c. Is $F(n)$ a cumulative distribution function?
d. Find $E(N)$.

3. Assume the glimpse probability, g, has a constant value of .2.

a. Tabulate values of $p(n)$ and $F(n)$, for $n = 1, 2, \ldots, 5$.
b. Sketch the graph of $p(n)$ and $F(n)$ for these five glimpses.
c. What is the numerical value of $F(2.5)$?
d. Why does the probability function $p(n)$ decrease as n increases even though g is constant?
e. If after making five glimpses the target has not been detected, what is the probability that detection occurs on the sixth glimpse?
f. What is the expected number of glimpses required for detection?

4. A radar is used to detect incoming enemy missiles at an anti-missile site. The maximum radar range is 140 N.mi. and detection must occur before a missile closes to a range of 100 N.mi. in order to destroy it.

Two alternatives have been considered since the radar is capable of two scan rates—fast and slow.

On *fast*, four glimpses (scans) of the target are possible, i.e., one every 10 N.mi. The probability of detection on each scan is:

.2 when the range is between 120 and 140 N.mi., and
.4 when the range is between 100 and 120 N.mi.

On *slow*, two glimpses of the target are possible, i.e., one every 20 N.mi. The probability of detection on each glimpse is:

.4 when the range is between 120 and 140 N.mi., and
.7 when the range is between 100 and 120 N.mi.

a. State the objective for the comparison of the two scan rates.

b. What would you use as a measure of effectiveness to compare alternatives?

c. What is the result of your comparison, i.e., for which scan rate is the measure of effectiveness highest?

5. To gain insight into what g_i represents and what independence means, let D_2 be the event that a detection occurs on the second glimpse and let D_3 be the event that a detection occurs on the third glimpse.

Consider simulating the process of detection by using a box in which are placed 100 slips of paper, one of which has *detection* written on it and the rest blank. An observer picks slips at random and records his results, until a detection slip is drawn.

For each of these three variations:

(1) After each slip is drawn it is discarded.
(2) After each slip is drawn it is replaced.
(3) After each slip is drawn it is replaced *and* another slip having *detection* written thereon is added to the box.

Determine:

a. Whether or not g is constant, and

b. Whether or not D_2 and D_3 are independent by comparing $P(D_3)$ and $P(D_3 | \bar{D}_2)$.

6. In this chapter the probability of detecting a given target in n glimpses was found to be $F(n) = 1 - (1 - g)^n$, if g is constant. Suppose N targets are present operating independently. What is the probability that at least one is detected in n glimpses?

7. Show that for g constant in the discrete glimpse model, the variance of N is $(1 - g)/g^2$.

8. Show that for γ constant in the continuous looking model, the variance of T is $1/\gamma^2$.

9. In a continuous search, $\gamma = .1$ detection/minute.

a. What is the probability that detection occurs in the first two minutes?

b. What is the probability that initial detection occurs between two and three minutes after the search starts?

c. What is the expected number of detections in the first 15 minutes?

d. How long, on the average, must looking continue in order to detect the target?

10. Assume the instantaneous probability of detection is not constant but is a function of time as follows:

$$\gamma(t) = \frac{2t}{t^2 + 1}$$

Find the mean time to detection.

11. Suppose the constant glimpse probability is .002 and the glimpse rate, a, is five glimpses/minute (so that $n = 60at = 300t$, where t is search time in hours).

a. What is the expected time to detection?

b. How many search hours would be required in order to provide an 80 percent chance of detecting the target?

c. What is the probability of detection if a search is conducted for the length of time you computed for the answer to part a?

12. Suppose a ship is searching visually for a liferaft and that γ is a function of range, r, as follows:

$$\gamma(r) = \frac{40}{r^3}$$

The ship starts the search at initial range of 2 N.mi. and approaches the liferaft on a direct course at a speed of 10 knots.

a. What is $\gamma(t)$?
b. What is the probability that detection will occur before the range decreases to 1 N.mi.?

13. In a continuous looking problem the maximum range of detection is 200 N.mi. and the target will approach directly at 400 knots. $\gamma(r) = 1000/r$, for $r > 0$.

a. Express range (in nautical miles) as a function of time (in hours).
b. Express γ as a function of time.
c. Find the probability that detection occurs by the time the range closes to 100 N.mi.
d. Find the probability density function, $f(t)$, and state the range of t for which it holds.
e. Write an expression which (if evaluated) would give $E(T)$.
f. Write an expression which (if evaluated) would give the variance of T.
g. Suppose in part e you found $E(T) = 1/7$. Find the expected value of the range of detection.

14. Two detectors are being considered for installation on a destroyer in order to provide early warning against enemy air targets. The co says he wants the device which will detect the most targets before they close to 300 N.mi. The targets are expected to be flying directly toward the destroyer at a speed of 800 knots.

Device I is of the continuous looking type, having a maximum range of 400 N.mi. and a detection rate of $(400 - r)/6.25$ detections per hour at range r.

Device II is of the glimpsing type, having a maximum range of 400 N.mi., a glimpse rate of two glimpses per minute and $g = .2$ on each glimpse.

Compare the effectiveness of the two detectors.

15. In this chapter the probability function, $p(n)$, was found to be

$$p(n) = P(N = n) = g_n \prod_{i=1}^{n-1} (1 - g_i).$$

Find the conditional probability function $P(N = n \mid N > n - 1)$.

16. Show that for any two events, A and B, where $P(A \cup B) = 1$,

$$P(\bar{A} \mid B) = 1 - P(A \mid B).$$

17. In this chapter the probability density function was found to be,

$$f(t) = \gamma(t)e^{-\int_0^t \gamma(t)\, dt},$$

so that

$$P[t < T < t + dt] = f(t)dt = \gamma(t)e^{-\int_0^t \gamma(t)\,dt}\,dt.$$

What is the conditional probability given by $P(t < T < t + dt \mid T > t)$?

[Note: the answer should justify the term *instantaneous probability density* or *conditional probability density function* used by some authors to describe $\gamma(t)$.]

18. From Table 4-2, determine what vibration parameters of amplitude and frequency should be especially avoided for a vigilance task, such as a radar watch.

19. (*Optional problem*) *Monte Carlo simulation of discrete glimpse detection process:* Design a computer program simulating a discrete glimpse detection process through five glimpses where g for each glimpse is constant and $g = G$. The output of this program is printed values of $p(1)$ through $p(5)$ and $F(1)$ through $F(5)$. The simulation is to be run N times, where N must be sufficiently large to get statistically meaningful output values. A flow chart of a simulation model oriented to BASIC or FORTRAN is provided.

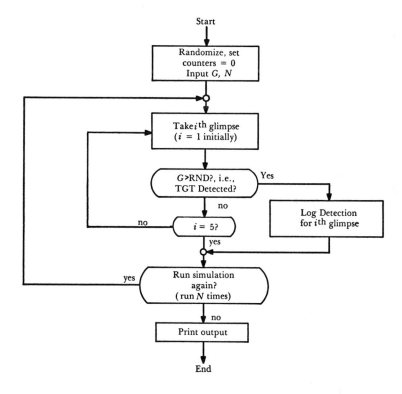

The output values of the simulation can be compared to the theoretical (mathematically calculated) values of $p(n) = g(1 - g)^{n-1}$ and $F(n) = 1 - (1 - g)^n$ for $n = 1, 2, 3, 4, 5$.

5 RADAR DETECTION THEORY AND ELECTRONIC WARFARE

All naval operations involving contact with an enemy depend upon the ability of the naval forces involved to locate the enemy and maintain contact. This is true on, under and above the surface of the sea. On and above the surface of the sea, the principal long-range sensor is radar. Determining the most effective employment of radar in naval operations is a continuing problem dating from the introduction of the first operational radar just prior to World War II. In fact, the history of Operations Analysis in the Navy began with the first applications of the scientific method to the operational use of radar at the time of its acceptance by the military.

The purpose of fleet radar is well defined. *It exists to detect and track targets on the sea or above it.* Major problems still to be solved are the *choice of a best measure of effectiveness* and *determination of the values for the measure chosen* for each radar. The measure may be maximum detection range of the radar, probability of detection of a target, probability of maintaining a track on a detected target or something else. In this chapter, measures of effectiveness based upon three operational theories will be presented and their applications to fleet radar discussed.

In order to comprehend the theories of radar operation, it is necessary to have some knowledge of the equipment and its operating environment; hence a description of the major components of radar equipment and a discussion of the physics of radar energy propagation in the atmosphere are included.

In the study of operational theory, a radar set can be regarded as a collection of black boxes. Broadly speaking, only the functions and the interactions of these boxes with the outside world of operators, targets, atmosphere, sea surface, maintenance men, and so forth, are of concern. The basic physics which is presented is associated solely with the interaction of the radar with the strictly physical aspects of its operational environment, the target and the propagation path.

501 DESCRIPTION OF A RADAR SYSTEM

The type of radar to be considered is a conventional pulse-modulated scanning system which is schematically illustrated in Figure 5-1.

The *timer* begins the cycle of radar operation by sending a pulse to the *modulator* and to the *indicator* to synchronize the time-measuring circuits with the departure of the transmitted *radio frequency* (RF) energy. The modulator provides a high voltage direct current pulse to the *transmitter,* causing it to run (oscillate) for the duration of the pulse. While oscillating, the transmitter generates the RF energy in the form of a short, powerful pulse. The time duration of the pulse is called the *pulse length*. The rate of its generation is called the *pulse repetition frequency* or pulse repetition rate.

The high energy pulse travels from the transmitter to the *antenna* through a switching mechanism called the *duplexer*. To permit the use of a single antenna for transmission and reception, the duplexer connects the transmitter to the antenna during transmission and at the same time isolates the *receiver* to protect its sensitive elements. In order to see a close target, the duplexer quickly disconnects the transmitter immediately after transmission and connects the receiver to the antenna. Thus the antenna both transmits the RF energy and receives echoes. The configuration of the antenna shapes the radio waves into a concentrated beam and points then in a particular direction. The direction of the beam is sent to the indicator as azimuth data.

The receiver amplifies incoming echo signals, which are relatively weak, and produces an output which approximates their envelope. The output of the receiver is normally used to control the intensity of the electron beam of the *cathode ray tube* (CRT) in the indicator. The indicator presents the display of radar information. When the indicator is told by the timer that a cycle has begun, it proceeds to record time. This is usually done by commencing a sweep of an electron beam across the face of a cathode ray tube. The displacement of the beam is then directly proportional to the elapsed time since cycle initiation, and a measure of distance to the target can be read directly from the cathode ray tube. At the same time, the indicator is receiving continuous information on the angular position of the antenna which it displays on a counter or by rotating the direction of travel of the sweep to match the antenna angle.

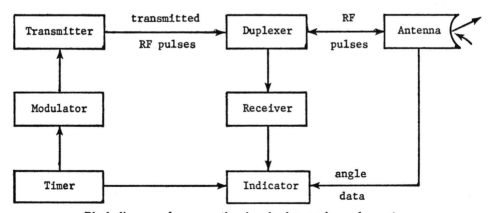

Block diagram of a conventional, pulsed, scanning radar system.

Figure 5-1.

502 BASIC PHYSICAL PARAMETERS

It is desirable next to introduce some symbolism to describe the basic physics of the radar process. The notation for, and definitions of, the basic physical parameters are as follows:

a. Radar frequency, f: number of electromagnetic energy cycles/second.
b. Range, R: range to the target.
c. Theoretical maximum range, R_m: maximum range obtainable based on the limitations of physical parameters. (See Figure 5-2.)
d. Wave length, λ: distance covered per cycle. $\lambda = c/f$, where c is the velocity of propagation of electromagnetic waves (186,000 statute miles/second or 161,500 nautical miles/second).
e. Pulse length, T: length of transmitted pulse in seconds. (See Figure 5-3.)
f. Pulse repetition frequency, f_p: number of transmitted pulses/second. Since pulses can be emitted no more frequently than the time required for the radiation to travel to the theoretical maximum range and return, $f_p = c/2R_m$. (See Figure 5-4.)
g. Duty cycle, α: ratio of pulse length to the length of a radar cycle (see Figure 5-5):

$$\alpha = \frac{\text{time on (seconds)}}{\text{cycle length (seconds)}} = \frac{T}{1/f_p} = f_p T.$$

h. Peak power, P_t: instantaneous power in watts generated by the transmitter while in oscillation.
i. Average power, P_a: power, averaged over a total cycle:

$$P_a = \frac{\text{Power during time } T + \text{power during time } 1/f_p - T}{\text{Total time } 1/f_p}$$

$$= \frac{P_t \times T + 0 \times (1/f_p - T)}{1/f_p} = \frac{P_t \times T}{1/f_p}$$

$$P_a = T \cdot f_p \cdot P_t = \alpha P_t.$$

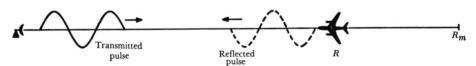

Transmitted pulse

Reflected pulse

R

R_m

Figure 5-2.

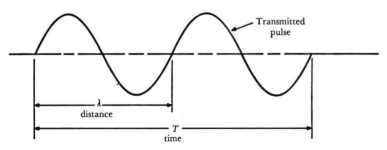

Transmitted pulse

λ
distance

T
time

Figure 5-3.

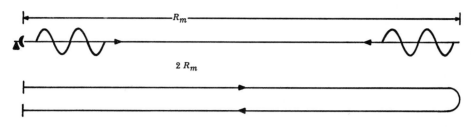

$$d = vt \qquad t \text{ from pulse to pulse} = 1/f_p$$

$$2R_m = c \times 1/f_p \rightarrow f_p = \frac{c}{2R_m}$$

Figure 5-4.

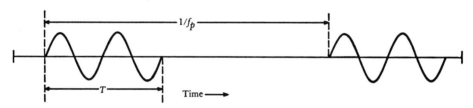

Figure 5-5.

j. Sweep speed, S_s: speed (inches/second) with which the electron beam is displaced across the face of the cathode ray tube. If d is the total displacement to correspond to a theoretical maximum range, R_m, then $c/2R_m = S_s/d$ and $S_s = cd/2R_m$. (See Figure 5-6.)

k. Antenna gain, G: ratio of the power density on the antenna axis to the power density produced at the same range by an omnidirectional radiator of the same output power. G measures the *focusing* effect of the antenna.

l. Effective area for reception, A_e: defined by,

$$A_e = \frac{\lambda^2 G}{4\pi}, \quad \text{or} \quad G = \frac{4\pi A_e}{\lambda^2}.$$

A_e usually varies between 50 and 85 percent of the geometric area of the antenna.

The pattern of energy created by a radar antenna consists of a sequence of reinforcements (called *lobes*) and cancellations (called *nulls*). For a particular antenna,

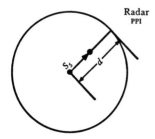

Radar
PPI

Figure 5-6.

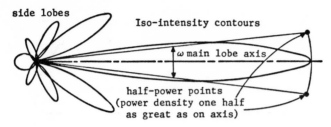

Lobe pattern for a conventional radar antenna.

Figure 5-7.

this pattern is often pictured by making a polar plot of iso-intensity lines as shown in Figure 5-7.

For a properly designed antenna, the side lobes are far less intense than the main lobe. The size of these secondary lobes and their number, as well as the fineness of the main lobe, are functions of the ratio of antenna dimensions (and shape) to wave length. A large antenna-size/wave-length ratio produces a fine main lobe and many much-suppressed side lobes. For approximate calculations the antenna pattern is idealized to a segment of a circle, of angular width ω, as shown in Figure 5-7. The angle ω is called the beam width. On the normal PPI-type indicator, the presented signal is the sum of the intensities received from many individual radar pulses which fall on the target as the scanning beam moves by. The intensities of these pulses are modulated by the beam pattern according to their angles of emission. Again, for approximate calculations, all pulses falling between the *half-power* points are treated as equal to the power density on the axis. This procedure is a compromise. It discards the energy from any pulses emitted outside the angles $\pm\omega/2$ and treats each pulse emitted inside this sector as being subjected to the maximum (axis) gain of the antenna. These considerations lead to the calculation of a fictitious number of *pulses on-target per scan*. If the *antenna rotation rate, a,* is in revolutions per minute, then the number of pulses on-target per scan is

Equation 5-1   Number of pulses/scan $= (f_p)\left(\dfrac{60}{a}\right)\left(\dfrac{\omega}{360}\right) = \dfrac{\omega f_p}{6a},$

where ω is measured in degrees.

The number of pulses on-target per scan can be increased, and range thereby increased, by increasing ω or f_p, or by decreasing a. The beam width, ω, is increased only at the expense of decreasing definition of the radar. The pulse repetition rate, f_p, usually cannot be increased because of travel time considerations. It may have to be decreased for increased range. Finally, if a is decreased, the penalty paid is decreased data rate. Thus, a fairly complex operational choice already exists in determining each of the basic system parameters.

This discussion, while not complete, will serve to introduce many of the basic operational parameters of pulsed, scanning radar systems. The following two sections present some of the physical principles affecting radar detection. These deal with deterministic rather than probabilistic concepts.

503 REFLECTIONS FROM THE SEA

For almost all operational situations a searching radar will provide substantial illumination of the earth's surface incidental to its search for air (or surface) targets. Much of the energy which reaches the sea surface will be reflected back to interfere with the directly radiated energy field, and thus set up an interference pattern in the atmosphere. This pattern has many operational implications.

The earth's reflecting surface is a sphere, but for wave propagation over distances which are not too great, it is usually considered a plane. Figure 5-8 illustrates the geometry of the situation; the physical principle involved is known as Lloyd's Mirror Effect.

The horizontal range, R, is measured in the reflecting plane (although it may be measured direct from radar to target, if the difference is insignificant). A ray from the radar antenna, incident on the plane at any angle θ, appears to come from the image of the antenna at A'. We are interested in finding the difference in the length of path $\overline{A'MB}$ and the length of the direct path $\overline{AB}$. The amount of extra travel, $\overline{A'B} - \overline{AB}$, will be important in determining the formation of fade zones.

The difference is most easily found by comparing the squared values between

$$\overline{A'B}^2 = R^2 + (h_1 + h_2)^2,$$

and

$$\overline{AB}^2 = R^2 + (h_2 - h_1)^2.$$

Subtracting yields

$$\overline{A'B}^2 - \overline{AB}^2 = 4h_1 h_2.$$

Factoring gives

$$(\overline{A'B} - \overline{AB})(\overline{A'B} + \overline{AB}) = 4h_1 h_2,$$

and

$$(\overline{A'B} - \overline{AB}) = \frac{4h_1 h_2}{\overline{A'B} + \overline{AB}}.$$

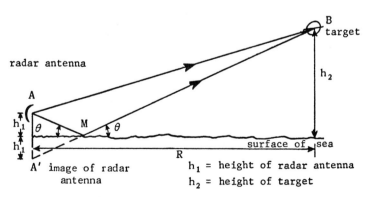

Diagram illustrating the geometry of Lloyd's Mirror Effect.

Figure 5-8.

Assume that h_1 and h_2 are very small compared to R so that

$$R \cong \overline{A'B} \cong \overline{AB}; \text{ and } \overline{A'B} + \overline{AB} \cong 2R.$$

Then

$$(\overline{A'B} - \overline{AB}) = 4h_1h_2/2R = 2h_1h_2/R = \text{extra travel, } \Delta.$$

Let δ be the phase difference *in radians* due to extra travel. Then

$$\gamma = \left(\frac{2\pi}{\lambda}\right)(\Delta) = \left(\frac{2\pi}{\lambda}\right)\left(\frac{2h_1h_2}{R}\right) \text{ radians,}$$

where λ = wave length of the radar. Independent of this, there is a phase shift of 180 degrees (π radians) upon reflection at M. Thus, the *total phase difference* between direct and reflected paths is

$$\delta' = \delta + \pi = \left(\frac{2\pi}{\lambda}\right)\left(\frac{2h_1h_2}{R}\right) + \pi = \frac{4\pi h_1h_2}{\lambda R} + \pi \text{ radians.}$$

Reinforcement of the radar wave at the target occurs when δ' is an even number of π radians, i.e., extra travel, $\Delta = \dfrac{2h_1h_2}{R} = \dfrac{n\lambda}{2}$, for $n = 1, 3, 5, \dots$, which results in maximum signal strength back at the radar receiver. *Cancellation* occurs for even values of n and results in minimum (or zero) signal strength back at the radar receiver.

For a given radar installation, h_1 and λ are fixed while only target height, h_2, and range, R, vary. A plot of the lobe pattern of this radar would be approximately as shown in Figure 5-9.

Figure 5-9 is of real operational significance. An aircraft approaching the radar, at constant altitude, will fly through a sequence of lobes and interspersed nulls. Thus, the operator may not have a steady radar contact but one which will appear and disappear as the target approaches. Because of this, a well-defined lobe pattern plot can be used to furnish information on the approximate altitude of the target aircraft by noting the ranges at which it intercepts the various lobes and nulls. During these interceptions, the echoes on the scope will vary from maximum intensity to complete fading.

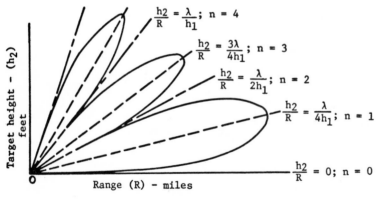

Vertical lobe pattern.

Figure 5-9.

504 RADAR HORIZON

While the path of the radar beam is relatively straight, there is some bending due to refraction. This causes the range to the radar horizon to be greater than it would be if the radar rays were perfectly straight. To demonstrate this, the range to the radar horizon will be computed in the case of straight rays, after which the equation applicable in the actual case will be developed. Figure 5-10 is a geometrical presentation of the pertinent relationships.

Analytically, $R^2_e + r^2_{Ho} = (R_e + h_1)^2 = R^2_e + 2R_e h_1 + h^2_1,$

and $r^2_{Ho} = 2R_e h_1 + h^2_1,$

or $r^2_{Ho} = h_1(2R_e + h_1) \cong 2h_1 R_e$

since h_1 is small compared to R_e.
Then,

$$r_{Ho} = \sqrt{2h_1 R_e}.$$

The bending of the radar rays causes them to follow the dash-lined path shown in Figure 5-10. To compensate for this effect, a different (larger) radius of the earth is assumed. For standard atmospheric conditions, the actual earth radius is replaced by a fictitious earth radius equal to $(4/3)R_e$. Then,

Equation 5-2 $r'_{Ho} = \sqrt{2h_1(4/3)R_e}.$

To get r'_{Ho} in miles, convert h_1, the antenna height in feet, to its height in statute miles, and observe that

$$r'_{Ho} = \sqrt{(2)\left(\frac{4}{3}\right)(3960) \text{ miles} \left(\frac{h_1 \text{ feet}}{5280 \text{ feet/mile}}\right)}$$

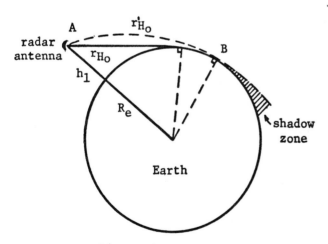

Diagram of radar horizon.

h_1: height of radar antenna (feet).
R_e: radius of earth (3,960 statute miles).
r_{Ho}: range to horizon (straight ray, statute miles).
r'_{Ho}: range to horizon (refracted ray, statute miles).

Figure 5-10.

or

$$r'_{Ho} = \sqrt{2h_1 \text{ (feet)}} \text{ statute miles.}$$

The result, range to the radar horizon, is in statute miles, while the height of the radar antenna is in feet. The range in statute miles at which one can expect a target at height h_2 to cross the radar horizon is found as follows:

$$r'_{Ho} = \sqrt{2h_1 \text{ (feet)}} + \sqrt{2h_2 \text{ (feet)}} \text{ statute miles.}$$

Example: Antenna height = 50 feet; target height = 800 feet.

$$r'_{Ho} = \sqrt{2(50)} + \sqrt{2(800)} = 10 + 40 = 50 \text{ statute miles.}$$

A consequence of the radar horizon is the existence of a *shadow zone* beneath the radar ray tangent to the earth at B, which is a distance r'_{Ho} from the radar, and into which very little energy goes by direct propagation. A target coming from the shadow zone into the directly illuminated region is said to have crossed the radar horizon. From calculations which produced the lobe pattern as depicted in Figure 5-9, it can be shown that the horizon ray is a null in the interference pattern. Operationally, this means that very low target altitudes give a low probability of detection by search radar.

Likewise, the increase of radar horizon with increasing antenna height provides motivation for airborne radar detection and control systems.

505 OPERATIONAL RADAR MODELS

In considering the physical aspects which determine how well, or how poorly, a radar system performs as a detection device, it is most important to recognize the influence of the human beings who operate and maintain the radar and interpret its outputs. The degradation of performance which results from a poorly tuned receiver, normal deterioration of electronic parts, water in the wave guides or from an inattentive or fatigued operator, is as real as, and often outweighs, the strictly physical considerations. However, the variation in radar performance which arises in the strictly physical area (that is, with perfect operators and maintenance) is very great and will be discussed in the following paragraphs. Also the performance of the human part of the system is subject to control and improvement, while the natural phenomena which affect performance are not. There are two areas of natural phenomena which profoundly affect detection. For convenience these are called *target physics* and *propagation physics*. Some effects of propagation physics have been discussed under reflections from the sea and the extension of the radar horizon due to refraction.

Target physics are those characteristics of the target which cause detection performance to vary. For example, a target is usually characterized by a parameter known as target echo-area, A_t, which will be defined later. While target echo-area is a widely fluctuating random variable, it is often treated as a constant in elementary radar models.

The random fluctuations of A_t result from the fact that most radar targets are complex collections of reflecting points and surfaces. In aircraft, the various nacelles, edges, surfaces, antennas and other appurtenances each act as reradiating points which return echoes to the radar. Further, the phase relationships of the various reradiations constantly change as the aircraft oscillates about its average flight path, and as its structure flexes and vibrates. This variable has time-period fluctuations which have a definite effect on detection.

Finally, the relative importance of the contributions of *target* and *propagation physics* to variations in detectability are unknown, so it is not possible to say one is minor with respect to the other.

All of the preceding discussion of natural causes of variability of radar detection needs to be put in proper perspective by pointing out that the absolute variability they contribute is dependent upon frequency. As the radar frequency decreases, so does the variation. Therefore, some point exists where increased power and reduced frequency would cause the variation in detection from these natural causes to be overcome. It is interesting to note that in the later stages of World War II there was a trend toward higher frequencies in air-search radar. This trend was reversed as more development and evaluation work was done.

The goal of a radar model is the prediction of a radar's ability to detect a target. A model which predicted this detection capability using only the elementary parameters of the radar system—such as pulse rate, pulse length, average power, sweep speed, antenna gain, etc.—would attempt to *determine* the range at which detection will occur, or the intensity of a signal returning to the antenna in terms of those basic parameters. Because of the elementary nature of its inputs, such a model is called *absolute* or *deterministic*.

The *radar equation* is clearly an attempt to formulate an absolute theory, and were it not for the random nature of target, propagation, maintenance, operation and background noise, it might well succeed. In the presence of variations in these quantities, the radar equation can be expected to yield, at best, an *estimate* of an average range of detection in terms of the *average* values of the other quantities. It may also be used to determine a *maximum possible* range of detection.

Another approach to the formulation of a radar theory is to seek a less sophisticated model which accepts a certain amount of operational data and attempts its extrapolation to more general operational situations. Two such theories, the *blip/scan* and the *direct method,* will be presented to predict the probability of detection for a radar. They lead to models which will be referred to as *relative* or *probabilistic*.

506 THE RADAR EQUATION

The reasoning which leads to the radar equation is analogous to that used for sonar in a later chapter. At the source, a radar signal of a certain strength is generated. It is beamed or focused toward a target by the antenna. Its intensity decreases while traveling through the atmosphere because of physical phenomena such as *spreading, absorption, scattering* and so on. A certain amount of energy from this reduced signal hits the target. Depending primarily on the size, aspect, construction and so forth of the target, some portion of this incident signal is reradiated or reflected in the direction of the receiver. As this signal returns, it is reduced again by travel through the atmosphere, and some portion finally reaches the antenna and is focused into the receiver.

The simplified radar equation developed here uses the basic parameters defined earlier and gives the amount of power received from the returning pulse, P_r, in terms of transmitted power, P_t, antenna gain, G, target area, A_t, effective antenna area, A_e, and range, R. To derive it the assumption is made that a radar pulse traveling through the atmosphere spreads omnidirectionally as on the surface of an expanding sphere and that effects of absorption, reflections from the sea and so on are negligible.

The intensity or power density of a signal at range R from an omnidirectional antenna is

Equation 5-3
$$I_0 = \frac{P_t}{4\pi R^2} \frac{\text{watts}}{\text{unit area}},$$

where P_t is the transmitted (peak) power in watts and $4\pi R^2$ is the surface area of a sphere of radius R. From the definition of G it follows that the power density on the axis of an antenna of gain G would be

Equation 5-4
$$I_g = \frac{P_t G}{4\pi R^2} \frac{\text{watts}}{\text{unit area}}.$$

Let A_t denote the target-echo area which collects energy from the incident wave and reradiates it *omnidirectionally*. This definition of target-echo area is somewhat arbitrary in that A_t is determined only by the solution of the full radar equation. With this definition, the power received by the target is

Equation 5-5
$$P_g = \frac{P_t G A_t}{4\pi R^2} \text{ watts},$$

and the power density returned to the radar, from the power reradiated omnidirectionally by the target is

Equation 5-6
$$I_r = \frac{P_t G A_t}{(4\pi)^2 R^4} \frac{\text{watts}}{\text{unit area}}.$$

Using the effective area of the antenna, A_e, as a collector of energy, the reradiated power collected by the antenna is

Equation 5-7
$$P_r = \frac{P_t G A_t A_e}{(4\pi)^2 R^4} \text{ watts}.$$

Solving for range, Equation 5-7 becomes

Equation 5-8
$$R^4 = \frac{P_t G A_t A_e}{P_r (4\pi)^2}.$$

If P_o is the minimum detectable power for the radar receiver, then the maximum range, R_m, for detection is the range at which $P_r = P_o$ and Equation 5-8 can be written

Equation 5-9
$$R^4{}_m = \frac{P_t G A_t A_e}{P_o (4\pi)^2}.$$

This may be modified, if desired, by substituting for G or A_e, which are related by the expression $A_e = \lambda^2 G / 4\pi$, as stated earlier. It is, of course, possible to be much more sophisticated in the model by regarding *second-order* effects, such as the absorption of energy by the atmosphere, but Equation 5-9 is in a basic form which furnishes much information immediately. It will be seen in Section 510 how the radar equation can be used to evaluate the effectiveness of jamming equipment carried by the target.

507 THE BLIP/SCAN THEORY

In searching for a target, a scanning radar *looks* repeatedly in the direction of the target. On some, but generally not all of these looks or scans, the radar echo from the target will be sufficient to produce a visible electronic response on the radar indicator. This may also be true of the individual pulses within one look, but the quantity treated here is the summation of the individual returns from this single look.

Detection of the target cannot be considered to have occurred until the human operator has *seen* the target indication and confirmed for himself, usually by more than one scan, that the original response was a target and not a random surge of noise. Thus, target detection is a probabilistic phenomenon compounded by many individual random events.

A simple and intuitively appealing relative theory can be constructed around the assumption that the outcomes on successive scans are independent. This theory has come to be known as the *blip/scan theory*. Its intended purpose is to permit the extrapolation of limited operational data, such as might be collected by conducting trial detection and tracking runs on aircraft, to cases not covered by the trials. Tests or trials of such a nature have long been conducted by COMOPTEVFOR, but such projects are costly in terms of time and services. This is an important reason for wanting to extract as much information as possible from each trial and, further, to feel reasonably sure that such data can be extrapolated to operational situations not covered by the trials. The data may thus be used for the purpose of evaluating the performance of a radar system and provide the basis for comparison of different systems.

To develop the theory, recall the glimpse model in Chapter four (Equation 4-3) where the probability of detecting a target in n discrete glimpses was

$$F(n) = 1 - \prod_{i=1}^{n} (1 - g_i).$$

Since for any positive number x, $e^{\ln x}$ is equal to x, $F(n)$ can be written as

Equation 5-10
$$F(n) = 1 - e^{\ln\left[\prod_{i=1}^{n}(1 - g_i)\right]},$$

and since the log of a product is the sum of the logs, Equation 5-10 becomes

Equation 5-11
$$F(n) = 1 - e^{\sum_{i=1}^{n}[\ln(1 - g_i)]}.$$

This can be further simplified by noting that if each g_i is small, the expression $\ln(1 - g_i)$ is approximately equal to $-g_i$. Using this assumption, Equation 5-11 simplifies to

Equation 5-12
$$F(n) = 1 - e^{-\sum_{i=1}^{n} g_i}.$$

The consequences of this assumption are not critical. It can be shown that for a typical case where a target closes on a radar, the value of $F(n)$ becomes large before the value of g_i increases enough to invalidate the approximation; and whether or not the approximation is good, Equation 5-12 is a *conservative* estimate of the *actual* probability given by Equation 5-11. In Chapter four it was assumed that each value of g_i was known and hence the probability of detection could be computed. The blip/scan theory provides a means for *determining* values for g_i in terms of other basic parameters, realizing that detection depends on three basic events: *blips must appear on the radar scope; the operator must see them;* and *the operator must identify these blips as the target.*

Let Ψ_i be the probability that on the ith glimpse (scan) the target will produce a recognizable blip on the radar scope, and let p_o, the *operator factor*, be the probability that the radar operator, not knowing the location of target, will see the blip. p_o will be assumed constant for a given operator. Suppose, now, that a blip appears on the scope and the operator sees it. Will he immediately report the blip as a target? Probably not, as too many false blips appear in a typical operational situation for one to be confident of identifying a target on the basis of a single blip. In the usual case an operator seeing a blip will suspect the possibility of a target but will verify its appearance on successive scans before identifying it as a target. On *how many* scans must he see a blip before identification takes place? The most common assumption and the one used here is known as the *double-blip hypothesis*. It assumes:

a. that a blip must be seen on *two successive* scans before it is recognized as a target,

b. that an an operator who is *alerted* by seeing one blip and suspecting a target will surely see a blip which appears in the same position on the following scan, and

c. that if a blip does not appear on the following scan, the operator immediately forgets the first and thus is no longer alerted.

For detection to take place under the double-blip hypothesis, a blip must appear, the operator (unalerted) must see it, a blip must occur on the next scan, and the operator now alerted must see it. The probability that an operator would detect a previously undetected target on the ith scan, g_i, would then be

Equation 5-13
$$g_i = (\Psi_{i-1})(p_o)(\Psi_i)(1),$$

(assuming the event that a blip appears on a particular scan is independent of the event that a blip appears on any adjacent scan). Equation 5-12 then becomes

Equation 5-14
$$F(n) = 1 - e^{-p_o \sum_{i=1}^{n} \Psi_{i-1} \cdot \Psi_i},$$

from the assumption that p_o is constant.

In order to apply this theory, operational data must be used to determine the value of the constant, p_o, and then for values of Ψ_i the probability of detection can be determined and extrapolated to other cases. Two types of operational data are required. For both, aircraft are used to approach the radar on a direct course from beyond the maximum radar range. Values of Ψ_i are then determined by use of *tracking runs* with an alerted radar operator. Values of $F(n)$ are determined using *detection runs* with an unalerted operator. These values can then be used in Equation 5-14, where the remaining unknown, p_o, can be determined.

In practice, to make data-gathering easier, instead of determining values of Ψ_i and $F(n)$ for every glimpse, the range (from maximum range, R_m, to zero range) is arbitrarily divided into intervals of length Δr. These intervals are numbered, starting with the outermost interval and working in, and are denoted by Δr_j for $j = 1, 2, 3, \ldots$. For example if $R_m = 100$ miles and Δr is chosen to be 10 miles, then Δr_1 is the interval from 90–100 miles, Δr_2 from 80–90 miles, and so on. Furthermore, since Ψ_i changes little from one glimpse to the next, the quantity measured will be the average value of Ψ_i in each range interval. All values of Ψ_i in the first range interval can then be approximated by their average value, denoted $\Psi_{\Delta r_1}$, and all values of g_i in the first range interval can be approximated by their average value, $g_{\Delta r_1}$. In the general case, for all range intervals, Δr_j, Equation 5-13 becomes

$$g_{\Delta r_j} = \Psi^2_{\Delta r_j} p_o.$$

For a given aircraft speed and radar antenna rotation rate, the number of glimpses or scans which occur while the aircraft is in each range interval can be computed. Let L be this number of scans per range interval, a the antenna rotation rate in revolutions per minute, v the target/radar relative velocity in knots, and Δr the length of each range interval in nautical miles. Then

$$L = \frac{60\, a\Delta r}{v} \text{ scans/range interval.}$$

Now if m range intervals contain n glimpses, then

$$\sum_{i=1}^{n} g_i = \sum_{j=1}^{m} L \cdot g_{\Delta r_j},$$

and the probability of detection by the time an aircraft passes through m range intervals becomes, from Equation 5-12,

Equation 5-15 $$F(m) = 1 - e^{-L \sum\limits_{j=1}^{m} g_{\Delta r_j}},$$

and Equation 5-14 becomes

Equation 5-16 $$F(m) = 1 - e^{-L p_o \sum\limits_{j=1}^{m} \Psi^2_{\Delta r_j}}.$$

To find values of $\Psi_{\Delta r_j}$ tracking runs are conducted in the following manner. An aircraft proceeds from maximum radar range directly at the radar. The radar operator is *alerted;* that is, he knows the exact position of the aircraft at all times and will surely see a blip if it is presented on the scope. He records the number of scans on which a blip appears while the aircraft is within each range interval. Several such tracking runs are made and the results averaged for each range interval. A typical set of data is presented in Figure 5-11, where the average number of blips received has been rounded to whole numbers.

If $a =$ six revolutions per minute, $\Delta r = 10$ N.mi. and $v = 180$ knots, then $L = 20$ scans per range interval and values of $\Psi_{\Delta r_j}$, $\Psi^2_{\Delta r_j}$ and $\Sigma \Psi^2_{\Delta r_j}$ can be computed and tabulated as well.

With *detection* runs both the radar *and* the operator are evaluated by varying the procedure somewhat. Aircraft approach the radar from well beyond maximum range at different bearings and times. An unalerted radar operator, not knowing where the

j	Δr_j	Average number blips received	Blip/scan ratio $\Psi_{\Delta r_j}$	$\Psi^2_{\Delta r_j}$	$\Sigma \Psi^2_{\Delta r_j}$
1	90–100	2	2/20	4/400	4/400
2	80–90	4	4/20	16/400	20/400
3	70–80	6	6/20	36/400	56/400
4	60–70	8	8/20	64/400	120/400
5	50–60	10	10/20	100/400	220/400
6	40–50	13	13/20	169/400	389/400
7	30/40	15	15/20	225/400	614/400
8	20/30	11	11/20	121/400	735/400
9	10/20	9	9/20	81/400	816/400

Tracking runs.

Figure 5-11.

j	Range interval Δr_j	Number of first detections in this interval	Cumulative number of first detections through j intervals	Cumulative probability of detection through j intervals
1	90–100	2	2	2/40 = .05
2	80–90	2	4	4/40 = .10
3	70–80	4	8	8/40 = .20
4	60–70	8	16	16/40 = .40
5	50–60	8	24	24/40 = .60
6	40–50	8	32	32/40 = .80
7	30–40	4	36	36/40 = .90
8	20–30	2	38	38/40 = .95
9	10–20	0	38	38/40 = .95

Detection runs.

Figure 5-12.

aircraft are, notes the range interval in which he first detects each aircraft as it approaches. Typical data for 40 detection runs are tabulated in Figure 5-12, where the cumulative number of detections and cumulative probability of detection are also computed.

For this example p_o can be computed for any value of m using $\sum_{j=1}^{m}\Psi^2_{\Delta r_j}$ as given in Figure 5-11 and F(m) as given in Figure 5-12. If the m used is six, then, from Equation 5-16,

$$F(6) = 1 - e^{-20p_o \sum\limits_{j=1}^{6} \Psi^2_{\Delta r}},$$

$$.80 = 1 - e^{-20p_o(389)/(400)} = 1 - e^{-19.45p_o},$$

$$.20 = e^{-19.45p_o}.$$

Taking the natural logarithm of both sides

$$\ln .20 = -19.45p_o,$$

and

$$p_o = \frac{-\ln .20}{19.45} = \frac{1.609}{19.45} = .083.$$

As long as p_o is fairly constant, it makes little difference which value of m is used to make the computation, although from statistical considerations the first few intervals may not contain enough data to be representative.

One of the uses for the blip/scan model is to develop a *lateral range curve* for a radar. Lateral range curves, which will be discussed in Chapter six, give the probability of detecting a target not only which passes directly overhead but also which passes by at lateral range (closest point of approach) x. The blip/scan model enables one to extrapolate such information by substituting

$$L = \frac{60a\Delta r}{v},$$

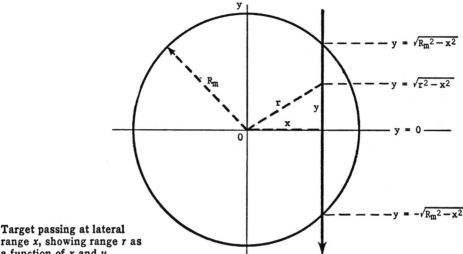

Target passing at lateral
range x, showing range r as
a function of x and y.

Figure 5-13.

so that Equation 5-16 becomes a function of range

$$P(r) = P\begin{pmatrix} \text{detection occurs} \\ \text{at range } r \text{ or greater} \end{pmatrix} = 1 - e^{-\frac{60ap_o}{v} \sum\limits_{\substack{\text{all } j \text{ for} \\ \text{ranges} \geq r}} \Psi^2_{\Delta r_j} \cdot \Delta r}.$$

Letting $\Delta r \to 0$, $P(r)$ becomes

Equation 5-17 $$P(r) = 1 - e^{-\frac{60ap_o}{v} \int_r^{R_m} \Psi^2(r)\, dr}.$$

For a given lateral range x, $r = \sqrt{x^2 + y^2}$ from Figure 5-13. If this value is substituted for r in Equation 5-17 and the integration performed over all values of y, then the resulting expression gives the desired probability (lateral range curve) as a function of the lateral range x.

508 DIRECT METHOD FOR RADAR EVALUATION

One of the assumptions of the blip/scan model which affects its validity is that of blip-to-blip independence. A model more recently developed for determining lateral range curves directly without using that independence assumption is referred to as the *direct method*. Recalling the lobe pattern resulting from Lloyd's Mirror Effect, it can be expected that as a target approaches a radar at a given altitude, there will be several successive blips produced on the scope at some intervals and no blips at other intervals. Furthermore, this pattern of dependence should be the same at any bearing from the radar.

To gather data for this model, the aircraft conducts an *actual* trial run, approaching the radar directly from beyond maximum range. An *alerted* operator records each blip as it appears on the scope as in Figure 5-14A and determines the annular rings shown in the shaded areas of Figure 5-14B.

If a simulated aircraft were to pass by the radar at the same altitude but at lateral range x, how many blips would appear on the scope? If it is assumed that the aircraft

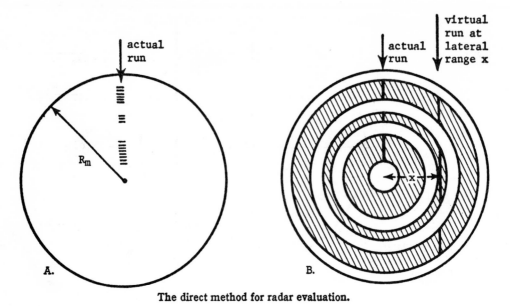

The direct method for radar evaluation.

Figure 5-14.

on this *virtual* run will produce blips while in *the same* annular rings, then the number of virtual blips can be computed geometrically. Each actual run can then be used to construct the rings and determine the number of blips which would be produced by a virtual run at any lateral range. The results from all the actual runs are averaged in the following manner.

Let p_o be the operator factor previously defined, and let $N(i, x)$ represent the number of virtual blips computed for lateral range x, based on the ith actual run. Also let $P(i, x)$ be the probability of detecting a target at lateral range x based on information obtained on the ith actual run. Then the probability the operator fails to detect all of the $N(i, x)$ blips is*

Equation 5-18 $$(1 - p_o)^{N(i,x)},$$

so that

Equation 5-19 $$P(i, x) = 1 - (1 - p_o)^{N(i,x)}.$$

If *n* actual runs are made, then

$$P(1, x) = 1 - (1 - p_o)^{N(1,x)},$$
$$P(2, x) = 1 - (1 - p_o)^{N(2,x)},$$
$$\vdots \qquad\qquad \vdots$$
$$P(n, x) = 1 - (1 - p_o)^{N(n,x)}.$$

*Independence *may* be assumed here. It can be shown, however, that Equation 5-18 results if p_0 is recognized as the probability an operator sees a blip when it appears *if he has not yet seen a blip produced by that target*. Then the development can be continued using conditional probabilities, as was done in Sections 402 and 403 of Chapter four.

The *average value* of $P(i, x)$ based on n actual runs is then

Equation 5-20
$$\overline{P}(x) = \frac{1}{n} \sum_{i=1}^{n} P(i, x).$$

Equation 5-20 gives, for each value of x, one point on the lateral range curve, and by repeated application of this procedure for a number of lateral ranges, the overall lateral range curve can be generated.

The operator factor may be arrived at separately from the direct runs made in the evaluation of the radar much as it was determined for the blip/scan model. It may also be obtained for each operator from laboratory experiments as a sonar operator's ability to distinguish sounds in the ocean is determined from sound laboratory testing.

The direct method furnishes a simple model for generating an estimate of the lateral range curve from a single collection of runs made at zero lateral range, i.e., overhead runs. The principal assumption which underlies this method is that if a blip appears at a given range on a direct run, then a similar target would produce a blip at the same range no matter what its bearing, aspect or speed relative to the radar.

Three radar theories have been briefly introduced, beginning with the radar equation and ending with the direct method. The present state of knowledge is not sufficient to indicate a choice between these theories. All are known to be imperfect, but until a better mathematical model can be formulated from increased knowledge, analysis of radar detection must make judicious use of all to formulate estimates of radar detection performance. Since radar is a primary sensory device in modern warfare, studies and analyses of the many facets of radar and radar performance are continually being made.

509 ELECTRONIC WARFARE

Electronic warfare (EW) is a distinct and well-defined major function in military operations. It is included in this chapter on radar because of its importance to the operational use of radar and because of the application of the radar equation itself to the use of jamming equipment. In its broadest sense, EW encompasses the employment of all devices and equipment which radiate or receive electromagnetic energy. This includes the tactical and strategic use of such equipments as radar; communications devices for the command, control, and exchange of information among friendly forces; and fire control equipment for the firing and control of weapons against the enemy. Thus the importance of EW, in the context of today's methods of waging war, becomes obvious when one realizes that virtually every weapons system, every detection system and every communication system relies heavily, if not totally, upon the use of electromagnetic energy as the link between vital phases of the operation of such systems. The inherent weakness of an electromagnetic radiation is its susceptibility to detection and interference because of its free-space propagation characteristics. And, it is the exploitation of this weakness which accounts for a major expenditure of effort in electronic warfare.

Electronic warfare can be defined in more specific terms as an interaction between two or more information systems for the purpose of gaining tactical or strategic advantage. An information system, as referred to here, is understood to be any electronic device that radiates and/or receives information (intelligence) by means of electromagnetic energy transmission. The problems concerned with when, where and how to generate this electronic interaction and the action to be taken to counter its detrimental effects, are fundamental to electronic warfare.

Electronic warfare is so important in U. S. defense that the Defense Department spends a significant portion of the defense budget in this field of military operations. The expenditure of this amount reflects the universal military dependence upon radar, radio and infrared electromagnetic propagation systems for target detection, surveillance, weapons guidance and communications.

Because of its direct relationship to virtually every type of warfare, EW must be fully considered when planning any operation. Particularly important is the application of the principles of EW to amphibious, antisubmarine and anti-air warfare—actions which call for a high degree of control and coordination. Limited (peacetime) electronic warfare is being carried on continuously as each military power probes the other's electronic defenses. The objective is to determine the location of every radar and radio transmitter, and to analyze its operating characteristics in order to develop equipment suitable for interfering with its proper operation in the event of a shooting war.

Electromagnetic energy is used to convey intelligence (ideas, information or instructions) from one point to another, just as a telephone wire might be used. The elementary form of this link is an alternating magnetic field (traveling at the speed of light) having a *basic frequency* (carrier), and a *basic relative amplitude* (energy level) which diminishes steadily as it moves away from the transmitting source because of divergence and absorption by the atmosphere. These two basic parameters are inherent in all electromagnetic transmission links. However, in order to convey intelligence from one point to another by this means, the basic *carrier* must be *modulated* (modified) in some specific way. This is done by several methods: *pulsing* the basic carrier (turning it off and on as with a Morse code key); changing the amplitude, *amplitude modulation* (AM); or changing the frequency around its basic frequency, *frequency modulation* (FM). Intricate combinations of these means of modification may be used in order to transmit complicated commands or instructions on a single carrier.

Thus, every transmission of electromagnetic energy has very definite and specific parameters which can be detected, analyzed and evaluated to indicate source and purpose. In many cases, the intelligence being conveyed by this method can be intercepted and used to the detriment of the originator.

Electronic warfare may be divided into two major areas of effort, *electronic countermeasures* (ECM) and *electronic counter-countermeasures* (ECCM).

a. Electronic countermeasures is defined as that major subdivision of EW which involves actions taken to prevent or reduce the effectiveness of enemy equipment and tactics employing or affected by electromagnetic radiations. To be effective, ECM must be used on a fleet-wide basis. It may be further classified as follows:

(1) *Passive* ECM. Electronic countermeasures are classified as passive when of a type which cannot be detected by the enemy. Thus their use requires no tactical disclosures, but does require extensive operator training. Examples of EW falling into this category are:

(a) *Intercept search* (electronic search and reconnaissance), which consists of search with proper receiving equipment for electromagnetic radiations to determine their existence, source and pertinent characteristics. The interception, analysis and evaluation of enemy electronic emissions is of major importance in any operation, and enables one's own forces to plan effective measures for countering enemy use of electronic systems. The result of intercept search is *electronic intelligence* (ELINT) concerning enemy electronic capabilities and employment. This information is collected, further analyzed, consolidated and disseminated through ELINT centers in both Atlantic and Pacific fleets.

(b) *Tactical evasion*, the taking of evasive actions to avoid or impede detection and/or tracking by the enemy. It depends upon knowledge of the capabilities and limitations of enemy detection and tracking equipment.

(2) *Active* ECM. Electronic countermeasures are classified as active when of a type which may be detected by the enemy. Because the enemy may be able to acquire intelligence about one's own forces from its use of active ECM, it requires comprehensive intelligence and demands careful advance planning in its application. In peacetime, very strict controls are placed upon the use of active ECM. Examples of EW falling into this category are:

(a) *Jamming*, the deliberate radiation or reradiation of electromagnetic signals with the objective of obliterating or obscuring signals which an enemy is attempting to receive. Electronic jamming is the direct radiation of a jamming signal, as opposed to nonelectronic jamming which utilizes the signal of the victim's transmitter reflected from physical objects, such as clouds of foil strips called *window* or long foil streamers referred to as *rope*.

(b) *Deception*, the deliberate radiation or reradiation of electromagnetic signals to mislead an enemy in the interpretation of data received by his electronic equipment, or to present false indications to his control systems. This may also be electronic by imitating radar pulses or other signals to present false targets or false information, or nonelectronic by use of physical objects, such as *kites* and *gulls*, which can reflect energy as if they were real ships or aircraft.

b. Electronic counter-countermeasures is defined as that major subdivision of EW which involves actions taken to ensure effective use of electromagnetic radiation in spite of the enemy's use of countermeasures. It may be assumed that an enemy will take advantage of every opportunity to jam radars, communications, guided missiles and other operational equipment; and that he will also use deception devices. The adverse effects of these anticipated measures should be assessed for every operation, and provision should be made for equipment and tactics for counteraction. Inherent in ECCM is the requirement for one's own forces to minimize the opportunity for the enemy to gain intelligence about one's capabilities and equipment through his use of passive ECM. The proper application of ECCM rests upon (but is not limited to) the following principles:

(1) Proper use of *emission control* (EMCON): a carefully planned restriction on the radiation of all transmitting equipment in an operating force in order to minimize the degree of intelligence that an enemy might gain by use of passive ECM. This restriction is implemented through a published EMCON plan. Each such plan is designed for the specific operation at hand. All naval forces now operate at all times under some type of EMCON plan.

(2) Recognition and analysis of the enemy's use of active ECM in order to gain the intelligence necessary to counteract its effects.

(3) Development and use of antijamming techniques and devices to minimize the effects of enemy active ECM.

(4) Development of a high degree of operator training in *reading through* enemy jamming and deception tactics by means of continuous exercises and updating of techniques.

510 APPLICATION OF THE RADAR EQUATION TO JAMMING

Jamming, in its crudest form, is the simple saturation of the radar system with sufficient noise power of the correct frequency to prevent detection of desired targets. Consider for the moment a target operating a jammer approaching the radar. At long range, as the radar antenna sweeps across the bearing of the jammer, it will receive a signal. This signal will not come in as a discrete timed pulse, but will flow in uniformly when the receiver is open. Thus the source will be identified only in bearing and will appear to be at all ranges. On a PPI this produces what is known as *strobe-jamming*. As the jammer closes, the strobe will widen as detectable energy becomes available at larger angles off the antenna axis. Next, there will be spill-over into side lobes as a detectable signal will be received when a side lobe is pointed toward the jammer. Ultimately, the entire scope face may be affected.

One objective of the jammer is to obscure the vehicle bearing it, but the phenomenon of spill-over into side lobes makes it possible to *cover* targets not on the same bearing. The first effect is known as *self-screening* and the second as *mutual-screening*. First, the case of self-screening using the radar equation derivation of Section 506 will be investigated.

Separate from the jamming noise coming into the radar receiver is the reflected radar signal from the bomber. This returned power density is (Equation 5-6):

$$I_r = \frac{P_t G A_t}{(4\pi)^2 R^4} \frac{\text{watts}}{\text{unit area}},$$

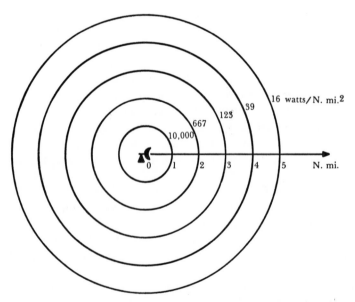

Figure 5-15. Circles are isointensities expected to be received back at the radar from a target at the indicated ranges (quantities assume $P_t G_t A_t = (4\pi)^2 (10{,}000)$ watt-N.mi.^{2})

in which the received *signal* intensity decreases proportionally to the *fourth power* of the range. (See Figure 5-15.)

If, however, the attacker is jamming, the intensity of the *noise* received by the radar decreases proportionally to only the *second power* of the distance from the jamming source (in this case, the bomber) according to the formula for omnidirectional jamming:

Equation 5-21
$$I_j = \frac{P_j}{4\pi R^2}.$$

If the jammer transmits with a directivity gain, G_j, then:

$$I_j = \frac{P_j G_j}{4\pi R^2}.$$

Assuming P_j for an omnidirectional jammer to be (4π) (1000) watts, then the signal intensity would decrease as shown by the isointensity lines of Figure 5-16.

Since the intensities decrease with range at unequal rates, *larger* ranges favor the *jammer;* at sufficiently large range I_r is less than I_j, and the jammer prevails. At such ranges, the target is screened. However, at sufficiently *small* ranges I_j is less than I_r and there is more power density available from the *reradiated radar pulse* than from the jammer. Thus, there is a unique value of range, called the *crossover* or *self-screening* range, inside of which the radar is back in business. Of course, with the proper values of P_j, P_t, A_t and G, this crossover range may be trivially small, but often it is not. Its value may be found by equating the expressions for I_r and I_j and solving for the range by:

Equation 5-22
$$R_{ss} = \sqrt{\frac{P_t G A_t}{P_j 4\pi}}.$$

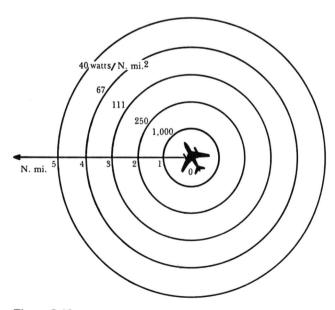

Figure 5-16.

If the jamming bomber has directive gain capability, then the self-screening range would also be found by setting the two intensities equal:

$$I_r = I_j$$

$$\frac{P_j G_j}{4\pi R_{ss}{}^2} = \frac{P_t G_t A_t}{(4\pi)^2 R_{ss}{}^4},$$

yielding:

$$R_{ss}{}^2 = \frac{P_t G_t A_t}{P_j G_j 4\pi}.$$

In the example given, $R_{ss}{}^2 = \dfrac{(10,000)(4\pi)^2}{(4\pi)^2(1,000)} = 10$ N.mi.^{2}; so $R_{ss} = 3.16$ N.mi.

That model is applicable to the situation where the attacker is doing his own jamming. However, the increased sophistication of modern EW equipment impels the following considerations:

The high costs of jamming equipment procurement;

The reductions of bombload to carry adequate jamming equipment;

The extra personnel demands and training time required to obtain an aircrew proficient in both the attack role and in jamming;

The inevitable degradation in performance of one function from the distraction by another.

These considerations suggest the allocation of the bombing and the jamming missions to *separate* aircraft, each dedicated to one of the tasks in terms of equipment and crew training. An additional benefit from this concept is the requirement for fewer total aircraft. Since more fuel is consumed in a bombing mission, a jammer aircraft might be able to cover several successive attack sorties.

The implication of this concept to the previous model is an invalidation of the mathematics which simplified the self-screening model. The *range R* from the radar to the bomber is *no longer equal* to that from the radar to the jammer. (See Figure 5-17.)

The crossover range from dominant jammer intensity to dominant signal return intensity may be visualized by superimposing the isointensity lines of Figures 5-15 and 5-16 with the jammer located a fixed distance (for mathematical convenience Figure 5-18 stations the jammer 5 N.mi. from the radar), with distances shown from the radar. The radar is assumed to utilize directional gain in whichever direction the bomber approaches.

If the jammer and the bomber are aligned with the radar, the jamming intensity received by the radar would be 40 watts/N.mi.^{2} The radar signal intensity returned by the bomber with corresponding intensity is seen as a distance just under 4 N.mi. from the radar. This apparent disadvantage in crossover range compared to the self-screen-

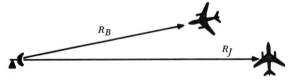

Figure 5-17. R_B denotes range from the radar to the bomber. R_J is range from jammer to radar.

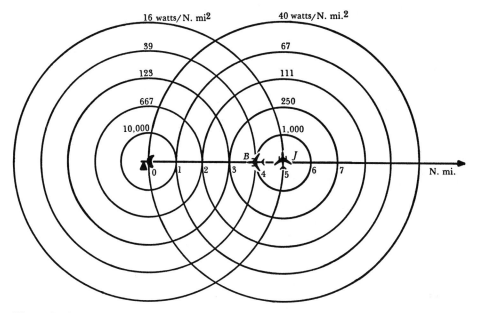

Figure 5-18.

ing example would be compensated for by the ability of the jammer-dedicated aircraft to carry equipment capable of higher power output.

The formulation for a crossover range in this situation would again be to find a range of equal intensities, where:

$$I_r = I_j$$
$$\frac{P_j G_j}{4\pi R_j^2} = \frac{P_t G_t A_t}{(4\pi)^2 R_B^4},$$

with R_j the range of the jammer constant; then the bomber's range when equal intensities are received would be:

Equation 5-23
$$R_B^4 = \frac{P_t G_t A_t R_j^2}{P_j G_j \, 4\pi}.$$

For the example values:

$$R_B^4 = \frac{10,000(4\pi)^2(25)}{1,000(4\pi)^2}$$
$$R_B = \sqrt[4]{250} = 3.97 \text{ N.mi.}$$

If the bomber attacked from a direction not aligned between the jammer and the radar, then the radar could increase the crossover range, by taking advantage of his receiving directivity gain, A_e. A resulting locus of crossover ranges for varying attack directions and stationary jammer would take on more of a kidney shape than a circle. (See Figure 5-19.)

This effect would be accentuated if the jammer also had directivity gain, so that his isointensity contours would not be concentric circles but elongated directionally. (See Figure 5-20.)

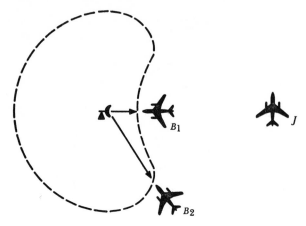

Figure 5-19.

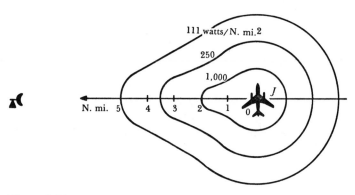

Figure 5-20.

511 THE EMPLOYMENT OF ECM AND ECCM

A classical example of move and countermove in electronic warfare is the operation of British ASW aircraft against German U-boats in the Bay of Biscay during World War II. The submarines, enroute to and from the Atlantic, would surface during darkness to recharge their batteries, replenish air in the boats and make radio reports to Germany.

These practices were comparatively safe for the submarines until 1942 when more and more submarines failed to report in by radio or return from patrol. After some investigation, the Germans discovered that the British were locating the general position of the submarines by triangulation on the radio signals. British patrol aircraft would then proceed to this general area, pinpoint the U-boat's position with airborne radar and attack.

The U-boats were soon able to counter this menace of aerial attack by installing L-band receivers (covering the frequency of the British airborne radar) to detect the approach of the aircraft. As a result of this move, German U-boat losses fell off significantly.

Then, early in 1943, the British began replacing the L-band radar installed in their night-flying aircraft with a radar of a different frequency. These modified aircraft were once again able to close and destroy surfaced submarines, free from detection by the U-boat until it was too late for the boat to submerge. The German submarine losses in the Bay of Biscay then increased rapidly.

The Germans, of course, were able to determine the reason for the new British success, but because of technical difficulties, the receivers necessary to counter the new British radar were not installed in the U-boats until late in 1943. The ultimate installation of the receivers, along with the practice of running submerged more of the time, soon cut down on the disastrous toll of U-boat losses.

This see-saw of equipment and tactics continued right to the end of the war, but other factors outside the realm of electronic warfare also entered into the U-boat problem in the latter years of the war. The point to note in this example of electronic warfare is that for every move made by one side, a countermove was soon instituted by the other. To nullify the countermove, the original force was constrained to develop a new piece of equipment or a new tactic. This is a typical pattern in EW.

To visualize what electronic warfare might be like today, one might imagine a hypothetical but realistic situation facing the Navy in one of the troubled areas of the world.

a. Reconnaissance. A constant ECM reconnaissance of the potential enemy is being conducted by periodic flights of ECM-equipped aircraft along the enemy's borders. This electronic search and analysis of resulting electronic intelligence will pinpoint the position and type of all active enemy electronic emitters. Information on the characteristics of the emitters will include what they are, e.g., radar, navigation aid; what their purpose is, i.e., air search, height finder; and characteristics of the transmissions (frequency, pulse repetition rate, pulse length, antenna rotation rate, pulse shape, and so forth).

b. Initial approach. Suppose an amphibious strike operation were scheduled at a point on the enemy coastline, and the enemy had modern long-range radar and effective ECM receivers. The task force must proceed under an emission control (EMCON) plan ordered by the Officer in Tactical Command (OTC). This plan would be a flexible means of minimizing the probability that electronic transmissions from friendly forces might be used by the enemy to give him information such as the size and position of the task force. The EMCON plan might range from complete electronic silence, to communications transmissions on UHF only (essentially line of sight), to an alternate radar time-sharing plan. In this latter case, radar pickets would operate their radar at random or at fixed intervals for a few sweeps and then shut down while another radar picket searched for a few sweeps. This procedure makes ECM direction finding and search by the enemy more difficult.

At the same time that the EMCON plan was in operation, a continuous passive ECM watch would be maintained. Based on electronic intelligence, the ECM receivers would monitor the radar frequencies used by the enemy airborne radar. In addition, those frequencies on which the enemy might pass communications between units would also be monitored to pinpoint ships and aircraft and to gain useful information. When an enemy radar signal was received, it would be analyzed immediately and the force notified of the frequency and bearing of the enemy signal. As soon as other ships intercepted the signal and reported its bearing, the position of the enemy radar would be determined by triangulation. Until it was determined that the enemy unit was a threat, this EMCON plan would remain in effect.

c. Close approach. When enemy aircraft constitute a threat to the force (a decision made by the OTC), the flexibility of the EMCON plan becomes important in permitting the force to turn on all necessary radars when electronic silence is no longer useful. Search, height finder and fire control radars may be activated selectively to intercept and destroy enemy raids.

As the aircraft are closing the task force, its radars may experience jamming. This might be electronic jamming or nonelectronic jamming such as chaff or rope. At the same time, the task force would be attempting to jam the enemy radar with appropriate jamming methods. Thus each side would be using active ECM in an attempt to weaken the other's electronic capability.

As the two opposing forces were using various forms of ECM against each other, they would also be employing principles of ECCM to counter the opponent's ECM. The primary tools used by the task force in ECCM are trained and alert operators, diversity of frequencies and special antijam (AJ) circuits in the radars. Most important among these is a good radar operator, one able to detect jamming and to continue to track a target in the midst of radar noise with some degree of effectiveness. The task force will have numerous radars, operating on different frequencies, so that if one or two experience jamming, control of friendly CAP may be conducted using some other radar. If all ECM and ECCM procedures and equipment are operating at maximum capacity, the task force should be able to successfully thwart the initial attempts of the enemy to destroy it or delay the amphibious landing.

d. Attack. During the landing operation, deception by the task force may play an important role in confusing the enemy and weakening his efforts at opposition. A small task element may approach the enemy from a direction other than the main invasion route, and with electronic devices trick the enemy into believing that this unit is actually the main attack force. The small element may have radar repeater transmitters and corner reflectors so that it appears to consist of more and larger ships than it actually does. The task element may also use many radio transmitters to simulate the radio traffic of a much larger force. In addition, the task force may confuse the enemy by sending conflicting radio messages over the enemy's own communications nets.

In summary, electronic warfare is a constant test of the ingenuity and ability of the forces involved. The naval commander must constantly be apprised of the status of his electronic equipment and make full use of all intelligence that may be available from his electronic equipment. He should make every effort to prevent the enemy from effectively using his electronic devices.

It may also be pointed out that inherent in effective employment of ECM and ECCM is a requirement for absolute coordination and familiarity with the details of the operation by *all* units in the task force. The planning and proper promulgation of the operation order leading to the actual execution of a complex naval operation, such as an amphibious operation, must provide for the smooth and expeditious continuation of the operation in the face of every tactic taken against it by the enemy's use of ECM and ECCM.

In most operational situations, the force commander will have certain numbers and specific types of electronic equipment available to him. His immediate response to an electronic threat will be in the form of selection of an established tactic to counter the threat or the development of a new ECM tactic. The steps in the development of an

ECM tactic will follow the same general pattern as applied to other tactical developments:

a. Evaluate the physical (electronic) environment in which the tactics are to be employed.

b. Select a proper (optimum) tactic to accomplish the mission.

c. Employ the tactic selected.

d. Evaluate the tactic's effect on the accomplishment of the mission, using an appropriate MOE.*

512 SOME SPECIFIC CONSIDERATIONS IN THE EMPLOYMENT OF ELECTRONIC WARFARE

Electronic warfare is a series of moves and countermoves by opposing forces to optimize the chances of success by each. The numbers and types of equipment available will impose limitations on the alternatives that a commander may consider. Three specific constraints which enter into the operational employment of EW are:

a. Allocation of resources. One of the primary problems involved in electronic warfare is that of allocation of resources. In a typical strike problem, the mission is that of delivering a maximum number of weapons to the target with the aircraft available. However, in the face of an expected electronic threat to the bombers from the enemy's radar, the logical defense would be to install electronic jamming equipment on the strike aircraft. The problem then arises as to just how much jamming equipment should be carried.

In the first extreme, the strike force could send no jammers at all, and load the aircraft solely with bombs, missiles or other weapons. In this case, the bombers could inflict maximum damage *if* they get to the target. But the risk is high that the aircraft will not get through a tight enemy defense which has unrestricted use of radar.

In the other extreme, the strike force could nullify or greatly diminish the effects of an enemy electronic threat by loading the attack aircraft with jammers and other ECM equipment, but the reduced payload of weapons would decrease the chances of a successful mission.

Obviously the solution to the problem of just how much jamming and other ECM equipment should be sent with the attacking aircraft should lie somewhere between these two extremes. The question is, where? The answer to a problem of this type might be approached through analytical methods as in the following example.

---

*A modern example of the difficulty in finding an acceptable measure of effectiveness is that used to compare jamming tactics against surface-to-air missiles (SAMs). An analysis based on combat data would logically first give consideration to the *purpose* of EW jamming as an MOE. The purpose of the jamming would be to protect those aircraft for which the jamming is in support. Then the MOE that would fall out at first cut would be losses (or hits) per sortie (or per attack sortie). With this lowest-values-optimal MOE, a comparison of the tactics could be made. Combat data would reflect missions being flown against different targets, each presenting differing degrees of SAM threat exposure. This would also be true for missions flown against the same targets at different times, or via different routes. So, would an MOE preferable to the first suggested be losses (or hits) per SAM fired (or reported)? Perhaps, but such an MOE assumes considerable consistency of tactics by the SAM sites. For example, more effective jamming might induce the SAM sites to hold fire, looking for a better opportunity. Or, to the contrary, the site might attempt to compensate for the low hit probability of each SAM against effective jamming, by firing more SAMs. Which response is more likely to effective jamming? The answer would be a function of SAM site tactics, which in turn would probably vary, at least according to the supply situation. A high degree of intelligence concerning the SAM tactics and supply would be necessary to make this a logical MOE.

Let

D = the event the target is destroyed;
S = the event the aircraft reaches the target, expressed as a function of ECM equipment load;
B = weapons load of strike aircraft in tons; and
J = ECM equipment load of strike aircraft in tons.

A typical function representing the relationship between $P(D|S)$ and aircraft bomb (weapons) load, B, is:

$$P(D|S) = 1 - e^{-\lambda_1 B},$$

where λ_1 is a constant reflecting the effectiveness of the particular weapons used. The graphical representation is:

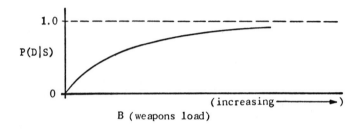

A typical function representing the relationship between $P(S)$ and the aircraft ECM equipment load, J, is

$$P(S) = 1 - ce^{-\lambda_2 J},$$

where c is a constant in the range zero to one representing the probability the aircraft fails to reach the target if it carried no ECM equipment; and λ_2 is a constant reflecting the effectiveness of the particular ECM equipment.
The graphical representation is:

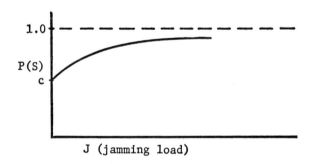

The physical limitations of the particular aircraft being used in the strike mission produce a further restraint that

$$\text{maximum load} = L_m = B + J.$$

To find the optimal balance between the bomb load, B, and the ECM equipment load, J, for each aircraft in the strike mission, subject to the maximum load restraint, the measure of effectiveness, M, would be

$$M = P(D) = P(S)P(D|S), \text{ since } D \subset S.$$

Substituting $P(S) = 1 - ce^{-\lambda_2 J}$, and $P(D|S) = 1 - e^{-\lambda_1 B}$, it is then a simple matter to determine those values of J and B which yield a maximum value of M through the application of the concept of differentiation in finding maxima and minima. If M were plotted as a function of the ratio of equipment loading to weapons loading, the graph would look something like that shown here:

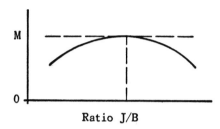

b. **Optimum time to energize active ECM.** In the use of electronic jammers, the problem arises as to the time when the jamming equipment should be energized. If the jammer is turned on too early, it provides a signal on which the enemy ECCM direction finders may triangulate to fix the force's position as it approaches. On the other hand, if the jammers are turned on too late, it is apparent that the enemy may already have received all the radar information needed to intercept the strike. Obviously, the first requirement to the solution of this problem is knowledge of the enemy radar's probable maximum detection range. Additionally, consideration must be given to the possibility that enemy weapons may possess a home-on-jam mode of operation. Jamming a strike with this capability might actually increase the enemy's probability of kill. This is another example of the improvement-counter-improvement nature of electronic warfare.

c. **Probability of signal intercept.** Another problem in the field of electronic warfare is that of predicting the success of the enemy's ECM reconnaissance and search efforts against one's own radar emissions during EMCON conditions. Specifically, the task force commander must have information concerning the probability of intercept by the enemy of his various radars which are turned on for specific lengths of time under the EMCON plan. Consider the following hypothetical problem:

A task force operates on a particular EMCON plan which specifies that a certain radar be turned on in a random fashion for an average of two sweeps every five minutes. The enemy is searching the radar frequency spectrum with a narrow band receiver that covers just one-tenth of that spectrum at a time. What is the probability that he will detect a certain radar of the task force within the time necessary to accomplish the mission of the task force—say two hours? The solution to this type of problem may be obtained from an application of the binomial probability distribution using the Poisson approximation as discussed in Section I-19 of Appendix I.

PROBLEMS

Conversion factors and useful constants:

$$c = 186{,}000 \text{ statute miles/second} \qquad \pi = 3.1416$$
$$= 161{,}500 \text{ nautical miles/second} \qquad \pi^2 = 9.870$$
$$= 3 \times 10^8 \text{ meters/second} \qquad \pi^3 = 31.01$$
$$= 3.28 \times 10^8 \text{ yards/second} \qquad 4\pi = 12.57$$
$$\text{one nautical mile} = 6080 \text{ feet} \qquad (4\pi)^2 = 157.9$$
$$= 2027 \text{ yards} \qquad (4\pi)^3 = 1984$$
$$= 1.1516 \text{ statute miles}$$

For Problems one through five assume a radar with the following characteristics:

Frequency	1.25×10^9 cycles/second
Peak power	8×10^5 watts
Pulse length	3.0×10^{-6} second
Radar antenna height	50 feet
Antenna rotation rate	10 revolutions/minute
Horizontal beam width	2.0 degrees
Pulse repetition frequency	500 pulses/second
Antenna gain	1000
Minimum detectable signal	10^{-11} watt

1. For the radar find:

    a. The wavelength in feet.
    b. The average power output.
    c. The number of pulses on target per scan.
    d. The maximum range in nautical miles allowed by the pulse repetition frequency.
    e. The effective antenna area for reception.

2. An F-4 is making a low altitude (200 feet) run directly toward the radar at 400 knots.

    a. What is the F-4's range to his visual horizon?
    b. At what range, in nautical miles, will the F-4 cross the radar horizon?
    c. How soon after crossing the radar horizon will the F-4 pass over the ship?
    d. At what range from the radar will the F-4 reach the first region where radar signals are reinforced by surface reflected signals?

3. As an enemy aircraft approaches the radar, at an altitude known to be below 15,000 feet, it presents a radar signal which becomes strong at a range of 120 N.mi. and then starts to fade out. Calculate the possible altitudes for the aircraft.

4. The radar is used to determine the average echo area of an F-4. The power density of the reflected radar signal is measured at the antenna to be 2×10^{-10} watt/yard^2 when the F-4 is at a range of 2×10^4 yards.

    a. What is the target area of the F-4?
    b. At a range of 20 N.mi., what would be the power received by the F-4?
    c. At a range of 20 N.mi., what would be the reflected power received by the radar?

   d. What is the maximum radar range computed for the given minimum detectable signal?

5. What would be the antenna gain if the antenna were omnidirectional?

6. One of the problems inherent in a deterministic model, such as the radar equation, is its use of average values to predict average results. For example, the radar equation uses an average target area and an average minimum detectable power to predict the range of detection. Realizing that both of these quantities vary about their mean value, the accuracy of such a deterministic model is dependent on *how much* such quantities vary, i.e., how large their variance. Consider the following example which is *unrelated* to the radar equation.

   Suppose the range of detection, R, is given by $R = 10\,x^2$, where x is known to have an average value of five.

   a. What range is determined (a deterministic model) using the average value of x for computations?
   b. What is the mean value of R if x is uniformly distributed between zero and 10?
   c. Does the deterministic model give a very accurate approximation of the probabilistic model?

7. During an exercise, aircraft made many tracking runs at various altitudes and 50 detection runs. The antenna rotation rate of the search radar was 9 revolutions per minute and the relative closing speed of the aircraft was 180 knots.
   Using the results of the exercise runs as tabulated:

j	Range interval in nautical miles Δr_j	Average number of blips received in each interval, from tracking runs	Number of first detections in each interval, with 50 detection runs
1	90–100	3	1
2	80–90	6	3
3	70–80	8	6
4	60–70	19	20
5	50–60	21	12
6	40–50	16	3
7	30–40	15	2
8	20–30	10	0
9	10–20	8	1
10	0–10	0	0

   a. Compute the number of scans per range interval.
   b. Compute and tabulate for each range interval, values for $\Psi_{\Delta r_j}, \Sigma^2_{\Delta r_j}, \Sigma \Psi^2_{\Delta r_j}$, and $F(m)$.
   c. Compute p_0 based on the information for ranges greater than 50 N.mi.
   d. Compute p_0 based on all information available.

8. In Problem seven:

   a. What is the *empirical* probability that detection occurs before a target penetrates to 40 N.mi. (based only on detection run data)?

b. What is the theoretical probability that detection occurs before a target penetrates to 40 N.mi. (using tracking run data, the blip/scan model, and p_0 determined in Problem seven)?

c. Compute $g_{\Delta r_1}$.

d. What is the largest value of $g_{\Delta r_j}$ in this example?

e. Does the approximation that $\ln(1 - g_i) = -g_i$ appear to be justified in this example?

9. In the blip/scan model, the double-blip hypothesis leads to the expression $g_{\Delta r_j} = p_0 \cdot \Psi^2_{\Delta r_j}$. Write an expression for $g_{\Delta r_j}$ if:

a. A triple-blip hypothesis is used.

b. Detection requires that blips appear and be seen on *any two* and *only two* of five successive scans.

10. As an aircraft approaches the radar on a direct run, 10 blips appear on the scope at the position indicated in the figure.

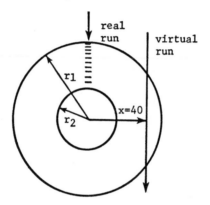

If $r_1 = 50$ N.mi. and $r_2 = 20$ N.mi., find, using the assumptions of the *direct method:*

a. The number of virtual blips if the aircraft were to pass at 40 N.mi. lateral range.

b. The number of virtual blips for an aircraft passing at zero N.mi. lateral range.

c. The lateral range for which the probability of detection would be the greatest.

11. Using the direct method for radar evaluation, find $\bar{P}(x)$ for each run shown in the figure, and sketch the lateral range curve (use $p_0 = .10$).

i	$N(i,0)$	$N(i,10)$ Number of virtual blips	$N(i,30)$	$N(i,50)$	$N(i,70)$	$N(i,100)$
Run number	Twice the number of real blips	at 10 nautical miles	at 30 nautical miles	at 50 nautical miles	at 70 nautical miles	at 100 nautical miles
1	12	12	7	4	2	0
2	14	13	8	5	2	1
3	14	13	8	5	3	2
4	15	13	9	6	3	1
5	11	10	7	3	2	0

12. As task force commander you have at your disposal an aircraft in which is installed a radar system with the following capabilities:

$$P_t = \text{one megawatt}, \ G = 1000, f = 80.8 \text{ megacycles}, \ P_0 = 10^{-10} \text{ watt}.$$

If the reflective area of the target, A_t, is 4 square yards, calculate:

a. The maximum range of the radar in yards using the radar equation.
b. The minimum height at which the aircraft should be stationed in order to detect low flyers and surface vessels at maximum range.
c. The self-screening range of the radar system (in yards) if it is being jammed by an omnidirectional jammer of 100 watts.

13. The following information is known concerning the air search radar at a particular SAM site.

$$A_e = 200 \text{ feet}^2$$
$$f = 3 \times 10^8 \text{ cycles/second}$$
$$P_a = 400 \text{ watts}$$
$$f_p = 800 \text{ pulses/second}$$
$$T = 1 \times 10^{-6} \text{ second}$$

What is the minimum jamming power, P_j, necessary so that an aircraft ($A_t = 80$ feet^2) attacking the SAM site will not be detected outside of 5 N.mi.?

14. Using the allocation example between bombs and ECM equipment in this chapter, where $\lambda_1 = 1$, $\lambda_2 = 1$, $c = .1$, and $L_m = 2$ tons:

a. Find the values of B and J which maximize the chance of destroying the target.
b. What is the probability of destroying the target for the optimal values of B and J?

15. In designing an air-to-air missile, the maximum total weight is limited to 1,000 pounds and the weight of the propellent section is fixed at 360 pounds. If

$$G = \text{weight of guidance and control section},$$
$$W = \text{weight of warhead section},$$
$$\text{P(hit)} = \left(\frac{G}{640}\right)^2, \text{ and P(kill|hit)} = \frac{W}{640}:$$

a. How much weight should be allocated to the warhead section and to the guidance and control section?
b. What is the maximum possible P(kill) using the optimum weight allocation?

16. Show that if $\lambda_1 = \lambda_2 = \lambda$ in the allocation example between bombs and ECM equipment, the maximum P(D) is obtained when

$$\frac{J}{B} = \begin{cases} \dfrac{\lambda L_m + \ln c}{\lambda L_m - \ln c}, & \text{for } e^{-\lambda L_m} < c \\ 0 & , \text{ otherwise} \end{cases}$$

17. Show that the expression for F(n) in Equation 5-12 is a conservative estimate of the actual probability of detection given by Equation 5-11, using the fact that for $0 < g_i < 1$, $\ln (1 - g_i) \leq -g_i$.

18. Let

D_n be the event that detection occurs on the nth scan,
A_n be the event that a blip appears on the nth scan, and
B_n be the event that the operator sees a blip on the nth scan.

Using Equation I-8 in Appendix I, show that Equation 5-13 holds for the assumptions given, where

$$D_n = A_{n-1} \cap B_{n-1} \cap A_n \cap B_n \text{ and } g_n = P[D_n | \bar{D}_1 \cap \bar{D}_2 \cap \cdots \cap \bar{D}_{n-1}].$$

Note that the intersection of several events $\bar{D}_1 \cap \bar{D}_2 \cdots \cap \bar{D}_n$, can be abbreviated using the symbol $\cap_{i=1}^{n} \bar{D}_i$.

19. A jammer with 5,000-watts power is standing off 10 N.mi. in support of an attack against a surface-to-air missile radar which has parameters $P_t G_t A_t = 4\pi \times 100,000$ watt-N.mi.^{2} Assume that the jammer gain effect G_j varies as a function of α, the attack angle off the direction from radar to jammer, by a factor $\dfrac{1}{1.1 - \cos \alpha}$.

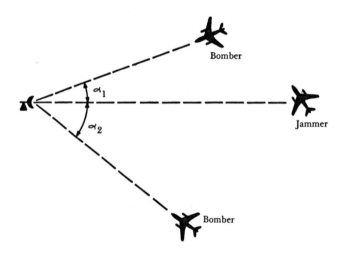

Sketch the locus of crossover ranges for varying attack angles, by determining R_B for α values of 0°, 30°, 60°, 90°, 120°, 150° and 180°.

6 Lateral Range Curves and Sweep Width

In the discussion of the direct method radar detection model in the previous chapter, the term *lateral range* was introduced. The *lateral range curve,* a graphical display of the probability of detecting a target which passes at any lateral range from the radar, was also mentioned. In this chapter, these two concepts will be more fully elaborated because of their importance to all situations in which a detection device is used to search for a target. A parameter called *sweep width,* another very important term in target detection, will be introduced to provide a necessary quantitative measure of the effectiveness for a detection device.

601 LATERAL RANGE

In searching for targets with any kind of detection device, it will almost always be the case that either the target or the detector, or both, will be in motion. Detection becomes possible because the relative motion between target and detector brings them sufficiently close together for the target to pass into and through the zone of possible detection.

The target's relative motion will rarely bring it *directly* toward the detector. Generally, the target moves along a line of relative motion through the zone of possible detection of the searcher. The range to the target at its *closest point of approach* (CPA) to the searcher is defined as *lateral range.* It is used to define the position of a particular line of relative target motion with respect to a detection device searching for the target. Lateral range is a physical parameter usually denoted by the symbol x.

The region or zone of possible detection is within a circle around the detection device having a radius equal to the maximum possible detection range, R_m. A geographic presentation of the movement situation is shown in Figure 6-1.

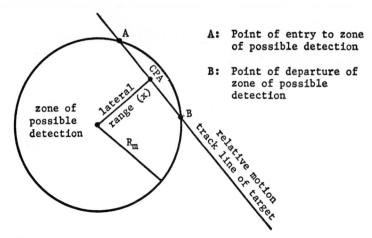

A: Point of entry to zone
      of possible detection

B: Point of departure of
      zone of possible
      detection

Figure 6-1.

602   LATERAL RANGE CURVE

How does one predict the chances of detecting a target which enters and traverses the detection envelope of the sensor in a straight line? In other words, what is the probability of detecting a target which passes at lateral range x?

Suppose a target is moving along a line which will cause it to pass at some lateral range within the detection zone of a particular detection device. For a fixed set of environmental conditions, the cumulative chance of detecting the target increases from the time the target enters the detection zone at point A in Figure 6-1, until the moment it reaches the point of departure from this zone at point B. At that time, all chance (probability) of detecting the target has passed. This cumulative probability is denoted by $\overline{P}(x)$. The graphical representation of $\overline{P}(x)$ for all values of x is known as a *lateral range curve*. The proper interpretation of $\overline{P}(x)$ is the conditional probability of detection, given that the target's range at CPA is x. A typical lateral range curve is shown in Figure 6-2.

How is a lateral range curve made? Any of the problem solution techniques listed in Chapter four, or combinations of them, might be used. As an example, the cumulative probability of detecting a target, using either the separate glimpse model or the continuous looking model [$F(n)$ or $F(t)$] of Chapter four could be employed and denoted $\overline{P}(x)$, since the number of glimpses or the time in the detection envelope is a function of lateral range. If, however, the g_i or the $\gamma(t)$ required are not known, then *statistical estimates* for the lateral range curve might be made, ideally from real world data already available, otherwise generated as part of trials or exercises.

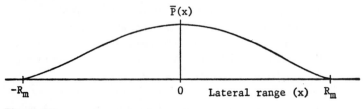

Figure 6-2.

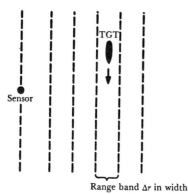

Range band Δr in width

Range band $\Delta r = 5$ kyds	# Runs of TGT thru Δr	# Det. in band Δr	P_D
0– 5	15	15	1.0
5–10	10	8	0.8
10–15	12	6	0.5
15–20	16	4	0.25

Figure 6-3.

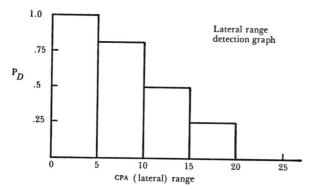

Figure 6-4.

If a target makes numerous runs past a detection device in various CPA (lateral) range bands, then by recording the number of detections per number of runs of the target in each range band, a graph can be developed which depicts the resulting estimated probabilities of detection (P_D) in each range band. (See Figures 6-3 and 6-4.)

If a continuous curve is faired through the lateral range graph, the resulting curve estimates a *lateral range curve*. (See Figure 6-5.) This curve depicts the probability that a sensor will detect a target as a function of the lateral range (or CPA) of the relative target track.

One important point must be kept in mind when a specific lateral range curve is discussed. That curve represents the cumulative probability of detection for a *particular target*, under a *particular set of environmental circumstances*, with a *particular detection device*. Any change in these conditions will result in a different lateral range curve. The point to be made is that one detection device will have a family of lateral range curves, each

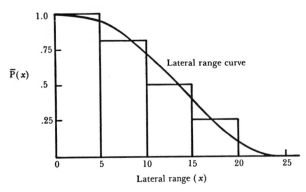

Figure 6-5.

representing different combinations of target type and size under a variety of environmental conditions. The dilemma of developing and maintaining an almost infinite number of lateral range curves for each of the large number of detection devices in the fleet (including the eyeball for visual search) is overcome by grouping targets into basic types (such as small, medium and large), and environmental conditions into basic categories (such as smooth sea, moderate seas and high seas), with one lateral range curve representing the average conditions existing within each grouping.

It will be seen in the following section that it is possible to make the problem of tabulating all these lateral range curves even simpler by carefully choosing a single expression to represent an entire lateral range curve, making unnecessary the tabulation of the curves themselves.

The lateral range curve is generally represented as a symmetric curve about the detection device, from maximum range on one side to maximum range on the other, as in Figure 6-2. One may think of a sensor platform as moving through an area containing potential targets. In this sense, the platform is *sweeping* through the area. This concept may be applied even though the platform is stationary with the targets moving past it, or when *both* target and platform are moving, as is generally the case in naval operations.

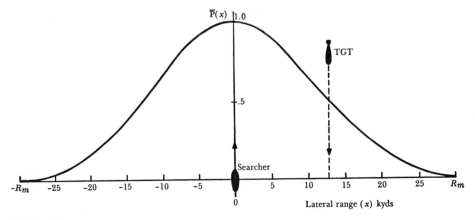

Figure 6-6.

It should be noted that the lateral range curve is *neither* a probability density function *nor* a cumulative distribution function. Actually it is a conditional-probability function. Using this curve, we can pick any lateral range x and find the probability that a target will be detected if it passes at CPA $= x$ from the sensor. (See Figure 6-6.)

For example, if a searcher has a lateral range curve as depicted in Figure 6-6 and a target passes the searcher at a lateral range $= 13$ kyds, the probability that the target will be detected is $\overline{P}(13) = .5$. Note that beyond some max range R_m, the probability that the target will be detected is zero.

603 DETECTION OF RANDOMLY DISTRIBUTED TARGETS

Consider the case of target search in which it is assumed that the target is *randomly positioned* in an area through which the detection device is sweeping. This is often a valid assumption since the location of the target is not usually known and the movement of the target is at best an estimate. Consider that this target has some chance of being detected, i.e., its lateral range is some value between $-R_m$ and $+R_m$. This target is just as likely to follow a relative track line through the zone of detection at one lateral range as at any other lateral range. Mathematically, this means that if a random variable, X, is defined as the lateral range to this target, then X has a *uniform probability distribution* over the range of values from $-R_m$ to $+R_m$. It follows (from basic probability theory) that the *probability density function* of the random variable X is

$$f(x) = \begin{cases} \dfrac{1}{2R_m}, & -R_m < x < +R_m \\ 0, & \text{elsewhere.} \end{cases}$$

Now, recall that the function $\overline{P}(x)$ gives the probability of detecting a target which transits *at some specific lateral range x*. The probability of detecting a target whose lateral range is *not* known, i.e., is random, is the *expected value* of $\overline{P}(x)$, where x may assume *all possible* values of lateral range; or, according to the formula for the expected value* of a function of a continuous random variable:

Equation 6-1.a
$$E[\overline{P}(x)] = \int_{\text{All } x} \overline{P}(x) \cdot f(x)\, dx.$$

In this case, since x is uniformly distributed between $-R_m$ and $+R_m$, the expected value becomes

Equation 6-1
$$E[\overline{P}(x)] = \frac{1}{2R_m} \int_{-R_m}^{R_m} \overline{P}(x)\, dx,$$

noting that $1/(2R_m)$ is a constant. This gives, then, the probability of detection of a target which randomly transits the zone of possible detection.

Now suppose we have an SSK conducting a stationary patrol in the center of a barrier of length L, and it is not known exactly what track (lateral range or CPA) a target will have in passing through the barrier. (See Figure 6-7.) If it is assumed that a

---

*The mathematical quantity $E[\overline{P}(x)]$ can and should be considered a bona fide probability itself, as Equation 6-1.a also represents the "rule of total probability" for a continuous random variable (lateral range x).

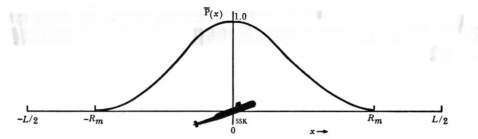

Figure 6-7.

target is equally likely to come through the barrier at any point along L, then the target's lateral range or CPA from the SSK can be assumed to be uniformly distributed and, if $f(x)$ is the probability density function of the target's lateral range, then:

$$f(x) = \begin{cases} \dfrac{1}{L}, & \text{for } \dfrac{-L}{2} \le x \le \dfrac{L}{2} \\ 0, & \text{elsewhere.} \end{cases}$$

One can now compute the *probability of detecting* the target, assuming that the target is equally likely to transit through the barrier starting at any point along the barrier front L:

$$E[\overline{P}(x)] = \int_{-\infty}^{\infty} f(x) \cdot \overline{P}(x)\, dx,$$

Now if $L/2 \ge R_m$, we have

Equation 6-2 $$E[\overline{P}(x)] = \frac{1}{L} \int_{-R_m}^{R_m} \overline{P}(x)\, dx.$$

The integration yields zero over the intervals $-\infty$ to $-R_m$ and R_m to ∞. This is also intuitive to the situation, as regions beyond the maximum detection range of the sensor would not contribute to the expected probability of detection. For a target track interval L beyond the maximum detection range, the expected probability of detection for the same sensor is less than the first case wherein L coincided with $-R_m$ to R_m.

For example, assume that an SSK has a lateral range curve described as in Figure 6-8:

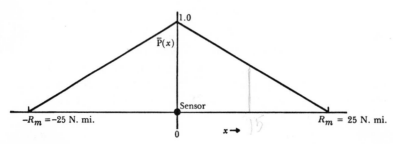

Figure 6-8.

$$\overline{P}(x) = \begin{cases} 1 + \dfrac{x}{25}, & \text{for } -25 \le x \le 0 \\[2mm] 1 - \dfrac{x}{25}, & \text{for } \quad 0 \le x \le 25 \\[2mm] 0, & \text{elsewhere,} \end{cases}$$

and suppose the target transit track is uniformly distributed along $L = 60$ N.mi. centered at the sensor. Then:

[handwritten margin note: derivitive takes form $\frac{x^2}{2}$]

$$E[\overline{P}(x)] = \int_{-\infty}^{\infty} \frac{1}{L} \cdot \overline{P}(x)\, dx = \frac{1}{L} \int_{-R_m}^{R_m} \overline{P}(x)\, dx$$

$$= \frac{1}{60}\left[\int_{-25}^{0} \left(1 + \frac{x}{25}\right) dx + \int_{0}^{25} \left(1 - \frac{x}{25}\right) dx \right] = \frac{1}{60}\left[\int_{-25}^{0}\left(x + \frac{x^2}{25\cdot2}\right) + \int_{0}^{25}\left(x - \frac{x^2}{25\cdot2}\right) \right]$$

$$= \frac{1}{60}\left[x + \frac{x^2}{50} \right]_{-25}^{0} + \left[x - \frac{x^2}{50} \right]_{0}^{25} = \frac{1}{60}\left(\left(0 + \frac{0^2}{50}\right) - \left(-25 + \frac{625}{50}\right) + \left(25 - \frac{625}{50}\right) - \left(0 - \frac{0^2}{50}\right) \right)$$

$$E[\overline{P}(x)] = \frac{1}{60}[25 - 12.5 + 25 - 12.5] = \frac{25}{60} = .42.$$

Symmetry can often be used to reduce the computational workload of these problems.

Observe the situation of Figure 6-9. Here, several searchers are conducting a search at a distance apart, *track spacing*, denoted by S, such that there is no overlap of detection zones, i.e., $S > 2R_m$. If the target is randomly located in the area being searched, what would be the probability of detecting a given target as it passes through the line of searchers? In this case let X be the lateral range of the target from the nearest searcher. Then the value of X is uniformly distributed between $-S/2$ and $+S/2$, and $f(x)$ has the value $1/S$. The expected probability of detection by one searcher would then be

$$E[\overline{P}(x)] = \int_{\text{All } x} \overline{P}(x) \cdot f(x)\, dx,$$

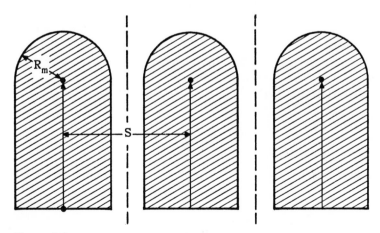

Figure 6-9.

which becomes

Equation 6-3
$$E[\overline{P}(x)] = \frac{1}{S} \int_{-R_m}^{R_m} \overline{P}(x) \, dx,$$

since for all values of x outside these limits, $\overline{P}(x) = 0$.

Finally, consider the situation where all of the target track interval L is *within* the $-R_m$ to R_m range. This can occur when the target is constrained, for example, by a narrow channel. Here the expected probability of detection.

$$E[\overline{P}(x)] = \int_{\text{All } x} \overline{P}(x) \cdot f(x) \, dx$$

is evaluated more precisely as

Equation 6-4
$$E[\overline{P}(x)] = \frac{1}{L} \int_{-L/2}^{L/2} \overline{P}(x) \, dx,$$

reflecting the fact that the detection capabilities of the lateral range curve $\overline{P}(x)$ where the target is not going to pass do not make contributions to the expected probability of detection.

604   SWEEP WIDTH

It would be desirable, where possible, to characterize each detection device (radar, sonar, eyeball, and so on) by some quantity that is physically meaningful. One such quantity might be the effective range of detection. Another might be the range for 50 percent probability of detection. Still another could be that range beyond which as many targets are detected as are missed at lesser ranges. Such a quantity would be useful, for instance, in deciding how far apart searchers must be stationed and still effectively conduct a search. Whatever the quantity used, it must be precisely defined and understood by those who use it. (The mathematical equivalence of the first and the third quantifications is demonstrated by Problem eight at the end of the chapter.)

One widely used concept to measure a sensor's capability in terms of distance is *sweep width*. This concept assumes that as a detection device searches for targets through an area, it effectively sweeps out a path of a certain width. Using the third example of Section 603, the problem is to detect targets which pass within a distance $S/2$ on either side of the sensor. In Figure 6-10 only one of the several searchers is shown, since the situation is the same for each of the others. If all targets within the sweep width were detected and none detected outside, then the probability of detection of a single target would be just the fraction of all targets within the sweep width, which for this case is

$$\overline{P}(\text{det}) = \frac{\text{sweep width}}{S}.$$

However, from Equation 6-3 it is seen that this probability of detection is

$$E[\overline{P}(x)] = \frac{\int_{-R_m}^{R_m} \overline{P}(x) \, dx}{S}.$$

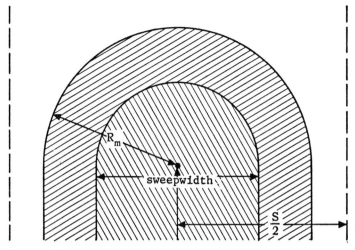

Figure 6-10.

Notice in this example that if only *the area under the lateral range curve* were known, the probability of detection could be determined without reference to the lateral range curve itself. Search for targets which can be considered to have random locations is a common operational situation and a mathematical fortuity, since it allows us to work with a single quantity, the *area* under a lateral range curve. This quantity, denoted by W, is

Equation 6-5
$$W = \int_{-R_m}^{R_m} \overline{P}(x)\, dx. \qquad = \overline{P}(o)\, R_m \;?$$

In measuring the effectiveness of a detection device, the probability of detection is an important consideration. From Equation 6-3 it can be seen that for a *nonoverlapping* search, the probability of detection is directly proportional to the area, W, under the lateral range curve. *Hence this area, W, is as good a measure of detection capability as the probability of detection itself.* Therefore, to be consistent, the sweep width must be defined in magnitude as equal to the area, W, under the lateral range curve. (In essence, this defines an equivalent "cookie cutter" lateral range curve with a base of width W and height $\overline{P}(x) = 1$.) The symbol W then physically represents the *effective* width of the sensor's detection zone. Its value is found by computing the *area under the lateral range*

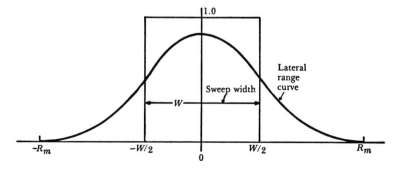

Figure 6-11.

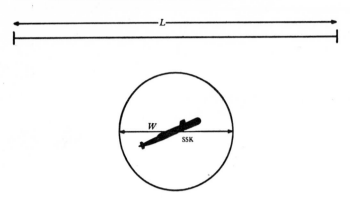

Figure 6-12.

curve. The average probability of detecting a randomly distributed target with sensors whose detection zones do *not* overlap is then

Equation 6-6 $$\bar{P}(\text{det}) = \frac{W}{S}.$$

In the earlier example of an SSK patrolling a barrier of width L where target transits are uniformly distributed along L, using sweep width W (Figure 6-12), the expected probability of detecting a target $E[\bar{P}(x)]$ becomes simply:

Equation 6-7 $\quad E[\bar{P}(x)] = W/L$, provided that $L/2 \geq R_m$.

It can easily be shown that using sweep width W in the above fashion yields the same answer as when the complete functional form of the lateral range curve, $\bar{P}(x)$, is used; i.e.:

$$E[\bar{P}(x)] = \frac{W}{L} = \int_{-\infty}^{\infty} f(x) \cdot \bar{P}(x)\, dx = \frac{1}{L}\int_{-R_m}^{R_m} \bar{P}(x)\, dx,$$

provided of course that $L \geq 2R_m$.

Using the same parameters as the SSK example in Figure 6-13:

$$\bar{P}(x) = \begin{cases} 1 + \dfrac{x}{25}, & \text{for } -25 \leq x \leq 0 \\[2mm] 1 - \dfrac{x}{25}, & \text{for } \quad 0 \leq x \leq 25 \\[2mm] 0, & \text{elsewhere,} \end{cases}$$

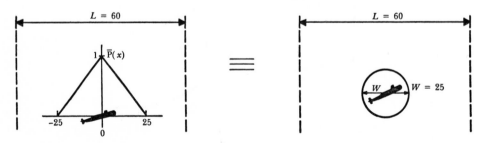

Figure 6-13.

$$W = \int_{-R_m}^{R_m} \bar{P}(x)\,dx = \int_{-25}^{0} \left(1 + \frac{x}{25}\right) dx + \int_{0}^{25} \left(1 - \frac{x}{25}\right) dx$$

$$W = 25 - 12.5 + 25 - 12.5 = 25 \text{ N.mi.}$$

Then:

$$E[\bar{P}(x)] = \frac{W}{L} = \frac{25}{60} = .42.$$

In actual practice, values of the sweep width, W, are usually computed and tabulated for various detection devices against different classes of targets under various (average) environmental conditions. It should be noted that so far only searches in which there is no overlap of detection zones have been discussed. The situation in which searchers are placed closer together so that overlap occurs will be discussed in Chapter seven.

PROBLEMS

1. A target is 20 N.mi. bearing 000 degrees true from the detector. Target course and speed are 090 degrees true, 10 knots. If the detector's course and speed are 000 degrees true, 10 knots:

   a. What is the relative speed of the target?
   b. What is the target's direction of relative movement?
   c. When will it be at CPA?

2. The lateral range curve, $\bar{P}(x)$, for certain radar is represented by

$$\bar{P}(x) = .9 \left[1 - \left(\frac{x}{50}\right)^2\right], \quad -50 < x < 50.$$

   a. If targets pass the radar with lateral ranges uniformly distributed between -50 and 50, what is the probability of detecting a given target?
   b. If targets pass the radar with lateral ranges uniformly distributed between -100 and 100, what is the probability of detecting a given target?
   c. If targets pass the radar with lateral ranges uniformly distributed between -25 and 25, what is the probability of detecting a given target?
   d. What is the sweep width of this radar?

3. If, in Problem two, the lateral range curve were

$$\bar{P}(x) = \begin{cases} .8\left(1 - \dfrac{x}{75}\right), & 0 < x < 75 \\[2mm] .8\left(1 + \dfrac{x}{75}\right), & -75 < x < 0, \end{cases}$$

what answers would be different? (Note: if the curve is sketched, integration will be unnecessary.)

4. The lateral range curve of a particular radar can be represented by the following figure:

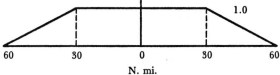

N. mi.

   a. What is the maximum range, R_m, of the radar?
   b. What is the probability that the radar will detect a target passing at a lateral range of 45 N.mi.?
   c. What is the sweep width of the radar?
   d. What is the probability of detecting a target which will pass in a random manner within 60 N.mi. of the radar?
   e. What is the probability of detecting a target which will pass randomly between 30 and 60 N.mi. from the radar?
   f. What is the probability of detecting a target which will pass randomly within 45 N.mi. of the radar?

5. A radar which is located at the center of a 100-N.mi.-wide channel has the following lateral range curve:

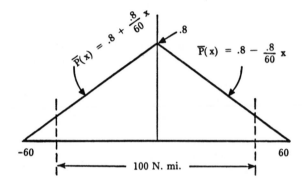

   a. What is the probability of detecting a target which passes down the channel at a distance of 10 N.mi. from the edge of the channel?
   b. What is the probability of detecting a target which is as likely to transit the channel at one point as any other?
   c. If the target has a greater probability of transiting near the center of the channel than near the edges, would you expect the probability of detecting the target to be higher, lower or the same as in part b?

6. Suppose a target is more likely to transit near the center of the channel than near the edge as indicated by the following probability density function:

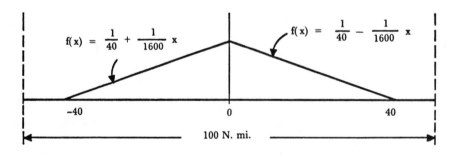

Using the lateral range curve from Problem five, what is the expected probability of detecting such a target?

7. A division of destroyers using visual means, is searching in a line abreast for a small liferaft. Course is 000 degrees true. The liferaft passes exactly between the two easternmost destroyers as shown in the figure.

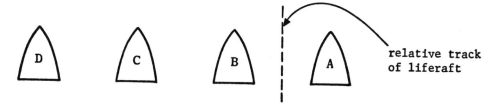

From the lateral range curve for visual detection of this target under existing conditions, it is determined that destroyers A and B each have a probability of detection of .6, destroyer C has a probability of detection of .1, and destroyer D has a probability of detection of zero. The probability of detection by each destroyer is independent of the other.

   a. What is the probability that the liferaft is *not* detected?
   b. Compute the probability of detection of the liferaft by the division of destroyers.
   c. What is the probability that destroyers A, B and C each detect the liferaft?
   d. What is the probability that both destroyers A and B, but no others, detect the liferaft?

8. The sweep width, W, can be defined as the quantity such that as many targets are missed at lateral ranges less than $W/2$ as are detected at lateral ranges greater than $W/2$. One hundred targets pass the detector at lateral ranges uniformly distributed between $-R_m$ and R_m.

   a. Compute the number of targets *missed* which pass at lateral ranges between $-r_0$ and r_0, where r_0 is some range between zero and $\pm R_m$.
   b. Compute the number of targets *detected* which pass at lateral ranges between $-R_m$ and $-r_0$ or between r_0 and R_m.
   c. Show that if the answers to a. and b. are equal,

   then

$$r_0 = W/2 = \frac{1}{2} \int_{-R_m}^{R_m} \overline{P}(x) \, dx.$$

   d. Show that the definition of W given in this problem is equivalent to that given in the text.

Hint: Let A be the event the target passes in the interval $-r_0$ to r_0. Let B be the event the target passes in the interval $-R_m$ to $-r_0$, or r_0 to R_m. Let D be the event the target is detected, and $\bar{D}$ be the event it is not detected.

7 Search and Patrol

Since World War II, the combat capabilities of modern naval units have increased considerably. Nuclear submarines can travel at much greater submerged speeds than the older types. They can submerge to greater depths and remain at sea longer than any of their predecessors. Missiles have increased the fire power of every unit capable of launching them. Jet aircraft are a much greater threat than aircraft of the earlier piston types because their higher speeds require faster defensive reaction times.

Scouting in the form of search and detection must improve in order to keep pace with technical developments and perform effectively as the electronic and sonic eyes and ears of the fleet. Tactical, i.e., short-term, decisions made to counter a threat are dependent on fleet capabilities to locate a hostile unit before it can maneuver into a position to attack.

Searching for, and detecting, an enemy unit before it can inflict serious damage in a surprise move is as important now as it has always been in naval history. The difference between what has happened in past warfare and what could happen in warfare using the latest weapons systems is one of degree—damage inflicted by missiles with nuclear warheads, at short or long range, would be beyond all comparison to damage inflicted in naval actions of the past.

The obvious goal of search and detection is to deter hostile units from staging a threat or to make neutralization of the threat possible. The existence of a threat in specified areas may or may not be known; consequently all means of search must be evaluated with this objective in mind. While the uncertainty of the presence of a threat may be surmised, the uncertainty of detection in terms of probability of success should not be overlooked.

The success of a search depends upon or is affected by one or more of these factors:

a. Nature of the target.
b. Environmental conditions.
c. Sensor equipment available.
d. Tactics employed.

The *target* may be any type of naval unit which in one way or another can constitute a threat. Submarines, influence mines, surface vessels or aircraft are common types of potential threats. In time of *peace* the search leads to detection; in time of *war* a threat must be detected and neutralized by deterrent action or destruction.

The environmental conditions which must be carefully considered in this type of naval operation are represented not only by oceanographic conditions—sea state; water conditions in terms of pressure, temperature, salinity, and so on; smooth or rocky sea bottom—but also climate, illumination in and above the water, cloud formations and many others.

The types and performance characteristics of the sensor equipment available play an important part in search and detection. The more powerful and sensitive the equipment is, the greater the probability of accomplishing the mission. The greater the reliability and effectiveness of the equipment, the greater the expectation of reducing the uncertainty of the outcome.

The alternatives in some operations may include the procurement of new or different systems, more men and ships, and so forth. In other cases, the alternatives will be limited to possible search tactics and dispositions using the forces at hand.

This chapter begins with a discussion of various alternative tactics in target search. The emphasis will be placed on analyzing these different types of search in order to derive means (measures of effectiveness) for evaluating the effectiveness of each particular type.

The student should endeavor to understand clearly the reasoning used in these developments so that he can apply the same principles in other situations which may be encountered. The principles learned will also enable him to make later use of operational search plans and patrols with a greater degree of effectiveness.

701   RANDOM SEARCH

Suppose it is known only that a target is somewhere in a given region of total area A. For lack of information to the contrary, its position is assumed to be uniformly randomly distributed in A, i.e., as likely to be found in one part of A as in any other.

Suppose also that the observer searches the area using no systematic plan or method. In this random search, what is the probability that detection will occur by the time the observer has traveled L N.mi. through the area?

Let $\overline{P}(x)$ again be the lateral range curve for the observer and this particular target in the existing environment. Divide the observer's path into N segments of equal length L/N, each approximating a straight line as in Figure 7-1. For detection to occur in the *first segment* two events must take place. Let B be the event that the target is *in* the area of length L/N and width $2R_m$, so that there is some chance of detection occurring, and let C be the event that the target *is detected;* then

$$P(B) = \frac{2R_m L/N}{A},$$

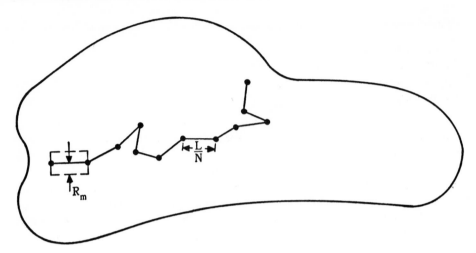

Figure 7-1.

and from Equation 6-1

$$P(C|B) = \frac{1}{2R_m} \int_{-R_m}^{R_m} \overline{P}(x)\, dx.$$

Therefore, the probability of detection $P(C)$ is given by $P(C \cap B)$, since $C \subset B$, that is, the target cannot be detected when it is not within maximum detection range; or:

$$
\begin{aligned}
P(\text{detection}) &= P(C|B)\, P(B) \\
&= \frac{2R_m L/N}{A} \cdot \frac{1}{2R_m} \int_{-R_m}^{R_m} \overline{P}(x)\, dx, \text{ for the first segment of search} \\
&= \frac{L}{NA} \cdot \int_{-R_m}^{R_m} \overline{P}(x)\, dx = \frac{WL}{NA}.
\end{aligned}
$$

Now in general for the ith *segment* of search,

$$P(\text{detection occurs on } i^{\text{th}} \text{ segment} \,|\, \text{no detection so far}) \geq \frac{WL}{NA},$$

since the remaining area of equally-likely target location $\leq A$ during subsequent segments (failure to detect in earlier segments reduces the likelihood of target location in such segments).

$$P(\text{detection } \textit{fails} \text{ to occur on } i^{\text{th}} \text{ segment} \,|\, \text{no detection so far}) \leq 1 - \frac{WL}{NA}.$$

Thus, $\left(1 - \dfrac{WL}{NA}\right)$ is an *upper bound* for failure on the ith segment.

Using the chain rule of conditional probabilities, an upper bound for

$$P(\text{no detection}) = \prod_{i=1}^{N} \left(1 - \frac{WL}{NA}\right) = \left(1 - \frac{WL}{NA}\right)^{N}, \text{ for the whole search.}$$

Thus a *lower bound* for

Equation 7-1 $P(\text{det}) = 1 - \left(1 - \dfrac{WL}{NA}\right)^{N}$, for the whole search.

A further refinement is usually made in this model by noting that

$$\left(1 - \frac{WL}{NA}\right)^{N} = e^{N \ln (1 - WL/NA)}$$

which is approximately equal to $e^{-WL/A}$, since when WL/NA is small

$$\ln \left(1 - \frac{WL}{NA}\right) \cong - \frac{WL}{NA}.$$

A *lower bound* for the probability of detection in this *random search model* then becomes

Equation 7-2 $P(\text{det}) = 1 - e^{-WL/A}$,   *conservative estimate*

provided the fraction of the area effectively covered on each segment, WL/NA, is small.

It should be made clear that this development is based on the following assumptions:

a. The target's position is randomly distributed in A.
b. The search is conducted in a random manner.

The significance of this model is not that it represents a particular type of operational search, but that it represents a theoretical search in which the least information is known about a target and no systematic search plan is used. Hence, *in the case where more is known about a target and a systematic means of searching is used, an equal amount of search effort should yield a higher probability of detection.*

The quantity WL/A in the exponent is called the *coverage factor*. It is the ratio of area swept, i.e., the area which lies within the sweep width to the total area. This coverage factor then measures the amount of effort spent searching. It may take on values of one, two or more in a search where a high probability of detection is necessary.

Figure 7-2 shows the way in which the probability of detection in a random search increases with the coverage factor. It can be seen that when the coverage factor is small, the probability of detection is approximately equal to the coverage factor itself. When

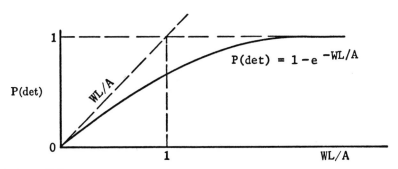

Figure 7-2.

the coverage factor is larger, this probability approaches unity, exhibiting a *saturation* or *diminishing returns* effect, due in part to an increase in overlapping of swept areas.

The coverage factor WL/A at values less than 1.0 represents an *optimistic* or upper bound for the probability of detection, as opposed to the *conservative* estimate of the random search (Equation 7-2). If the searcher's lateral range curve is relatively steep (such as for the definite range law), if the target is stationary and if the searcher(s) *never overlap* coverage, then we would have mutual exclusiveness between segments for detection. Thus the P(det) over the N segments would be strictly additive, yielding P(det) $= WL/A$. Such an approximation becomes unrealistic for high values of WL/A where overlap becomes inevitable.

702   UNIFORM RANDOM SEARCH

It is useful to consider another case of random search in order to see a different aspect of coverage factor. Suppose the area of search were divided into n strips of width S and length b, so that $A = nSb$ (Figure 7-3). Suppose the searcher attempted to cover the area somewhat more uniformly by conducting part of his random search in each strip. An equivalent coverage of the area could be obtained by using n observers to search the area, one traveling down the center of each strip. In such a search, to be considered in the next section, each observer would travel a distance b and the total search path in the area would be nb.

In order that the total search efforts be comparable, let the total search path for this uniform random search be nb. If the observer spent equal time in each strip, the search path in each strip would be b, but conducted randomly as in Figure 7-3. Now $L = nb$ and $A = nSb$ so that the coverage factor becomes

$$\frac{WL}{A} = \frac{W(nb)}{(nSb)} = \frac{W}{S},$$

and Equation 7-2 for a *uniform random search* becomes

Equation 7-3 $$P(\text{det}) = 1 - e^{-W/S}.$$

This uniform random search model gives the same *lower bound* to the probability of detecting a target as the random search model, for an equal expenditure of search effort. This uniform plan may cause less overlap in execution, thereby causing the real probability of detection to be greater.

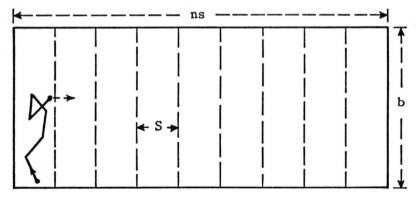

Figure 7-3.

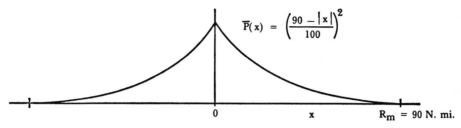

$$\overline{P}(x) = \left(\frac{90 - |x|}{100}\right)^2$$

0   x $R_m = 90$ N. mi.

Figure 7-4.

703 PARALLEL SWEEPS

Suppose again a target is known to be located in some particular area of the ocean and is as likely to be in one part as in any other part of that area. A common method of search employed in such a case, in order to systematically cover the area, is known as *parallel sweeps*. Such a search is conducted by several observers searching on parallel tracks through the area, their common distance apart, or *track spacing*, being S N.mi.

The objective of this section is to provide a method of arriving at the probability of detection when the lateral range curve is known.

Assume the lateral range curve for each observer is as given by Figure 7-4, and that several observers are used simultaneously to search the area in Figure 7-3. Each observer covers his strip by traveling down its center line. The probability of detection when the lateral range curves of adjacent observers do not overlap is given by Equation 6-6.

If the track spacing were less than $2R_m$, more than one of the observers could detect the target. Consider the detection potential between any two of the searchers, when the conditions include equal spacing and the target being equally likely to pass between any two, also equally likely at any point between two. If the lateral range curves of the sensors are *at least alternately* identical, that is, the second sensor away from each sensor is the same, then the probability of detecting a target which passes between any two is the same as the overall probability of detection of the sweep.

Conventionally setting lateral range zero at one of a pair of sensors, and lateral range S at the other (Figure 7-5), the formula applied for this probability of detecting the target which passes between them would be

$$E[P(x)] = \int_0^S P(x)\frac{1}{S}\,dx.$$

The individual lateral range curves which are factors in this $E[P(X)]$ between 0 and S are seen to be the right side of $\overline{P}_1$ and the left side of $\overline{P}_2$. However, these lateral range curves are originally listed for the sensors each at a range zero. So while $\overline{P}_1(x)$ is

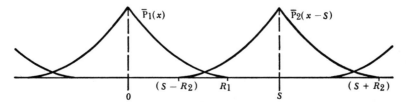

$\overline{P}_1(x)$ $\overline{P}_2(x - S)$

$(S - R_2)$ R_1 $(S + R_2)$
0   S

Figure 7-5.

a valid input, $\bar{P}_2$ inputs must be transformed, specifically by representing its input as $\bar{P}_2(x - S)$.

Furthermore, discontinuities exist in the composite $P(x)$, specifically at $S - R_2$ and at R_1, where R_1 and R_2 are the respective maximum ranges of sensors one and two. Therefore, the integral is composed of the parts of continuity, and

Equation 7-4

$$E[P(x)] = \frac{1}{S} \left\{ \int_0^{S-R_2} \bar{P}_1(x) \, dx + \int_{R_1}^S \bar{P}_2(x - S) \, dx \right.$$

$$\left. + \int_{S-R_2}^{R_1} [\bar{P}_1(x) \cup \bar{P}_2(x - S)] \, dx \right\}$$

For the case where the track spacing is less than R_m, the target could be detected by more than two observers. Let S, for example, be 60 N.mi. so that the overlapping lateral range curves would be as shown in Figure 7-6. Here the tracks for different observers are numbered arbitrarily, and track one is used as the reference. Notice that although observers are positioned 60 N.mi. apart, the pattern mirrors itself every 30 N.mi., and a target 20 N.mi. to the right of track one has the same probability of detection as a target 20 N.mi. to the left of track two, and so on. Every target then will pass within 30 N.mi. of the nearest observer.

First consider a target whose lateral range, x, is between zero and 30 N.mi. to the right of the observer on track one. Such a target could be detected by any or all of the observers on tracks one, two and three.

Let $\bar{P}_i(x)$ be the probability this target is detected by the observer on the ith track. Since x represents the lateral range measured from the first track, a transformation must be made to relate all lateral range curves to this common reference. The reader may verify that in the following example:

$$\bar{P}_1(x) = \bar{P}(x) = \left[\frac{90 - x}{100} \right]^2,$$

$$\bar{P}_2(x) = \bar{P}(S - x) = \left[\frac{90 - (60 - x)}{100} \right]^2,$$

and

$$\bar{P}_3(x) = \bar{P}(S + x) = \left[\frac{90 - (60 + x)}{100} \right]^2.$$

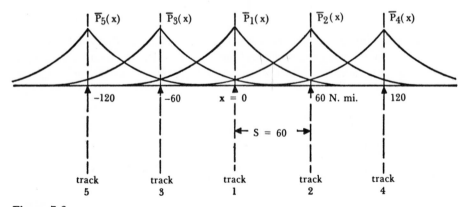

Figure 7-6.

Now let P(x) be the probability that a target, passing x N.mi. to the right of observer one, is detected. For $0 \leq x \leq 30$, this probability is one minus the probability of failing to detect on all three tracks. Assuming independence, this becomes

Equation 7-5 $P(x) = 1 - [1 - \overline{P}_1(x)][1 - \overline{P}_2(x)][1 - \overline{P}_3(x)]$.

When the individual $\overline{P}_i(x)$ of the example are substituted in Equation 7-5, they can be combined and simplified to give

$$P(x) = .843 - [1.49 \times 10^{-2}]x + [1.24 \times 10^{-4}]x^2 + [3.92 \times 10^{-6}]x^3$$
$$- [2.37 \times 10^{-8}]x^4 - [1.8 \times 10^{-10}]x^5 + 10^{-12}x^6.$$

The average probability of detection for this search can be found by taking the expected value of P(x), i.e.,

$$E[P(x)] = \int_{\text{All } x} P(x) \cdot f(x)\, dx$$

where $f(x) = 1/30$, since x is uniformly distributed between zero and 30. Therefore

$$E[P(x)] = \int_0^{30} P(x) \cdot \left(\frac{1}{30}\right) dx.$$

If P(x) found from Equation 7-5 is used and the integration performed, the result is .6785. Since this same result would be obtained had the target been assumed zero to 30 N.mi. left or right of *any* track (except near the end observer), the average probability of detecting a target is the same. *For a given lateral range curve,* this average probability of detecting a target depends only on the track spacing and hence is denoted $\overline{P}(S)$. In this example, using $S = 60$ and the lateral range curve given, $P(S) = .6785$.

This result may be compared with the previously discussed *random search* model by computing the sweep width for the lateral range curve in Figure 7-4.

$$W = \int_{-90}^{90} \left(\frac{90 - |x|}{100}\right)^2 dx = 2\int_0^{90} \left(\frac{90 - x}{100}\right)^2 dx = 48.6 \text{ N.mi.}$$

The *coverage factor* W/S would then be

$$\frac{W}{S} = \frac{48.6}{60} = .81,$$

and for an equivalent search effort a uniform random search would yield a minimum (lower bound) probability of detection of

$$1 - e^{-W/S} = 1 - e^{-.81} = .5551,$$

compared with the exact value .6785 for the systematic coverage given by parallel overlapping sweeps.

The parallel sweep method was developed assuming enough observers in a line abreast to cover the area by sweeping through it once. Nothing was assumed about the target's position or motion except that it remained in the area throughout the search. It can be seen that if the target were assumed stationary, then a *single* observer could make successive parallel sweeps through the area at a distance S apart and the same result would be obtained. Another equivalent situation would occur if several stationary observers were placed across a channel at a distance S apart to detect transiting targets. Many other types of searches and patrols are nothing more than parallel sweep coverage adapted to a particular situation.

The model developed in this section has led to the computation of the average probability of detecting a target. While this will serve as a useful measure of effectiveness in many problems, it may be better to use the minimum probability of detection in others. If, for example, a target had the capability to track the searchers, he could maneuver into the most advantageous position to avoid detection, and a better measure of effectiveness for the search would be the minimum probability of detection. This position is usually, but not always, located halfway between adjacent searchers. The minimum probability occurs at that range which yields the minimum value of $P(x)$ from Equation 7-5.

704   INVERSE CUBE LAW

In the previous section a method for finding the probability of detection with parallel sweeps was demonstrated. In the example, using a particular lateral range curve, the probability of detection $\overline{P}(S)$ was found to be .6785 for a track spacing, S, of 60 N.mi. The student can see that for other possible lateral range curves and different track spacings the method would be applicable, although graphical approximations or the use of a computer might be necessary to carry through the calculations.

The question arises as to whether the shape of the lateral range curve would significantly influence the result, e.g., for a search with a lateral range curve of a different shape but whose sweep width is the same, would $\overline{P}(60)$ still be .6785? The answer, for typical lateral range curves, is that the result would *not* differ significantly. This makes it possible to predict with some confidence the probability of detection, using the coverage factor, without knowing the shape of the lateral range curve from which the sweep width was computed.

One model, of particular value in predicting the probability of detection for parallel sweeps where the coverage factor is known, is developed through application of the *inverse cube law of detection* which was previously discussed in Chapter four. Its derivation, which is beyond the scope of this text, may be found in OEG Report Number 56, *Search and Screening*. It requires the use of normal probability tables and is determined from:

Equation 7-6 $$\overline{P}(S) = 2 \int_0^z f(t)\, dt,$$

where $f(t)$ is the *standardized normal distribution* with *mean* zero and *variance* one, and

$$z = \sqrt{\frac{\pi}{2}\frac{W}{S}} = 1.253\frac{W}{S}.$$

If this model were used to compute the probability of detection in the example of the previous section where $W = 48.6$ and $S = 60$, then

$$z = 1.253\frac{W}{S} = 1.015,$$

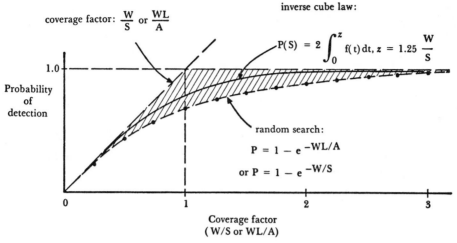

Figure 7-7.

and

$$\overline{P}(60) = 2\int_{0}^{1.015} f(t)\,dt$$

$$= 2(.3449) \text{ from normal tables,}$$

$$= .6898$$

which agrees closely with the previously computed value of .6785.

Figure 7-7 summarizes the models discussed thus far. The coverage factor itself gives a good estimate of the probability of detection when its value is small or when there is no overlapping of possible detection zones. The random search models estimate the probability of detection when little is known about the target, no systematic search plan is used, or essentially no overlapping of adjacent swept areas occurs. The inverse cube law is a model which agrees closely with the parallel sweep model and is perhaps the best theoretical predictor of operational results because of its "middle" location between the two extremes.

In operational situations, a given coverage factor should yield a probability of detection somewhere in the shaded area between the conservative random search model and the optimistic coverage factor.

705 A POSTERIORI PROBABILITY OF TARGET LOCATION

There are many operational situations in which an essentially stationary target is the object of a search based upon initial (a priori) estimates of target location probabilities. For example, an area known to contain the target could be subdivided and each subarea assigned an estimate that the target is within that division. A simple case would be as follows: the target is known to lie within the rectangle depicted in Figure 7-8 and is further assumed to be within subarea 1 with .7 probability and 2 with .3 probability.

Subarea 1	Subarea 2
$L_1 = .7$	$L_2 = .3$
100 sq. N. mi.	150 sq. N. mi.

Figure 7-8.

The L_i value is the initial, or a priori, likelihood that the target is within the ith subarea. It should be noted that for n subareas:

$$\sum_{i=1}^{n} L_i = 1.$$

Now suppose that one or more of the subareas are searched and the target is *not* found after the search effort. Suppose, for example, that subarea 1 in the rectangle above is searched to a great extent because of L_1 being greater than L_2, and that there is no sign of the target. It is reasonable to assume that the fact that the target was *not* found should lead to a revision of the initial or a priori estimates of target location probability. In fact, by applying Bayes' theorem, one can revise the a priori probabilities, L_i, and come up with new (revised) or *a posteriori* probabilities that the target lies within each subarea.

Recall Bayes' theorem (Appendix I, Section I-8):

$$P[A_j|B] = \frac{P[B|A_j]P[A_j]}{\sum\limits_{i=1}^{n} P[B|A_i]P[A_i]},$$

where all A_i are mutually exclusive events, i.e., for all $i \neq j$, $P[A_i \cap A_j] = 0$, and all of these events make up the sample space, i.e.,

$$\sum_{\text{all } i} P[A_i] = 1.$$

Now consider an area of target uncertainty subdivided into n subareas and let:

A_j = Event [target is in j^{th} subarea]
B = Event [target not detected in search of area of uncertainty].

Define the following:

L_j = a priori P[target in j^{th} subarea]
L_j' = a posteriori P[target in j^{th} subarea|target not detected in search area]
P_j = P[target detected|target in j^{th} subarea]
$\quad = 1 - P[B/A_j]$

It should be noted that:

$$L_j \equiv P[A_j] \quad L_j' \equiv P[A_j|B] \quad (1 - P_j) = P[B/A_j]$$

Then referring to Bayes' theorem:

Equation 7-7
$$L'_j = \frac{(1 - P_j)L_j}{\sum\limits_{i=1}^{n} (1 - P_i)L_i}.$$

If it is assumed that an area of uncertainty is searched for an essentially stationary target; and that given the target lies in a particular subarea of that total area, then it is *uniformly distributed* within that subarea; and if a further assumption is made that search in any subarea is considered to be random, then to be most conservative,

Equation 7-8
$$P_j = 1 - e^{-WVT_j/A_j},$$

where another form of the coverage factor is apparent:

$$\frac{WVT_j}{A_j} \equiv \text{search coverage factor in subarea } j \text{ (of size } A_j).$$

As an example, in the area previously given which was subdivided into two subareas (subareas 1 and 2), the initial a priori estimates were that the target was in subarea 1 with probability .7 ($L_1 = .7$) and subarea 2 with probability .3 ($L_2 = .3$). Whichever subarea the target happens to be in, it is assumed that the target's position within that subarea is uniformly distributed. Now suppose that a search vehicle with search speed $V = 10$ knots and sweep width $W = 2$ N.mi. conducts a random search of the total area spending 12 hours searching subarea 1 and 4 hours searching subarea 2. For this illustration, suppose also that the size of subarea 1 (A_1) is 100 sq. N.mi. and subarea 2 (A_2) is 150 sq. N.mi. If the target is not found in this initial search effort, one could re-evaluate the probabilities associated with the target being in each subarea as follows:

$$P_1 = 1 - e^{-wvt_1/A_1} = 1 - e^{-(2)(10)(12)/100} = 1 - .09$$
$$P_1 = .91$$
$$P_2 = 1 - e^{-wvt_2/A_2} = 1 - e^{-(2)(10)(4)/150} = 1 - .59$$
$$P_2 = .41$$
$$L'_1 = \frac{L_1(1 - P_1)}{L_1(1 - P_1) + L_2(1 - P_2)} = \frac{(.7)(.09)}{(.7)(.09) + (.3)(.59)}$$
$$L'_1 = .26$$
$$L'_2 = \frac{L_2(1 - P_2)}{L_1(1 - P_1) + L_2(1 - P_2)} = \frac{(.3)(.59)}{(.7)(.09) + (.3)(.59)}$$
$$L'_2 = .74.$$

Thus, after the initial search effort resulting in no detection of the target, one could calculate the re-evaluative (a posteriori) probabilities associated with the subarea in which the target lies. Here, the a posteriori probability that the target is now in subarea 1 (L'_1) is computed to be .26 and L'_2 computed to be .74. Subsequent search effort might be concentrated within subarea 2, as this area is now more likely to contain the target. One should realize that this entire process is iterative, i.e., if the target is not found in subsequent search effort, new a posteriori probabilities should be calculated using the previously computed a posteriori probabilities as a priori probabilities.

This application of Bayes' theorem has had several successful operational uses. It merely permits the analyst to take advantage of updated information, and this is an offer that should not be refused.

706 RANDOM SEARCH OF AN EXPANDING AREA (EVADING TARGET)

The formula studied previously for random search of a *fixed* area for an essentially stationary target whose position is considered to be uniformly distributed within the area is given as:

$$P_D(T) = 1 - e^{-wvT/A},$$

where v is the search velocity and T is the search time, causing wvT/A to be coverage factor.

It appears that the above formula is a special case of a more *general* formula for random search of an area given as:

Equation 7-9 $$P_D(T) = 1 - e^{-\int_0^T wvdt/A(t)},$$

where w is the sweep width of the search vehicle, v is the search speed of the search vehicle, and $A(t)$ is size of area as a function of time.

Area Expanding as a Circle

One of the most frequent cases of an expanding area is one in which the area of uncertainty of the target *expands circularly* and target position remains uniformly distributed within the expanding area. If a target is known *initially* to be uniformly distributed within a circle of radius R, and thereafter can be *evading* in any direction at a maximum speed U, then:

$$A(t) = \pi(R + Ut)^2$$

and

$$\int_0^T \frac{dt}{A(t)} = \int_0^T \frac{dt}{\pi(R + Ut)^2} = \frac{T}{\pi R(R + UT)}.$$

The probability of detection as a function of time can then be written:

Equation 7-10 $$P_D(T) = 1 - e^{-c}$$

where:

Equation 7-10.a $$c = \frac{wvT}{\pi R(R + UT)}$$

In *prolonged search,* that is as t approaches infinity, the term R *inside* the parentheses becomes insignificant compared to the term UT, so that:

Equation 7-10.b $$\lim_{T \to \infty} c = \frac{wv}{\pi RU}$$

Suppose a submarine periscope is sighted and a VP aircraft is sent to datum to conduct a random search. The submarine can be evading datum at a maximum speed of 10 knots and the VP aircraft arrives at datum 30 minutes after the submarine was

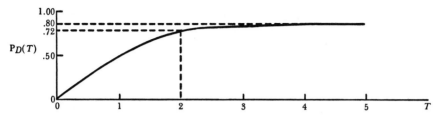

Figure 7-9.

sighted. The VP aircraft conducts a random search about the datum at a speed of 250 knots, and its sweep width is estimated to be 2,000 yards (1 N.mi.).

In this problem, upon commencing search, the target is assumed to be initially uniformly distributed within a circle whose radius is $R = UT_L$; where T_L is the "time late" at datum of the searching aircraft. Therefore, $R = (10 \text{ knots})(.5 \text{ hour}) = 5$ N.mi. In prolonged search about datum, i.e., no matter how long the VP aircraft conducts a random search about the increasingly expanding area of uncertainty, the probability that the evading submarine will be detected can be computed as (see Figure 7-9):

$$P_D(T \to \infty) = 1 - e^{-\frac{wv}{\pi RU}}$$
$$= 1 - e^{-(1)(250)/\pi(5)(10)}$$
$$= 1 - e^{-1.59}$$
$$= 1 - .20$$
$$P_D(T \to \infty) = .80.$$

The probability that the aircraft will detect the target within the initial two hours of search time after arrival at the datum area can be computed as:

$$P_D(T) = 1 - e^{-wvT/\pi R(R + UT)}$$
$$P_D(T = 2) = 1 - e^{-(1)(250)(2)/\pi 5[5 + (10)(2)]}$$
$$= 1 - e^{-1.27}$$
$$= 1 - .28$$
$$P_D(T = 2) = .72.$$

As can be seen, if the target continues to open (evade) datum as described, the area of uncertainty rapidly becomes very large and, if the target is not detected early, say within the initial two hours after search commences, the chance of detecting the target with continued search effort becomes marginal. By decreasing the variable T_L and calculating the corresponding value of $R = UT_L$, one can readily perceive the importance that time late at datum has in target detection capability.

PROBLEMS

1. An aircraft is conducting a completely random visual search over an area of 20,000 square N.mi. Assume that the search, which covers a total distance of 800 N.mi, consists of a total of 20 random legs of equal length. For the prevailing conditions, the visual sweep width of the searching unit is 15 N.mi.

   a. What is the probability of detecting the target on one leg of the search?
   b. What is the probability that the target is *not* detected on any of the 20 legs?
   c. What is the probability that the target is detected (using Equation 7-1)?
   d. What is the probability of detection if Equation 7-2 is used?

2. Three aircraft operating independently are assigned to conduct random search sorties in an area 600 N.mi. by 300 N.mi. The search speed of the aircraft is 180 knots. For the prevailing conditions, the sweep width of the aircraft radar is determined to be 60 N.mi. Fuel considerations limit the on-station time for each aircraft to 3 hours.

   a. What is the probability that the first aircraft detects the target during a single sortie?
   b. If each aircraft flies a single sortie, what is the probability that the target is detected?
   c. How many aircraft are required, each flying a single sortie in a completely independent manner, in order to achieve a probability of detection of .9?

3. A parallel-sweep search is to be flown to cover a rectangular area 300 N.mi. by 600 N.mi. Track spacing, S, for the search will be 60 N.mi. For the prevailing conditions the sweep width, W, of the aircraft radar is determined to be 60 N.mi. A graphical representation of the search is given by the following:

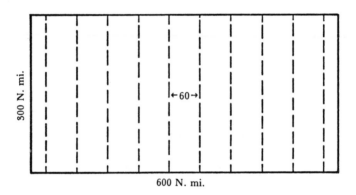

600 N. mi.

   a. What total distance is traveled in the area?
   b. Estimate the probability of detection using the random search model.
   c. Does the random search model provide an estimate which is too high or too low?
   d. What is the coverage factor?

4. Which of the two following expressions is a more conservative estimate of the probability of detection,

$$1 - e^{-WL/A} \quad \text{or} \quad 1 - (1 - WL/NA)^N?$$

Does your answer to this question depend on N? Explain.

5. An S2F aircraft with an APS-38 radar is assigned to conduct a search for a large liferaft located somewhere in an area 500 N.mi. by 200 N.mi. in size. Search speed, V, of the aircraft is 150 knots. Under the prevailing conditions and considering the characteristics of the target as well as search altitude, the sweep width of the radar is determined to be 50 N.mi. Fuel considerations limit the aircraft time on station (in the area) to 4 hours.

a. Using the random search model, compute the probability that the aircraft will detect the liferaft in a single sortie.

b. How many aircraft-hours in the area would be required to achieve a probability of detection of .95?

c. What is the *average number* of aircraft-hours, T, required in the area to detect the liferaft?

$$\text{(Note that } P(T \le t) = 1 - e^{-WVT/A}.)$$

6. Suppose six radars are placed across a channel, as shown, to detect targets which are as likely to transit the channel at one point as any other. This situation is similar to a parallel sweep search in which the targets are stationary and each radar moves up the channel.

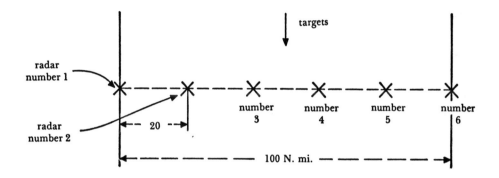

Each radar has the following lateral range curve, $\overline{P}(x)$, and detects independently of any other radar.

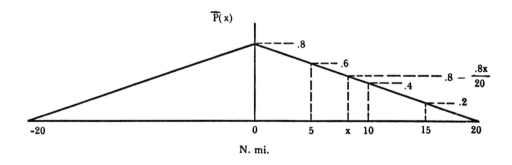

a. What is the probability that a target will be detected which transits the channel:
   (1) at the left edge zero N.mi. from radar number one?
   (2) 5 N.mi. to the right of radar number one?
   (3) 10 N.mi. to the right of radar number one?
   (4) 15 N.mi. to the right of radar number one?

    (5) 20 N.mi. to the right of radar number one?

    (6) x N.mi. to the right of radar number one? Find the answer in terms of x where $0 \leq x \leq 20$.

  b. Could you now easily extend this for a target passing at some other point in the channel?

  c. What is the average probability of detecting a target which may pass at any point between zero and 20 N.mi. to the right of radar number one? Would the answer to this question change if radars number two, three, four or five were substituted for radar number one?

  d. What would be the coverage factor?

  e. Using the inverse cube law, compute the probability of detection and compare the answer to that for c.

7. A square area 200 N.mi. by 200 N.mi. is completely searched one time by means of parallel sweeps using a track spacing of 40 N.mi. Sweep width for this particular search is determined to be 30 N.mi.

  a. Estimate the probability of detecting a randomly located target using the random search model.

  b. Using the inverse cube law, compute the probability of detecting the target.

  c. What track spacing would be required to produce a probability of detection of .95 (using the inverse cube law)?

8. A pilot returning at night from a strike has been forced to "punch out" over water. Prior to ejection, the pilot reported his course, speed and position but not his altitude. Based upon intuition, you feel that he most likely ejected at an altitude of 2,000–5,000 feet or possibly at 5,000–10,000 feet. He would not have been above 10,000 feet. Constructing an area within which the pilot might have landed, you subdivide the area into four squares and assign a priori probabilities that the pilot landed within each square as follows:

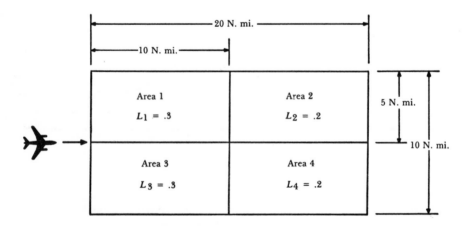

    The decision is made to immediately send a single A/C to search for the downed pilot and, at the same time, detach a screening DD to proceed toward the area.

Initial search by the A/C will be visual (the downed pilot has a light). It is assumed that the sweep width of this visual search is 7 N.mi. and that search can be considered to be essentially random in nature. The A/C conducts a search as follows:

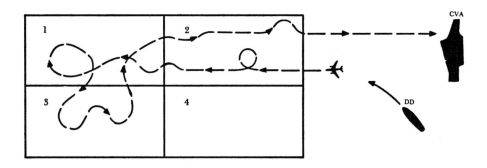

$$D_1 = 14\ \text{N.mi.}$$
$$D_2 = 20\ \text{N.mi.}$$
$$D_3 = 12\ \text{N.mi.}$$
$$D_4 = \ 0\ \text{N.mi.}$$

D_i = length of search track flown in subarea i

In the event that the above search by the A/C does not find the downed pilot, re-evaluate the likelihood that the pilot is in each subarea in order that the DD might conduct a follow-on search most effectively.

8 Barrier Patrols

In planning a search, the nature of the target is usually known and its general position and intended movements may be more or less known. However, unless a fairly definite estimate of its motion can be made, the plan of search will have to be designed so as to be effective against a target having any one of many different sorts of motion. The emphasis of this chapter is on the situation which arises when both the *intent* and the *capabilities* of the target are known. To know the intent of the target is to know something about where it is going, through what part of the ocean it passes or from what geographical locality it comes. To know the target's capabilities is to have a reasonably good estimate of its speed as well as its endurance.

Attention will be confined in this chapter to the case in which the detectability of the target does not change during the search or patrol. In the case of visual or radar detection, only surface craft (including surfaced submarines) are considered. In the case of sonar detection, the submarine target is regarded as constantly submerged. This avoids the complication which would occur, for example, in the case of a submarine whose times of submergence and surfacing are not known.

While three cases are of importance in naval warfare, only the first will be studied in this chapter.* In the first, the target's intention is to traverse a fairly straight channel (which may be a wide portion of the ocean). The vector velocities at all points are parallel and equal, a *translational vector field*. The associated search is called a *barrier patrol*. In the second case, the target is proceeding from a known point on the ocean, e.g., a point of fix, an island, or a harbor. The vector velocities are of a definite magnitude equal in length but are all directed away from this point, a *centrifugal radial vector field*. In this class of search belong the *expanding square* and the *retiring search* when

*A complete analysis of all three cases may be found in OEG Report 56, *Search and Screening,* Chapter seven.

the approximate time of departure is known, and the *closed barrier* in other cases. In the third case, the target's intention is to reach a definite point, e.g., the objective area of landing operation, an island needing supplies, or a harbor. The vector velocities are equal in length but directed inward toward this point, a *centripetal radial vector field*. Again the method of reacting to this intention may be the *closed barrier*.

In the case in which the target intends to reach a point moving on the ocean (a ship, convoy or task force), the vector field is of an entirely different character. The form of patrol used is called a *screen* and is the subject of Chapter ten.

801 CROSSOVER BARRIER PATROL

Under a wide variety of circumstances, the problem of detecting a target in transit through a channel by means of an observer whose speed, v, considerably exceeds the speed, u, of the target, e.g., an airborne observer and ship target, can be simplified to the following mathematical statement. Given a channel bounded by two parallel lines D miles apart (the vertical lines of Figure 8-1) and a target moving through this channel and parallel to it at a fixed speed, u (downward in Figure 8-1B), how shall the observer fly from one side of the channel to the other and back, etc., in order to be most effective in detecting the target?

It is necessary to orient the flights relative to a fixed reference point, O_1, from which they start or take their direction. Thus O_1 may be a convenient geographic point at or near the narrowest part of the actual channel. The line $\overline{O_1 O_1'}$ (in Figure 8-1) is drawn across the perpendicular to the channel as a purely mathematical reference line called the *barrier line*.

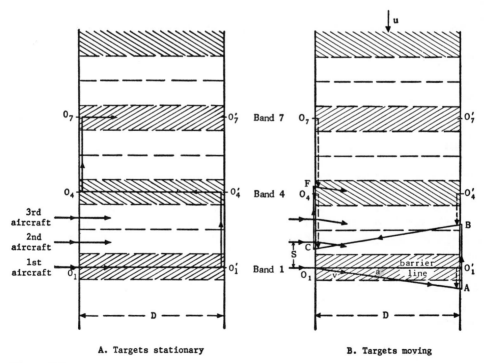

A. Targets stationary   B. Targets moving

Figure 8-1.

For convenience of wording, the target will be referred to as a ship and the observer as an aircraft. While this corresponds to the most prevalent situation, others will be considered later. The same mathematical ideas apply in all cases.

Suppose three aircraft are available to prevent targets from transiting the channel undetected. Let S be the track spacing used between aircraft and consider this problem as a special case of *parallel sweeps*. In Figure 8-1, the channel is divided into several bands of width S. If targets are stationary, as in Figure 8-1A, the three aircraft could search the first three bands while crossing the channel, then move up the opposite side of the channel and search bands four, five and six on the return trip, etc., with the first aircraft taking each third (shaded) band. However, with targets moving down the channel, as in Figure 8-1B, such a search would let some targets transit with an unnecessarily low probability of detection. With slight modification, the parallel sweep method can be made more effective.

Let the first aircraft fly the pattern O_1, A, B, C, F, as indicated by Figure 8-1B, where the angle, a, is computed such that a target originally at O_1' would be at A when the aircraft reaches A. The location of point A then depends on u, v and D. In effect, the first aircraft has searched for targets originally located in band one and now desires to search for targets which originally were located in band four. He must fly up the channel to intercept at B, any target originally at O_4'. After flying the *upsweep*, $M = \overline{AB}$, he returns across the channel at the necessary lead angle to keep him over the collection of possible targets which originally were in band four. Finally, he flies an upsweep leg up the channel from C to F where he intercepts the position of a target originally at O_7, thus completing one *basic element* of the search. At point F, he begins another cycle identical to the first, covering targets originally in band seven, etc.

At the same time, the second and third aircraft, flying parallel to the first, cover bands two and three on the first leg, five and six on the return, etc. Before computing the times and distances involved, it should be pointed out that there are three possibilities:

a. The barrier may progress further *up* the channel with each basic element flown. This is called an *advancing barrier*.

b. The barrier may retire *down* the channel with each succeeding element. This is referred to as a *retiring barrier*.

c. The barrier may remain stationary. This is called a *symmetric barrier*.

Which of these three types of barrier results depends on u, v, D, S and the number of aircraft, n.

To proceed further, it is necessary to develop certain relationships which follow logically from the preceding description. The angle, a, is dependent solely on the two speeds, v and u, of aircraft and target respectively. From the requirement that the aircraft reaches point A when a target originally at O_1' also reaches point A, it can be seen in Figure 8-1B that $\sin a = \overline{O_1'A}/\overline{O_1A}$, where $\overline{O_1'A} = ut_1$ and $\overline{O_1A} = vt_1$, when t_1 is the time required for the aircraft to reach point A.

Equation 8-1
$$a = \sin^{-1}\frac{u}{v}.$$

To find the *time, T_0, for an aircraft to complete one basic element* requires some intermediate computations.

$$D = \sqrt{(vt_1)^2 - (ut_1)^2} = t_1 \sqrt{v^2 - u^2};$$

therefore:

$$t_1 = \frac{D}{\sqrt{v^2 - u^2}}.$$

When the first of n aircraft (and also a target originally at O_1') is at point A, it proceeds next to intercept a target *originally* located n bandwidths, nS miles above point O_1'. This target must *now* be a distance nS above point A and traveling down the channel with speed u. Let t_2 be the time it takes for the aircraft to proceed up the channel to intercept such a target. Then

$$t_2 = \frac{nS}{u + v}$$

and the total time for the first aircraft to reach B is the sum $t_1 + t_2$, or

$$t_B = \frac{D}{\sqrt{v^2 - u^2}} + \frac{nS}{u + v}.$$

The *length of the upsweep*, $M = \overline{AB}$, is the distance traveled by the aircraft in the time t_2 so that $M = vt_2$ or

Equation 8-2
$$M = \frac{vnS}{u + v}.$$

This completes half of one basic element and the remaining half is seen to be identical. Therefore the time for one complete basic element, T_0, is given by $2t_B$ or

Equation 8-3
$$T_0 = \frac{2D}{\sqrt{v^2 - u^2}} + \frac{2nS}{u + v}.$$

802 SYMMETRIC CROSSOVER PATROL

The question arises as to whether the resulting barrier with n aircraft flying parallel is advancing, retiring or symmetric. It would be symmetric only if the starting point for the second element were the same as the first, i.e., if F and O_1 coincided. Note carefully that the time for a target originally at O_7 in Figure 8-1B to reach point F is equal to T_0, the same time as that required for the aircraft to reach F. If F were located at O_1, the target originally at O_7 would have to travel six bandwidths to reach point F. If n aircraft were used, the number of bands swept during one basic element is $2n$ and the first unswept band is the one originally located a distance $2nS$ above the barrier line. When will this band, or rather a target in this band, reach the barrier line? Let T_t represent the required time, i.e.,

T_t = time required for a target originally in the first unswept band to reach the barrier line, and is

Equation 8-4
$$T_t = \frac{2nS}{u}.$$

For an *advancing* barrier, as in Figure 8-2A, F is above O_1; therefore:

$$T_t > T_0.$$

5   4.5

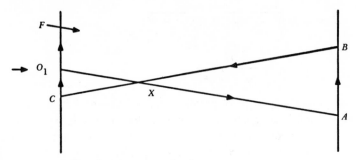

A. The advancing crossover barrier

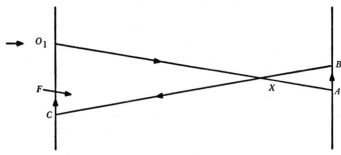

B. The retiring crossover barrier

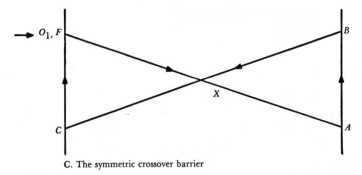

C. The symmetric crossover barrier

Figure 8-2.

For a *retiring* barrier, as in Figure 8-2B, F is below O_1; therefore:

$$T_t < T_0.$$

For a *symmetric* barrier, as in Figure 8-2C, F and O_1 coincide; therefore:

$$T_t = T_0.$$

From these relationships, it is possible to determine the number of aircraft required or the track spacing necessary for a symmetric barrier to be maintained. For this case it is required that

$$T_t = T_0;$$

therefore

$$\frac{2nS}{u} = \frac{2D}{\sqrt{v^2 - u^2}} + \frac{2nS}{v + u}.$$

Solving for n, and letting $K = \sqrt{(v + u)/(v - u)}$ gives

Equation 8-5
$$n = K\frac{D}{S}\frac{u}{v},$$

or solving for S gives

$$S = \frac{KDu}{nv}.$$

803 ADVANCING CROSSOVER PATROL

The advancing barrier represents a situation in which more than enough aircraft-hours are available to produce the required coverage. Advantage can be taken of this circumstance by flying only during favorable periods; in daylight, if visual detection is used, or for a photographic mission; at night with radar, if the element of surprise is important; and so on. After advancing the barrier sufficiently during the favorable period, flights can be discontinued and targets in the next unswept band can be allowed to proceed down the channel until reaching the barrier line $\overline{O_1O_1'}$, at which time the patrol must be started again.

Suppose n aircraft flying parallel have *each* flown N basic elements. The first unswept band of potential targets is then the one originally located $2nN$ bands above the barrier line $\overline{O_1O_1'}$. The equivalent distance to be traveled is $2nNS$, and these targets will reach the barrier line at time $2nNS/u$, or NT_t.

With reference to the observer, the search time or *patrol period* for N basic elements is NT_0, except that the last upsweep on the last element can be omitted since it contributes no additional coverage. Thus:

Equation 8-6
$$\text{patrol period} = NT_0 - \frac{nS}{u + v}.$$

The allowable *no patrol period* (NPP) during which the search may stop without allowing unswept targets to pass the barrier line may now be found from

Equation 8-7   patrol period + no patrol period $= NT_t$,
so that,

$$\text{no patrol period} = NT_t - \text{patrol period}$$
$$= NT_t - NT_0 + \frac{nS}{u + v}.$$

Collecting terms gives

Equation 8-8
$$\text{NPP} = N(T_t - T_0) + \frac{nS}{u + v}.$$

804 NONCONTINUOUS PATROL

The possibility of using an advancing barrier to avoid a continuous patrol may now be discussed. Suppose that for A hours it is expedient to patrol, whereas during B hours it is inexpedient. B might be the hours of darkness when visual detection is not possible.

Usually such a patrol would be conducted on a daily cycle so that $A + B = 24$, but other cycles may be required on occasion.

The following conditions must hold:

- Patrol period $\leq A$,
- No patrol period $\geq B$,
- Patrol period + no patrol period $= A + B$.

If, however, the last two expressions hold, the first must also hold, so the last two are sufficient. The third condition (using Equation 8-7) becomes

$$NT_t = A + B,$$

which can be written (using Equation 8-4) as

$$\frac{N(2nS)}{u} = A + B$$

or

Equation 8-9
$$nS = \frac{u(A + B)}{2N}.$$

The second condition (using Equation 8-8) becomes

Inequation 8-1
$$N(T_t - T_0) + \frac{nS}{u + v} \geq B.$$

A solution to this *noncontinuous* patrol problem then consists of values of n, N and S so that *both* Equation 8-9 and Inequation 8-1 hold. There may be several combinations which qualify as a solution. A trial and error procedure will ultimately produce a solution, though it may be time consuming. It is possible to simplify the effort by eliminating from Inequation 8-1 any values of N which cannot satisfy Equation 8-9. This is done by substituting into Inequation 8-1 values for T_t, T_0 and nS from Equations 8-4, 8-3 and 8-9 respectively, and multiplying through by $-N$. The resulting quadratic inequality then simplifies to the following:

$$N^2 - c_1 N - \frac{c_2}{4} \leq 0,$$

where

$$c_1 = \frac{Av - Bu}{2DK},$$

$$c_2 = \frac{u(A + B)}{DK} \quad \text{and} \quad K = \frac{\sqrt{v + u}}{\sqrt{v - u}}, \text{ as before.}$$

A solution to the quadratic inequality, giving the desired positive values of N which satisfy the Inequation 8-1 and allow Equation 8-9 to hold, is

Inequation 8-2
$$N \leq \tfrac{1}{2}[c_1 + \sqrt{c_1^2 + c_2}].$$

No trial and error is involved in using Inequation 8-2 since values of n and S are not required. A solution may then be determined quickly as follows:

a. Solve Inequation 8-2 to find the *maximum* value of N (reduce to an integer).
b. Using that maximum value of N and the *maximum* desired track spacing (usually

determined from a required probability of detection), solve Equation 8-9 to find the *minimum* value of n (increase to an integer).

c. Using the maximum desired track spacing, solve Equation 8-9 for the *minimum* value of nN (increase to an integer).

d. Any allowed values of n and N, whose multiple is large enough, become a solution to the problem. The track spacing to be used must be determined by again using Equation 8-9. A numerical example is given in the next section.

805 BARRIER PATROL SELECTION CONSIDERATIONS

For a crossover barrier patrol, the probability of detection is exactly the same as for parallel sweeps for the same track spacing, S. However, the accuracy of the computed probability of detection depends on two additional variables, the estimated *target course* and estimated *target speed*.

If the target's speed, u, has been *overestimated*, some portions of each band will be searched more than once and the true probability of detection will be higher than computed. The true probability of detection will *not*, however, be as high as it would be if the search were planned (and S reduced) for the correct value of u. Underestimating the target speed produces the opposite effect, and the probability of detection will be less than predicted.

If the target is moving obliquely down the channel instead of exactly parallel to the banks as we have been assuming, the effective value of the target speed as far as the tightness of the barrier is concerned is the downward component of the speed. This reduces the effective speed and produces the same result as when the target speed is overestimated.

There are two general types of problems which require a solution:

a. Given a required effectiveness, i.e., *probability of detection* $\overline{P}(S)$, design a barrier to most efficiently produce it, specifying n, N, S, patrol time.

b. Given the resources available, i.e., time, number of aircraft, etc., design a barrier with maximum effectiveness, specifying N, S, $\overline{P}(S)$.

The following examples are illustrative:

a. It is desired to close a 300-N.mi. channel with a barrier having an 87 percent chance of detection. The speeds are $v = 150$ knots and $u = 14$ knots. The sweep width is 20 N.mi., and the inverse cube law is assumed. How many aircraft are needed in order to have a symmetric barrier, and how should the flights be conducted?

Using the inverse cube law, S is required to be 16.6 N.mi. With this value for S the number, n, of aircraft must be the smallest *integer*, not less than that required for a symmetric barrier in Equation 8-5, i.e.,

$$n = K \frac{D}{S} \frac{u}{v} = \sqrt{\frac{164}{136} \frac{(300)(14)}{(16.6)(150)}} = 1.85.$$

In other words, two aircraft are necessary. But with two aircraft, an advancing barrier will result because T_t will be greater than T_0. To have a stationary barrier, the two aircraft must fly closer together, their track spacing determined by solving the same equation for S, with $n = 2$:

$$S = \frac{KDu}{nv} = \sqrt{\frac{164}{136} \frac{(300) \times (14)}{(2) \times (150)}} = 15.4 \text{ miles.}$$

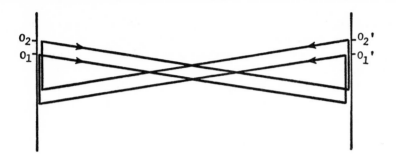

Symmetrical barrier flown by two aircraft.

Figure 8-3.

With this reduced track spacing, the barrier gains in tightness. In fact the probability found from the inverse cube law now becomes 90 percent, which is all to the good. The length of upsweep given by Equation 8-2 is $M = 28.2$ N.mi. Finally, the lead angle given by Equation 8-1 is $a = 5° 21'$. These quantities determine the basic element for the two symmetrical crossover paths shown in Figure 8-3.

In determining force requirements, additional factors must be considered. With $n = 2$, $S = 15.4$, etc., it can be found that $T_0 = 4.38$ hours. A long-range patrol aircraft may have an endurance sufficient for two basic elements, although time must be allowed for flying to and from the base, investigation of contacts, and so on. Two other aircraft must then continue the barrier, beginning the third basic element at points O_1 and O_2, as before.

b. Under the assumptions of the last example, let it be required to fly a barrier of the advancing type with n aircraft during the $A = 12$ hours of light and no flights during the $B = 12$ hours of darkness. The method at the end of Section 804 can be applied to find the solution. First, Inequation 8-2 is used to determine $N \le 2.57$, and hence, the maximum number of basic elements *for which the patrol period is less than A is two*. Then using $N = 2$ and $S = 16.6$, Equation 8-9 gives $n = 5.05$, so the *minimum number* of aircraft flying abeam is six. The same equation solved for nN, using the maximum allowed track spacing, becomes $nN = 10.1$, which means the product nN must be 11 *or greater*. In summary, any combination of n and N is a solution provided the following hold:

$$N = 1 \text{ or } 2,$$
$$n = 6, 7, 8, \ldots,$$
$$nN \ge 11,$$

and
$$S = \frac{168}{nN} \text{ from Equation 8-9.}$$

Two of the possible solutions are tabulated in Figure 8-4.

The officer who must decide how to conduct the barrier can use this information along with subjective considerations, such as operator fatigue, to make an intelligent decision.

n	N	S	$\bar{P}(S)$	T_O	Patrol period	Total aircraft hours on station
6	2	14.0	.93	5.02	9.55	57.3
11	1	15.3	.90	6.01	5.02	55.2

Figure 8-4.

806   BARRIER WHEN TARGET SPEED IS CLOSE TO OBSERVER'S SPEED

So far it has been assumed that v considerably exceeds u. When $v \leq u$, the crossover type of barrier is *impossible*. Even when u is nearly as great as v, the angle a is so large that a crossover barrier is inefficient. This does not arise when the observer is airborne and the target is a ship, but when both observer and target are units of the same type (both ships or both aircraft), the situation excluded heretofore becomes important. Although many barrier plans for a channel can be devised for this case, attention will be confined here to the very simple case in which the observer moves back and forth across the channel on a straight path perpendicular to its (parallel) edges. Such a barrier, called a *linear patrol*, is always possible as its design does not involve the speed ratio, u/v.

This linear patrol will be compared with the symmetrical crossover patrol (when $u < v$), and since only a rough comparison is sought here, the definite range law will be assumed, i.e., the fraction of targets coming within the sweep width will be used for the probability of detection. A more sophisticated detection law is not likely to alter the comparison appreciably.

The diagrams in Figure 8-5 show the geographic as well as the relative tracks for the two types of patrol. In both cases the observer moves only to a distance $W/2$ from the channel edge, so that for the crossover patrol some coverage is obtained on each upsweep. Only one observer is used in each case, and for the crossover patrol S is adjusted to provide a symmetric barrier.

In each relative track, the swept area is shaded and a representative half cycle selected. The probability of detection for each case has been taken as the ratio of the shaded area to the total area in the channel between the two dashed lines marking off the half cycle.

The solid segments at the exterior corners of the relative tracks of Figure 8-5 are of mainly academic interest. They would be areas of nondetection if the definite range law were assumed omnidirectional, giving a circular detection envelope at any time. However, if the fore-aft and the sideways detection ranges are assumed independent, a square detection envelope exists about the searcher, and these regions would be areas of detection. The detection equations of this section assume the latter, and more simple, square. Section 807 uses the more complex but more precise circular detection envelope. The mathematical difference resulting from the different assumptions underlying the two models is very small for the probability of detection by a linear patrol which reverses course at distance $W/2$ from the boundary.

It is convenient to introduce two new variables to describe the probability of detection, $r = v/u$ and $\lambda = D'/W$. For the case of the crossover patrol, the probability of detection, $P_{\bowtie}$, is given by

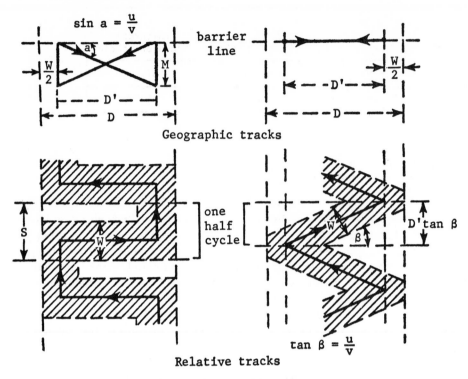

A comparison of barrier patrols.

Figure 8-5.

Equation 8-10

$$P_{\bowtie} = 1, \quad \text{or} \quad \left(1 + \frac{r\sqrt{r^2 - 1}}{r + 1}\right)\frac{1}{\lambda + 1},$$

whichever is smaller. For the linear patrol, the probability of detection, $P_{\leftrightarrow}$, is given by

Equation 8-11

$$P_{\leftrightarrow} = \begin{cases} 1 - \left[\left(\lambda - \dfrac{\sqrt{r^2 + 1} - 1}{2}\right)^2\Big/\lambda(\lambda + 1)\right], & r \leq 2\sqrt{\lambda(\lambda + 1)}, \\ 1 & , r > 2\sqrt{\lambda(\lambda + 1)}. \end{cases}$$

In Figure 8-6, the values of P for the two cases are plotted as a function of r with λ kept fixed for a given curve. In comparing crossover patrols with linear patrols, curves having the same value of λ should be compared. The solid curve passes through the points of intersection of the curves being compared and marks the boundary between the regions where linear is preferable and where crossover is preferable.

In order to facilitate the selection of the preferable type of patrol, Figure 8-7 is included. This curve shows the relation between λ and r for the points of intersection of curves in Figure 8-6. An example will illustrate the use of the curves. Suppose a ship making 12 knots is trying to prevent undetected penetration of a barrier by a submerged submarine traveling at six knots. Assume further that the channel being guarded is 8 N.mi. wide and that the sonar sweep width, W, is 2 N.mi. Then $D' = 8 - 2 = 6$, $\lambda = 6/2 = 3$, $r = 12/6 = 2$. Entering Figure 8-7 with these values for λ and r, one discovers that a crossover patrol is preferred.

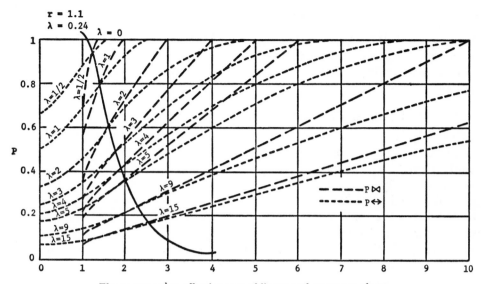

The comparative effectiveness of linear and crossover plans.

Figure 8-6.

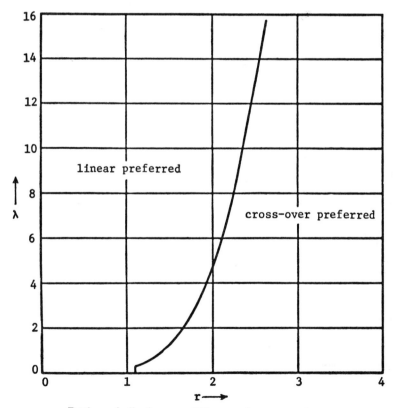

Regions of effectiveness of linear and crossover plans.

Figure 8-7.

807   KINEMATIC ENHANCEMENT OF LINEAR PATROLS

This section will use only plane trigonometry to derive the theoretical probabilities of detection using back-and-forth searches for an SSK reversing course *at the patrol area boundary,* and for an SSK reversing course when the effective *sweep radius reaches the area boundary.*

Case 1. SSK Reverses Course at Patrol Area Boundaries

Refer to Figure 8-8. A patrolling submarine (SSK) is to protect a patrol area with a certain length front D by proceeding at constant speed on courses parallel to the patrol front, traveling back and forth between area boundaries and reversing course at each area boundary. Transitors enter the area uniformly distributed across the patrol front on a course perpendicular to the patrol front. Any transitor that closes the patroller to within his sweep radius R is detected. It is convenient in this section to work with R, one-half the sweep width W.

In this approach to detection probability determination, submarines are assumed to have the capability of "sweeping" a patrol area, detecting all targets within the swept area and failing to detect all those outside. This is equivalent to assuming the definite range law of detection, where definite range, or sweep radius, is obtained (from actual at-sea results) by integrating under the lateral range curve and calculating the

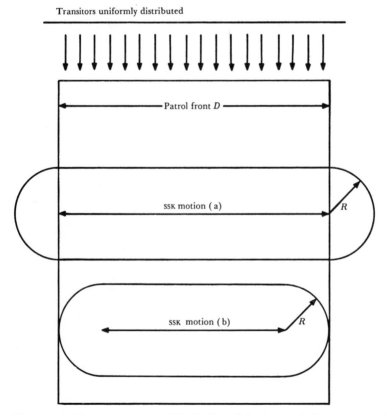

Figure 8-8. True areas covered by back-and-forth search for SSK reversing course at area boundary and when sweep radius reaches area boundary.

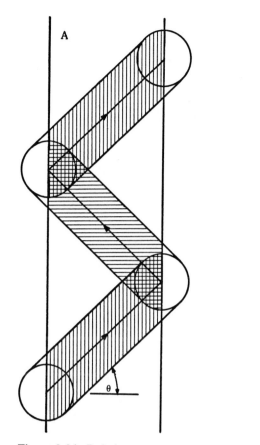

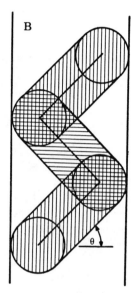

Figure 8-9A. Relative area swept for SSK reversing course at area boundaries.

Figure 8-9B. Relative area swept for SSK reversing course when sweep radius reaches area boundary.

range corresponding to an equal area under a curve of probability one. This is mathematically easy to handle, and the resulting detection probabilities for back-and-forth search, while not exact, are sufficiently accurate.

The method used here for the kinematics between transitor and SSK is to keep the transitor position fixed with only the SSK and its detection circle moving relatively to the transitor. The relative areas swept after several cycles of back-and-forth search will appear as in Figure 8-9A, for SSKs reversing course at the boundary. The angle θ is determined by transitor and SSK speeds, i.e., $\theta = \tan^{-1}(u/v)$, and Figures 8-9A and B depict the case where $u \simeq v$.

Probability of detection determination In Figure 8-10A the portion of the shaded area that lies within the patrol area front D represents the relative area swept for one SSK trip between boundaries. The angle θ establishes the direction of relative motion between SSK and transitor, and $\tan \theta = u/v$. A brief inspection of Figures 8-9 and 8-10 will reveal that consideration of one or any number of SSK search legs will result in the same effectiveness for search.

Referring back to Figure 8-10A, the probability of detection can be seen to be the ratio of the swept area (within the patrol area) to the total relative area for the leg. The

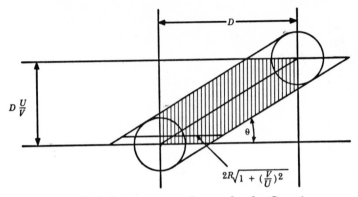

Figure 8-10A. Relative area swept for one leg for Case 1.

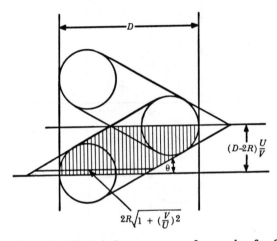

Figure 8-10B. Relative area swept for one leg for Case 2.

method used here is to determine the shaded area (parallelogram minus the areas of the triangle that fall *outside the patrol area*) and then divide by the total relative area.

The area within the parallelogram of Figure 8-10A is *base* times *height*. Referring to Figure 8-11:

$$\sin \theta \text{ can be seen} = R/\text{half the base}$$

but:

$$\tan \theta = \frac{u}{v},$$

so:

$$\sin \theta \text{ also} = \frac{u}{\sqrt{u^2 + v^2}} = \frac{1}{\sqrt{1 + \frac{v^2}{u^2}}};$$

then:

$$\text{half the parallelogram base} = R/\sin \theta - R\sqrt{1 + \frac{v^2}{u^2}}$$

and the whole parallelogram base is $2R\sqrt{1 + \left(\frac{v}{u}\right)^2}$.

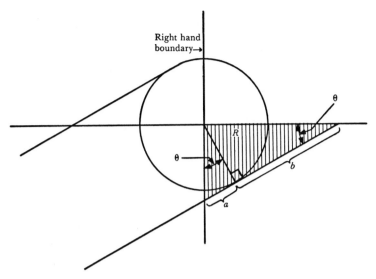

Figure 8-11.

The parallelogram height is shown in Figure 8-10A to be a function of the patrol front length D and the angle θ. Specifically, $\tan \theta = \dfrac{\text{height}}{D}$, also $= \dfrac{u}{v}$, so height $= D\dfrac{u}{v}$. The area of the parallelogram, then, is *base* times *height*, or

$$2RD\frac{u}{v}\sqrt{1 + \left(\frac{v}{u}\right)^2}.$$

The shaded area of Figure 8-11 shows the area to be subtracted from the parallelogram area at one end of the patrol leg. See also Figure 8-10A for comparison.

Dropping a perpendicular from the center of the search area circle to the hypotenuse of the triangle in question makes the solution simple. The length of that line is R, which can be thought of as the height of the triangle. The base of the triangle is the sum of the lengths of a and b, which resulted from the drop of the perpendicular R. Since $\tan \theta = a/R$ in one subtriangle and R/b in the other, the base of the triangle becomes $R \tan \theta + R/\tan \theta$; the area of the triangle is:

$$R^2(\tan \theta + 1/\tan \theta)/2,$$

which reduces by trigonometric identity to $R^2(u^2 + v^2)/2uv$, and the total shaded area outside the patrol zone is $R^2(u^2 + v^2)/uv$.

The total relative area for one ssk search leg is seen to be the length of the patrol front D times the height of the parallelogram Du/v, or D^2u/v.

Finally, probability of detection for back-and-forth sweep where the ssk reverses course at the patrol area boundary is found:

Equation 8-12 $\quad P_{\nleftrightarrow} = 2\dfrac{R}{D}\sqrt{1 + \left(\dfrac{v}{u}\right)^2} - \dfrac{R^2}{D^2}\left[1 + \left(\dfrac{v}{u}\right)^2\right]$

Case 2. SSK Reverses Course When Effective Sweep Radius Reaches Area Boundary

A patrolling submarine is to protect a patrol area under the same conditions as those in Case 1 except that its course reversal is to occur when the effective sweep radius reaches the area boundary.

Probability of detection determination The basic concepts are the same as for Case 1. The SSK sweeps a relative area on each of his back-and-forth legs, and the relative area swept would appear similar to that shown in Figure 8-9B. Notice that when comparing Case 1 and Case 2, if the ratio of the transitor-to-SSK speeds remains the same, the angle θ does also.

Probability of detection can again be seen in Figure 8-10B to be the ratio of that swept area to the total relative area for the leg. The method used herein is to determine the shaded area (parallelogram minus the areas that fall *outside the swept area* of the advancing circle) and divide by the total relative area.

The area within the parallelogram of Figure 8-10B is determined by *base* times *height*. The base is seen to be the same as for Case 1:

$$2R\sqrt{1 + \left(\frac{u}{v}\right)^2}$$

Parallelogram height is the same as for Case 1 except that it is shortened by twice the sweep radius: $(D - 2R)\frac{u}{v}$. The area of the parallelogram is:

$$2R(D - 2R)\sqrt{1 + \left(\frac{v}{u}\right)^2}\left(\frac{u}{v}\right).$$

The shaded area of Figure 8-12 shows the area to be subtracted at one end of the patrol leg. Also see Figure 8-10B for comparison. That area can be determined by first determining the area in the triangle ACE and subtracting the area of the sector ABE.

The area of the triangle is $(R/2)\,(R/\tan\theta)$, or $(R^2/2)\frac{v}{u}$.

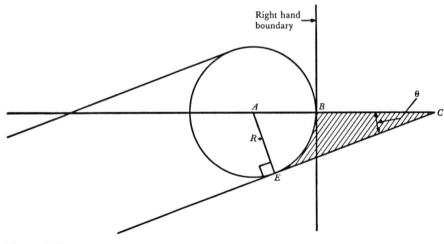

Figure 8-12.

The area of the sector is $\pi R^2 \left(\dfrac{90 - \theta}{360}\right)$.

The swept area of interest, then, is the area of the parallelogram, less twice the triangle, plus twice the sector, or:

$$2R(D - 2R)\sqrt{1 + \left(\frac{v}{u}\right)^2}\left(\frac{u}{v}\right) - R^2\left(\frac{v}{u}\right) + 2\pi R^2\left(\frac{90 - \theta}{360}\right).$$

The total relative area for one SSK leg is seen to be the length of the patrol front D times the height of the parallelogram $(D - 2R)\dfrac{u}{v}$ or $D(D - 2R)\dfrac{u}{v}$.

Finally, the probability of detection for back-and-forth sweep where the SSK reverses course when effective sweep radius reaches the area boundary is seen to be:

$$P_{\leftrightarrow} = \frac{2R(D - 2R)\dfrac{v}{u}\sqrt{1 + \left(\dfrac{v}{u}\right)^2} - 2R^2\left[\dfrac{1}{2}\dfrac{v}{u} - \pi\left(\dfrac{90 - \theta}{360}\right)\right]}{D(D - 2R)\dfrac{u}{v}},$$

which reduces to:

Equation 8-13

$$P_{\leftrightarrow} = \frac{2R}{D}\sqrt{1 + \left(\frac{v}{u}\right)^2} - \frac{R^2}{D(D - 2R)}\left(\frac{u}{v}\right)^2 + \frac{R^2\phi}{D(D - 2R)}\left(\frac{v}{u}\right)$$

where ϕ is the complement of θ, expressed in radians.

Detection probability determination for Case 2 is correct by this method for the cases of interest to submarines; i.e., $1/4 < u/v < 4$, and $D/R > 2$. In certain cases outside of these bounds, this particular method of swept area determination is incorrect.

Even when the parameters fall into valid ranges for these models, a decision between the two tactics of this section may not be a simple comparison. For many mobile detection platforms, the sweep width (radius) is a nonlinear function of speed v.

PROBLEMS

1. A single patrol aircraft is assigned to fly a crossover barrier across a channel 150 N.mi. wide to detect surface vessels transiting parallel to the channel boundaries on course 225 degrees true. The following parameters prevail.

> Visual sweep width: 15 N.mi.
> Track spacing: 25 N.mi.
> Maximum expected target speed: 20 knots
> Aircraft cruising speed: 120 knots

   a. What is the initial true heading of the aircraft on the first leg if the barrier starts on the northwest side of the channel?
   b. What is the time (in hours) required to fly one upsweep along the channel boundary?
   c. What is the time (in hours) required to fly one complete basic element?
   d. What type of crossover barrier results?

    e. What courses of action are open to the patrol squadron commander which would result in an advancing barrier?

2. Preliminary calculations by a task force staff operations officer indicate that utilizing one aircraft under the conditions given, a retiring crossover barrier would result.

Time for target to move two track spacings:	2.50 hours
Time for aircraft to complete one basic element:	2.65 hours
Channel width:	175 N.mi.
Track spacing:	25 N.mi.
Target speed:	20 knots
Aircraft speed:	150 knots

    a. What is the minimum number of aircraft which will change the retiring barrier into either a symmetric or an advancing crossover barrier?

    b. With the number of aircraft determined in part a, how long is the no patrol period if six basic elements are completed (less the last upsweep)?

3. A merchant ship, with an estimated speed of 20 knots on a westerly course, is expected to pass through an approach zone to Haiphong extending 150 N.mi. to the east. A patrol squadron, utilizing aircraft with a cruising speed of 160 knots, has been assigned the task of searching this approach zone and taking photographs of all merchant vessels for intelligence purposes. The time available for visual search and taking photos is from 0600 to 1800 daily, with patrolling to continue for several weeks.

    Assuming the squadron can maintain one aircraft on station for 6 hours at a time, and using a track spacing of not more than 16 N.mi.:

    a. How long will it take the aircraft to fly one complete basic element of its patrol if the approach zone is 100 N.mi. wide?

    b. What type of crossover barrier results?

    c. How many complete basic elements can the aircraft fly within its 6-hour patrol period?

    d. If the aircraft starts its first basic element at 0600, flys its maximum number of complete basic elements, then is relieved on station by a second aircraft which flies the same number of complete basic elements (except the last upsweep), can the mission be fulfilled if patrolling is stopped at this point, then resumed at 0600 the following day?

    e. Explain in what manner the squadron can utilize a number of aircraft to accomplish the mission during the specified daylight hours, specifying n, N and S.

    f. If three aircraft fly parallel sweeps, how many basic elements can they complete before they must be relieved on station by three fresh aircraft?

4. The coverage of a 500-N.mi.-wide channel is required using a barrier with a 95 percent chance of detection. Aircraft search speed will be 190 knots. The best estimate of enemy transiting speed is 18 knots. For existing conditions, the sweep width is 25 N.mi. The inverse cube law for detection is assumed.

    a. What is the maximum track spacing which can be used?

    b. How many aircraft are needed in order to have a symmetric barrier?

c. Using the minimum number of aircraft required, what must be the values of S, M and a?

d. What is the probability of detection?

5. You have been assigned to provide a 90 percent chance of detecting and photo-graphing, during daylight hours, any ship which transits a certain channel for the next two-week period. You must decide how to use your squadron of ten patrol planes most effectively to accomplish the objective. The inverse cube law applies and the following data are known or assumed.

Channel width	100 N.mi.
Maximum search speed	226 knots
Maximum expected target speed	30 knots
Time of sunrise	0430
Time of sunset	2030
Predicted sweep width	30 N.mi.
Aircraft endurance (take-off to landing)	12 hours
Distance of base to channel	80 N.mi.
Maximum number of aircraft airborne at one time	four

a. State the objective of the operation.
b. What measure of effectiveness can be used?
c. What is the maximum allowable track spacing?
d. What is the maximum number of basic elements that can be flown each day?
e. What is the minimum number of aircraft that must be on station?
f. List several possible alternatives. (One, for example, would be to conduct an advancing crossover barrier beginning at 0430 each day using four aircraft, each completing four basic elements with track spacing 22.5 N.mi.)
g. Complete the numerical value of your measure of effectiveness for each alternative.
h. What is the best alternative?

6. A number of aircraft are to be used in a crossover barrier to search a channel during the 14 hours of daylight, and avoid searching during the 10 hours of darkness. Given: The inverse cube law holds, at least a 90 percent probability of detection is required, $u = 20$ knots, $v = 150$ knots, $W = 40$ N.mi., $N \le 4.36$.

a. What is the maximum allowable track spacing?
b. What is the minimum number of aircraft required?
c. Find three different combinations of n, N, S and P(det) that satisfy the requirements and complete the table.

	n	N	S	P(det)
1				
2				
3				

7. An advancing crossover patrol is conducted by n aircraft.

   a. How far up the channel is the first aircraft when N basic elements (less the last upsweep) have been completed?

   b. If the aircraft are based D_2 N.mi. from the channel and the barrier line is placed so that the distance to O_1 from the base is minimum, how long will it take for the aircraft to return to the base after completing the patrol?

   c. If the aircraft are based D_2 miles from the channel, where should the barrier line be placed in order to minimize the distance traveled getting to and from the channel?

8. A destroyer is capable of sonar search at speeds of up to 18 knots. It is to prevent undetected penetration of a barrier by a submerged submarine traveling at 10 knots. The barrier is to be set up in a 10-N.mi.-wide channel and the sonar sweep width at 18 knots is 2 N.mi. What patrol type (crossover or linear) is preferred?

9. a. Compare the probabilities of detection using Case 1 with using Case 2 for a stationary detection platform ($v = 0$).

   b. Which of the answers seems more in accord with earlier models?

   c. Why does the other one differ?

10. a. An ASW helicopter is to protect an area with patrol front length D by dipping its active sonar for time T_{dp} at intervals $2R$ between dips, while traveling parallel to the front at speed v back and forth between boundaries. Transiting submarines enter the area at speed u uniformly distributed across the patrol front on a perpendicular course. Any transitor that closes the helo to within its sweep radius R is detected. Assuming $D \gg R$, derive an expression to estimate the probability that the transitor will be detected.

    b. Use this model to compute the probability of detection where

$$u = 10 \text{ knots} \qquad R = 3 \text{ N.mi.}$$
$$v = 60 \text{ knots} \qquad D = 60 \text{ N.mi.}$$
$$T_{dp} = 0.1 \text{ hour}$$

11. (*Optional problem*) *Monte Carlo computer simulation of back-and-forth patrol:* Develop and use a Monte Carlo computer simulation model.

$$N = \# \text{ of trials (Monte Carlo runs)}$$
$$D = \text{width of patrol front in yards}$$
$$L = \text{length of patrol area in yards}$$
$$W = \text{sweep width of patroller in yards}$$
$$u = \text{transitor speed in knots}$$
$$v = \text{patroller (SSK) speed in knots}$$
$$X1, Y1 = \text{patroller position}$$
$$X2, Y2 = \text{transitor position}$$

Referring to the flow chart that follows, the program logic has:

- Used a 3-minute time step, i.e., moved SSK and transitor in jumps (distances) equivalent to 3 minutes; for example, a ship doing 5 knots would move $5 \times 100 = 500$ yards every 3 minutes.
- Included a step to check the range (C) between SSK and transitor after each move; note that if $C < W/2$, then a detection would occur.

- Started a new run either if a detection occurs *or* if the transitor gets through the patrol (a total length of *L*) without being detected.
- Made provisions to have patroller reverse course each time he reaches the end of his patrol area. A direction value *M* is used to accomplish this; when $M = +1$, the patroller moves in one direction and when $M = -1$, the patroller moves in the other. Note that multiplying *M* by -1 each time the patroller reaches a boundary alternately changes the sign of the direction vector *M*.

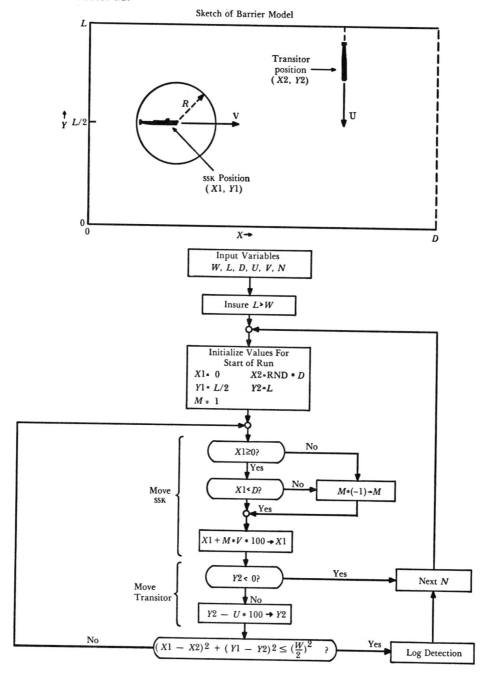

Sketch of Barrier Model

Compare the output values of the simulation with the theoretical (mathematically calculated) values of

$$P_\oplus = \sqrt{1 + \left(\frac{v}{u}\right)^2 + \frac{W^2}{4D^2}\left[1 + \left(\frac{v}{u}\right)^2\right]}.$$

Would you expect the simulation values to be more than, less than or the same as the theoretical values? Why?

9 Sonar Detection

Before a submarine can be attacked, it must be detected and its subsequent positions determined within the requirements of the available weapons system. Detection and position fixing can take place in two ways. There may either be some transfer of energy from the submarine to the searcher, or else the submarine may disturb one of the natural, static, spatial fields, such as the earth's magnetic field, thereby betraying its presence. These magnetic field distortions are detectable at short ranges. However, the anomaly diminishes proportionally with the inverse of the range cubed. Hence, a detection and tracking system which depends upon magnetic anomalies is quite limited in range. For longer range detection and tracking some other natural phenomenon must be exploited.

Electromagnetic waves are propagated with extreme rapidity and to great distances through certain media. However, sea water is essentially impervious to electromagnetic waves for most frequencies. Acoustic pressure waves, while lacking the propagation velocity of electromagnetic waves, are capable of being transmitted through the sea to distances which are operationally significant. Because of this, sonar is the primary sensing system used for antisubmarine warfare, underwater communications and underwater nagivation. Even though sonar is the best existing underwater sensing system, there are many limitations to its effective employment.

The optimal use of sonar requires a thorough understanding of its limitations so that these effects may be minimized. For example, sea water is not uniform in density, pressure, temperature or salinity, and all these characteristics have important effects on sound propagation through the sea. The requirement for predicting these effects on sonar performance has become a necessity, and a difficult one at that. Other operational factors must also be taken into account, such as the size and shape of the enemy submarine, the speed of the searching unit, and so on. This chapter will investigate several of the factors involved in sonar detection and the operational employment of sonar.

901   FUNDAMENTAL CONCEPTS AND UNITS

Consider a vibrating flat plate in the water. As the plate moves back and forth, it pushes the water one way and then the other. As it moves to the right in Figure 9-1, the plate causes an increase in pressure in the water just to its right. This increased pressure is propagated through the water at a certain velocity depending on the temperature, pressure and other conditions of the water. As the plate moves to the left, a region of decreased pressure is created at its right face, and this negative pressure effect is also propagated through the water. If the motion of the plate back and forth is periodic, or more particularly harmonic, the pressure disturbance in the water at a distance, r, from the plate can be expressed as

Equation 9-1 $$p(r,t) = p(r) \sin\left[2\pi\left(ft - \frac{r}{\lambda}\right)\right],$$

where $p(r,t)$ is the pressure expressed as a function of r, the distance from the plate, and t, the time since a particular wave departed the plate. On the right $p(r)$ is the pressure amplitude expressed as a function of r, f is the frequency of vibration in cycles per second and λ is the wavelength. Note the dependence of the amplitude on the distance from the source. The amplitude of a pressure disturbance will always diminish, if interference effects are neglected, with increasing r. The nature of this diminution is an important factor in the discussion which follows.

If the distance is held constant the pressure becomes solely a function of time, and Equation 9-1 simplifies to

Equation 9-2 $$p(t) = p_A \sin\left[2\pi(ft)\right],$$

where p_A is now a constant amplitude.

Each pressure wave, as it passes a point, is capable of causing pressure fluctuations in a small volume of water. It is also capable of moving it back and forth slightly and is thus capable of doing work. Hence, the acoustic wave is a carrier of energy. Imagine a surface perpendicular to the direction of propagation of the wave train, and on this surface consider an area, A, as shown in Figure 9-2. The time rate of energy transfer is power, and the power divided by the area through which it is flowing is termed the

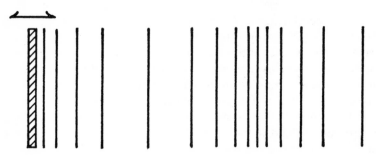

Figure 9-1.

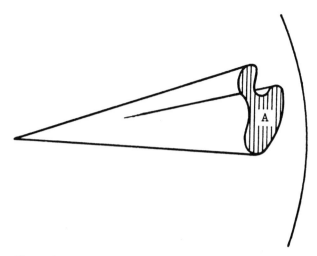

Figure 9-2.

power density, or intensity. It can be shown that the average intensity is related to the pressure at any point in the ocean by

Equation 9-3
$$I = \frac{p^2_{rms}}{\rho c},$$

where p_{rms} is the *root mean square* pressure, ρ is the density of the water and c is the velocity of sound in the water. The root mean square pressure is the square root of the average instantaneous pressure squared during one cycle of vibration. This term is often encountered in acoustics and other engineering fields. For the remainder of this chapter, whenever the term pressure is used, it will be understood to mean the average intensity. The product of the two terms ρ and c in Equation 9-3 is known as the *specific acoustic impedance*. The importance of Equation 9-3 is that it clearly shows the dependence of the power transmitting capacity of a train of acoustic waves on the pressure. If the *rms* pressure in the water can be measured, then the sound intensity can be determined. One way to do this is by means of a hydrophone. A hydrophone is merely an electrical-acoustic device, much like a microphone, which transforms variations in water pressure into a variable electric voltage. Thus, after appropriate calibration, p_{rms} can be read directly from a voltmeter attached to the output of a hydrophone.

A convenient system is needed in order to measure and discuss these quantities. In general, the metric system is used in the field of underwater acoustics. Pressure is expressed in dynes per square centimeter and intensity defined in terms of ergs per second per square centimeter or watts per square meter. A frequently encountered unit of pressure is the *microbar,* which is equivalent to *one dyne/cm².*

A fact of considerable importance is the range of pressures over which the human ear is sensitive. The ear can hear and withstand pressure disturbances up to 1,000 microbars, and can hear pressure disturbances as small as .0001 microbar. A problem is encountered when discussing pressures that vary over so great a range—the minimum audible disturbance is one ten millionth that of the maximum. In underwater acoustics useful pressures having even greater variations in magnitude are commonly encountered. In order to make the numbers more manageable, the logarithms* are used rather than the numbers themselves. Suppose two acoustic signals are to be compared, one having an *rms* pressure of 10,000 microbars, the other .0001 microbar. Their ratio would be

$$\frac{p_1}{p_2} = \frac{10,000}{.0001} = 100,000,000,$$

a very cumbersome number. Notice the simplification, however, when the logarithm of these ratios is taken:

$$\log \frac{p_1}{p_2} = \log (p_1) - \log (p_2) = 4 - (-4) = 8.$$

It is customary in engineering work to multiply the logarithm by a multiple of 10, such as,

$$10 \log \left(\frac{x_1}{x_2}\right) = 80, \; 20 \log \left(\frac{p_1}{p_2}\right) = 160, \text{ etc.}$$

and to refer to the result as the number of *decibels*. Note that in actuality the result is dimensionless, since it involves the logarithm of a ratio of two quantities having identical units.

In underwater acoustics, the attribute of primary interest is *intensity*. Acoustic intensity comparisons are expressed in decibels. Comparisons may be made at some point in the sea between sounds originating from different sources, or at different points in the sea between sounds from the same source. Comparisons can also be made between the acoustic intensity of a sound and a *standard intensity*, denoted I_0,

$$10 \log (I/I_0) \text{ db} = \text{sound intensity } level.$$

The word *level* is italicized here to emphasize that it is associated with the decibel scale. Thus, one speaks of a sound intensity *ratio*, I/I_0, but the sound intensity *level* would always be

$$10 \log (I/I_0).$$

The intensity is most often expressed as a function of pressure. Recalling Equation 9-3,

$$I = \frac{p^2}{\rho c},$$

so that

$$I_0 = \frac{p_0{}^2}{\rho c},$$

and this ratio in decibels would be

$$10 \log (I/I_0) = 10 \log \left(\frac{p^2}{p_0{}^2}\right)$$

$$= 10 \log \left(\frac{p}{p_0}\right)^2$$

$$= 20 \log \left(\frac{p}{p_0}\right).$$

*The term *log* in this text denotes a logarithm to the base 10. The term *ln* denotes the natural or Napierian logarithm.

Two equivalent expressions have now been defined, which can be used interchangeably when the units are compatible. They are

Equation 9-4 $\text{sound intensity level} = 10 \log \left(\dfrac{I}{I_0} \right),$

and

Equation 9-5 $\text{sound pressure level} = 20 \log \left(\dfrac{p}{p_0} \right).$

The *pressure* and *intensity standards* for underwater acoustics are generally taken to be *one microbar* and *one watt/cm²*, respectively. For airborne sounds, the standards are .0002 *microbar* and 10^{-16} *watt/cm²*, respectively. Care must be exercised that the correct standards are used.

It may be that an acoustic signal is amplified by some device. Consider a sound having an intensity I_s in the sea just adjacent to a hydrophone. The hydrophone converts the sound to an electrical signal which might then be amplified and fed into a set of earphones which convert the electrical signal back to airborne acoustic waves. If the output of the earphones has an intensity of I_a, then the *gain* of the hydrophone-amplifier-earphone system is

Equation 9-6 $\text{gain} = 10 \log \left(\dfrac{I_a}{I_s} \right).$

If $I_a > I_s$ the gain is positive, if $I_a < I_s$ the gain is negative, and if $I_a = I_s$ the gain is zero.

A hydrophone and an earphone are both examples of *transducers,* a device which converts power from one transmission medium to another. Converting waterborne acoustic power to electrical power is the function of the hydrophone, a receiving transducer. In the example, the earphone was a transmitting transducer. The sonar transmitting transducer is referred to simply as the transducer as a matter of custom.

902 SOUND PROPAGATION THROUGH THE SEA

Consider a source of sound located in the sea. The intensity of the sound can be measured at any point in the sea, near to or far from the source. For purposes of measuring intensity at the source, the intensity measurement is generally taken at one unit from the source and labeled I_S. The intensity can then be measured at any distant point where a hydrophone is located and denoted I_R. It is operationally significant to compare the two values. One way to do this is to form the ratio I_S/I_R. Note that if the ratio, denoted n, is greater than unity, the intensity at the source is greater than at the receiver. Furthermore, by comparing the measured intensities to a standard intensity we find that

$$I_S/I_R = \frac{I_S/I_0}{I_R/I_0},$$

and if we let

$$n = \frac{I_S/I_0}{I_R/I_0},$$

then

$$10 \log n = 10 \log (I_S/I_0) - 10 \log (I_R/I_0)$$
$$= \text{sound intensity signal level at the source minus}$$
$$\text{the sound intensity level at the receiver.}$$

10 log n is called the *transmission loss* and is labeled N_W. Thus

$$N_W = \text{(signal level at source)} - \text{(signal level of receiver)},$$

or

Equation 9-7 $$N_W = L_S - L_R,$$

where L_S and L_R stand for the signal level, i.e., sound intensity level of the acoustic signal, at the source and receiver respectively.

Most of the factors that influence transmission loss have been accounted for by scientific research. It is known that *spreading loss, surface boundary loss, bottom boundary loss, sound velocity distribution* and *attenuation due to absorption and scattering* all have significant effects, and each of these factors will be discussed separately.

903 SPREADING LOSS

To understand *spreading loss,* it is convenient to imagine a theoretical ocean which has no boundaries and in which every point has the same physical properties as any other point, i.e., an infinite, homogenous medium. In such a medium, sound energy would propagate from a point source in all directions along straight paths and would have a spherical wave front.

Assuming no losses due to absorption, the change in intensity with radial distance from the point source would be due only to the spherical divergence of energy, i.e., there would be no loss of energy due to spherical divergence as might be implied by the term *spreading loss,* but the energy would be spread over a larger surface area, thus reducing the intensity. For this model, the intensity of energy passing through the surface of a sphere of radius r, centered at a point source, is expressed by

$$I_r = \frac{P_t}{4\pi r^2} \text{ watts/m}^2,$$

where P_t is the acoustic power radiated omnidirectionally from the source. The intensity of this sound at a distance of one unit from the source will be labeled I_S, and is given by

$$I_S = \frac{P_t}{4\pi(1)^2}.$$

The transmission loss is therefore

$$10 \log \left(\frac{I_S}{I_r}\right) = 10 \log r^2,$$

or

Equation 9-8 $$N_W = 20 \log r.$$

Equation 9-8 represents *spherical divergence* of sound energy. The power per unit area decreases as the area of the sphere encompassing the wave front increases, i.e., is inversely proportional to the square of the distance.*

The ocean is not an unbounded medium however, and all sources are not omnidirectional point sources. For sources that radiate energy only in a horizontal direction,

---

*Any units for range may be used provided the reference intensity is measured in the same units.

sound energy diverges more like the surface of an expanding cylinder. Also, since the ocean is bounded at the surface and bottom, *cylindrical divergence* is usually assumed for ranges that are large compared to the depth of the water. The transmission loss for cylindrical divergence is given by

Equation 9-9 $N_W = 10 \log r.$

904   SURFACE BOUNDARY

The surface boundary acts as a perfect reflector of sound energy when the sea surface is relatively smooth. When the surface is rough, there is scattering of incident energy in various directions. There is also some scattering of sound energy because of the formation of air bubbles in rough seas.

To illustrate the effect of surface reflection, assume that a point source radiates energy in a homogeneous medium bounded only at the surface. The sound pressure reaching a point of reception at a distance r from the source would be a combination of the pressure wave traveling via the surface reflection and the pressure wave traveling directly from the source. The surface reflected wave would experience a 180-degree phase shift at reflection and possibly some loss in amplitude due to scattering. Since the phase of a pressure wave at the point of reception is a function of the distance traveled, the difference in path length also contributes to the difference in phase of the two pressure waves. Therefore, it is very likely that the two pressure waves arriving at the point of reception are not in phase. The combined pressure wave could vary from smaller than to larger than that received via the direct path. The effect of surface reflection is sometimes attributed to the *Lloyd's Mirror Effect* which was discussed in Chapter five.

The amount of sound transmitted into the air at the surface is comparatively negligible, and one may assume that all of the incident energy is reflected.

905   BOTTOM BOUNDARY

The bottom boundary affects the transmission of sound in much the same way as the surface boundary. The sound energy loss due to scattering at bottom reflection is related to wave length and bottom roughness. However, it is not a perfect reflector; a considerable amount of the incident energy is absorbed by the bottom material. There may or may not be a phase shift at bottom reflection, depending upon the characteristics of the bottom and the angle of incidence of the sound wave front.

The depth of the water also has important effects on the amount of energy received via the bottom reflected path. In deep water, with the source and receiver relatively near the surface, there are intervals between bottom reflections where the only sound energy present is that propagated via other paths. A plot of sound intensity versus range will show fluctuations at certain range intervals due to the arrival of bottom reflected energy.

In shallow water, sound energy is reflected back and forth between the surface and the bottom to such an extent that the mathematical models used to describe the propagation of sound in such cases become extremely complicated.

906   SOUND PROPAGATION CHARACTERISTICS

Contrary to the assumptions made up to this point, the ocean is not a homogeneous medium, and the velocity of sound varies from point to point in the ocean. This variation in sound velocity is one of the most important characteristics affecting the transmission of sound.

The three main factors affecting the velocity of sound in the ocean are *temperature, salinity* and *pressure*. The relationship of these factors is given empirically by

Equation 9-10 $c = 1448.6 + 4.63t - 0.0538t^2 + 0.000354t^3 + 1.307(s - 35)$
$$- 0.0170t(s - 35) + 0.01815z$$

where

$c =$ sound velocity in yards per second,
$t =$ temperature in degrees Fahrenheit,
$s =$ salinity in parts per thousand, and
$z =$ depth in yards.

Of these three factors, temperature has the greatest effect on the variation in sound velocity. Near the surface, large variations in temperature are common, because of the heating, cooling and mixing of the surface water. Sound velocity varies almost in proportion to the temperature variations in the upper part of the ocean. In the deep ocean, below approximately 500 fathoms, temperature is almost constant and the sound velocity gradient is fairly stable, with the change due mainly to pressure.

The rate of change of the velocity of sound in any one of the three space coordinates is called a *velocity gradient*. For almost all operational problems, the velocity gradient with respect to horizontal changes of location can be taken as being zero. The major gradient of interest is the vertical gradient, dc/dz, where z is distance below the surface. If a source of sound at the surface of the sea radiates omnidirectionally, a wave front expanding from this source in all directions transfers energy from one particle in the water to another, and by this means the wave is propagated. If we select some point on this wave front and from it draw a line in the direction of energy propagation, then connecting these points as the wave expands in space will result in a line called a *ray* (Figure 9-3).

The angle that any ray makes with the vertical is called the angle of incidence and is related to the velocity of propagation at any point by Snell's Law,

Equation 9-11 $$\frac{\sin \theta}{c} = \text{constant, for any ray.}$$

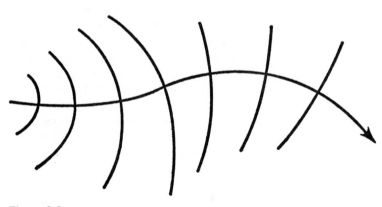

Figure 9-3.

This important relationship states that for any particular ray with velocity of propagation equal to c, the angle of incidence will always be θ, regardless of the position along the ray. It follows that the direction of energy propagation will vary as the sound velocity varies. In antisubmarine warfare, this variation can produce pronounced operational effects, as will be seen shortly.

Consider the comparatively simple situation wherein the velocity gradient is constant, i.e., the incremental change in velocity for each unit increase in depth is the same. This might occur if the water temperature and salinity were constant in the surface layer. In this layer the pressure will, of course, increase as the depth increases, resulting in a constant positive velocity gradient. For such a situation, the velocity at any depth would be given by

Equation 9-12 $$c(z) = c_0 + gz$$

where $c(z)$ is the velocity at depth z; g is the velocity gradient, dc/dz, which is a constant; and c_0 is the velocity at the surface. The problem is to determine what happens to the rays of acoustic energy in this environment. From Snell's Law

$$\frac{\sin \theta}{c} = \frac{\sin (\theta + \Delta\theta)}{c + \Delta c}.$$

In this expression $\Delta\theta$ and Δc are merely changes in the angle of incidence and the propagation velocity, respectively. Cross multiplying yields

$$c \sin \theta + \Delta c \sin \theta = c \sin (\theta + \Delta\theta).$$

Transposing and dividing both sides by $\Delta\theta$ gives

$$\frac{c [\sin (\theta + \Delta\theta) - \sin \theta]}{\Delta\theta} = \frac{\Delta c}{\Delta\theta} \sin \theta.$$

It can be seen from Equation 9-11 that in the limit as Δc approaches zero, $\Delta\theta$ will approach zero. Then, recalling the definition of a derivative,

$$\frac{c [d(\sin \theta)]}{d\theta} = \frac{dc}{d\theta} (\sin \theta),$$

which is

Equation 9-13 $$c \cos \theta = \frac{dc}{d\theta} (\sin \theta).$$

Applying the chain rule of derivatives and letting s denote the path length,

$$\frac{dc}{d\theta} = \frac{dc}{dz} \cdot \frac{dz}{ds} \cdot \frac{ds}{d\theta}.$$

Substituting this for $dc/d\theta$ in Equation 9-13 and letting $dc/dz = g$, the gradient, and $dz/dx = \cos \theta$ gives

Equation 9-14 $$c \cos \theta \frac{d\theta}{ds} = g \sin \theta \cos \theta.$$

Canceling $\cos \theta$ on both sides and noting that the radius R of any curve is $ds/d\theta$, gives the important result

Ray Radius (handwritten)

Equation 9-15
$$R = \frac{c}{g \sin \theta},$$

which can be seen to be a constant since we have assumed g to be constant and, from Equation 9-11, $c/\sin \theta$ is a constant for any particular ray. Hence the radius of any ray path can be calculated by taking c and θ for the ray at *any point* along the ray. The ray path can be plotted by swinging an arc of the correct radius through the point at which c and θ were observed. When the gradient is positive, the rays curve upward, i.e., away from the region of higher velocity. When the gradient is negative, the rays curve downward.

4-37 (handwritten)

The situation is illustrated in Figure 9-4, which depicts two sources of sound, one at the surface, the second deeper. At the left of the figure are shown three gradient profiles, each with respect to depth. One of these, shown by the solid line, is the temperature gradient. It can be seen that the temperature is constant in the layer of water near the surface. This constant temperature, or isothermal condition, is caused by the mixing action of wind and waves and is common over much of the surface of the ocean. Below this isothermal layer, the temperature can be seen to fall off at a more or less constant rate. The pressure gradient is shown by the broken line. The pressure increases constantly with depth. The combination of these two gradients leads, through Equation 9-10, to the idealized velocity gradient shown by the dashed line. In the surface layer, the temperature is constant and the pressure increase with increasing depth causes a slightly positive velocity gradient. Below the isothermal layer, the effect of temperature predominates over the pressure effect producing the negative gradient of velocity. In this discussion the salinity effect has been neglected.

From the surface sound source in Figure 9-4, the ray, emanating from that source at the lowest angle, has an angle of incidence equal to θ. The dashed line is tangent to this ray at the source. Perpendicular to this dashed line, hence also to the ray at the source, is a radius line extending upward to the right and having a length given by

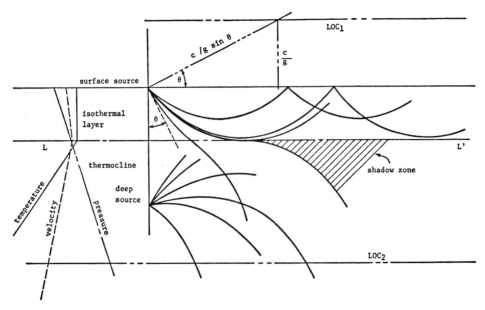

Figure 9-4.

Equation 9-15, where c is the velocity of sound at the surface. The ray follows the path of an arc of radius R downward until it reaches the boundary, denoted LL', separating the isothermal layer from the region below. At this boundary, the radius of curvature changes because the gradient changes and the ray begins to curve downward. The region below this boundary is called the *thermocline*.

The two lines labeled LOC_1 and LOC_2 are the loci of centers of curvature for ray paths emanating from the surface source. LOC_1 is the locus of centers for the ray paths as they traverse the isothermal layer, while LOC_2 is the locus for surface source rays propagated through the thermocline. Each of the loci is positioned above or below the depth level at which the rays either originate or enter a region of constant velocity gradient. The distance above or below the appropriate level is given by c/g, where c is the velocity at the point of ray origin or entry into the region in which the gradient, g, prevails.

The behavior of the rays emitted by the deep source are identical in principle to those emitted at the surface. Some of them are emitted at a high enough angle so that they enter the surface layer and are refracted upward. The rest are refracted downward.

The vertical scale in Figure 9-4 has been exaggerated for purposes of illustration. In actuality, the radii of curvature are on the order of 50 miles from the sources; hence the curvatures of the rays, while very significant operationally, would look very much like straight lines if plotted to scale. The radius of curvature of a ray emitted in a horizontal direction is less than that of any other ray emitted from the same source. The radius of a ray emitted vertically is infinite, i.e., the ray goes straight up or down without refraction. For any other ray, the radius lies somewhere in between. Owing to exaggeration of the vertical scale, the impression is given that some of the rays not emitted vertically will be refracted to the vertical direction. Inspection of Equation 9-15 shows that this cannot happen unless the velocity falls to zero, which is an impossibility in the ocean.

It is fairly easy to construct ray paths when the velocity gradient is a constant. This is rarely the case; but if the gradient is measured, it can be approximated by a succession of constant gradients. The rays can then be drawn as arcs in each of the regions approximated by the linear gradients. Consider Figure 9-5, in which a typical velocity gradient is shown on the left as a solid line and its linear approximations are shown alongside as dashed lines. The ray which emerges from the source and is just tangent to the bottom of the isothermal layer splits. Some of its energy is refracted back

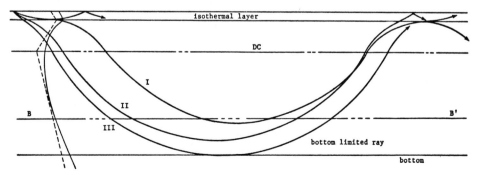

Figure 9-5.

to the surface where it is reflected, and some of it penetrates the layer boundary and is refracted into the deeper water. That part of the ray which is refracted downward, labeled I, curves downward until it crosses the horizontal broken line labeled DC, which is the depth corresponding to minimum sound velocity. At this depth the ray begins to curve upward because the effects of water density have begun to dominate the effects of temperature gradient. As it becomes horizontal, at its greatest depth, the velocity of sound is the same as it was when the ray was horizontal to the bottom of the isothermal layer. This is in accordance with Snell's Law. Another ray, starting out at the lower angle and labeled II, is refracted along a path similar in shape to the first. The two rays separate at first and then converge near the surface to the right. This convergence represents an increase in acoustic intensity, since the closer together the ray paths the greater the intensity of the acoustic waves. The ray labeled III, called the *bottom limited ray,* is the lowest convergent ray. There may be several such *convergence zones* as these rays are reflected from the surface and undergo similar refraction paths farther from the source. Notice that the existence of the convergence zones depends on the velocity gradient and the water depth. If the bottom were located along the line labeled BB', no convergence zone could exist because the rays would strike the bottom before they could become horizontal. As will be shown subsequently, the greater the acoustic intensity arriving at a target, the greater the probability of its being detected. Hence the existence of these convergence zones is of utmost importance in antisubmarine warfare.

Rays which do strike the bottom are also of considerable interest. Such rays may be reflected back towards the surface. They may also experience re-reflection downward after reaching the surface. It is not unusual for a ray to travel several times between the bottom and surface, and for detection of submarines to take place in a *shadow zone* as shown in Figure 9-4, by means of rays following such an indirect route.

In Figure 9-6, the *bottom bounce* phenomenon is illustrated. The bottom bounce ray path can be seen making several reflections off the surface and bottom. At each reflection, there is a loss of acoustic intensity from scattering, and additionally at the bottom from absorption of sound energy.

Notice the rays originating at the source located on the line labeled DC. Rays having an initial direction above the horizontal are refracted downward until they cross DC. They are then refracted back upward, and so on. Rays starting in a direction below the horizontal are refracted upward. It can be seen then that some rays originating from this source are trapped, thus suffering very little decrease in intensity due to surface scattering and bottom absorption. Their spreading loss will be cylindrical rather than spherical. Under these conditions propagation of sound to great

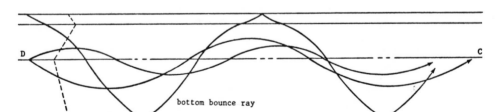

Figure 9-6.

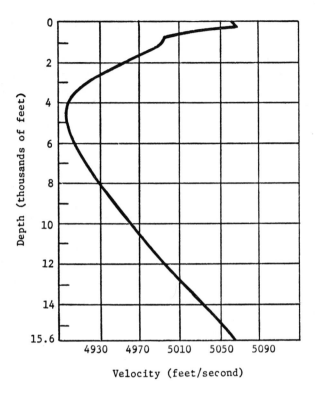

Velocity profile used for ray-diagram computations.

Figure 9-7.

distances is possible. The *SO*und *F*ixing *A*nd *R*anging system (SOFAR) utilizes this *deep channel* for very long-distance underwater detection and communications. It would be possible for survivors of a shipwreck to detonate a four- or five-pound charge of TNT in this channel and have it heard at distances of 1,000 miles. The sound of the explosion could be triangulated by SOFAR stations, thus fixing the position of the survivors.

The ray paths illustrated here are idealized approximations to those found in the oceans of the world. The principles of refraction discussed are precise however, and are used by acoustic engineers and scientists to predict and plot ray paths. Figure 9-7 is a typical sound velocity profile. This profile can be closely approximated by a series of straight lines. The greater the number of line segments used, the more accurate will be the approximation. For each such region of constant (approximately straight line) velocity gradient, the circular ray paths can thus be plotted. One ray-plotting technique uses a computer program to plot the rays as short straight line segments. [1]

907 ATTENUATION

Attenuation of sound energy in sea water arises through the action of two independent factors, *absorption* and *scattering*.

a. Absorption. The primary causes of absorption have been attributed to *viscous absorption*, *thermal relaxation* and *chemical relaxation*. All three of these forms of absorption are caused by the repeated pressure fluctuations in the medium as sound waves are propagated. The frequency of the sound wave, temperature of the water and the amount of $MgSO_4$ (magnesium sulfate) appear to be the primary factors influencing the variation in the magnitude of the loss due to absorption. Of these three factors, the frequency of the sound wave causes the most significant variation in the attenuation. Fortunately, frequency is a controllable variable in the design of active sonar systems. **b. Scattering.** Foreign bodies influence the transmission of sound primarily by the scattering of sound energy, i.e., by reflection and refraction. The amount of energy scattered is a function of size, density and concentration of foreign bodies present in the sound path, as well as the frequency of the sound wave. These foreign bodies are usually in the form of suspended particles, marine life or bubbles.

Attenuation increases rapidly as the frequency of the sound wave increases. For frequencies below 100 kilocycles, the attenuation coefficient, a, is approximately

$$a = 33.0 \times 10^{-6} \ f^{3/2} \, db/yd, \quad \text{where } f \text{ is the frequency in kilohertz.}$$

This relationship is of major importance to the naval tactician. It tells him that if higher frequencies are chosen for sonar operation in order to achieve greater target definition, the price he must pay is greater attenuation. The higher the frequency, the greater the attenuation and, in general, the less the range of detection, all other things being equal.

908 TRANSMISSION LOSS MODEL

It would be useful to have a simple mathematical relationship that would describe the effects of the various factors influencing transmission loss as they occur in the ocean. But the state of the physical conditions encountered in the ocean is very complex and not at all easy to represent. A few mathematical models do exist which provide close approximations for some sets of conditions, but, at present, no single model accounts for all the conditions encountered.

A simplified model used to obtain approximate values of transmission loss is

Equation 9-16 $N_W = 20 \log r + ar + A$

where $20 \log r$ is due to spreading, ar is due to attenuation, and A is the transmission anomaly which takes into account all the other factors such as refraction and reflection.

It is also important to realize that sound transmission in the ocean is three-dimensional, and the transmission loss versus horizontal range alone is not sufficient information for most operational situations. Areas of no sonar coverage occur at various intervals of range because of refraction, reflection and interference between waves traveling via different paths.

909 PASSIVE SONAR EQUATION [2]

The key to success in antisubmarine warfare is initial detection. For this work, the major sensor in use today is sonar, both active and passive. An understanding of sonar can only be achieved through a comprehension of the *sonar equation* and the concept called *figure of merit*. Unfortunately, the majority of operators in the Navy today, both senior and junior, have not taken time out to think through and learn these two simple concepts. Therefore, the purpose of this section is to spell out the sonar equation and figure of merit, to state the specifics of their usefulness and to indicate how the various parameters in the sonar equation, including the figure of merit, can be measured.

The possible detection range of particular equipment should be known, so that a tactician will then have a measure of the sonar's capability and a feel for what the sonar can do in a given tactical situation. Unfortunately, with *no* change in basic sonar capability, its detection capability in yards of range can change by a factor of two to six or even greater, simply because the ocean itself has changed. To state this another way, sonar equipment can only be designed to detect the arrival of a certain sound energy intensity. The range from which that sound intensity arrives is highly dependent on how much energy was lost en route. So *do not* try to measure the capability of sonar by detection range, but *do* try to understand that the capability of a sonar can only be measured by its ability to detect a certain level of sound energy intensity just outboard of its hydrophone array. Detection range is therefore a poor measure of sonar capability. There is, in fact, a much better measure. The key to this better measure is to separate in your mind the sonar from the ocean in which it must operate. Then sonar capability can be discussed in terms of the unchanging sonar hardware and ship as distinguished from the ever-changing ocean.

The *better* measure for sonar capability is called *figure of merit*. It is *not* range-dependent, and yet it can be related to range when propagation loss is known in terms of range. It is a direct and measurable indication of sonar capability.

The figure of merit is actually the sum of several parameters in the *passive sonar equation*. The sonar equation itself is mainly a specialized statement of the law of conservation of energy. To develop the sonar equation, the following thought steps must be taken:

a. Consider that the target radiates a certain sound energy intensity level. This is labeled L_S and measured in decibels.

b. En route to the ship, the sound intensity is diminished because of any one or more of the following: *spreading, ray path bending, absorption, reflection* and *scattering*. The decrease in intensity level due to this propagation loss is labeled N_W and is also measured in decibels. Hence the intensity level of the signal arriving at the ship is $L_S - N_W$.

c. The immediate surroundings of the ship's sonar array are noisy because of any one or more of the following: *sea state, own machinery, water flow past the array hydrophones* and *biologics*. The sonar can only detect that signal which is of an appropriate value relative to its background noise. This *background noise* is usually measured by an omnidirectional hydrophone and its value is labeled L_N. The array itself is directional and will discriminate against omnidirectional noise. Hence, the background noise measured inboard of the hydrophone array will actually be less than the noise measured by an adjacent omnidirectional hydrophone. The background noise measured on the inboard side of the ship's hydrophone array circuitry is given by $L_N - N_{DI}$, where N_{DI} is the measure of the advantageous effect of the array directivity. N_{DI} is called *directivity index*.

d. Consider now the value of a signal arriving at the ship which is greater than the ship's background noise measured inboard of the hydrophone array. This is:

$$L_S - N_W - (L_N - N_{DI}).$$

Arriving   Background
signal   noise
intensity

This in effect is the signal-to-noise ratio which is *provided* to the sonar operator. If the average value of this *provided* signal-to-noise ratio is exactly equal to what an operator *requires,* i.e.,

$$provided = required,$$

then it follows that a detection should occur. Thus, one can write

Equation 9-17 $(L_S - N_W) - (L_N - N_{DI}) = N_{RD}.$

N_{RD} is the label for *recognition differential,* which is defined as the *signal minus noise level required inboard of the hydrophone array in order that an operator can detect a target.* Actually, the business of detecting a sonar signal is a chance process for several reasons, one of which is that a human being is involved. Hence, the definition of N_{RD} is normally qualified by adding *in order than an operator can detect a target on* 50 *percent of those occasions for which a target presents itself.*

Thus if the average value of provided signal/noise *equals* the average of required signal/noise, then a detection occurs in 50 percent of the times that a detection could occur.

If (average) provided is *greater than* (average) required, the detection probability increases up to 100 percent, while if (average) provided is *less than* (average) required, the detection probability decreases down to zero percent. In summary:

Average provided = Average required, detection probability 50 percent;
Average provided > Average required, 50 percent to 100 percent;
Average provided < Average required, 50 percent to zero percent.

Note that the instantaneous value of the provided or required values of signal to noise can vary over a wide range of values because of the variability of operators and operators' moods, as well as time fluctuations in propagation loss, target radiated signal and own ship noise. Hence, while the average value of provided signal to noise may be less than the average value of required signal to noise, at times provided (instantaneous) may be greater than required (instantaneous), and a detection may occur. Thus a probability greater than zero exists even though the provided (average) is less than the required (average).

This section and the following section assume these average values consistently to be the precise values, thereby employing a *deterministic* approach.

Equation 9-17 is called the *passive sonar equation.* It expresses the relationship between all the parameters involved for a passive sonar detection.

The sonar equation as written in Equation 9-17 can be made more useful and meaningful by placing all range-dependent terms on one side. Thus we have

Equation 9-18 $N_W = L_S - (L_N - N_{DI}) - N_{RD}.$ = Figure of merit

All the parameters on the right side of the equation can be determined with no knowledge of range. To review:

L_S is target radiated noise,
L_N is the omnidirectional background noise,
N_{DI} is directivity index, and
N_{RD} is the operator's recognition differential, i.e., the
    required signal/noise.

The expression $L_S - (L_N - N_{DI}) - N_{RD}$ is given the name *figure of merit*. It follows that:

a. Figure of merit is allowable transmission loss, N_W, for 50 percent probability of detection.

b. Figure of merit can be measured by:

  (1) assuming a value for L_S, and
  (2) measuring N_{DI}, L_N, N_{RD}.

To illustrate how figure of merit can be used to specify sonar capability, consider the following example:

We wish to compare equipment A's detection capability to that of equipment B. Both sonars are on ships operating in sea state two, with own ship's machinery and flow noise less than sea state noise, and both against a submarine target making 5 knots (noncavitating).

a. For equipment A (at a frequency of 2 kilohertz):

L_N as specified by sea state two	$= -43$ db
N_{DI} might be	$= +12$ db
N_{RD} for an average operator using audio detection	$= -\ 3$ db
L_S for the submarine target at 5 knots	$= +14$ db
Figure of merit, $L_S - (L_N - N_{DI}) - N_{RD}$	$=\ \ \ \ 72$ db

b. For equipment B (at a frequency of 2 kilohertz):

L_N is same	$= -43$ db
N_{DI} might be higher because of sophisticated processing equipment	$= +21$ db
N_{RD} for average operator using special processing equipment	$= -15$ db
L_S for the same submarine target at 5 knots	$= +14$ db
Figure of merit	$=\ \ \ \ 93$ db

Hence, the equipment B sonar in a sea state two against the submarine target is 21 decibels better than using equipment A under similar conditions.

Remembering the figure of merit equals N_W, the example can be interpreted as follows:

a. Equipment A (with parameters as defined) can suffer a propagation loss of 72 decibels and still obtain a detection (probability 50 percent).

b. Equipment B (with parameters as defined) can suffer a propagation loss of 93 decibels and still obtain a detection (probability 50 percent).

c. Equipment B (as defined) can suffer 21 decibels greater propagation loss than equipment A (as defined) and still make a detection (probability 50 percent).

Hence, with *no* knowledge of the intervening propagation path between the ship and target, a quantitative comparison of two sonars has been made. To interpret this comparison in terms of range, a quantitative knowledge of range versus propagation loss must be known. Herein lies the complication of using range as a criterion for sonar capability, for detection range versus propagation loss varies widely in the various ocean operating areas of the world. Furthermore, a very small change in the figure of merit can sometimes mean a great change in detection range.

Propagation loss always increases with range. However, in different ocean areas and for different modes of sound transmission, the rate of increase of propagation loss with range varies dramatically. In the previous example, it was shown that the higher figure of merit gear can detect much farther than the other gear if both equipment must face the same propagation loss versus range. Moreover, equipment B can operate in a higher loss area than equipment A and still perhaps make a detection at a comparable range. To determine the exact numerical difference in detection range performance, a curve of propagation loss versus range is needed. A typical curve is shown in Figure 9-8 for propagation loss in water adjacent to Iceland. (Note that receiver and source were both at 50 feet for these measurements and frequency of transmission is specified at 2 kilohertz.) There are actually three different modes of sound transmission: *direct path, bottom bounce,* and *convergence zone propagation.* Hence, three curves or sets of curves are needed to relate propagation loss versus all ranges.

To estimate an initial detection range prediction for equipment A, enter the curve at 72 decibels propagation loss since figure of merit equals N_W (propagation loss). For direct path transmission, the detection range is 3,500 yards (upper square in Figure 9-8, probability 50 percent). A range by bottom bounce and by convergence zone is impossible. For equipment B at 93 decibels (lower squares in Figure 9-8), the following detection ranges can be found (probability 50 percent): direct path 18,000 yards; bottom bounce 41,000 yards (via the first bottom bounce); and convergence zone path 70,000 yards (out to first convergence zone).

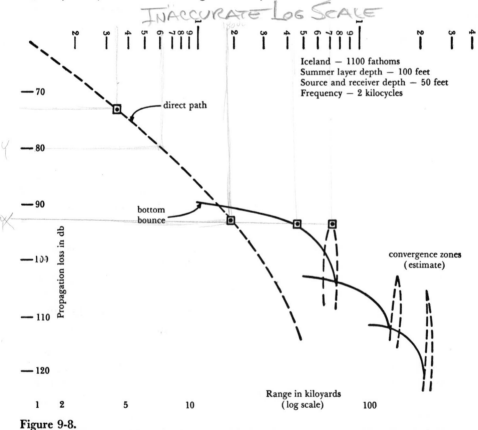

Figure 9-8.

It can be seen that the difference in 21 decibels of figure of merit can make a tremendous difference in initial detection range.

In fact, if equipment A's figure of merit were increased by the following steps:

a. **A signal processing** procedure used instead of the operator's ear for initial detection, N_{RD} might then be -15 decibels vice -3 decibels;

b. **The submarine target** increases its speed to perhaps 16 knots (still managing not to cavitate), L_S might then be 23 decibels vice 14 decibels; then,

the net increase in equipment A's figure of merit would be $12 + 9$ or 21 decibels. The new figure of merit would now be 93 decibels, and under the new conditions, equipment A would make detections at the same range as equipment B had under the old conditions.

Figure 9-9 shows the value of propagation loss versus range for a different area, the Norwegian Sea. The layer depth is still at 100 feet, the season still summer. However, now the receiver is below the layer, while the source is above. The tabulated results of the two figures of merit [72 for equipment A (circle); 93 for equipment B (asterisks)] in the Norwegian Sea area are listed and the values for the Iceland area are repeated for comparison in the table (Figure 9-10).

If propagation loss versus range were examined for other geographic areas, *or* for other layer depths, *or* for situations where the source and receiver were not as specified

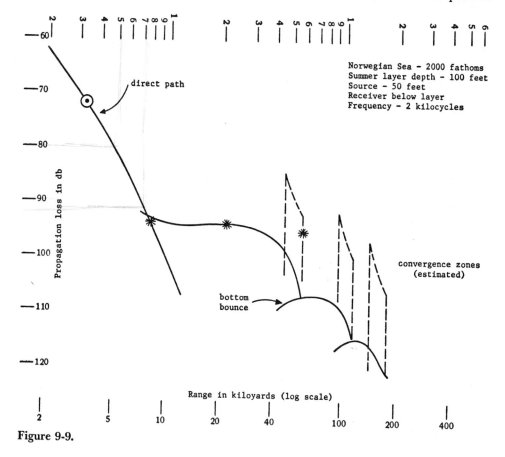

Figure 9-9.

	Equipment A Audio	Equipment B Signal Processing	Equipment A Audio	Equipment B Signal Processing
Figure of merit in db	72	93	72	93
Area	Norwegian Sea		Iceland area	
Direct path	3,300	8,000	3,500	18,000
First bottom bounce	impossible	22,000	impossible	41,000
First convergence	impossible	58,000	impossible	70,000
Points labelled on figure				

Figure 9-10.

in these examples, it would be found that propagation loss versus range continued to vary widely with the changing environment. A ship, sonar and target, placed in each of these environments in turn, would experience entirely different detection ranges in each case with no change in actual sonar capability.

Since the capability of sonar is finally determined by the amount of signal it can detect just outboard of its hydrophone array, and since this capability is completely independent of range or propagation loss, the figure of merit, which provides a numerical value for the capability, is a far more meaningful measure of sonar performance. Naturally, to the tactician, detection ranges are of prime importance. The figure of merit is readily usable to convert directly to range *if* propagation loss versus range can be determined by some other means. The nature of the many factors affecting transmission or propagation loss becomes more apparent if discussed in terms of the three modes of sound transmission.

Direct path is, as its name indicates, direct from target to receiver. The direct path is affected drastically by ray path bending due to the change in sound velocity with ocean temperature. In isovelocity water, the major cause of energy loss is due to spreading of the energy as it travels farther from the source. In highly refractive water (larger thermal gradients), the spreading loss is compounded by ray path bending. While the sound velocity profile can be measured accurately near the ship, to obtain a similar measurement of any reasonable accuracy at points in between the ship and target is almost impossible. Hence, in using the previously measured results of some other person, or in predicting propagation loss by tracing out ray paths, there will always be a certain inaccuracy resulting from an ignorance of the actual detailed water conditions.

The direct path sometimes provides very unusual sound propagation because of surface trapping. This situation can only come about if the sound velocity increases with depth. An isothermal or slightly positive BT followed by a negative trace can create the requisite conditions. The quantitative relationship between surface trapping propagation loss in decibels versus range in yards seems difficult to predict, and very few data are available.

Bottom bounce propagation is by a path which is either beamed or bent towards the ocean bottom and results in energy being bounced off the ocean bottom. This form of energy travel is relatively free of the thermal conditions in the ocean, but is highly dependent on ocean depth and the losses which occur on the bottom when the ray bounces. As an example, a beam which is depressed 15 degrees from the horizontal will bounce a ray off the bottom about 12,000 yards away in 1,500 fathoms of water. A detection range of 24,000 yards can thus be obtained with sonar of the proper figure of merit. If one reduces the operating depth to 150 fathoms, the range is correspondingly dropped to 2,400 yards for this single bounce. Propagation is possible with two or three bounces, but the energy loss is, of course, considerably greater for each successive bounce off the bottom or surface. However, in shallow water with a flat and sandy bottom the sound energy loss due to multiple bounces is sometimes compensated for by the flat angle of incidence. Thus bottom bounce propagation is possible in shallow water with the low losses usually associated with propagation in a surface channel.

Convergence zone propagation takes place in very deep water where the sound velocity decreases with depth because of decreasing temperature, reaches a minimum and then starts to increase because of increasing density with depth. This minimum velocity point is called the deep sound channel depth and results in a focusing of energy about the deep channel. In the Atlantic, the deep channel exists at about 400–500 fathoms. There must be approximately this depth or greater below the deep channel to permit convergence zone propagation. The sound energy leaving the target at all angles is bent down, goes past the deep channel and is bent back up to be refocused near the surface at about 30 miles.

In summary for *passive sonar:*

a. Figure of merit is defined as $L_S - (L_N - N_{DI}) - N_{RD}$.
b. Figure of merit can be measured and is independent of range.
c. Figure of merit is a direct and quantitative measurement of sonar capability.
d. Figure of merit equals the propagation loss possible which still permits a detection (with probability 50 percent).
e. If propagation loss versus range is known from previous at-sea measurements, then figure of merit versus range is known.

Range is a *poor* measure of sonar capability and figure of merit is a *good* measure of sonar capability.

910   ACTIVE SONAR EQUATION [2]

The details concerning the passive sonar equation relate directly to active sonar with some notable exceptions. In the main, however, all things said about the usefulness of figure of merit as a measure of sonar capability apply directly to the active sonar case.

To develop the active sonar equation, the following thought process takes place:

a. L_S is not now the radiated signal from the target, but is the radiated signal from the pinging ship.
b. The radiated signal, L_S, leaves the ship and is diminished in intensity en route to the target by an amount N_W. Hence $L_S - N_W$ arrives at the target.
c. The target as a whole reradiates the received echo. The ratio of reflected intensity to incident intensity is called *target strength* and is labeled N_{TS}. Hence, the returning sound intensity, measured by convention at one yard away from the target, is $L_S - N_W + N_{TS}$.
d. En route back from the target, the propagation loss, N_W, again has its effect. Hence, the signal arriving just outboard of the ship is

$$L_S - N_W + N_{TS} - N_W.$$

e. As in the passive case, concern should be taken with the value of returning signal intensity minus background noise. For active sonar, the background noise is determined by the loudest of the contributing factors (if the loudest is approximately 9 decibels or higher than the rest) or by the summation of all factors. The contributing factors are *machinery noise, sea state* and *flow over the hydrophones.* These were also factors involved in passive self-noise. In addition, active sonar self-noise may be affected by *volume-reflected reverberations* and *surface-reflected reverberations.*

Volume reverberations are due to back-scattered sound from the discontinuities in the body of the ocean, while surface reverberations are due to back-scattering from discontinuities caused by the rough ocean bottom or surface. The omnidirectional self-noise due to isotropic noise caused by hull, machinery, sea state or water flow over the hydrophones is labeled L_N. The hydrophone array directivity can discriminate against a portion of this, and hence own self-noise in the array is labeled $L_N - N_{DI}$, where N_{DI} is again the directivity index. Reverberations are not isotropic; hence, the array directivity does not distinguish against reverberation noise as for the other type. For the case of the reverberations-limited active sonar, i.e., reverberations are the loudest source of self-noise, a special directivity index must be defined. Considering only the machinery or sea noise-limited case, the signal-minus-noise equation is

$$L_S - N_W + N_{TS} - N_W - (L_N - N_{DI}).$$

signal arriving outboard own self-noise
of the ship's hydrophones measured inboard of
          hydrophone array

f. As for passive sonar, if the average value of *provided* signal/noise equals the average of the *required* signal/noise, then a detection will occur (probability 50 percent).

N_{RD} is the label used for the average value of the *required* signal/noise and is called the recognition differential as before.

The active sonar equation is thus:

$$L_S - N_W + N_{TS} - N_W - (L_N - N_{DI}) = N_{RD}.$$

Rewriting the equation, and placing all range-dependent terms on one side, we have

Equation 9-19 $2N_W = L_S + N_{TS} - (L_N - N_{DI}) - N_{RD}.$ =figure of merit

To compute the figure of merit for an active sonar in a ship on station, the following figures might be typical:

L_S sonar radiated signal level	= +140 db
N_{TS} target strength	= + 15 db
L_N as specified by sea state two	= − 43 db
N_{DI} for the sonar at 2.0 kilohertz	= + 25 db
N_{RD} for sonar at 2.0 kilohertz	= + 27 db
Figure of merit, $L_S + N_{TS} - (L_N - N_{DI}) - N_{RD}$	= 196 db

In order to determine what this figure of merit means in terms of range, it is necessary to recall the relationship that active figure of merit equals two times propagation loss. Entering Figure 9-9 with the propagation loss (196/2), the active detection ranges (probability 50 percent), not indicated in the figure, would be:

Direct path	9,400 yards,
Bottom bounce	48,000 yards,
First convergence	58,000 yards.

In summary for active sonar:

a. Figure of merit equals $L_S + N_{TS} - (L_N - N_{DI}) - N_{RD}$.

b. Figure of merit is *not* dependent on range and hence avoids the vagaries of propagation loss versus range in various ocean areas under changing environmental conditions. Figure of merit is therefore a *good* indicator of sonar capability.

c. Figure of merit equals the total propagation loss $(2N_W)$ which can be suffered and still achieve a detection (with probability 50 percent).

d. If propagation loss versus range is known, the figure of merit versus range is known.

If figure of merit can be measured while underway, the commanding officer of a ship can do these important things:

a. Determine that his sonar is or is not operating as designed.

b. Predict the detection ranges possible in various areas *if* propagation loss versus range curves are available.

With the figure of merit concept in mind, the war planner can do these things:

a. Compare the capabilities of various sonars on various units either actual or assumed.

b. Predict the detection ranges possible in various areas *if* propagation loss versus range curves are available.

Sonar is the key to ASW success. A quantitative knowledge of sonar performance can be obtained by measuring the figure of merit at sea. With this knowledge, a CO can ensure that his equipment is peaked, and also predict detection ranges against possible enemy targets. The war planner can do likewise for either a real or hypothetical enemy. Because the changing ocean results in dramatic changes in propagation loss versus range, to state a sonar's capability in terms of range is only half the story, and may even be misleading. A better method for defining a sonar's capability is by figure of merit. This can then be related to range for a particular geographical area or specific sea conditions.

BIBLIOGRAPHY

[1] R. J. Urick, *Caustics and Convergence Zones in Deep Water Sound Transmission*, The Journal of the Acoustical Society of America, Volume 38, Number two, page 349, August 1965.
[2] This section is based on an article by Captain Frank A. Andrews, U. S. Navy, Retired (Ph.D., Yale, 1950).

PROBLEMS

1. The root mean square pressure of a sonar signal arriving at an omnidirectional hydrophone is one dyne/cm^2. The root mean square pressure of the background noise arriving at the same hydrophone is 0.01 dyne/cm^2. The acoustic impedance, ρc, of the water is 1.5×10^8 dyne-sec/cm^3.

a. Compute the intensity of the signal arriving at the hydrophone.
b. Compute the intensity of the background noise arriving at the hydrophone.
c. Compute the *level* of the signal relative to one microbar.
d. Compute the *level* of the background noise relative to one microbar.
e. Compute the ratio of signal intensity to background noise intensity, i.e., the signal-to-noise ratio.
f. Compute the *relative intensity level* of the signal-to-noise.
g. Compute the *relative sound pressure level* using the pressures given for the signal and noise.
h. Compare the results of f and g.

2. The source level for a nuclear submarine traveling at 20 knots is given as 150 decibels relative to 0.0002 dyne/cm². What is the source level expressed in decibels relative to one dyne/cm²? Derive mathematically.

3. For an isothermal layer, the temperature is constant with depth throughout the layer. Assuming salinity also to be constant with depth,

a. What is the primary variable influencing the velocity profile within the layer?
b. Is the slope of the velocity profile constant within the layer? If so, what is the slope?
c. Draw a rough plot of the velocity profile within the layer.

4. Using the velocity profile given here:

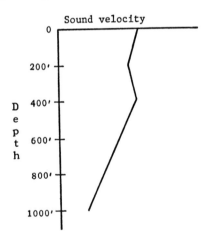

a. Draw a ray path plot of the sound energy directed in a horizontal direction from a source located 200 feet deep.
b. Draw a ray path plot of the sound energy directed in a horizontal direction from a source located 800 feet deep.
c. What will happen to most of the sound energy propagated in a horizontal direction from a sound source located between zero and 400 feet?
d. What will happen to most of the sound energy propagated in a horizontal direction from a sound source located between 400 and 1,000 feet?

5. Under the assumption that the ocean is an isovelocity medium, derive an expression for determining horizontal range, R_h, in terms of the water depth, D, and the

transducer tilt angle, θ, to the point where the energy bounced off a flat bottom will reach the surface again.

6. Using the result of Problem five and the same conditions, a water depth of 2,000 fathoms and a target at a horizontal range of 20,000 yards, what would be the optimum tilt angle for bottom bounce detection?

7. Assuming that detection range can be computed using the equation $N_W = 20 \log r + ar$, what effect does changing the frequency of the sound source from 10 kilohertz to 5 kilohertz have on the range of detection? What do each of the two terms on the right side of the equation represent?

8. A well-trained alerted operator has undergone tests to determine what fraction of signals he will detect as a function of the signal-to-noise ratio at a specific sound frequency. The results of the tests are represented by the graph.

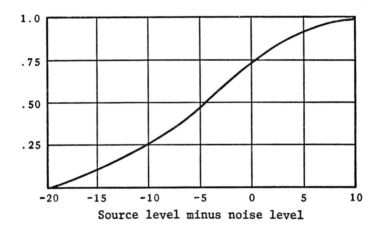

Source level minus noise level

   a. This operator should detect a signal level of 10 decibels when the noise level is 10 decibels what percentage of the time?
   b. What is this operator's recognition differential?

9. A particular omnidirectional hydrophone is most sensitive to frequencies in the region of one kilohertz. This hydrophone is located at a depth of 90 feet in an area where the background noise level has just been measured to be -45 decibels. The output from the hydrophone is fed into a series of signal processing stages and finally presented to an operator who must determine (yes or no) whether a true submarine signal is being presented at any given time. From past performance, it has been determined that this operator can detect a true submarine signal in the region of one kilohertz about half the time when the signal-to-noise intensity ratio is 1/20.

   a. What is the figure of merit for this hydrophone when searching for a submarine target traveling at a speed of 10 knots and producing a noise level of 25 decibels for frequencies in the region of one kilohertz?
   b. Assuming that transmission loss, N_W, can be determined by the equation,

$$N_W = 20 \log r + ar,$$

at what range would you expect detection to occur against the submarine target described in part a?

c. How much noise would a submarine have to make in order to make detection expected at a range of 20,000 yards?

10. An echo-ranging sonar produces a 20-kilohertz signal with a source level of 100 decibels. From past experience, it has been determined that the average operator can make detections with this sonar with a recognition differential of 0 decibels. The directivity index for this sonar is +15 decibels. A new sonar, in the research and development stage at the present time, is designed to produce a 10-kilohertz signal with a source level of 150 decibels and to have a directivity index of 25 decibels, and it is predicted that the average operator will be able to detect with a recognition differential of +5 decibels. The target strength expected for 20-kilohertz signals is 20 decibels and for 10 kilohertz is 15 decibels.

Using information on the average water conditions in the deep ocean, it is found that the average background noise level at 20 kilohertz is −65 decibels and at 10 kilohertz is −60 decibels.

a. Compute the figure of merit for the 20-kilohertz sonar.
b. Compute the figure of merit for the 10-kilohertz sonar.
c. Using the transmission loss equation, $2N_W = 40 \log r + 2ar$, compute the expected detection range for each of the two sonars.
d. For a measure of potential sonar capability, would you use the difference in figure of merit or the difference in expected detection range? Why?

10 SCREENING

The importance of antisubmarine warfare today results from continued increase in size and quality of the Soviet submarine fleet, which must be considered a potential enemy. The Navy must meet the challenge posed by this threat in order to ensure control of the seas to ourselves and our allies in time of war. Part of the challenge lies in developing more capable detection and weapons systems; the other in utilizing most effectively those systems currently available.

Operations against submarines fall into two categories:

a. Offensive operations which actively seek to destroy submarines and their support facilities.

b. Protective operations which seek to defend against submarine attack.

This chapter shows how the protective operation of screening a convoy or task force can be analyzed in order to provide a commander with a basis for decisions concerning the optimum disposition of his protective forces. Such an analysis has been conducted for typical situations and the screen plans tabulated in tactical publications. A naval officer who understands how these plans were developed can carry out naval operations more intelligently, especially when the situation encountered is not exactly the same as one for which a screen plan is available.

When a formation of ships, such as a task force or merchant convoy, is in transit, the danger from enemy submarines can be greatly diminished by providing for their detection and destruction at as great a range as possible from the formation. With present technology, submerged submarines can be detected at a sufficient range only by passive or active sonar equipment. Consequently, it is necessary that sonar equipment be used by highly maneuverable and appropriately armed craft such as destroyers, destroyer escorts or helicopters stationed at a suitable distance from the formation.

Such an arrangement of escorts is called a *sonar screen*, and has the dual functions of *detection* and *attack*.

The *objective* of an antisubmarine screen is to provide maximum protection for the ships being screened. This objective can be stated in another way, i.e., to minimize the submarine's chances of scoring a torpedo hit on ships in the formation. Here the destruction of a submarine is of secondary importance since the objective can also be achieved in other ways.

The placement of the screening units is the primary controllable variable. In other words, the various possible positions of the screening units represent the *alternative courses of action* that are available to the operational commander when ordering the screen.

The problem is to determine the placement of the screening units which will minimize the submarine's chances of scoring a hit.

With a screen in place, the opposing submarine commander has two basic alternatives:

a. To attempt penetration of the screen and fire from inside at close range.
b. To fire his weapons from outside the screen.

In order to determine what placement of the screen will hold the submarine's chances of success to a minimum, it is necessary to be able to predict the outcome for each of the submarine commander's alternatives as the placement of the screen is varied. The *measure of effectiveness* used will be the probability that the submarine will hit one of the protected ships with a single torpedo. If the submarine attempts to penetrate the screen before firing, this probability of hit must include the probability of successfully penetrating the screen as well.

The following sections will develop theoretical models from which the above probabilities can be computed.

1001   PROBABILITY OF PENETRATING THE SCREEN UNDETECTED

The probability of detecting a submarine which chooses to penetrate the screen is referred to as the *line efficiency* (*L.E.*) of the screen. Therefore, the probability of a submarine penetrating undetected is one minus the line efficiency $(1 - L.E.)$.

The primary variables affecting line efficiency are the spacing between screening units and the detection system effectiveness for a specified set of conditions. The spacing between screening units is a controllable variable determined by the placement of the screen. The detection system effectiveness is a function of the many environmental variables, equipment availability and operating conditions. A method is needed to determine line efficiency as a function of screen spacing (the controllable variable) for a specified set of conditions. There are two general approaches that can be used, an empirical method and a theoretical method involving the use of lateral range curves.

The empirical method involves collecting data on the number of submarine screen penetrations detected and the number of submarine penetrations attempted under relatively constant conditions. The line efficiency is then estimated simply by taking the ratio of the number of penetrations detected over the number of penetrations attempted. It is important that these data be collected under the same, or approximately same, set of conditions that they will later be used to represent. In order to determine which value of screen spacing provides the best line efficiency, it is necessary

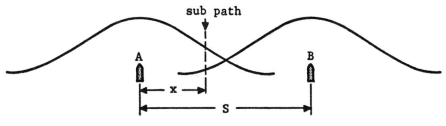

Detection probability for two screen units.

Figure 10-1.

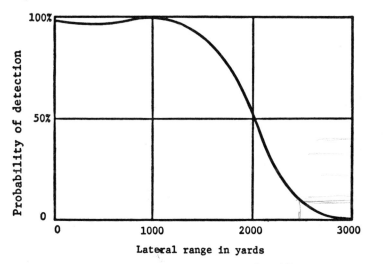

Lateral range curve for screen units A and B.

Figure 10-2.

to take data at each of several screen spacings, i.e., a range of values, under the same conditions.

The theoretical method involving the use of lateral range curves can also be used to determine line efficiency as a function of screen spacing. Since different lateral range curves result from different environmental and operational conditions, the curve which most closely approximates the existing conditions must be chosen.

Consider two screening units, A and B, stationed a fixed distance S apart, and a submarine penetrating somewhere between them at a lateral range x from unit A (Figure 10-1). The probability of detecting the submarine, given that it passes at lateral range x from A, is the probability of detecting the submarine by either *unit A* or *unit B* or *both*. This probability can be computed as was done in Section 703 for a parallel sweep search. For active sonar under relatively constant conditions, the event of detection by A and the event of detection by B are assumed to be independent* and

*These probabilities are not necessarily independent. For a passive sonar, the probability of detection for each screening unit would depend on the distribution of submarine generated sound. If the variable conditions are the same for screening units, then under certain conditions a submarine that is noisy for A would also be noisy for B. In this case, the probabilities would be highly dependent and the overall probability of detection would be

$$\overline{P}_{DET}(x) = \overline{P}_A(x) + \overline{P}_B(S - x) - P[\text{det by } A \text{ given det by } B] \cdot P[\text{det by } B].$$

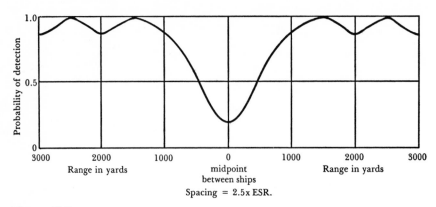

Figure 10-3.

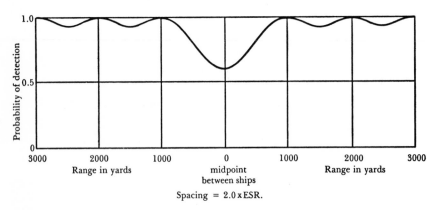

Figure 10-4.

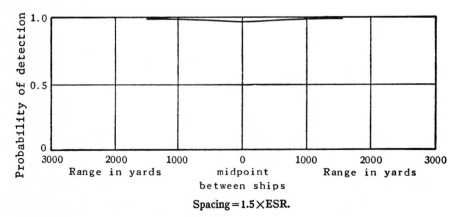

Figure 10-5.

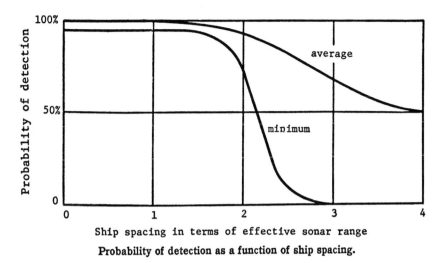

Ship spacing in terms of effective sonar range

Probability of detection as a function of ship spacing.

Figure 10-6.

therefore the overall probability of detection can be determined by

Equation 10-1 $\overline{P}_{DET}(x) = \overline{P}_A(x) + \overline{P}_B(S - x) - \overline{P}_A(x)\overline{P}_B(S - x).$

Conditions, however, are rarely truly fixed. An example of this is the depth of a submarine which is not usually known and may vary during the penetration. Normally, the lateral range curve for the submarine at best depth to avoid detection is used. This would result in a relatively tight and conservative ship spacing.

Lateral range curve information is not usually available to an operational commander. However, there does exist a geometrical measure of sonar effectiveness that is used and understood by operational commanders and defined in present tactical publications, i.e., *effective sonar range* (ESR). If each specific lateral range curve could be represented by one particular ESR, then results derived from lateral range curve inputs could be represented in units of effective sonar range. As a usable approximation, the effective sonar range is equivalent to that lateral range x for which the probability of detection is 0.5. It should be clearly understood that ESR information is not in itself sufficient to construct a lateral range curve; therefore, an exact one-to-one relationship does not exist. The ESR for the typical symmetrical lateral range curve shown in Figure 10-2 (see page 193) is the same for units A and B, i.e., 2,000 yards.

Overall probability of detection curves for adjacent screening units, which are spaced multiples of ESR apart, can be constructed using Equation 10-1. The curves for three different spacings are shown in Figures 10-3, 10-4 and 10-5.

Line efficiency can be determined from these curves for each of two assumptions concerning enemy capability. If the submarine can determine and choose the best point to penetrate, then the *minimum* probability on the curve should be used as the line efficiency. If, on the other hand, its point of penetration is more or less random, then the *average* probability should be used.

The effect of ship spacing on the line efficiency is summarized in Figure 10-6.

To determine which spacing is optimal, the length of the line to be screened, the submarine's ability to end-run and choose weak points in the screen and the number of screening units available for use in the screen must be considered in conjunction with the information from the curves.

1002   CONSTRUCTION OF PROBABILITY OF HIT CONTOURS

In designing antisubmarine screens, it is essential to determine the areas from which the submarine has a good chance of scoring a torpedo hit upon one of the screened units. The *torpedo danger zone* about an individual ship or group of ships is the region (thought of as moving along with the ships, i.e., it is fixed relative to them) within which a torpedo must be fired if it is to have *any* chance (probability) of scoring a hit. The shape and size of the zone will, of course, depend on the speed and type of torpedo, as well as the speed and disposition of the ships. The submarine's firing point, relative to the ship or formation reference point, can be characterized by two variables:

a. R_f **is the range** at which the torpedo is fired (firing range).
b. θ **is the angle measured,** port or starboard, from the bow of the target ship to the intended relative torpedo track (angle on the bow).

For a given firing range and angle on the bow, it is possible to find the probability, $P(R_f, \theta)$, that a torpedo fired from that point will hit the target. The boundary of the torpedo danger zone is the smallest closed curve representing the locus of points $P(R_f, \theta) = 0$. Similar curves or *contours* can be determined which represent the locus of all points about a ship or force where the probability of hit is any other constant value, $C, 0 \leq C \leq 1$. Three such contours are depicted in Figure 10-7, where $P(R_f, \theta) = C$ for $C = 0$, $C = .25$, and $C = .5$.

The primary factor involved in the determination of the enemy's chance of success, $P(R_f, \theta)$, is the type of weapon he uses. If the lethal coverage of the weapon is high, the chance of success is correspondingly greater. Consider, for example, three types of torpedoes. The first runs at a 45-foot depth and explodes after a given length of run. The second is at 5 feet and explodes on contact. The third is at 5 feet, exploding on contact, but provided with a homing device so that when it passes within 500 yards of a ship, it will home into the ship and score a hit. It is obvious that the first will have a rather small lethal coverage since only a ship at a particular point will be affected by the explosion. The coverage of the second is greater because any ship along the entire run of the torpedo may be hit. The homing feature of the third will give it by far the greatest coverage because the ships need only be within 500 yards of the torpedo track

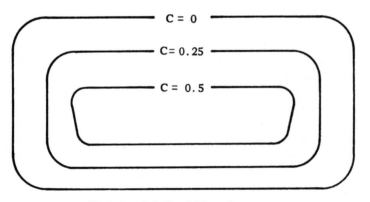

Typical probability of hit contours.

Figure 10-7.

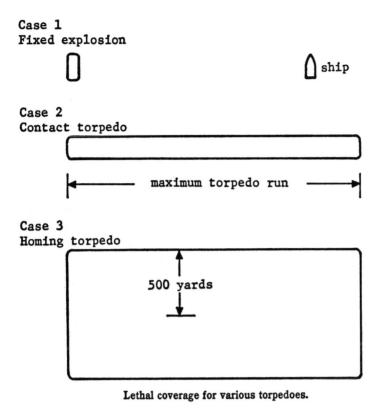

Case 1
Fixed explosion

ship

Case 2
Contact torpedo

|← maximum torpedo run →|

Case 3
Homing torpedo

500 yards

Lethal coverage for various torpedoes.

Figure 10-8.

for a hit to be scored. These cases can be demonstrated qualitatively in Figure 10-8. The lethal areas shown are for a torpedo proceeding at right angles to a ship. The areas shown have the property that any ship whose center lies in the area will be hit by the torpedo. For case one, this area is slightly larger than the plan view of the ship, since a torpedo exploding up to about 10 yards away might sink the ship.

Lethal coverage alone does not determine the enemy's chance of a hit. His firing errors must be taken into account. If these errors are so great that there is only a small probability that the target lies in the lethal area, his chance of a hit is correspondingly smaller. For any given accuracy, however, the weapon with the largest lethal coverage will be the most effective.

The foregoing discussion applies only to a single target. When fired at a convoy or group of ships, the torpedo will be successful if it hits any member of the group, i.e., if any of them lie in the lethal area. In general, the torpedo will actually be fired at a particular ship, but it may miss that ship and hit another one purely by chance. For long-range torpedoes fired at large convoys, the chance of such an event may be considerable. In such a case a torpedo may actually be fired as a *browning shot* from a far distance, aimed at the convoy as a whole, on the chance of a random hit. Because of the importance of browning shots with large, closely spaced convoys, the probability of achieving a hit in a merchant convoy is quite different from that on a single ship. Section 1003 will discuss the case of the single ship. The probability of a hit in a large convoy will be discussed in later sections.

5-27

1003   PROBABILITY OF HITTING A SINGLE SHIP OF A TASK FORCE WITH A SINGLE TORPEDO

While the general practice is to fire torpedoes in salvo, the probability that a salvo of a given number of torpedoes will hit, sink or damage to some extent a ship in a convoy, depends on the probability of scoring a hit with a single torpedo. It also depends on the damage assumed as a result of a given number of hits, e.g., the damage being different for merchantmen and for cruisers. The one torpedo hit probability becomes, therefore, the fundamental quantity to be found as a preliminary to any study of the probability of damage.

In general, the following method can be used to determine the probability of hit when the desirability of hitting a single specific target is the overriding consideration. This might occur when the submarine is interested only in a prime target or the formation has large spacing between ships. A good example is the situation in which a submarine is attacking a carrier task force, and has as its prime target the carrier. The submarine would most likely take a position such that chances of hitting the intended single target are the highest.

Consider a submarine firing at a single ship from point F relative to the target. Figure 10-9 is drawn to depict this situation in *relative space,* i.e., as the ship is moving. All relationships (such as the torpedo track) are plotted with reference to an observer standing on the target ship.

The angle ω represents the angular limits of the relative torpedo tracks that will hit the ship. ω is a function of R_f, L and θ, where L is the length of the target ship. If R_f is much greater than L, then $S \cong L \sin \theta$ giving

Equation 10-2
$$\omega = \frac{L \sin \theta}{R_f} \text{ in radians,}$$

$$= \frac{57.3 L \sin \theta}{R_f} \text{ in degrees, or}$$

Equation 10-3
$$R_f = \frac{57.3 L \sin \theta}{\omega}.$$

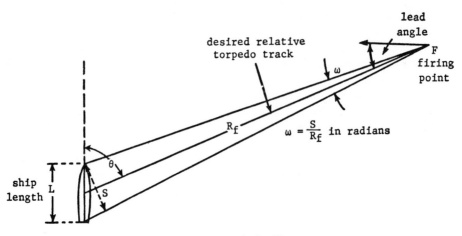

Torpedo fired at a single ship.

Figure 10-9.

A hit will occur *if and only if* the torpedo travels a relative path within the angular limits of ω. Let the random variable X be the angular firing error, i.e., the number of degrees the relative torpedo track deviates from the desired relative track. The probability of hit then depends on the probability distribution of X. It is generally the case that X has a normal probability distribution, with a mean of $\mu = 0$, and whose variance, σ^2, is a function of the angle θ. The square root of the variance, or standard deviation, σ, is a measure, in degrees, of the deviation of a torpedo from its desired track. This deviation may result from firing inaccuracies in equipment or personnel error, but mostly from inaccuracies in determining the correct lead angle from estimates of the course, speed and range to the target.

Determining a particular value of σ as a function of all the conditions affecting it will not be attempted in this text. Methods have been devised for determining σ, and are discussed in OEG Report No. 56. Operationally, the values of σ for various torpedoes and firing situations have been tabulated and are available on board ship. For the purpose of the remaining discussion, it will be assumed that the values of σ are known.

The probability of obtaining a hit from relative range R_f at bearing θ can be expressed symbolically as

$$P(R_f, \theta) = P[-\omega/2 \leq X \leq \omega/2]$$
$$= \int_{-\omega/2}^{\omega/2} \frac{1}{\sigma\sqrt{2\pi}} e^{-x^2/2\sigma^2} dx.$$

The value of this probability of hit can be found using standardized normal distribution tables after making the following transformation of variables:

Equation 10-4 $$Z = \frac{X - \mu}{\sigma} = \frac{X}{\sigma}, \text{ recalling } \mu = 0.$$

Then the desired probability of hit is

Equation 10-5 $$P(R_f, \theta) = P[-\omega/2 \leq X \leq \omega/2]$$
$$= P[-\omega/2\sigma \leq Z \leq \omega/2\sigma]$$
$$= 2P[0 \leq Z \leq \omega/2\sigma],$$

which can be found from tables that tabulate the shaded area of the normal distribution shown in Figure 10-10.

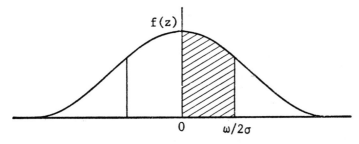

Area under the normal curve.

Figure 10-10.

If the tabulated values are for the standardized normal distribution function, $F(z)$, given in Appendix I, Section I-23, then

Equation 10-6
$$P(R_f, \theta) = 2P(0 \leq Z \leq \omega/2\sigma)$$
$$= 2[P(-\infty \leq Z \leq \omega/2\sigma) - P(-\infty \leq Z \leq 0)]$$
$$= 2\left[F\left(\frac{\omega}{2\sigma}\right) - .5\right].$$

To find the locus of all points (probability of hit contour) about the target where the probability of hit is some constant value C, it is necessary to find the value of $\omega/2\sigma$ for which $P(R_f, \theta)$ is equal to C, using Equation 10-5 or 10-6.

For example, to construct the contour for $C = 0.25$, where $L = 250$ yards and σ is known as a function of θ, the following table of values for ω and R_f can be computed from Equations 10-3, 10-6 and the normal tables:

θ	30°	60°	90°	120°	150°
σ	5.4°	6.3°	7.9°	9.9°	11.6°
ω	3.46°	4.03°	5.06°	6.33°	7.42°
R_f	2,080 yards	3,100 yards	2,850 yards	1,970 yards	965 yards

From the data in this table, the isoprobability of hit contour can be constructed (Figure 10-11).

A template, drawn to the proper scale and having the shape of this curve, can be used to determine the probability of hit contour about a task force of several such ships. Figure 10-12 illustrates the use of such a template for a task force in a circular disposition. The envelope of all the individual curves is the desired contour for the task force.

In the next three sections, theoretical models will be presented for determining probability of hit contours about a convoy in which ships are closely spaced and, hence, more than a single target must be considered in computing the overall probability of a hit.

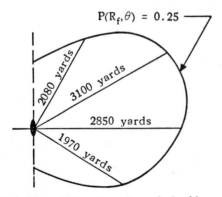

Probability of hit contours for a single ship.

Figure 10-11.

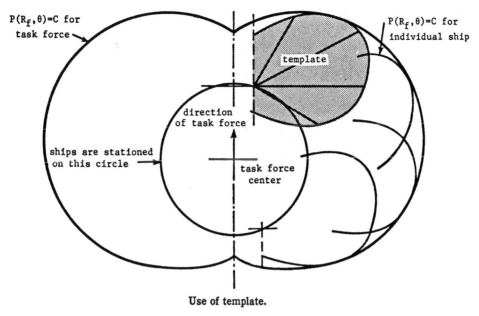

$P(R_f, \theta) = C$ for task force

$P(R_f, \theta) = C$ for individual ship

template

direction of task force

ships are stationed on this circle

task force center

Use of template.

Figure 10-12.

1004 SIMPLE COUNTING MODEL

In a large convoy, ships are usually spaced closely and in a regular pattern. Assuming each ship is on station, it would be possible to plot their positions with their lengths drawn to scale as in Figure 10-13.

The overall probability of hit is determined by extending the method discussed in the last section for a single ship. This probability of hit is the probability that a torpedo's relative track was in any one of the shaded sectors.

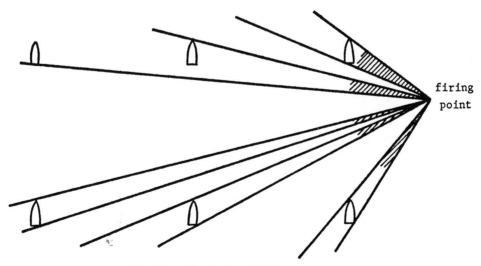

firing point

Possible paths for torpedo hit on convoy.

Figure 10-13.

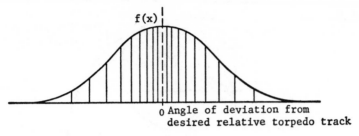

Torpedo firing errors.

Figure 10-14.

The probability of hit obviously depends on the aim point for an individual target, and it may be necessary to compute the probability for several aim points in order to find a submarine's maximum overall probability of hit on the convoy.

A simpler way of determining the probability of hit on the convoy makes use of a geometric approximation.

The angular deviation, X, of a torpedo from its desired relative track is assumed to have a normal distribution with mean zero and standard deviation σ. The density function can be divided graphically into a number of equal-sized areas. In Figure

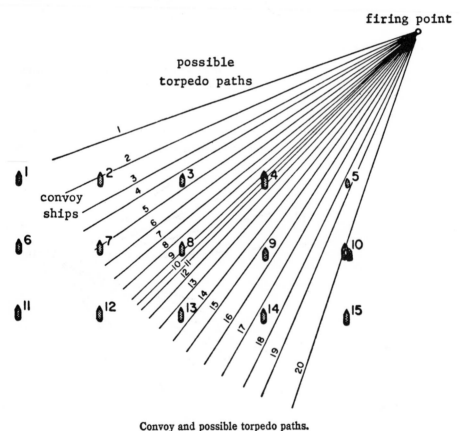

Convoy and possible torpedo paths.

Figure 10-15.

10-14, the number arbitrarily used is 20. Since the areas are equal, the probability is 1/20 that X will have a value within any increment. Assuming that a torpedo will follow any one of the 20 possible tracks, the angular deviation of a track may be represented by the average angle off the mean point of aim for that area. These 20 possible torpedo tracks would then be spaced closer together near the center as in Figure 10-15.

By superimposing the torpedo diagram on the convoy and counting the number of torpedo paths that intersect ships, the chance of a hit can be estimated. If a path intersects more than one ship, the path is still counted only once. In the example shown in Figure 10-15, six out of the 20 possible paths would result in a hit, so that the probability of a hit from that firing point is 30 percent.

$\frac{6}{20} = .30$

In deciding on the probability of a hit from any particular point, however, it is necessary to pick out the submarine's best shot. Should it aim at ship number four, as shown in Figure 10-15, or at number five which is closer but presents a less favorable target aspect? It is usually possible to pick out the best shot by eye after a little experience, but sometimes several possible aim points must be investigated.

This method is extremely simple and direct, but it has some disadvantages. It involves careful drawing and positioning of the diagrams. Then a great deal of inspection of the diagrams is required. In this example, where 20 possible torpedo paths are used, the answer is only accurate to about 5 percent and may show considerable fluctuation for very small changes in firing position. If a greater number of paths were used, the accuracy would increase somewhat.

1005   DIFFUSE TARGET MODEL

An obvious extension of the simple counting method can be used to reduce the fluctuations in the probability of hit which are caused by the screening effect of a regular lattice of ships. It takes into account the possibility of irregularity in the convoy formation, that is, of ships being somewhat out of their proper convoy station. Each ship is considered to have a *diffuse target length* equal to the ship's length plus the amount the ship varies in position as shown in Figure 10-16. Then the probability that a torpedo passing through the diffuse target length will actually hit the ship is $P(\text{hit}) = L/l$.

531

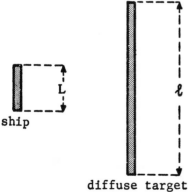

diffuse target length.

Diffuse target length.

Figure 10-16.

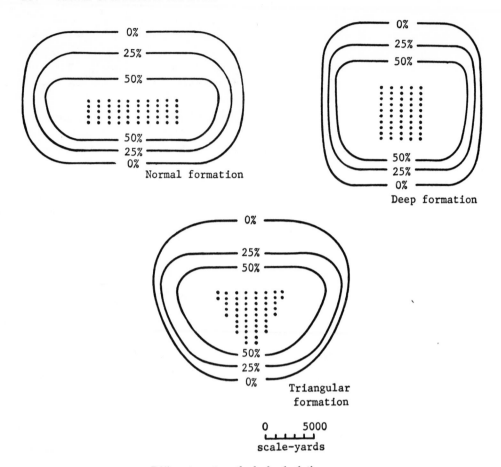

Diffuse target method of calculations.
Probability of hit contours for different convoy formations and a 5,000-yard
range contact torpedo.

Figure 10-17.

Consider now the ith torpedo path ($i = 1, 2, \ldots, m$; m being the number of possible torpedo paths) and the jth diffuse target ($j = 1, 2, \ldots, n$; n being the number of ships in the convoy). Let the number h_{ij} be the probability that a torpedo traveling along the ith path will pass through the jth diffuse target length. From a diagram analogous to Figure 10-15, h_{ij} can be evaluated as equal to either one or zero by inspection. Then the probability that a torpedo following the ith path will hit the jth ship (given it hits no previous ship) is

Equation 10-7
$$P_{ij} = h_{ij} \frac{L_j}{l_j}.$$

Hence, the probability of hitting any ship on the ith path (which mathematically reduces to at least one hit on the ith path) is

Equation 10-8
$$P_i = 1 - \prod_{j=1}^{n}(1 - P_{ij}),$$

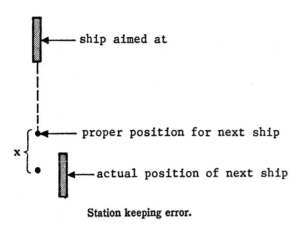

Station keeping error.

Figure 10-18.

and the overall probability of a hit from the particular firing point is

Equation 10-9
$$P(R_f, \theta) = \frac{1}{m} \sum_{i=1}^{m} \left[1 - \prod_{j=1}^{n} (1 - P_{ij}) \right]. \quad = \frac{1}{m} \sum_{i=1}^{m} P_i$$

This probability of hit is smoother and more realistic than that obtained by the simple counting method. Several contours determined using this method are shown in Figure 10-17. The diffuse target method is considerably more laborious however, and involves a good deal of arithmetic calculation.

It should be pointed out that the choice of the lengths of the diffuse targets is rather arbitrary. A plausible assumption is that each ship may be out of station with respect to its neighbor by a given amount which may be denoted x. (See Figure 10-18.) Then the diffuse length, l, for the nearest neighbors to the ship fired at will be $L + 2x$.

In a like manner, assuming random station keeping errors, the diffuse lengths for the next nearest neighbors may be computed. This compounding of position errors continues to a point until the whole column essentially becomes one large diffuse target.

The position of the ship at which the torpedo is aimed can be thought of as being fixed and the positions of other ships becoming increasingly uncertain the farther they are from the target ship. It is evident that the actual formation pattern from the submarine's point of view is something of this sort, though the specific way in which the position uncertainty increases may vary considerably.

1006 RANDOM COLUMN MODEL

If the calculations required by the diffuse target model are prohibitively lengthy, a simplification is possible. Treat each column of the convoy as a single diffuse target in which the individual ships are distributed more or less at random. The probability that a torpedo, passing through the column, will hit a ship is given by $P(\text{hit}) = L/a$, where a is the average ship spacing in the column.

This random column method is very simple and convenient, but is *not* accurate at close ranges where the actual probability of hitting the ship aimed at is considerably increased. For browning shots fired at a substantial distance from the convoy, however, the method is very satisfactory.

The simple counting, diffuse target and random column methods are directly applicable to straight running torpedoes. If a torpedo enters a convoy and then zigzags or circles to increase its chance of a random hit, the resulting diagrams become increasingly confusing. Some calculations have been carried out for pattern running torpedoes against a single target using the direct method, but the combination of a pattern running torpedo (or salvo thereof) and a multiplicity of targets is very difficult to evaluate in this way. It is possible, however, to write explicit expressions for the probability of a hit by a torpedo having generalized performance characteristics. The development and analysis of these more sophisticated models is beyond the scope of this text.

1007 THE SUBMERGED APPROACH REGION

If a submarine is to have the chance, C, of scoring a hit with one torpedo, it must reach a point on the contour $P(R_f, \theta) = C$. Since this point will usually be within visual or radar range of the formation, the submarine must generally make its approach to the firing position submerged. Let the submarine speed be u, the formation speed be v, and assume that, as in the case of a conventional submarine, $u < v$. Then it is not necessarily possible for the submarine to reach all points on the curve $P(R_f, \theta) = C$. The area of the ocean in the vicinity of the formation from which it is possible to reach a firing position is called the submerged approach region, R_C. It is determined by drawing a tangent to either side of the curve $P(R_f, \theta) = C$ at an angle of $\psi = \sin^{-1}(u/v)$ degrees, measured from the formation's course line. The shaded area shown in Figure 10-19 is the submerged approach region.

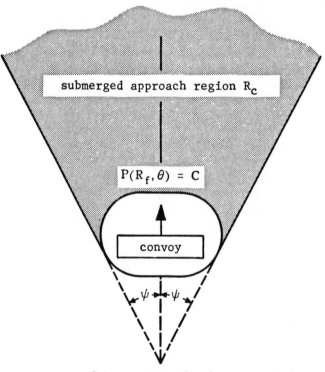

Submerged approach region.

Figure 10-19.

The angle and the tangents are the limiting (submerged) approach angle and lines respectively. With the advent of submarines capable of very high submerged speeds, the submarine may be able to attain the curve $P(R_f, \theta) = C$ submerged from virtually any point in the immediate area of the formation, thus extending the submerged approach region throughout 360 degrees.

1008 OPTIMAL PLACEMENT OF THE SCREEN

As stated previously, the objective of the screen is to minimize the enemy submarine's chance of scoring a hit on one of the ships in the formation. With a screen in place, the submarine has two alternatives:

a. To penetrate the screen and fire its weapons from inside.
b. To fire its weapons from outside the screen.

The screen should be placed so that the submarine's maximum chance of success, considering both alternatives, is minimized. This is a conservative decision criterion corresponding to the <u>maximin</u> criterion discussed in Chapter three. If the screen is *not* placed according to this criterion, the submarine's probability of success by one of his alternatives will be greater than necessary.

For each probability of hit contour $P(R_f, \theta) = C$, the submarine's submerged approach speed, u, and formation speed, v, a corresponding submerged approach region, R_C, can be determined. Only those submarines lying within the submerged approach region, R_0, corresponding to the probability of hit contour $C = 0$, will pose a threat to ships in the formation. Two cases: $u < v$ and $u > v$ will be discussed.

If $u < v$, the submerged approach region, R_0, is restricted by the limiting lines of submerged approach. In this case, the screen line shown by the line $S_0S'_0$ in Figure 10-20 need only extend between the limiting lines of approach so as to intercept

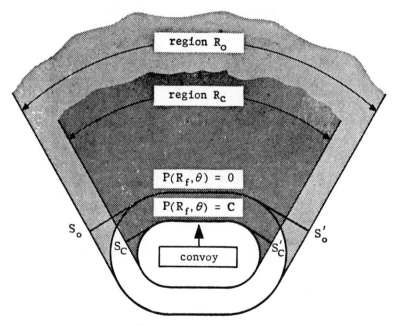

Placement of screen.

Figure 10-20.

submarines making a submerged approach from the region R_0. Such a line is constructed by stretching a string around the probability of hit contour $P(R_f, \theta) = 0$, its two ends terminating on the limiting lines of approach and perpendicular to them. The result is the *bent* screening line $S_0 S'_0$. A similar screening line can be constructed for any particular probability of hit contour, $P(R_f, \theta) = C$. Such a line is shown in Figure 10-20, i.e., $S_C S'_C$. Notice that the limiting lines of approach have the same angle ψ for both $S_0 S'_0$ and $S_C S'_C$, but the difference is due to the size and shape of the contour curve for different values of C. Thus, for a given u and v, the problem is to determine around which contour, C, to place the screen line.

First, consider placing the screen along the line $S_0 S'_0$. If a line efficiency of 1.0 could be maintained for this placement, the probability of success for each of the submarine's alternatives would then be:

$$P[\text{hit given the submarine fires from outside the screen}] = C = 0,$$

and

$$P[\text{penetrating the screen undetected}] \times g = (1 - L.E.)g = 0,$$

where g = probability of the torpedo hitting a ship given an undetected penetration by the submarine.

Unfortunately, the number of screening units available, coupled with less than perfect sonar effectiveness, does not normally allow a line efficiency equal to 1.0. If the screen is placed around the contour $C = 0$ and the line efficiency is less than 1.0, it is obvious that the submarine can maximize its probability of success by choosing to penetrate the screen and fire from inside, e.g., if $L.E. = 0.15$:

$$P[\text{hit from outside}] = C = 0$$

and

$$P[\text{penetrating undetected}]g = (1 - L.E.)g = 0.85g.$$

Note that if a contour, C, is chosen that represents a higher probability of hit for the submarine, the major effect this would have on line efficiency is to allow a shorter screen line. Decreasing the length of the screen line will increase line efficiency because of closer spacing between screening units. Then, for a higher value of C (closer screen) the line efficiency increases while the submarine's probability of hitting from outside the screen is increased. The effect of varying C for each of the submarine's two alternatives is shown in the graph (Figure 10-21).

The dashed line labeled $1 - L.E.$ in Figure 10-21 would apply if $g = 1.0$. This may not be true, but if the submarine is able to penetrate the screen undetected, it will be able to fire from close range. If g is known to be other than one, its effect on the submarine's probability of success given that he chooses to penetrate should be considered, i.e., $(1 - L.E.)g$. The solid line in Figure 10-21 shows the effect of a g less than 1.0.

Assuming that the only consideration of the submarine commander is his desire to score a hit and that safety of his ship is of no concern, then the best course of action is to attempt to penetrate the screen whenever $(1 - L.E.)g$ is greater than C, and to fire from just outside the screen if C is greater than $(1 - L.E.)g$. In either case, the submarine's maximum probability of scoring a hit is the greater of the two quantities $(1 - L.E.)g$ or C. This maximum probability of scoring a hit is represented as a function of screen radius in Figure 10-21 by the heavy solid line. Thus, the minimum of these

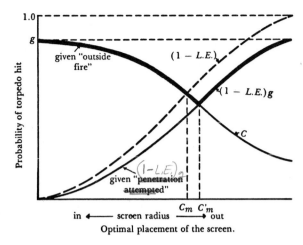

Optimal placement of the screen.

Figure 10-21.

maximums (the low point of the heavy solid line) occurs where the two curves, $(1 - L.E.)g$ and C, intersect. The value of C corresponding to the intersection is labeled C_m', and this value of C represents the contour line around which the screen should be placed. If g is equal to one, the intersection occurs at that value of C labeled C_m. This leads to the following criterion for the optimal placement of the screen: *Place the screen so that the probability of a submarine penetrating undetected and scoring a hit is equal to the probability of that same submarine scoring a hit from a point just outside the screen.*

If $u > v$, the region R_0 is *not* restricted by limiting lines of approach. Since the submerged approach region in this situation includes all points outside the probability of hit contour, the screen line must extend 360 degrees around the force. A circular screen that approximates the size and shape of the appropriate probability of hit contour is normally used in such a case. The same reasoning and decision criteria are used to decide which value of C is appropriate.

1009 EFFECT OF SIMPLIFYING ASSUMPTIONS

First, submarines actually do give consideration to their own safety. Thus, if the screen were placed by the preceding criteria, it would be more favorable to them to fire from outside the screen than to try to penetrate it. For convenience, the screen line representing $C = C_m$ in Figure 10-21 will be referred to as $S_{cm}S_{cm}'$. Hence, the best screen line would be somewhat farther out than $S_{cm}S_{cm}'$; just how much farther is a difficult matter to estimate.

Additional considerations which affect the actual screen line positions are:

a. The submarine can be expected to have more than one torpedo, whereas it has been assumed implicitly in the foregoing probabilities that only one torpedo was fired. Firing several torpedoes would enlarge the area within a given hit contour, and to a lesser extent would also increase the damage done by a close range submarine. These two effects would operate in opposition to one another in their effects on optimal screen placement.

b. It was assumed that a submarine attempting to penetrate the screen does so with equal detection probability over the screen's entire length. Yet, it is markedly advantageous to the submarine to operate near the sides of the screen so as to facilitate its escape after firing. The normal attacking procedure used by submarines tends to bring them into contact nearer the wings than the van of a convoy of any size. For both these reasons, it is important to avoid lessening the screen's line efficiency near its wings.

c. In the case of screening a fast ship or task group which may be zigzagging or maneuvering radically, the limiting approach angle is increased and the limiting lines of approach are farther apart. Hence, the screen must extend through a greater angle off either bow, but the principles developed earlier still apply. The extreme case is that of the fast carrier task force which must be prepared to change its course radically, even to backtrack at short notice, in order to launch planes into the wind or to avoid or surprise the enemy. Circular screens around the whole task force are frequently used in such cases, either with equally spaced escorts or with closer spacing in the forward parts of the circle. Even when a circular distribution is not necessary, turning the group into unswept waters must be avoided. The screen should be extended in the direction the formation expects to turn so as to detect any submarines possibly present. This is particularly important in view of the tendency of submarines to attack from the flank.

d. It may be objected that the reasoning upon which the choice of $S_{cm}S'_{cm}$ was based assumes that the submarine commander knows the values of the various probabilities involved, a thoroughly unrealistic assumption. Actually, this does not invalidate the reasoning. Lack of knowledge can only result in his taking a less favorable course of action which will reduce his chances of success.

1010   INCREASING SCREEN EFFECTIVENESS

When the number of escorts is insufficient to provide a reasonably high line efficiency without moving the screen line too close to the main body of the formation for safe maneuvering, it is possible to increase the average probability of detection of the screen by directing the individual units to *patrol station*. Patrolling stations causes the individual units to randomly maneuver within a fixed radius, e.g., 500 yards, around their assigned screen stations while at the same time conforming to the overall course and speed of the formation. This action causes the location and value of the point of minimum probability of detection between adjacent screen units to shift constantly as the screen spacing varies. Operationally this means that the submarine will be forced to make a random penetration of the screen and the average rather than minimum probability of detection will prevail. Of course, the submarine may be able to pick his point of penetration at a time when the escorts are their maximum distance apart, and thus increase his chances of undetected penetration. However, as long as the screen units patrol randomly and independently of each other, it is less likely that the time of occurrence of this maximum separation will be predictable to the extent that the submarine will be able to take advantage of it.

When a limited number of additional screening ships or ASW helicopters are available, it may be more advantageous to increase the probability of detection in the direction from which the threat is most likely. This can be accomplished in one way by stationing additional ASW units, called *pickets,* outside the screen in advance of the formation to provide greater depth to both radar and sonar coverage. A second alternative is to place the additional units, called *pouncers,* between the screen and the main body of the formation to ensure greater depth of sonar coverage.

PROBLEMS

1. The ships in Destroyer Division 99 are equipped with two different types of sonar. The lateral range curves associated with each type sonar are shown here:

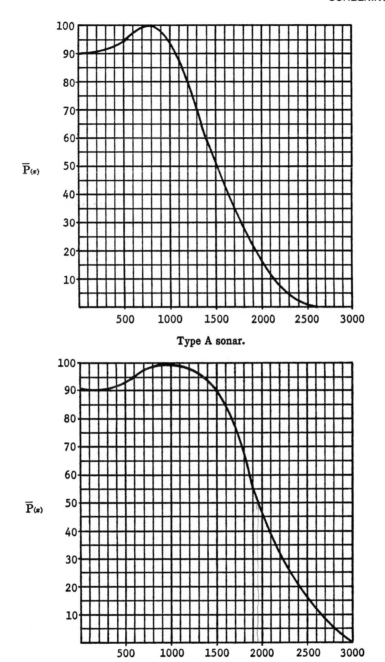

Type A sonar.

Type B sonar.

a. What is the effective sonar range for type *A* sonar?
b. What is the effective sonar range for type *B* sonar?
c. Two ships, one equipped with type *A* sonar, the other with type *B* sonar, are to conduct a parallel sweep search. Using the average of the two effective sonar ranges as the spacing between the ships, determine the probability of detection of a submerged target which passes between the ships at various points, and plot

the results on graph paper (as in Figures 10-3, 10-4 and 10-5) for ship spacings of 1.5, 2.0 and 2.5 ESR.

2. Two screening ships are equipped with identical sonar whose lateral range curve for the particular day is as follows:

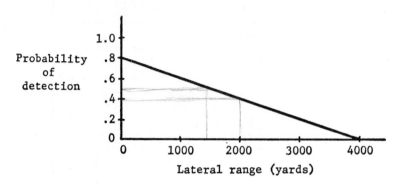

a. If the ships are stationed 8,000 yards apart, what is the line efficiency if the submarine knows the location of weakest point in the screen?

b. With the ship spacing still 8,000 yards and the submarine unaware of the line's weakest point, assume it therefore attempts to penetrate the screen at random. What is the line efficiency now? AT LATERAL RANGE = 2000 = .4

c. What can the screen commander do to improve the line efficiency regardless of the submarine's tactics, assuming that he is committed to the ship spacing of 8,000 yards because of a limited number of escort ships available?

3. A single torpedo is to be fired at an aircraft carrier which is 1,000 feet (333 yards) long. The torpedo firing errors are normally distributed according to the following table:

θ	30°	60°	90°	120°	150°
σ	2.0°	2.4°	2.7°	3.0°	3.5°

a. Calculate the firing range for which the probability of hit is 0.5 if the angle on the bow is 30 degrees.

b. Calculate the probability of hit from a range of 3,000 yards, if the angle on the bow is 120 degrees.

4. In determining the probability of hit contours for a formation of closely spaced ships, three methods were presented, each using a discrete simulation of the normal distribution. Suppose only five lines are to be used to represent possible torpedo tracks, and the angle on the bow is 60 degrees for which $\sigma = $ six degrees. Compute the number of degrees each of the five lines would vary from the desired relative torpedo track in order to simulate the normal distribution.

5. Consider the following diagram showing five possible torpedo tracks for a single torpedo. The on-station position of ships is shown along with their diffuse target

length and the length of the random columns. Each ship is approximately 200 yards in length.

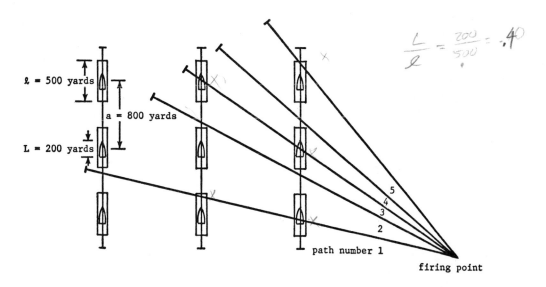

$$\frac{L}{\ell} = \frac{200}{500} = .4$$

a. What is the probability that a torpedo aimed as indicated will follow path number one?

b. Assuming each ship is on station, what is the probability of a hit from this firing point?

c. Assuming that each ship is in its diffuse target area of length 500 yards, what is the probability of hit?

d. Assuming random locations of ships in their respective columns, each of which is approximately 2,400 yards long, what is the probability of hit?

e. Explain why the different possible torpedo paths should be drawn with different lengths.

6. A single carrier is to be screened from enemy submarines by five destroyers each having a lateral range curve as given in Problem two. The carrier is 333 yards long and the formation speed is 20 knots. Submarine submerged speeds of up to 10 knots are estimated, and torpedo accuracy is as given in Problem three.

Determine the optimum screen stations of the five destroyers in providing the protection for the carrier. (A maneuvering board sheet will make plotting simpler.)

7. COMDESDIV 99 decides to arrange his ships in such a manner that the ships with type B sonar will, in every instance, separate two ships with type A sonar. He has five ships, two with type B and three with type A sonar. The lateral range curves are as shown in Problem one. Thus the screen formation will be of this general arrangement (use ESR from type A sonar):

    Type A   Type B   Type A   Type B   Type A

The wing ships are stationed on the limiting submerged approach lines, and the line $S_{(0 \cdot 5)}S'_{(0 \cdot 5)}$ is 14,000 yards in length.

a. What will be the distance between ships (in yards)? What is this spacing in terms of ESR?

b. What will be the line efficiency of such a screen if the submarine picks his optimal penetration point?

c. Assuming the submarine has no intelligence regarding the installed equipment or the location of ships, what is the line efficiency of the screen?

d. List in ATP-1 notation, the screening station assignment for ships in DESDIV 99.

e. If the submarine had a probability of 0.90 of scoring a hit once it penetrated the screen: (Assume the submarine will penetrate at his optimal point.)

   (1) Is the screen placement on the $S_{(0 \cdot 5)}S'_{(0 \cdot 5)}$ line optimal?

   (2) What is the submarine's best alternative?

f. What effect, if any, would patrolling of stations by the DESDIV 99 ships have on screen placement? Explain your answer.

8. Operations Evaluation Group Study Number 377 is concerned with predicting the improvement in performance which might result from changes in streamlining and battery power for a given submarine. The following are some basic relationships between *battery energy* (E), *power* (P), *time* (T), *speed* (S), *auxiliary power* (A) and *distance* (D):

$E = PT$, E is constant for a given battery;

$P = KS^\sigma + A$. K and σ are constants characterizing the submarine.

$D = ST$.

From these relationships, find the expression for the maximum value of distance (D_m) in terms of E, K, A and σ. (Hint: eliminate T, find dD/dS and, finally, D_m.)

11 Anti-Air Warfare

The most valid evaluation of a weapons system's effectiveness comes from observing its performance in actual combat against an enemy. Experience thus gained is invaluable in developing and predicting the effectiveness of new systems. When such direct experience is not available, however, other methods for analysis must be given a more active role. In this chapter several examples are given. One illustrates the use of fleet exercises in evaluating the *anti-air warfare* (AAW) effectiveness of fleet units. Another illustrates the use of a theoretical analysis to determine the optimum disposition of *combat air patrol* (CAP) about a task force. *Surface-to-air missile* (SAM) firepower is analyzed; then the problem of defense posture concerns trade-offs in maximizing the measures of effectiveness against the air threats of this chapter or against the surface and subsurface threats of the preceding chapter.

The general objective of the commander responsible for AAW is to protect the task force from enemy air attack. Each of his alternative methods of defense must specify values for the many controllable variables, from disposition of ships and aircraft to training of operators and procedures for repair and maintenance of equipment.

A measure of effectiveness must be chosen to compare the effectiveness of various alternatives in protecting the task force from air attack. Frequently, however, the measure of effectiveness used, in order to be measurable, must be one which measures only part of the overall objective.

1101 THE AAW EXERCISE

The fleet AAW exercise serves two very valuable purposes. First, it provides the pilots, air controllers, commanding officers and, in fact, all fleet personnel involved with the *training* essential to fleet combat readiness. Second, and equally important, it provides the *data base* from which the fleet commander may make a realistic appraisal of the capabilities of his command. Shortcomings revealed by close analysis of these data may be corrected, and the readiness of the fleet for future operations thereby improved.

An AAW exercise is designed to simulate the defense of a task force against an enemy air attack by using friendly aircraft to simulate the enemy. Some artificialities exist, of necessity, since friendly aircraft cannot actually be destroyed, and any means of countering a given raid must cease prior to the actual firing of weapons. Even so, the AAW exercise, if properly analyzed, yields much valuable information concerning fleet readiness.

Exercises are expensive; hence they require careful planning, data collecting and post-exercise analysis in order to derive maximum benefit from the cost and time incurred. In all exercises some sacrifice in realism must be made in order to reduce time and expense. Other means of simulating air defense operations are available in the form of war gaming and computer simulations which are much less expensive, but also less realistic because actual forces are not involved. Such techniques do afford valuable insight and a basis for prediction in areas where exercises are not feasible.

Complete and detailed instructions for the conduct of exercise analyses, as appropriate to the scope and objectives of the exercise and the size and character of the forces involved, are promulgated by the various numbered fleets, fleet commanders in chief, force and type commanders and the Chief of Naval Operations. The basic reference for the conduct of all fleet exercises is the *Conduct of Fleet Exercises* (FXP-5) series published by the Office of the Chief of Naval Operations.

It should be noted that the great bulk of exercise planning and analysis is done by line officers, not just OA qualified specialists, although the latter may be responsible for certain features of pre-exercise planning and for more sophisticated post-exercise evaluation. Experience in exercise analysis is part of the professional education of all line officers. Information garnered through thorough, thoughtful analysis is extremely valuable, while, conversely, the consequences of slipshod data recording and analysis can be serious and far-reaching in estimating the readiness and effectiveness of the forces afloat.

1102   EXERCISE ANALYSIS

In this example of an AAW exercise, 200 *enemy* aircraft attempted to penetrate the force AAW defenses which were composed of CAP interceptors and SAMs. In order to gain maximum training and collect more data in a limited time, each raid aircraft continued on to the center of the force whether or not it was successfully countered (intercepted) by CAP. For simplicity, the number of raids detected includes only those detected early enough to be opposed by both CAP and SAMs. The data collection was designed to provide information on the following sequence of events:

a. Raid detected. A raid was detected by the task force radar.
b. CAP assigned. A specific CAP was vectored toward the incoming detected raid.
c. Tally-ho. The CAP visually sighted the raid or *locked on* with its own fire control radar.
d. Intercept. The CAP successfully maneuvered into *position to fire* a weapon.

As the raid proceeded inbound to within missile range, another sequence of events was necessary for the raid to be successfully opposed by SAMs.

e. Raid designated. The raid was assigned to a specific missile system within the ship. This assignment was made by transmitting range, bearing and altitude of the raid to the weapons system fire control equipment.

f. Raid acquired. The weapons system fire control radar had begun to track the target, i.e., *locked on.*

g. Raid fired on. The raid was within firing range, the fire control solution complete and a missile ready for launch.

In Figure 11-1 basic data were collected simply by recording the number of raids for which each successive step was accomplished.

One use for such information is to point out which steps in the air and surface sequences are weakest. For example, it may be of interest to know the probability of detection resulting from a certain tactical disposition of the air search radar available to the force. Viewed in a strictly mathematical sense it is, of course, impossible to arrive at this number precisely. But when one considers the results obtained from the exercise as a statistical sample, then the data obtained may be used as a *best estimate* of the true, but *unknown,* probability of detection. In the discussion which follows, it will be understood that such terms as probability of detection, probability of intercept given tally-ho, and so on, will be best estimates of these probabilities based upon data obtained from this exercise. If data were available from several exercises, the results might be averaged in order to refine these estimates.

From the data in Figure 11-1, it is seen that of 200 raids, 160 were detected. Thus an estimate of the probability of detection can be obtained by taking the ratio of these two numbers,

$$P[D] = \frac{160}{200} = .80.$$

In a similar manner, conditional probabilities concerning the various phases of the air and surface problems can be computed.

Air Problem

Conditional probability of CAP assigned, given detection,

$$P[C|D] = \frac{120}{160} = .75.$$

Conditional probability of tally-ho, given CAP assigned,

$$P[T|C] = \frac{90}{120} = .75.$$

Air Problem		*Surface Problem*	
Number of raids	200	Number of raids	200
Number of raids detected	160	Number of raids detected	160
Number of CAP assigned	120	Number of raids designated	155
Number of tally-ho's	90	Number of raids acquired	120
Number of intercepts	40	Number of raids fired upon	115

Tabulated exercise data.

Figure 11-1.

Conditional probability of intercept, given tally-ho,

$$P[I \mid T] = \frac{40}{90} = .44.$$

Surface Problem

Conditional probability of designating a raid, given detection,

$$P[DES \mid D] = \frac{155}{160} = .968.$$

Conditional probability of acquisition, given designation,

$$P[ACQ \mid DES] = \frac{120}{155} = .774.$$

Conditional probability of SAM fired, given acquisition,

$$P[SAM \mid ACQ] = \frac{115}{120} = .958.$$

With a view to strengthening AAW, the above ratios might have provided an argument for improvement in certain factors of the air problem.

A useful *measure of effectiveness* which can be computed from these data is the probability that a raid can reach the task force without being either intercepted by CAP or fired on with SAMs. This probability is called the factorized probability of an unopposed raid, $P(u_f)$, and can be determined as follows:

$$P(u_f) = 1 - P(I \cup SAM)$$
$$= 1 - P(D)P(I \cup SAM \mid D)$$
$$= 1 - P(D)[1 - P(\overline{I} \cap \overline{SAM} \mid D)]$$
$$= 1 - P(D)[1 - P(\overline{I} \mid D)P(\overline{SAM} \mid D)], \text{ which gives}$$

Equation 11-1 $P(u_f) = 1 - P(D)\{1 - [1 - P(I \mid D)][1 - P(SAM \mid D)]\}.$

For this exercise where $P(D) = 160/200$, $P(I \mid D) = 40/160$, and $P(SAM \mid D) = 115/160$, the factorized probability of an unopposed raid is

$$P(u_f) = .369.$$

Notice that in developing Equation 11-1 independence was assumed in order that $P(\overline{I} \cap \overline{SAM} \mid D) = P(\overline{I} \mid D)P(\overline{SAM} \mid D)$. More precisely this implies that *once a raid is detected,* the event that the raid is fired on by SAMs is independent of whether or not the raid was intercepted by CAP. For an exercise of the type just described, this assumption seems valid, whereas if all detected raids were *not* presented to both CAP and SAMs (because some raids were either detected late or destroyed early) the assumption would not be warranted.

If the exercise provided for keeping track of each raid as it approached the task force, some data may be available in addition to the basic information tabulated for the air and surface problem. In this exercise, it was determined that the number of raids both intercepted by CAP and fired on by SAMs, $n(I \cap SAM)$, was 30. The detected raids can then be further broken down as in Figure 11-2.

Number both intercepted and fired on, $n(I \cap SAM) = 30.$

Number intercepted but *not* fired on, $n(I \cap \overline{SAM}) = 40 - 30 = 10.$

Number *not* intercepted but fired on, $n(\overline{I} \cap SAM) = 115 - 30 = 85.$

Number *neither* intercepted nor fired on, $n(D \cap \overline{I} \cap \overline{SAM})$

$$= 160 - (30 + 10 + 85) = 35.$$

Analysis of detected raids.

Figure 11-2.

The probability of an unopposed raid, $P(u)$, can now be found more simply using this additional information:

Equation 11-2 $$P(u) = \frac{n(\overline{D}) + n(D \cap \overline{I} \cap \overline{SAM})}{\text{number of raids}}.$$

For this exercise

$$P(u) = \frac{40 + 35}{200} = .375.$$

Considering that opposition to a raid not only could result in killing it before it reached the task force center, but could benefit the task force by other means (such as driving it away sooner or impeding the accuracy of its weapons delivery), the probability of an unopposed raid is a meaningful "inverse" measure of effectiveness. A better measure of effectiveness, however, might be the probability of a raid reaching the task force center without being destroyed, taking into account the kill probabilities for air and surface fired weapons. If these kill probabilities were known, they could be used with the exercise data to provide the probability of survival. Let S be the event a raid survives and K the event that a raid is killed or destroyed. Then the probability of survival is

Equation 11-3

$$P(S) = 1 - P(K)$$
$$= 1 - [P(K \cap I \cap \overline{SAM}) + P(K \cap I \cap SAM) + P(K \cap \overline{I} \cap SAM)]$$
$$= 1 - [P(K|I \cap \overline{SAM})P(I \cap \overline{SAM}) + P(K|I \cap SAM)P(I \cap SAM)$$
$$+ P(K|\overline{I} \cap SAM)P(\overline{I} \cap SAM)]$$

If the CAP's air-to-air weapon has a .7 kill probability and a SAM has a .4 kill probability, and we use the exercise data in Figure 11-2, substituting all into Equation 11-3 gives:

$$P(S) = 1 - \left\{ (.7)\left(\frac{10}{200}\right) + \left[1 - (.3)(.6)\right]\left(\frac{30}{200}\right) + (.4)\left(\frac{85}{200}\right)\right\}$$

$$= .672.$$

If the exercise data in Figure 11-2 are not known, then the probability of survival may be approximated by making the same independence assumption as before—this time to estimate the inputs for Equation 11-3.

It should be noted that time effects are ignored in the analysis; one would not apply these percentages with a linearity assumption to predict oppositions or kills if the raids were to come in such dense rates as to saturate the capability of some part of the AAW system.

Even considering the *constraints, artificialities* and *assumptions* controlling the conduct of this exercise, a probabilistic analysis serves its purpose quite well. It presents the weak areas in the air defense problem that have the most degrading influence on the overall air defense posture, and points out those areas where further study, modification, improved tactics or equipment needs to be investigated.

1103   DISPOSITION OF CAP

In warfare, and planning for warfare, the conservative approach is to base decisions on the capabilities of the enemy rather than on his intention. More often than not his capabilities are directly related to the position of his forces with respect to one's own forces. For example, there is cause for apprehension, at least, if an enemy aircraft is at the bomb release point. It may be that he intends not to attack, but prudence requires that one's defenses be designed in such a way as to prevent his gaining a position where the option belongs to him.

Consider the center of the task force as the origin of a cylindrical coordinate system. Label the coordinates horizontal range, bearing and altitude. Within this system can be located not only the enemy air forces but also one's own defensive forces, such as one's combat air patrol. It is in terms of these variables that a discussion of the most effective placement of the CAP can best be presented.

In order to investigate this problem, let us make some assumptions supported by operational experience. For example, it is well known that air search radar does not detect all air targets at the same range. In fact, some are not detected at all. Therefore, there must exist some function, $f(r)$, which describes the likelihood of detecting an approaching air target at range r. Experience has often shown this function to have the form of Figure 11-3. Such a function as this would depend on the type of radar, the type of aircraft, meteorological conditions, and so on. It is not too difficult to imagine a family of such curves, similar in shape to that found in Figure 11-3, resulting from variations of these parameters.

If the random variable, R, is defined as the horizontal range at which detection takes place, the function $f(r)$ should have the property that

Equation 11-4
$$P[R \geq r] = \int_r^\infty f(r)dr.$$

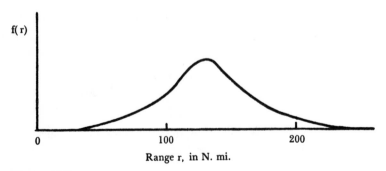

Range r, in N. mi.

Figure 11-3.

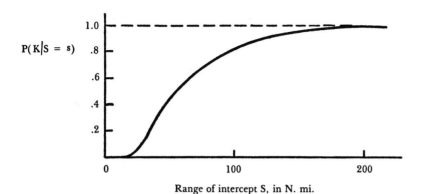

Figure 11-4.

But note that

$$\int_0^\infty f(r)dr = c, \text{ for } 0 \le c \le 1,$$

since detection is not absolutely certain.

Similarly, a function can be defined which will give the kill probability of enemy aircraft as a function of range from task force center at time of interception. Note that the kill probability should be higher the farther out interception takes place, as the CAP will have a longer period of time in which to carry out their attack.

Let S represent the range at which an incoming raid aircraft is intercepted. Then let $P(K|S = s)$ be the probability of kill, given that the range of intercept is equal to s. It is worth emphasizing that S is a random variable.

Figure 11-4 is a graph of $P(K|S = s)$ derived from combat data. It should be clear that a different function would result for different aircraft and weapon capabilities.

These two functions, $f(r)$ and $P(K|S = s)$, may be used to arrive at an optimal disposition of the CAP. Consider that n CAP aircraft can be kept on station at any one time to meet and oppose incoming raids. The following assumptions are made:

a. The n CAP will be stationed equidistantly on a circle of radius ρ from the task force center.
b. Only the CAP aircraft nearest to a raid will engage that raid.
c. The CAP will intercept at a speed equal to that of the enemy raid.

Figure 11-5 shows the geometry involved when an enemy raid, detected at range R, is intercepted by the nearest of the three CAP on station.

R is the range of radar detection, a random variable. The angle Φ between the bearing of the incoming raid and the bearing of the nearest CAP, is also a random variable. From the assumption of equal velocities, the distance flown by the nearest CAP to the point of interception is the same as that flown by the incoming raid, i.e., $R - S$. Applying the law of cosines to the triangle:

$$(R - S)^2 = \rho^2 + S^2 - 2\rho S \cos \Phi,$$

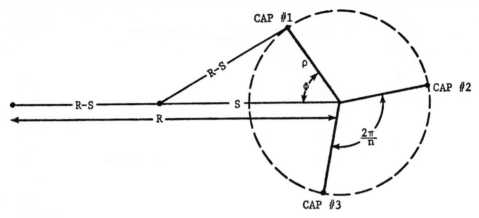

Figure 11-5.

which when solved for S yields

Equation 11-5

$$S = \frac{R^2 - \rho^2}{2(R - \rho \cos \Phi)}.$$

$P(K|S = s)$ was previously defined as the probability of kill if the range of intercept is equal to s. If the probability density function of S were known, the expected value of $P(K|S)$ could be found:

$$\overline{P}(K) = E[P(K|S)] = \int_{\text{all } s} P(K|s)f(s) \, ds.$$

In general, $f(s)$ will not be known explicitly. The functions $f(r)$ and $f(\phi)$ should be known, however—$f(r)$ from tests under controlled conditions or from past data as in Figure 11-3, $f(\phi)$ estimated from the expected tactical situation. Suppose $f(r)$ and $f(\phi)$ are known, and $f(r)$ is indeed a probability density function. Since S is a function of R and Φ, $P(K|S = s)$ can be written as a function of R and Φ, i.e., $P(K|R = r, \Phi = \phi)$.

The expected value of a function of any two independent random variables, X_1 and X_2, can be determined from

Equation 11-6 $\quad E[g(X_1, X_2)] = \int_{\text{all } x_1} \int_{\text{all } x_2} g(x_1, x_2)f(x_1)f(x_2) \, dx_2 \, dx_1$

$$= \int_{\text{all } x_1} f(x_1) \left[\int_{\text{all } x_2} g(x_1, x_2)f(x_2) \, dx_2 \right] dx_1.$$

Hence the expected probability of kill, $\overline{P}(K)$, can be found as

Equation 11-7

$$\overline{P}(K) = E[P(K|R, \Phi)] = \int_{\rho}^{\infty} f(r) \left[\int_{-\pi/n}^{\pi/n} P(K|r, \phi)f(\phi) \, d\phi \right] dr,$$

where $f(r)$ is found from Figure 11-3, and $P(K|R = r, \Phi = \phi)$ from Figure 11-4 after substituting for all the values S in Equation 11-5. The density function, $f(\phi)$, can be found if raids are assumed as likely to approach from one direction as from any other. Then Φ is uniformly distributed between $-\pi/n$ and π/n, giving

Equation 11-8 $$f(\phi) = \frac{n}{2\pi}, \text{ for } -\frac{\pi}{n} < \phi < \frac{\pi}{n}.$$

The limits of integration on r become ρ to ∞ since for any detection range less than ρ interception is not possible (at equal speeds) and $P(K|r, \phi)$ would be zero.

The overall probability of kill, computed using Equation 11-7, would not be a function of R and Φ, since these quantities are *integrated out*. However, this probability of kill still depends on n and ρ and, hence, can be written $P(K|n, \rho)$. For a given number of CAP, n, the probability of kill could be plotted as a function of ρ and the optimal value of ρ found. The computations conducted for the situation given in Figures 11-3 and 11-4 yield the results shown in Figure 11-6. It can be seen that the optimal CAP stationing distance for this example varies from zero to about 70 miles, depending on the number of CAP airborne.

For other typical situations, the integration in Equation 11-7 can become very difficult to complete by hand, although employment of computer techniques makes such computations routine.

1104 FIREPOWER EQUATION [1]

The probability of kill would be expected to be a nondecreasing function of detection range and/or the range of first interception, not only for CAP but for the SAM scenario as well. Therefore, it is desirable to construct a firepower equation that will determine the maximum number of missile salvos that can be fired at an incoming raid. The raid could be either an aircraft or a missile. In this derivation, the flight path is assumed directly toward the SAM firing ship, and the following sections will consider the more complex model when that assumption does not hold. The missiles fired are assumed to have a maximum intercept range and a minimum firing range. To get the maximum number of salvos, a salvo must be fired so that it will intercept exactly at its maximum

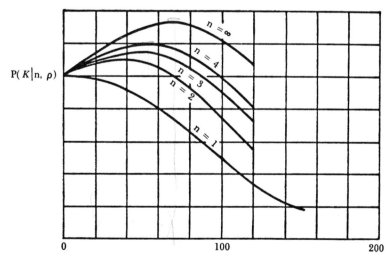

Mean patrol distance of CAP unit from task force, ρ

Figure 11-6.

range. Then salvos must be fired as fast as possible until the raid has closed within the minimum firing range.

In developing this equation, a *shoot-look-shoot* policy has been used with no delay times taken into account (look time = 0). In other words, as soon as one missile intercepts the raid, another is instantaneously fired.

The shoot-look-shoot model is especially valid when only one fire control radar or guidance system is available for that particular target.

Before we derive the equation, we define the following terms:

T = Threatening raid

X = SAM ship

RX = Maximum range of SAM

RN = Minimum firing range of SAM

V = Speed of SAM

U = Speed of raid

t = Time

x_1 = Distance of raid from ship at i^{th} intercept after passing R

n = Number of salvos after initial intercept

M = Total number of salvos fired at inbound raid

The firing geometry is illustrated in Figure 11-7.

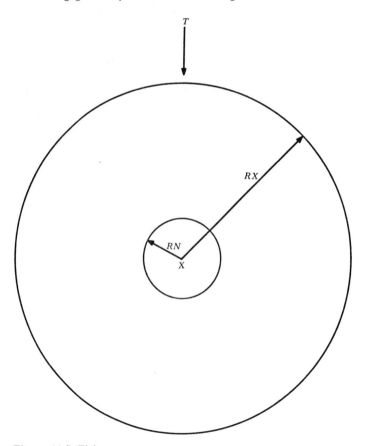

Figure 11-7. Firing geometry.

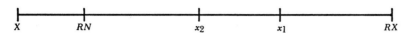

Figure 11-8.

As was stated before, the first salvo must be fired so that it will intercept at the maximum range of the missile. An equation will be derived for the additional number of salvos fired after the raid has reached RX, and one salvo will be added to this number to take into account the intercept which took place exactly at RX. [This means that the ith intercept is the intercept of the $(i + 1)^{\text{st}}$ salvo fired.]

With the raid at RX proceeding toward the ship, a salvo is fired. The missile travels a distance x_1, while the raid travels a distance $RX - x_1$ in Figure 11-8. The time of flight for each is the same. Therefore:

$$Vt = x_1 \quad \text{and} \quad Ut = RX - x_1.$$

Solving for the time and equating the two:

$$t = \frac{x_1}{V} \quad \text{and} \quad t = \frac{RX - x_1}{U},$$

or:

$$\frac{x_1}{V} = \frac{RX - x_1}{U}.$$

Solving now for x_1:

$$Ux_1 = V(RX - x_1)$$
$$x_1(V + U) = RX \cdot V.$$

Thus:

Equation 11-9.a
$$x_1 = RX \frac{V}{V + U}.$$

Similarly, for the second shot after the raid has passed R:

$$Vt = x_2 \qquad \text{thus} \quad t = x_2/V,$$
$$Ut = x_1 - x_2 \quad \text{thus} \quad t = \frac{x_1 - x_2}{U}.$$

Therefore:

$$\frac{x_2}{V} = \frac{x_1 - x_2}{U}.$$

Solving for x_2:

Equation 11-9.b
$$x_2 = x_1 \frac{V}{V + U}.$$

But from 11-9.a:

$$x_1 = RX \frac{V}{V + U}.$$

Substituting this into 11-9.b:

$$x_2 = RX \left(\frac{V}{V + U}\right)\left(\frac{V}{V + U}\right)$$

or:

Equation 11-9.c

$$x_2 = RX\left(\frac{V}{V+U}\right)^2.$$

For the third shot, again:

$$Vt = x_3 \qquad \text{thus } t = \frac{x_3}{V},$$

$$Ut = x_2 - x_3 \quad \text{thus } t = \frac{x_2 - x_3}{U}$$

Therefore:

$$\frac{x_3}{V} = \frac{x_2 - x_3}{U}.$$

Solving for x_3:

$$x_3 = x_2 \frac{V}{V+U}.$$

Substituting for x_2 from 11-9.c:

Equation 11-9.d

$$x_3 = RX\left(\frac{V}{V+U}\right)^3.$$

It is easily seen that this can be continued for $x_4 \ldots x_n$. By induction:

Equation 11-10

$$x_n = RX\left(\frac{V}{V+U}\right)^n.$$

Since the minimum missile range is RN, it will only be practical to shoot when $x_n \geq RN$. When $x_n < RN$, the missile cannot intercept the raid.

So:

$$x_n = RN \text{ and } RN = RX\left(\frac{V}{V+U}\right)^n.$$

Now solving for n by using logarithms:

$$\left(\frac{V}{V+U}\right)^n = \frac{RN}{RX}$$

$$n \log_{10} \frac{V}{V+U} = \log_{10} \frac{RN}{RX}$$

$$n = \frac{\log_{10} \dfrac{RN}{RX}}{\log_{10} \dfrac{V}{V+U}}.$$

Remembering that n tells the number of salvos that can be fired after the raid has passed R, one salvo must be added for the intercept that was made at R.

Therefore:

Equation 11-11

$$M = \left[\frac{\log \dfrac{RN}{RX}}{\log \dfrac{V}{V+U}} + 1\right],$$

where the square brackets denote the greatest integer contained within (since it would not be possible to fire a fraction of a missile).

Thus, given the maximum range of the missile, the minimum firing range of the missile, the speeds of the missile and the incoming raid, the maximum number of shots can be found by simply substituting the given values in the above formula and taking the greatest integer.

Since the SAM ship may be a picket stationed out on the axis of expected threat direction, it is also worth knowing the total number of salvos M^1 that could be fired at the raid after it has passed overhead the ship and headed outbound. A different equation could be derived in a manner similar to the incoming derivation. This would yield:

Equation 11-12
$$M^1 = \left[\frac{\log \dfrac{RX}{RN}}{\log \dfrac{V}{V-U}} + 1 \right].$$

The total number of salvos $(M + M^1)$ is then:

Equation 11-13
$$\left[\frac{\log \dfrac{RN}{RX}}{\log \dfrac{V}{V+U}} \right] + \left[\frac{\log \dfrac{RN}{RX}}{\log \dfrac{V-U}{V}} \right] + 2.$$

For ease in finding the number of salvos that can be fired at a raid inbound or outbound, Figure 11-9 graphs these numbers as functions of the speed and range

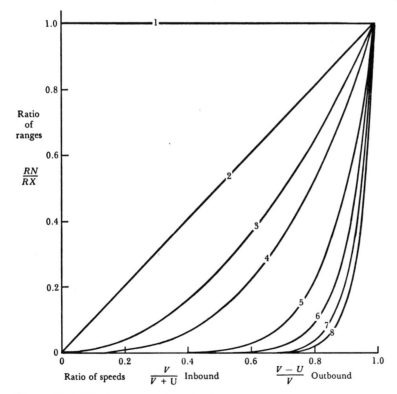

Figure 11-9. Maximum number of salvos.

ratios. By entering the graph with the calculated ratios of RN/RX and either $V/(V + U)$ or $(V - U)/V$, one locates a point, and the nearest curve above and to the left of this point tells the maximum number of salvos that can be fired inbound or outbound, respectively.

1105   AAW-ASMD SCREENING WITH SAM SHIPS

Firepower Analyzer

To make effective use of SAM-equipped ships in screening a convoy or task force from air attack (either aircraft or missiles), a method of determining the effect of various ship dispositions on the *overall* AAW-ASMD screen effectiveness is necessary. One model that can be used in determining AAW-ASMD screen effectiveness is called a firepower analyzer. This model simply determines the number of shots (or salvos) a SAM ship can get off at a given air target as a function of the target's closest point of approach (CPA) to the SAM ship. Figure 11-10 shows the geometry involved in the firepower analyzer model.

The *number of shots* that the SAM ship can fire during the time the target is within range is a function of maximum SAM range, target speed, SAM speed, SAM refire rate and the SAM ship firing doctrine. As seen from Figure 11-10, the smaller the range at CPA, the longer the target track length through the SAM firing envelope will be. This implies that regardless of the values of the variables discussed above, the number of possible shots will increase as CPA decreases.

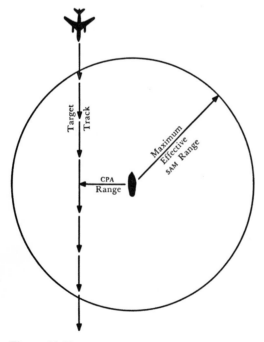

Figure 11-10.

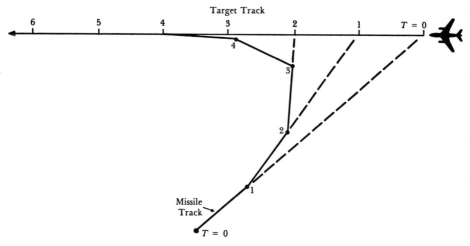

Figure 11-11. Pursuit course geometry.

SAM Flight Geometry

To determine mathematically the actual number of possible shots under a given set of conditions, a knowledge of the missile flight geometry is required. Two general types of flight geometries exist, *intercept* and *pursuit*. A pursuit geometry exists when a missile is guided or homes by constantly traveling in the direction of the current bearing to the target. Figure 11-11 illustrates the pursuit course of a missile. The distance traveled between missile course updates is exaggerated in Figure 11-11 for illustrative purposes. Actually, the missile is constantly turning as the target bearing changes.

An intercept course geometry is shown in Figure 11-12. To determine an intercept course, the target's speed must be known, which is not required for a pursuit geometry. In an intercept course situation, a lead angle (LA) is computed, based on target angle (TA), target speed (U) and SAM speed (V) such that the missile intercepts the target at a predetermined point along the target track.

As can be seen from Figures 11-11 and 11-12, the intercept course is *more efficient* in terms of the SAM *time of flight* before it reaches the target. Since maximizing the number of shots implies minimizing the time between shots, an intercept geometry will be preferred.

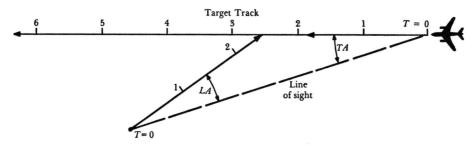

Figure 11-12. Intercept course geometry.

Number of Shots as a Function of CPA Range

Figure 11-13 illustrates the problem to be solved in calculating the number of possible shots as a function of CPA. The initial target angle can be defined as:

$$TA_1 = \sin^{-1} \frac{R_{CPA}}{RX},$$

where R_{CPA} = the range from SAM ship to target at CPA and RX = maximum range of SAM. The initial lead angle can be found from the following relationship:

$$LA = \sin^{-1} \frac{U \times \sin TA}{V}.$$

This lead angle relationship is derived as shown in Figure 11-14. For an intercept course to exist, the component of target speed across the line of sight (S_{TA}) must equal the component of missile speed across the line of sight (S_{MA}):

$$S_{TA} = U \times \sin TA$$
$$S_{MA} = V \times \sin LA$$
$$U \times \sin TA = V \times \sin LA$$
$$\sin LA = \frac{U \times \sin TA}{V}$$
$$LA = \sin^{-1} \frac{U \times \sin TA}{V}.$$

This relationship is valid as long as the target is closing the SAM ship. When the target has passed CPA and is opening, the situation shown in Figure 11-15 exists. Using the criterion for an intercept course to exist, $S_{TA} = S_{MA}$, the lead angle relationship for an opening target is derived as follows:

$$S_{TA} = U \times \cos (TA - 90°)$$
$$S_{MA} = V \times \sin LA$$
$$U \times \cos (TA - 90°) = V \times \sin LA$$
$$\sin LA = \frac{U \times \cos (TA - 90°)}{V}$$
$$LA = \sin^{-1} \frac{U \times \cos (TA - 90°)}{V}.$$

The lead angle relationships for an intercept course having been defined, the problem of Figure 11-13 can be solved for R_T, the distance traveled by the target between successive intercepts, and R_I, the range of the target from the SAM ship at a given intercept.

Knowing both lead angle and target angle, the third angle (ϕ) of the triangle described by RX, $R_{T(1)}$ and $R_{I(1)}$ in Figure 11-13 can be determined by subtraction:

$$\phi = 180° - (TA + LA).$$

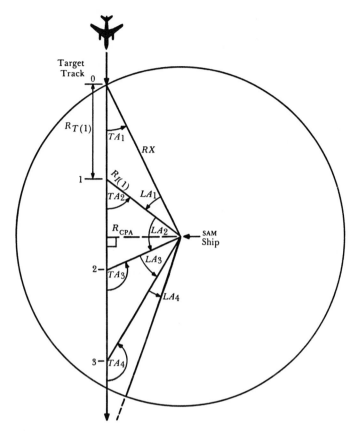

Figure 11-13.

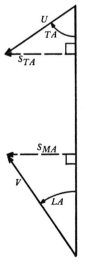

Figure 11-14.

Figure 11-15.

Then $R_{T(1)}$ and $R_{I(1)}$ can be found by the law of sines:

$$\frac{\sin \phi}{RX} = \frac{\sin TA}{R_{I(1)}} = \frac{\sin LA}{R_{T(1)}}$$

$$R_{I(1)} = \sin TA \times \frac{RX}{\sin \phi} = RX \frac{\sin TA}{\sin \phi}$$

$$R_{T(1)} = \sin LA \times \frac{RX}{\sin \phi} = RX \frac{\sin LA}{\sin \phi}.$$

If a shoot-look-shoot firing doctrine is used, and a zero time delay between shots is assumed, then the intercept range for the previous shot becomes the initial range for the succeeding shot, and the target angle for the succeeding shot can be expressed as:

$$TA_{(N)} = \sin^{-1} \frac{R_{\text{CPA}}}{R_{I(N-1)}} \quad \text{for a closing target,}$$

and:

$$TA_{(N)} = 180° - \sin^{-1} \frac{R_{\text{CPA}}}{R_{I(N-1)}} \quad \text{for an opening target.}$$

Now the lead angle can be calculated and $R_{T(2)}$ and $R_{I(2)}$ calculated, and so on until the target has flown out of SAM range.

To get the maximum number of salvos, a salvo must be fired to intercept exactly at maximum SAM range. Therefore, each intercept calculated in Figure 11-13 is in addition to the initial intercept at maximum range. The number of salvos that can be fired before the target passes out of range is found by solving the triangles of Figure 11-13 until the total of distance traveled between intercepts by the target, ΣR_T,

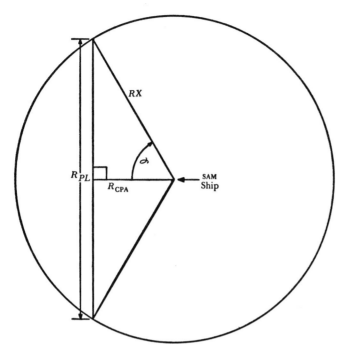

Figure 11-16.

exceeds the total path length of the target through the SAM envelope. This total path length is found as follows:

$$R_{PL} = 2 \times RX \times \sin \alpha,$$

where:

R_{PL} = Total path length of target through SAM envelope,

$$\alpha = \cos^{-1} \frac{R_{CPA}}{RX}.$$

Figure 11-16 illustrates the geometry leading to the preceding equation.

If $\Sigma R_T > R_{PL}$, then the last intercept calculated cannot be accomplished before the target is out of range and the last valid salvo is the preceding one.

Firepower Plot

Figure 11-17 is a plot of a SAM envelope for a ratio of $U/V = 0.8$, showing the locus of intercept points for each possible shot as calculated by the method discussed above. Two scales are shown in Figure 11-17, R_{CPA}/RX, the ratio of CPA range to maximum SAM range, and RS/RX, the ratio of SAM ship station range from force center to maximum SAM range. Both of these ratios are important in terms of the average number of shots expected against a target.

As can be seen from Figure 11-17, as the ratio of R_{CPA} to RX increases, the number of possible shots against the target decreases until, when the ratio is 1.0, only one shot is possible. If the ratio is greater than 1.0, the target never comes within SAM range, and it cannot be engaged. Conversely, as the ratio of RS to RX increases, the number of

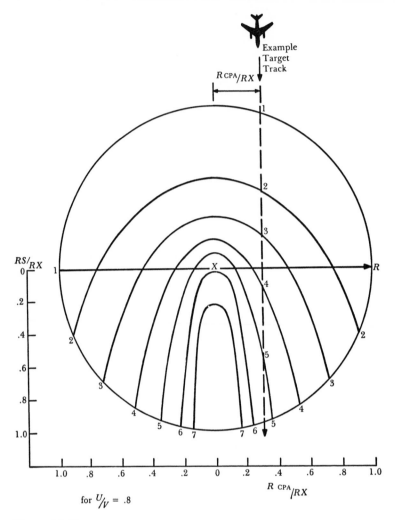

Figure 11-17.

possible shots increases until the maximum limit is reached at a ratio of 1.0. This occurs because as the distance of the SAM ship's station from force center is increased, the SAM ship has a longer time to engage the target before it reaches force center. The firepower analyzer here assumes that the incoming missile detonation point (or airborne weapons release point) is at the force center. The limit is reached when RS/RX is equal to 1.0 because the SAM ship now has the maximum possible time to engage the target. Any further increases in RS will not increase the number of shots, because the target already has to transverse the entire SAM envelope when $RS/RX = 1.0$.

Optimum Station Range

To optimize the distance from center at which the SAM ships should be stationed, the ratio RS/RX should be maximized while the ratio R_{CPA}/RX should be minimized. RS/RX can be optimized by stationing SAM ships a distance equal to RX, the maximum

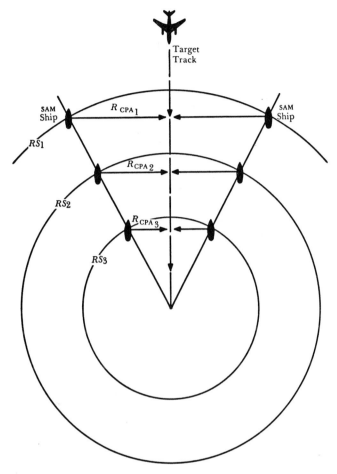

Figure 11-18.

effective SAM range from force center. However to optimize R_{CPA}/RX, the SAM ships must be stationed in as close as possible to force center, thereby minimizing the CPA of the target from the nearest SAM ship. Figure 11-18 illustrates this problem and shows how, for the same angular separation between SAM ships, decreasing RS (the station range) decreases R_{CPA}.

Then the two conditions for maximizing the number of shots are conflicting; to optimize RS/RX, RS would be equal to or greater than RX, and to optimize R_{CPA}/RX, RS must be as small as possible. To find the RS that provides the maximum expected number of shots, both of these competing effects have to be accounted for.

Relationship of RS and $R_{\text{CPA}_{\text{MAX}}}$

The relationship between RS and the maximum R_{CPA} is illustrated in Figure 11-19. Assuming an equally spaced circular screen of SAM ships, the angular separation between ships is given by:

$$\theta = \frac{360°}{NS},$$

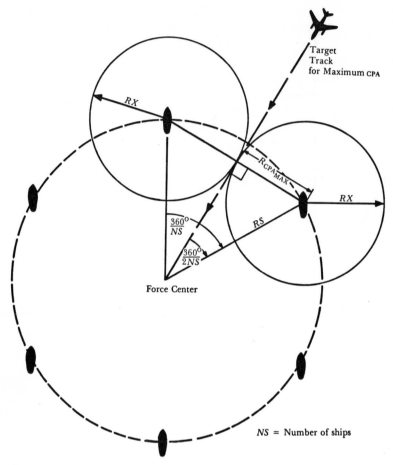

Figure 11-19.

where θ is angular separation between ships, and NS is the number of ships in the screen. The relationship between $R_{CPA_{MAX}}$ and RS is then:

$$\frac{\sin \theta}{2} = \frac{R_{CPA_{MAX}}}{RS},$$

or:

$$R_{CPA_{MAX}} = RS \times \sin \frac{360°}{2NS}.$$

The case illustrated in Figure 11-19 is that $R_{CPA_{MAX}} = RX$, the maximum effective SAM range. This case is for the maximum value of RS, because any further increase in RS leaves gaps in the SAM screen, and some targets would be able to reach force center without being engaged. As can be seen in Figure 11-19, the ratio RS/RX is greater than one. From the previous discussion of this ratio, a value greater than 1.0 does not increase the number of shots above the number of shots when the ratio is 1.0. Therefore, RS can be decreased until it is equal to RX without reducing the number of shots, and by decreasing RS the maximum value of R_{CPA} is reduced (see Figure 11-18), thereby increasing the number of shots expected against a target. By moving the SAM ships in until $RS = RX$, the ratio of RS/RX is still optimized and the ratio R_{CPA}/RX is reduced; and the combined effect is to increase the number of shots.

However, if the SAM ships are moved even closer in, the ratio of RS/RX becomes less than 1.0, which tends to decrease the number of shots. But at the same time, by decreasing RS, we are still decreasing $R_{\mathrm{CPA_{MAX}}}$, thus decreasing the ratio R_{CPA}/RX, which tends to increase the number of shots. The question is, at what point does the effect which decreases the number of shots become greater than the effect which increases the number of shots? RS is to be reduced until the decreasing effect of RS/RX becomes greater than the increasing effect of R_{CPA}/RX.

Number of Shots Versus R_{CPA}/RX and RS/RX

To answer the question posed above, it is necessary to know the magnitude of the sensitivity of the number of shots to changes of the ratios RS/RX and R_{CPA}/RX. Figure 11-20 is a plot of the number of shots versus the ratio R_{CPA}/RX. The different curves are shown for various values of the ratio RS/RX. Figure 11-20 is constructed from

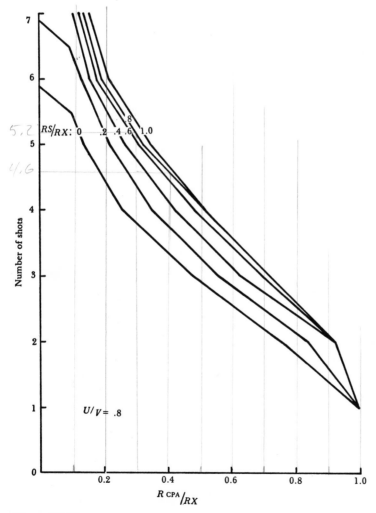

Figure 11-20.

Figure 11-17 by plotting the value of R_{CPA}/RX at which each of the curves for a given number of shots intersects either the line for a given value of RS/RX or the edge of the SAM envelope (whichever intersection occurs first). For example in Figure 11-17, the curve for two shots intersects the $RS/RX = 0$ line at a value of R_{CPA}/RX equal to 0.76. In Figure 11-20 then, for the curve when $RS/RX = 0$, two shots are plotted at an R_{CPA}/RX value of 0.76.

Average Number of Shots

Now, from Figure 11-20 and the relationship between RS and $R_{CPA_{MAX}}$ developed previously, the optimum value of RS can be calculated. It is assumed that incoming targets are randomly spaced around the screen perimeter so that any value of R_{CPA} between 0 and $R_{CPA_{MAX}}$ is equally likely. With this assumption the average number of shots against a target for a given value of RS/RX can be computed from Figure 11-20 by averaging the number of shots on the curve for the given RS/RX, across the range of R_{CPA}/RX values from $R_{CPA}/RX = 0$ to $R_{CPA}/RX = R_{CPA_{MAX}}/RX$. For example, if RS/RX is equal to 0.6, from the relationship $R_{CPA_{MAX}} = RS \sin \dfrac{360°}{2NS}$,

$$R_{CPA_{MAX}} = .6RX \sin \frac{360°}{2NS} \text{ and } R_{CPA_{MAX}}/RX = .6 \sin \frac{360°}{2NS}.$$

Optimum Station Range Example

Suppose three SAM ships are to be placed in an equally spaced circular screen. The relationship between RS/RX and $R_{CPA_{MAX}}/RX$ is then

$$R_{CPA_{MAX}}/RX = RS/RX \times \sin \frac{360°}{2 \times 3}$$
$$= RS/RX \times \sin 60°$$
$$= RS/RX \times .865.$$

Then the following relationships exist:

RS/RX	$R_{CPA_{MAX}}/RX$
1.0	0.865
0.8	0.69
0.6	0.53
0.4	0.35
0.2	0.17
0	0

The curves of Figure 11-20 for each value of RS/RX are averaged out to the appropriate value of $R_{CPA_{MAX}}/RX$, resulting in the following values:

RS/RX	Average number of shots, $\overline{N}$
1.0	4.6
0.8	5.1
0.6	5.5
0.4	5.9
0.2	6.3
0.0	5.9

For $RS/RX = 0.8$, $R_{CPA_{MAX}}/RX = 0.69$.

Therefore the curve for $RS/RX = 0.8$ is averaged from $R_{CPA}/RX = 0$ to $R_{CPA}/RX = 0.69$ as follows:

R_{CPA}/RX From - To	Number of Shots	x Weight =	
0 - .1	7.00	1.0	7.00
.1 - .2	6.75	1.0	6.75
.2 - .3	5.55	1.0	5.55
.3 - .4	4.90	1.0	4.90
.4 - .5	4.35	1.0	4.35
.5 - .6	3.85	1.0	3.85
.6 - .69	3.35	.9	3.02
		6.9	35.42
			$5.13 \cong 5.1$

Figure 11-21. Sample calculation for average number of shots.

An example of the calculation to obtain average number of shots is shown in Figure 11-21.

Figure 11-22 is a plot of the average number of shots as a function of RS/RX for the three-ship case calculated above. The dashed line shows the combined effects of decreasing RS/RX and decreasing R_{CPA}/RX as RS is decreased. The optimum value of RS/RX appears to be at about $RS/RX = 0.2$.

The solid curves in Figure 11-22 depict the two competing effects which combine to produce the dashed curve. The upper solid curve shows the increase that would be expected in number of shots caused by decreasing $R_{CPA_{MAX}}$ as RS decreases. The lower solid curve shows the decrease that would be expected in number of shots due to less engagement time as RS/RX decreases below 1.0. When the relationship between RS and $R_{CPA_{MAX}}$ is accounted for, as in the calculations of the example, the dashed curve is the result of interest.

1106 TRADE-OFF ANALYSIS—TORPEDO VERSUS AAW THREAT

If both a submarine and an aircraft or a missile threat exist simultaneously, then the screen placement should be optimized against the combined threat. It has been shown previously, in Chapter 10, that the submarine's probability of scoring a *torpedo hit* is a *function of the range* of the screen from the screened force. Section 1105 has shown that the *number of SAM shots* possible at an aircraft or missile target is also a *function of the screen's range* from the force screened. If the same ships are to provide both ASW and AAW protection, then the *optimum* screen radius will be the one that *minimizes the combined probability* of a hit from either a torpedo or an aircraft or a missile.

Probability of a Hit from the Air

To obtain the probability of being hit by an aircraft or a missile as a function of screen range, the number of shots versus screen range must be converted to a probability of shooting down the missile or aircraft. If the probability of shooting down the aircraft or missile with one shot is P_{Kss}, then the cumulative probability of shooting the target down is:

$$P_{K(N)} = 1 - (1 - P_{Kss})^N,$$

where $P_{K(N)}$ is the cumulative probability of kill with N shots, and N is the number of SAM shots at target.

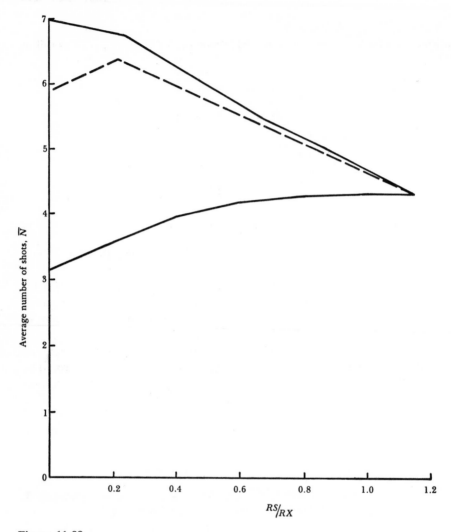

Figure 11-22.

If it is assumed that any missile or aircraft surviving the SAM screen will hit the screened force, then the probability of a hit from the air $P(H_A)$ is:

Equation 11-14 $$P(H_A) = 1 - P_{K(N)} = (1 - P_{Kss})^N,$$

where N, the number of SAM shots, is a function of the screen's range from the screened force.

Probability of a Torpedo Hit

A method of optimizing the screen radius (as shown in Chapter 10) against torpedo attack is to choose a screen radius that gives the submarine an equal probability of success from firing outside the screen or from penetrating the screen and then firing. Figure 11-23 is a graphical presentation of this torpedo screen optimization model.

The linearly decreasing function C is the submarine's probability of hitting the screened force with a torpedo as a function of firing range. The S-shaped curve is the

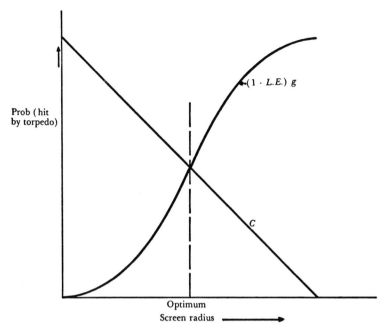

Figure 11-23.

probability of the submarine's successfully penetrating the sonar screen, $1 - L.E.$ (line efficiency), times the probability of a torpedo hit, g, given that the submarine fires from a given close range after penetrating the screen. The optimum screen radius is then the range at which these two functions have the same value. If the screen is stationed closer in, the submarine can fire from outside the screen and have a higher probability of hit than if the screen were stationed at the optimum range. Similarly, if the screen is stationed farther out than the optimum range, the submarine can more likely penetrate the screen, thereby attaining a higher probability of success than if the screen were optimally stationed.

Minimizing the Expected Number of Hits

To find the optimum screen radius when both submarine and air threats are present, the screen position that yields the lowest expected number of hits from both torpedoes and the air threat must be found. The number of torpedo hits expected for a given screen radius is combined with the number of hits expected from the air threat with the screen at that same radius to determine the total expected number of hits at a given radius. When the total expected number of hits is plotted against screen radius, the optimum screen position against the combined air and submarine threat can be found.

If the expected number of torpedo hits is:

Equation 11-15
$$E(H_T) = \sum_{\text{all } n} P_n(H_T) \times n_T$$

where $E(H_T)$ is the expected number of torpedo hits, $P_n(H_T)$ is the probability of a hit for the nth torpedo attack and n_T is the number of torpedoes fired in the nth attack, and the expected number of hits from the air is:

Equation 11-16
$$E(H_A) = \sum_{\text{all } n} P_n(H_A) \times n_A$$

where $E(H_A)$ is the expected number of hits from the air, $P_n(H_A)$ is the probability of a hit for the nth air attack and n_A is the number of weapons delivered in the nth attack; then the total expected number of hits for the screen at a given radius is:

Equation 11-17
$$E(H_{\text{TOT}})_R = E(H_T)_R + E(H_A)_R$$

where $E(H_{\text{TOT}})_R$ is the total number of expected hits with the screen at radius R, $E(H_T)_R$ is the expected number of torpedo hits with the screen at radius R and $E(H_A)_R$ is the expected number of hits from the air with the screen at radius R.

Example of Optimum Stationing against Air and Submarine Threat

If the probability of a submarine torpedo attack or an attack from the air is equally likely, and the probability of hit, $P_n(H_T)$ and $P_n(H_A)$, does not vary from attack to attack, then the total number of expected hits can be computed on the basis of one attack from the air and one submarine torpedo attack. If either of these assumptions is not true, the total expected number of hits must be computed on the basis of the expected number of air and submarine attacks.

Making the assumptions of equally likely attack from air or submarine, and no variance in attack-to-attack hit probability, then the expected number of hits is the product of probability of hit and the number of weapons launched in an attack. If it is further assumed that the number of weapons delivered by each threat in each attack is the same and is equal to one, then the total expected number of hits is the sum of the probability of a hit from the air and the probability of a hit from a torpedo.

Figure 11-24 is the plot of torpedo hit probability versus screen radius for a torpedo with maximum range of 6,000 yards and two sonar screens, one with an effective sonar range (ESR) of 2,000 yards and one with an ESR of 4,000 yards. Figure 11-25 is a plot of probability of a hit from the air versus screen radius. Figure 11-25 is derived from Figure 11-22 by using Equation 11-14,

$$P(H_A) = (1 - P_{Kss})^N,$$

where Figure 11-22 gives N as a function of screen radius, and assuming a SAM range of 20 miles.

Using Figures 11-24 and 11-25, one can plot the expected number of total hits versus screen radius. Figure 11-26 is such a plot. The lower curves are derived when the assumption is made that both types of attack are equally likely and the same number of weapons (one) is launched by each type of threat. The upper curves assume that the threat from air attack is tenfold (either ten weapons per attack or ten attacks with one weapon) and the submarine torpedo threat remains at one.

As can be seen from Figure 11-26, local minima occur at the screen radii corresponding to the minima that occur in Figure 11-24 for torpedo attack and to the minimum of Figure 11-25 for air attack. At each of those ranges, the curvature from one threat is not sufficient to offset the cumulative minimum caused by the other. When the threats are equally likely and deliver the same number of weapons, the local cumulative minimum occurring at the radius corresponding to the minimum torpedo hit probability is much lower than the local cumulative minimum at the minimum air

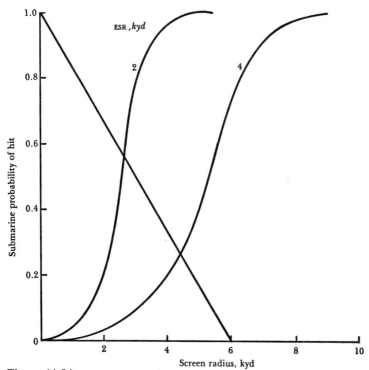

Figure 11-24.

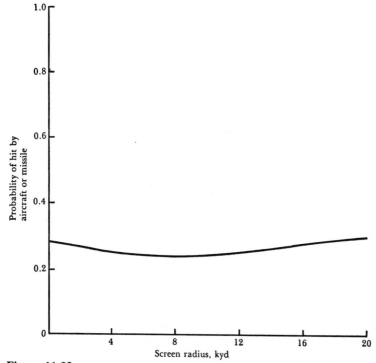

Figure 11-25.

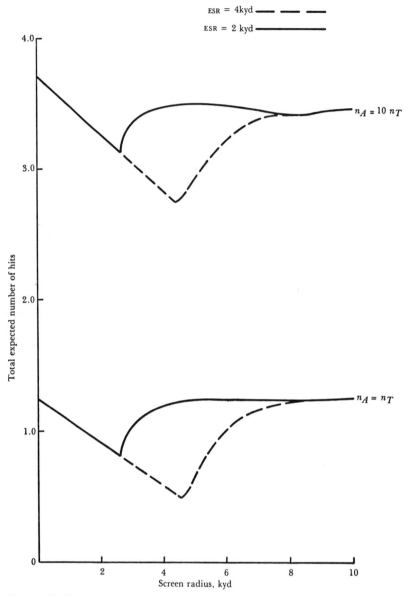

Figure 11-26.

hit screen radius. In fact, the local cumulative minimum corresponding to the mini-mum air threat radius is barely discernible. When the air threat is ten times as great as the submarine torpedo threat, the local cumulative minimum for the minimum air threat radius is much more evident; however, it is still greater than the cumulative minimum corresponding to the minimum torpedo hit radius.

A conclusion from this illustration would be that, for the parameters of the example, the screen should be optimized against the torpedo threat to optimize against both torpedo and air threats. This conclusion would be valid at least to the point where the air threat was ten times as great as the torpedo threat.

BIBLIOGRAPHY

[1] This section taken from a paper by Commander John G. Burton, USN, and others.

PROBLEMS

1. Given the following data for an AAW exercise conducted as described in this chapter:

Air Problem

Number of raid aircraft 225
Number of detections 210
Number of CAP assigned 150
Number of tally-ho's 125
Number of intercepts 100

Surface Problem

Number of raids designated. 200
Number of raids acquired 150
Number of raids fired upon. 100

> Number intercepted by CAP and fired upon by SAMs 45
> Probability of a kill for CAP weapons 3/4
> Probability of a kill for SAMs 3/4

Determine:

a. The factorized probability of an unopposed raid, $P(u_f)$.
b. The simple probability of an unopposed raid, $P(u)$.
c. The probability of survival of a raid.

2. From a different AAW exercise, the following data were collected:

Air Problem

Number of raid aircraft 200
Number of detections 160
Number of CAP assigned 130
Number of tally-ho's 115
Number of intercepts 88

Surface Problem

Number of raids designated 155
Number of raids acquired 120
Number of raids fired upon. 115

> Probability of kill with CAP weapons 1/2
> Probability of kill with SAM 1/2

a. Determine factorized probability of an unopposed raid, $P(u_f)$.
b. Estimate the probability of survival of a raid, $P(S)$.

3. In the CAP stationing model in this chapter, if CAP speed is K times the speed of the enemy aircraft, where $K > 0$:

a. Find the range of intercept, S.
b. What is the minimum range of detection for which a raid can be intercepted before reaching the task force center?

4. The probability of kill as a function of range of intercept, S, is $P(K|S) = 1 - e^{-.02s}$ where s is in N.mi.; detection range R has a density function given by $f(r) = .01(1 - .005r)$ for $0 < r < 200$; and four CAP are airborne. Write an expression which, if evaluated, would give the probability of kill in terms of CAP stationing distance, ρ, using the assumptions given in this chapter.

5. (*Optional Problem*) CAP *stationing computer simulation.* Develop a Monte Carlo computer simulation model of CAP intercept for the following situation: An aircraft carrier is

in midocean and an attacking aircraft may come from a random direction. A given number of aircraft, n, can be kept in the air continuously to defend the carrier. In considering where to put them, it is obvious to space them equally; the question is the best value of ρ, the stationing radius.

From Section 1103, a complete solution of the problem would seem to require already knowing the probability of detection as a function of target range R; also the probability of destroying the intruder before he reaches the carrier as a function of how far out he is intercepted, distance S. Assume that P[Det] $\simeq f(R)$ is a normal distribution with mean μ_R N.m. and standard deviation σ_R N.m. Consider a scenario wherein P[Kill] $\simeq f(S)$ is not known with any certainty, because a new air-to-air missile system has recently been installed in the fighter aircraft and operational data are lacking for combat conditions. However, it is reasonably certain that P[Kill] is a nondecreasing function of S. The task group commander reasons that, since the farther out the intercept, the higher the probability of shooting down the intruder, the ideal disposition (ρ) is that which maximizes the average value of the distance of the interception before the carrier, $\overline{S}$.

Utilize Z stationing radii increments of 1 N.mi. each. Next conduct a sensitivity analysis with respect to n, by comparing the optimum ρ for $n = 1, 3, 5$ and 24.

The model flow chart below oriented to BASIC or FORTRAN uses the variables designated above, plus the following:

$N =$ Number of CAP stationed
$M =$ Number of Monte Carlo trials
$B(\ ) =$ Array to keep the sum of ranges of interception S, for each of the CAP radii of station
$P =$ Randomly generated value of ϕ
$C =$ Cosine of random ϕ
$E =$ Sequential number of interceptor station
$F =$ Radius of interceptor station (ρ)
A: Average S for a particular ρ

Assumptions and Considerations

1. Let the speed of the intruder = the speed of the interceptor.
2. Program so that a value of n may be supplied without altering the program.
3. Because of the large amount of computer time used in generating normally distributed random variables (at least 12 RNDs each), the program utilizes each randomly generated target detection location for all the CAP station increments.
4. Notice that, at equal speeds, an interception before the attacker reaches the center cannot take place if the detection range R is less than ρ. Notice also that absolute application of Equation 11-5 for S could give negative values of S in certain instances. This is correct in that it signifies an interception *after* the intruder has passed the carrier. However, an interception after the carrier has been bombed is of no value. In this event, since the intruder is not intercepted before reaching the center, an S of 0.0 should be logged, to avoid biasing with negative S distances. Remember that such events do count as trials.

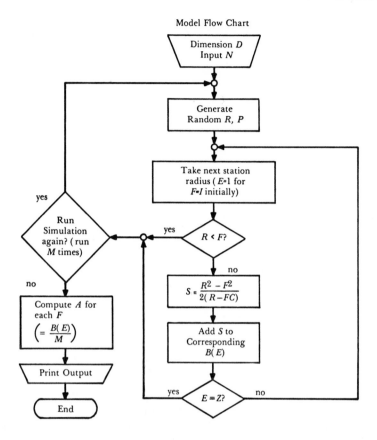

Model Flow Chart

Looking at the output, what conclusions can you draw from the rate of change in optimal stationing radius as the number of CAP is increased?

The task group commander is assuming that the expected value of a function of a random variable can be closely approximated by that function of the expected value of the random variable. Illustrate graphically how this could be wrong for this case.

12 Mine Warfare

In October 1950, an amphibious task force of 250 ships with some 50,000 troops embarked, steamed back and forth outside the approaches to Wonsan harbor in Korea. D-day for the landing at Wonsan had been set for 20 October, but a week after D-day the task force still marched and countermarched offshore while food supplies ran low. The landing was delayed because the approaches to Wonsan were mined. The situation was reported to the Chief of Naval Operations by Rear Admiral Allan F. Smith, U. S. Navy, in a message which began:

> The U. S. Navy has lost control of the sea . . . .

Admiral Forrest Sherman, U. S. Navy, who was then CNO, later explained Admiral Smith's shocking statement by saying:

> When you can't go where you want to, when you want to, you haven't got command of the sea.

Mine warfare had been used with great success long before Korea. Its origin can be traced back to 668 A.D., when Callinicus of Heliopolis invented *Greek Fire,* a highly inflammable mixture which burned underwater. Mines were talked about, and even used on occasion over the centuries, but were generally rejected for naval use because they were considered too clandestine for any chivalrous nation to use.

It was actually a minefield which Admiral Farragut so heartily *damned* at Mobile Bay. (The terms *mine* and *torpedo* were used interchangeably during that period.) Mines were used extensively by both Union and Confederate forces in the Civil War—by the South because they lacked naval forces and by the North because, in the words of Farragut:

> It does not do to give the enemy such a decided superiority over you.

248

The Civil War taught that, regardless of how distasteful mines may be as a weapon of war, navies must be prepared to defend against them and to use them whenever they can be employed productively.

Mine warfare was effectively waged in World Wars I and II by both sides. In June 1942, the German submarine U-701 planted 15 mines off the Chesapeake Capes. The results are described by Lieutenant Commander Arnold S. Lott, U. S. Navy, in his book *Most Dangerous Sea*. [1] It is an excellent example of how a very minimum expenditure of material and effort can produce tremendously effective results through the use of sea mines.

Late in the afternoon of June 15, Convoy KN 109, 18 ships and escorts, rounded Cape Henry enroute to New York from Key West. For a few minutes SS *Empire Sapphire* carrying the Convoy Commodore, waited off the entrance buoy for a pilot. The waiting convoy was a flock of sitting ducks for any lurking submarine, so at 1658, *Empire Sapphire* attempted to lead them in. Four minutes later an explosion shook the 11,000-ton tanker SS *Robert C. Tuttle*. U-701's first mine was found, and *Tuttle's* 142,700 barrels of crude oil never reached Philadelphia. PC-474 rescued the crew and the hulk was run ashore at Virginia Beach.

At this point Convoy 109 broke up into a confused melee of wandering ships. SS *Esso Augusta*, another 11,000-ton tanker loaded with fuel oil, began zigzagging and her Vice Commodore ordered the others to follow suit to avoid supposed submarine torpedoes. For half an hour she carried on around the entrance buoy until an explosion left her damaged, but not sinking. The second German mine had been found.

All the while, planes circled overhead and convoy escorts charged about hunting a submarine which had been long gone. Finally, at 1752, *Empire Sapphire* and the other ships picked up pilots and cleared out for Hampton Roads. Busily engaged in the submarine hunt, the destroyer *Bainbridge* got a contact about 1827 and dropped eight depth charges. Nine explosions followed. The extra one shook *Bainbridge* from stem to stern and laid her up for a six day repair job. The third German mine had been found. A mile or so away, *Esso Augusta* was still having her troubles. The escorting armed trawler, HMS *Lady Elsa*, had made three attempts to take her in tow, broken three tow lines, and finally gave up the whole idea. The Coast Guard sent a boat out to protect *Esso Augusta* and another to give a *mine warning* to three more ships coming up the coast and about to round the entrance buoy, where, it had finally been deduced, the Germans had planted mines in the channel.

The new arrivals, the armed trawler HMS *Kingston Ceylonite* and tug SS *Warbler* towing SS *De Lisle*, got the word too late. At 1915 a mine demolished *Kingston Ceylonite*. Her last bit of wreckage disappeared within two minutes. The fourth German mine had been found. That night SS *Keshena* and SS *Coyote* towed *Esso Augusta* into Hampton Roads. (*Keshena* was sunk by a United States mine in the Hatteras field a month later. A German mine got *De Lisle* off St. John's in November.)

On June 16th no ships moved out of Hampton Roads or Newport News, no incoming ships entered Chesapeake Bay. Sweepers checked the suspected area for magnetic mines and found five. More sweepers went over the usual ship channels but found no mines there. Then Mine Warfare School sweepers showed up to sweep for magnetic and acoustic mines. One, in error, swept for moored mines. All she caught was a harmless, old fashioned anchor. Finally, everyone swept for magnetics, found none, and the area was opened to shipping.

Next morning the regular southbound convoy sailed from Hampton Roads for Key West. At 0748, within two miles of the fatal entrance buoy, and in the area supposedly cleared, SS *Santore* was ripped open by a mine and went down with 11,095 tons of coal and three of her crew.

The Vietnam and Middle East conflicts illustrated once again the important role of mine warfare. During these conflicts both land and sea mines were used in both defensive and offensive tactical situations. Some of the weapons employed (representing the latest state of the art) were designed to be highly target-selective, highly reliable and very difficult to sweep or neutralize.

1201 OBJECTIVES

The minefield laid by the u-701 illustrates two main purposes which may be served by mine warfare:

a. To damage or destroy enemy shipping.
b. To deny the enemy use of certain waters, or at least hinder his operations in these waters by the threat presented by a minefield.

For a minefield to accomplish the first of these objectives, it must be laid in secret in a busy shipping lane. Secrecy is essential, for if the enemy suspects a minefield is present, he can sweep to eliminate the mines or perhaps simply reroute shipping around it. The fact that the field is laid in secret usually restricts the number of mines to be used; therefore a large number of ships must pass through the field before the probability of a hit becomes great enough to be significant.

Minefields laid to accomplish the second objective should be highly advertised after planting in order to deter enemy shipping. Knowing of its presence, the enemy will attempt to render the field harmless by sweeping operations. As a consequence, some effort must be devoted to keeping the field active. This means that the field must be reseeded at a rate equivalent to the sweeping rate of the enemy.

Deterrent fields may be used either offensively or defensively. An example of the former is the mining of an enemy's seaports in order to deny him effective use of those ports. Minefields may be used defensively around friendly ports to keep hostile submarines out of harbors or to deter an invasion force. They may also be used in a landing area to protect the ships of an amphibious force from counterattack by submarines or PT boats.

One general consideration which must be noted in mine warfare is that mines, once planted, do *not* distinguish between *friend* and *foe*. They will destroy one's own or neutral forces as indiscriminately as those of an enemy. It is therefore essential that the presence of minefields be carefully published to all friendly forces who may be apt to traverse the mined area. It is required by international law (The Hague Convention, 1907) that the presence of minefields which threaten neutral shipping be published to the neutrals concerned.

Careful thought must also be given to the possibility that some ports in enemy control today may reasonably be expected to be in friendly hands at some time in the future. Mines laid there to harass the enemy may require expensive and time-consuming sweeping efforts on the part of the minelayers in order to use the newly captured port.

1202 TYPES OF NAVAL MINES

Mines may be designed to lie on the bottom—even to bury themselves in the mud—to await a passing ship (*bottom mines*); they may be designed to float near, but just under, the surface while anchored to the bottom by a cable (*moored mines*); or they may be designed to drift with the current (*drifting mines*).

Depending on the objective of the minefield, the actuation of individual mines can be accomplished in one of three ways. *Controlled mines* are useful in defense of one's own ports. The field is controlled completely from an observation post ashore so that the mines may be set off electrically as desired, or control from the shore may be limited to arming or disarming to allow friendly shipping to pass safely through the field. *Independent mines* are those that are operated automatically by some device activated by the presence of a ship.

Independent mines are actuated either by physical *contact* with the target or by one of several *influence*-type exploder mechanisms which require only that a ship pass close by.

Although considered obsolete for years, the old-fashioned contact mine was used successfully as recently as the Korean War. A typical contact mine is a sphere with external projections called *horns*. These horns are made of a light material which bends easily on impact with a ship's hull. In each horn is a vial of electrolyte which, when broken, closes an electrical circuit and explodes the main charge of TNT inside the mine. There are three basic types of influence mines: *magnetic, acoustic* and *pressure*. Mines can also be constructed with a combination of two or more of the basic influence mechanisms. The magnetic mine is actuated by the passage of a metal-hulled ship which causes a disturbance of the vertical component of the earth's magnetic field. The acoustic exploder mechanism is equipped with hydrophones to detect the noise made by ship's machinery. Pressure mines react to the phenomenon that a ship in shallow water creates two pressure waves on the sea bottom, separated by a low-pressure (null) area. In the case of a *combination* mine, each influence criterion must be satisfied for mine detonation to be possible.

Although the area of influence for all these mines may be thought of as a circle around the mine, most are designed so that the explosion is delayed until the ship has reached its closest point of approach to the mine. Therefore, the activating area is reduced to a line extending on either side of the mine but perpendicular to the course of the ship.

The thought of mines lurking forever in the sea to destroy a ship unlucky enough to pass by brings terror to the heart of every seaman. Thus devices for rendering mines harmless after a specified period of time were developed almost concurrently with the invention of the exploder mechanisms. A natural sterilizing effect is provided in any device which depends on battery power for its operation, for as soon as the battery has run down the mine is harmless. More controllable sterilizing devices have been developed in the form of clock mechanisms and water-soluble collars which deactivate firing circuits after a preset period of time.

Delayed arming devices are provided as protection for the minelaying vessel, and as a countermeasure for minesweeping. Delay devices, in the form of clocks or water-soluble collars, cause a mine to activate after it has been in the minefield for a specified period of time. A more sophisticated device permits arming as a function of the number of ships passing within the influence area of the mine. It is usually in the form of a ratchet arrangement which may be set to delay detonation for any number of activations before the final firing circuit is completed. Each ship that comes within the mine's influence advances the ratchet to the next position until a detonation occurs.

1203   MINE DELIVERY

Ships have been designed and built to provide storage, servicing and minelaying facilities. However, the job of minelaying, per se, can be easily accomplished by almost any type of ship with very minor modifications. The North Koreans used sampans to lay the fields at Wonsan. The U. S. Navy used ferryboats as minelayers during both World Wars I and II. The destroyer is a useful vehicle when speed is essential in hostile waters. During World War II, a division of destroyers, rigged as minelayers (DMs), managed to lay 255 mines just six miles in front of a Japanese task force proceeding down *The Slot* between New Georgia and Santa Isabel Islands in the Solomons.

Surface delivery is most useful when it is essential to accurately position mines in a minefield and when the enemy forces in the area are weak or nonexistent. Surface minelayers are vulnerable to attack, however, by shore batteries, surface, air or subsurface units.

Minelaying by aircraft is especially useful in waters controlled by the enemy, even where formidable enemy defenses exist. Aircraft are most useful for replenishment of an already active minefield. Mines may be dropped from most bombers, or even transport aircraft, with very slight changes to existing configurations. Liberator bombers and B-29s were used effectively for this purpose during World War II. Air-dropped mines are often rigged with parachutes to slow their descent and reduce the impact velocity. The position accuracy of air-drop minefields is generally excellent if they are laid by aircraft with accurate air navigation and computer delivery systems. Some mines may be ineffective because of damage during the drop.

The Germans were the first to utilize the submarine to lay minefields covertly under the very noses of their enemy. The incident related earlier about U-701 is an excellent example. With mines designed so that they can be launched through the standard torpedo tubes, any attack-type submarine is a potential minelayer. Submarine minelaying is a means of obtaining very accurate positioning with greatly reduced probability that the delivery vehicle will be detected. It would be a mistake, however, to leave the impression that submarines are immune to detection in hostile areas. Submarines are most vulnerable to detection and attack when operating in waters shallow enough to be mineable. It is also quite likely that the very sea lanes which offer the best opportunity for mine warfare are the very waters where the enemy concentrates his ASW forces.

In summary, it is readily apparent that one advantage of mine warfare is that no specially designed vehicles are required for delivery. Any nation with ships, bombers or submarines has a potential minelaying force.

1204   MINE COUNTERMEASURES

Mine countermeasures are of three general types:

a. Special equipment installed on board ship to prevent the mine's actuating devices from functioning.

b. Physically removing, exploding or disarming mines in a minefield before friendly ships transit the field.

c. Circumnavigation of the field.

The last requires little comment. It is obvious that if a minefield's exact location is known and if shipping can be routed around it without undue inconvenience, the enemy will do so.

When it is necessary to use waters known or suspected to be mined, then sweeping or hunting operations are required to clear a channel through which shipping can pass. In shallow, clear waters moored mines may be visible from a boat or a helicopter. Hunting operations consist of locating individual mines and then disarming or destroying them.

Disarming or removing the mines is especially hazardous when the same areas have been bombed, as in the case of Vietnam anchorages and mud flats, since they are difficult to distinguish when mostly buried, and require different handling.

Sweeping operations vary with the type of mine. For moored mines, a cable with a paravane device to support the cable at its outer end and to hold it out at an angle to the sweeper is towed through the water. Spaced along the cable are cutting blades which sever the mooring lines of mines encountered. The mines then bob to the surface and can be destroyed by gunfire. [2]

Bottom mines are obviously not vulnerable to this type of sweeping activity. Certain types of influence mines may be destroyed, however, by towing a device to simulate the influence field of a ship and thereby cause the mines to explode. Noise-makers may be used to actuate acoustic mines. A device to create an electromagnetic field sufficient to disturb the vertical component of the earth's magnetic field may be used to actuate magnetic mines. The device can be towed by either ship or helicopter.

The most difficult mine to counter is the pressure mine. The difficulty lies in attempting to create the pressure disturbance of a large moving ship without using a large moving ship. Such sweeping devices are very expensive to consider. It may be worthwhile to note, however, that one mine defense tactic which could be employed is to move ships through a suspected minefield in column so that all but the lead ship would in effect be traversing waters already swept.

Minesweeping is a slow, expensive and nerve-racking business. It is successful only to some degree. The word *sterilized* is frequently used to describe a minefield presumably rendered harmless by minesweeping or hunting operations. However, one can never be 100 percent certain that all mines have been destroyed. It is only possible to reduce the probability of ships' being destroyed by mines to a level that is acceptable to the commander responsible for ordering forces into mined waters. With the delayed arming devices described earlier, it is possible for sweeping operations to go on repeatedly, only for it to be found that when shipping begins to move through the field, a new group of mines is active.

Passive measures on board a ship used to counter mine warfare vary with the type mine against which the ship is defending. As a defense against magnetic mines, *degaussing* coils are used to counter the disturbance which a metal ship would otherwise cause in the earth's magnetic field. Some limited defense against acoustic and pressure mines may be provided by moving very slowly with as little machinery noise and water disturbance as possible. Against moored contact mines, the best defense is to detect mines by sonar, helicopter or other visual means, and then maneuver the ship to avoid them.

1205 MINEFIELD PLANNING

From the foregoing discussion, it is obvious that a preliminary consideration in planning a minefield is the mineability of the waters. Two factors bear on this consideration:

a. Where the objective is destruction of shipping, it is essential that the plant not be detected by the enemy.

b. Where the objective is to deny the enemy use of certain waters, the commander must decide whether the objective justifies the risk to the minelaying force.

In order to use bottom mines effectively, one must be certain that the waters are shallow enough so that shipping will be within lethal range of the mine. The effect of tides and currents, as well as water depth, are important considerations in the use of moored mines. Where tidal variations are large, the moored mines may be submerged too deep to be effective at high tide and exposed on the surface at low tide. When tidal currents are strong, the moored mine may be dragged too far under the surface to be effective for several hours during the day.

Besides the preliminary consideration of mineability, the effectiveness of a minefield is a function of certain other factors:

a. Density of enemy shipping traffic.

b. Density of mines in the field, which in turn is a function of the number of mines and the area of the minefield.

c. Effective area of influence of the mines used.

d. The effective influence area of a transiting ship, which is a function of the length of path through the field and the width of the ship's influence area.

The problem confronting a minefield planner is one of levels of effectiveness under certain constraints:

a. Given specific minefield dimensions and traffic, what is the minimum number of mines required, and how should they be planted to obtain a predetermined level of effectiveness?

b. Given the same field and a specific number of mines, how should they be planted to achieve maximum effectiveness?

Consider the minefield for which the objective is destruction of enemy shipping. It might be hoped that several ships would blunder into the field before it is identified by the enemy and shipping warned away. Such was the case in U-701's minefield off the Virginia Capes. However, realistically one can only count on the first mine which is detonated. Thereafter, enemy countermeasures will attempt to render the field useless. Hence, a measurement of effectiveness for such a field is the probability that one ship will be sunk.

In general, this minefield model is based on the following **assumptions:**

a. Mines have been laid in secrecy and the enemy is unaware of the field's existence.

b. Ships traverse the field on one of two known headings, these being parallel but opposite.

c. Ships considered as traffic must pass within the outer limits of the field but are equally likely to enter the field at any point between the limits.

d. A ship which enters the mine's influence area will detonate the mine with certainty.

e. A mine which is detonated will sink the ship with certainty. This assumption is sometimes relaxed (as in Problem three).

1206 A PATTERN MINEFIELD

Consider a field where mines are laid in a series of lines perpendicular to the direction of traffic and with equal spacing between the mines in each line. The probability that a particular ship will be sunk while attempting to penetrate the first line is

$$p_1 = \frac{d}{D}, \qquad d < D$$
$$= 1, \qquad d \geq D$$

where

d = effective influence diameter of a mine, i.e., any ship whose centerline passes within distance $d/2$ of a mine, will actuate it, and

D = distance between mines.

Suppose the field consists of l such lines laid parallel to each other, and that the probability of successful penetration of each line is the same, assuming (given) the ship is not destroyed previously. The probability that a particular ship will survive one line is

$$1 - \frac{d}{D},$$

and the probability of surviving l lines is

$$\left(1 - \frac{d}{D}\right)^l.$$

If the mines are expected to remain active for m months and the traffic rate is t ships per month, then the probability that all ships survive all lines is

$$\left(1 - \frac{d}{D}\right)^{ltm}.$$

The probability that at least one ship is sunk, $P(S \geq 1)$, may then be seen as

Equation 12-1 $$P(S \geq 1) = 1 - \left(1 - \frac{d}{D}\right)^{ltm},$$

where S is the random variable denoting the number of ships sunk. If, after the first sinking, countermeasures render the field useless, then no more than one sinking is possible and Equation 12-1 represents the probability of *exactly one sinking* in m months.

Note that the term

$$\left(1 - \frac{d}{D}\right)^l$$

operationally says that the conditional probability that a ship which penetrated all previous lines of mines will penetrate the next line is a constant. This may not always be the case. For example, consider the minefield illustrated in Figure 12-1. In view of assumption b (on the parallelism of ship headings), a ship which successfully penetrates the first line will also penetrate all others successfully. On the other hand, if placement of mines within each line is staggered so that no line duplicates the threat presented by

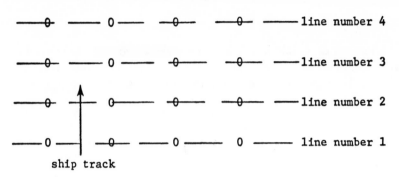

Figure 12-1.

any preceding line, the effect is similar to reducing D by an amount d for each succeeding line through which the ship passes. This, in effect, optimizes the field by reducing the probability of surviving a line, given successful penetration of previous lines.

1207 THE RANDOM MINEFIELD

In practice, it may not be possible or desirable to lay a pattern minefield, but rather to lay the mines at random in a prescribed area. Consider the case in which n mines are laid at random in a field of area A. Assumption b may be relaxed, but it will be necessary to know with some degree of accuracy the total distance, L, a ship must travel through the field. A potential target sweeps an area Ld through the field. The probability it will be sunk *by a particular mine* is equal to the probability that the mine is in the area swept, or

$$p_1 = \frac{Ld}{A},$$

since it is equally likely that the mine is at any point in the area. The probability that a ship survives the transit is

$$1 - \frac{Ld}{A}.$$

The probability the ship survives if n mines are in the field is

$$\left(1 - \frac{Ld}{A}\right)^n,$$

and the probability that all of the tm ships, which transit in m months, survive is

$$\left(1 - \frac{Ld}{A}\right)^{ntm}.$$

Finally, the probability that one or more ships are sunk is

Equation 12-2
$$P(S \geq 1) = 1 - \left(1 - \frac{Ld}{A}\right)^{ntm}.$$

Both this model and the pattern minefield model are applicable to all types of mines. If contact mines are used, the influence diameter of the mine becomes the width of the ship plus the physical diameter of the mine.

The development of the random minefield model is very similar to the derivation for the random search model.

BIBLIOGRAPHY

[1] Lieutenant Commander Arnold S. Lott, U. S. Navy, *Most Dangerous Sea*, U. S. Naval Institute, Annapolis, Maryland, 1959. A historical narrative of mine warfare from 668 A.D. through the Korean War.

[2] Captain J. S. Cowie, C.B.E., Royal Navy, *Mines, Minelayers, and Minelaying*, Oxford University Press, London, 1951. Mine warfare discussed from the point of view of an experienced naval officer.

PROBLEMS

1. A primary enemy shipping lane for coastwise traffic passes Bildau Point. It is estimated that traffic past Bildau Point averages 10 ships per month and that because of the particular geography, all of the ships pass between the 10- and 15-fathom curves. Although it is not considered safe for a submarine to risk firing torpedoes in the area, it is feasible for one to slip in, lay a minefield and retire to deeper waters. The plan is to lay magnetic mines equally spaced along a 3,000-yard line perpendicular to the shipping lane between the 10- and 15-fathom curves. Magnetic mines may be activated by the average merchant ship, if its keel passes within a circle of 45-foot radius centered over the mine.

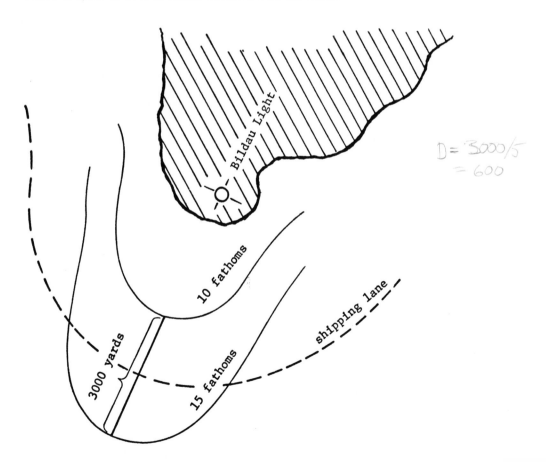

a. What mathematical expression would give the effectiveness of the field?

b. What will be the effectiveness of the field if five mines are used and if the mines remain effective for two months?

c. What is the minimum number of mines which must be used to obtain a probability greater than or equal to .9 that at least one ship is sunk?

2. The waters about Bildau Point are held by the enemy, and thus the decision is made for an air drop. Four A-6s are available for the drop.

a. If each A-6 can carry three mines and a single mine line is laid, what will be the effectiveness of the field if the mines remain effective for one month?

b. How many mines would be required to raise the effectiveness to at least .90? .95?

c. If it were possible to restrict all shipping to a channel 600 yards wide, and a field of 12 mines were then laid randomly in a 3,000-yard segment of the channel, how would the effectiveness of this field be changed?

3. A minefield is to be laid in secrecy with the objective of sinking one ship. As soon as the enemy is aware of the minefield's presence, he can easily reroute his shipping and thus render the minefield ineffective. Suppose the magnetic mines being used have an influence diameter of 45 feet but are not capable of sinking a ship unless its centerline passes within 15 feet of the mine.

a. If 10 such mines are laid equally spaced in a single line across a channel 1,000 yards wide, what are the chances of accomplishing the objective in two weeks or less if three ships transit the channel each week?

b. If the 10 mines were laid randomly in a 2,000-yard segment of the channel, what would be the probability of a sinking?

c. Is there a better way to lay the 10 mines?

13 System Effectiveness and Reliability

Previous chapters have discussed various naval operations. For each operation with its particular objective, measures of effectiveness were developed to predict the outcome of the operation for some of the alternatives available. In most of these operations, success depended not only on men and tactics, but also on sophisticated electronic systems. These systems were assumed to have a given performance capability in terms of characteristics such as speed, accuracy and range. It is necessary at some point in measuring a system's effectiveness to consider some additional factors. It is obvious that the best system available is worthless when it fails and replacement parts are not available, a technician cannot find the fault or the time for repair exceeds the mission length. These important elements and others will be considered more fully in the following discussion of logistic support.

1301 LOGISTIC SUPPORT

In any organization as large as the U. S. Navy, the problem of supplying a multitude of fleet units requires a far-flung and very effective logistic support organization.

As used here, *logistic support* may be defined as:

> The composite of action necessary to assure the effective and economical performance of the system and equipment which, functioning together, comprise a weapons system and, in turn, an operating force.

Logistic support implies supply, and according to official definition includes actions which cover:

a. Research, development, test and evaluation.
b. Requisition, storage, disbursement, distribution and maintenance of material.

c. Planning, recruiting, training, assignment and utilization of personnel.

d. Acquisition or construction and maintenance of facilities.

e. Budgeting, alloting and accounting for funds.

Naval logistic support recognizes a *user-producer* relationship. The *user* is the entity called the operating forces, and the supporting organization which fills the needs of the operating forces is referred to as the *producer*. The material and service support activities are under the command of the Chief of Naval Material, the Chief of Naval Personnel and the Chief of the Bureau of Medicine and Surgery.

The basic interrelationship between the *user* and the *producer* interests are always affected by the demand requirements voiced by the *user* and the limited resources available to the *producer*. Within these limitations, the elements of logistic support must be structured to meet the operational requirements of fleet units and their weapons systems.

The essential logistic and associated factors which affect a system's capability to perform a mission are shown in Figure 13-1.

The logistic support organization is committed to sustain the effectiveness of the weapons systems over the full duration of their mission requirements. Maximum sustained performance is equivalent to attaining the maximum possible operational effectiveness.

The primary measure of system effectiveness is termed *operational availability* and refers to the total time during the mission's duration when the weapons system or equipment is capable of meeting specified performance standards. Operational availability may be defined for continuously operated systems or equipment as the ratio of *time available when needed* to *total time needed*. Operational availability depends upon *reliability, maintainability* and *supply*. Reliability is the probability that the item will perform as expected for the entire period of the mission and is generally measured in terms of *mean time between failures,* which can be translated to a probability of failure *if*

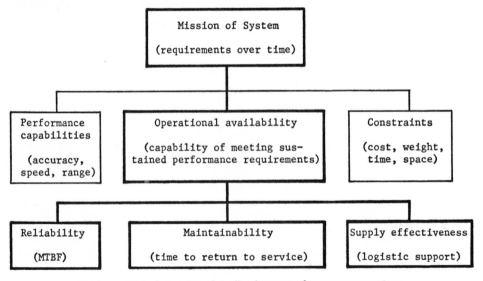

Factors which determine the effectiveness of a weapons system.

Figure 13-1.

a distribution of failures can be determined. Maintainability figures in this relationship as a major factor, and can be defined as the probability that a system, inoperable for any reason, can be returned to service in a given period. *Inventory* can be defined as the physical stock of goods kept on hand by an organization in order to promote the efficient running of its affairs.

1302   CLASSES OF FAILURE

Since reliability deals with performance for a given time or with the accomplishment of a certain mission of a specified duration, it is logical to study failures from a time-characteristic viewpoint. Failures are generally classified into three categories:

a. Initial failures are caused by a defect present at the time the equipment or part was first put into operation. Such defects result from an event in the pre-use life of the component, such as an error or mishap during manufacture, assembly, storage or transport of equipment. This initial failure will be observed during the very early life of the equipment's use and is usually eliminated by testing the components or equipment before they are put into operational use. Initial failures in such cases should not affect operational reliability to any extent. As the initial failures are corrected, the equipment failure rate will usually drop to a lower average value for the useful life of the equipment.

b. Chance or random failures result from unavoidable, unpredictable or unusually severe stresses that exceed the failure resistance of the part or component during its useful life period. The breakdown of a capacitor as result of a transient surge of voltage is an example.

c. Wear-out failures result from the depletion of some material or property necessary for the proper operation of a component. This depletion may be caused by abrasion, chemical reaction, etc. Examples are chemical exhaustion of dry cell batteries, embrittlement of wire insulation, fatigue of mechanical linkages and wear-out of bearings. In most cases, this type of failure can be reduced through improvement in design or replacement of components prior to expected wear-out.

These three types of failures can be represented in Figure 13-2.

This *bathtub* curve shows the *instantaneous failure rate* plotted against time. Of the three types of failures, only the last two, chance failure and wear-out, will be consid-

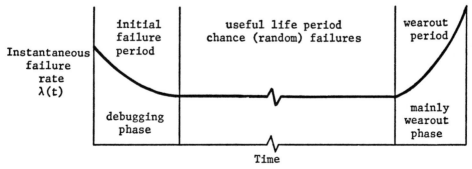

Bathtub failure rate curve.

Figure 13-2.

ered further in this chapter, since elimination of initial failures is a function of proper installation and testing.

Reliability is often measured in terms of the *mean time between failures* (MTBF), which is the expected time between failures. The mathematical relationship between MTBF, instantaneous failure rate and reliability in the case of chance or random failure is given in Section 1304. Simply stated, the value of the MTBF can be calculated by dividing the total hours of failure-free operation by the number of times the specific equipment failed. A typical component may have a mean life of 15,000 hours in a ship, 3,000 hours in an aircraft and 5 minutes in a missile. Therefore, for a meaningful statement of reliability the operational environment must also be stated. The currently accepted way of specifying environment is by a description of its operational use, that is, as ground equipment, shipboard, aircraft or missile. However, the handling, packing, transportation and storage—as well as operational conditions—constitute the environment, and thus affect the ultimate reliability. Sometimes rough handling in shipment constitutes the most severe environmental stress to which the components will be subjected. This explains the Navy's interest in all aspects of equipment container design, packaging, handling and shipping.

The various components and subsystems in a system may interact with each other. If a ship or aircraft is considered as a system, then the interaction of its components may be difficult to predict during manufacture, on a test stand or in a test vehicle. The importance of properly assessing the environment effects cannot be overemphasized.

1303   MATHEMATICS OF RELIABILITY

Reliability is a function of time, denoted $R(t)$, where $0 \leq R(t) \leq 1$. *$R(t)$ is the probability that a component will not fail before time t.* Thus, $R(t)$ is unity for $t = 0$ and approaches zero as time increases indefinitely.

Consider a theoretical experiment in which a number of like components are placed in a given environment. Let N_0 be the original number of functioning parts at the time the experiment starts, i.e., at $t = 0$. At intervals in operating time the number of parts still functioning is noted, where N_t is that number at any time t.

Consider an interval of time Δt. N_t is the number still functioning at time t, and $N_{t+\Delta t}$ is the number still functioning at time $t + \Delta t$. Then the difference between the two terms, $N_t - N_{t+\Delta t}$, would be the *number of failures* during that increment of Δt. The conditional probability of a part *failing* in the interval $[t, t + \Delta t]$, given that it *survived* in the interval $[0,t]$, is approximated by

Equation 13-1 $\text{P(failure in } \Delta t \,|\, \text{survival through } t) = \dfrac{N_t - N_{t+\Delta t}}{N_t}$,

which is the *fraction of failures* in the interval $[t, t + \Delta t]$.

Now, if $R(t) = \text{P (survival through } [0,t])$, then $R(t + \Delta t) = \text{P (survival through } [0,t] \text{ and no failure through } [t, t + \Delta t])$. If we use Equation 13-1, and the definition of conditional probability, $\text{P}(A \cap B) = \text{P}(A)\text{P}(B\,|\,A)$, for the events

A: a given component survived through time t [so $\text{P}(A) \equiv R(t)$],

B: the component does not fail in the interval $\Delta t \left[\text{so } \text{P}(B\,|\,A) = 1 - \dfrac{N_t - N_{t+\Delta t}}{N_t} \right]$,

then:

$$R(t + \Delta t) = R(t)\left(1 - \frac{N_t - N_{t+\Delta t}}{N_t}\right);$$

so the fraction of failures in the interval $[t, t + \Delta t]$ can be written as

Equation 13-2
$$\frac{N_t - N_{t+\Delta t}}{N_t} = -\frac{R(t + \Delta t) - R(t)}{R(t)}.$$

Dividing both sides of Equation 13-2 by Δt then gives the fraction failing *per unit time* during the interval $[t, t + \Delta t]$. This failure rate *as Δt approaches 0* is called the *instantaneous failure rate* at time t, and denoted by $\lambda(t)$. Thus

$$\lambda(t) = \lim_{\Delta t \to 0}\left[\frac{N_t - N_{t+\Delta t}}{N_t \cdot \Delta t}\right]$$

$$= \lim_{\Delta t \to 0}\left[-\left(\frac{1}{R(t)}\right)\left(\frac{R(t + \Delta t) - R(t)}{\Delta t}\right)\right], \quad \text{from Equation 13-2,}$$

$$= -\frac{1}{R(t)}\frac{dR(t)}{dt}, \text{ from the definition of a first derivative.}$$

Cross multiplying now gives

Equation 13-3
$$\frac{d[R(t)]}{R(t)} = -\lambda(t)\, dt.$$

Integrating over $[0, t]$,

$$\int_0^t \frac{d[R(t)]}{R(t)} = -\int_0^t \lambda(t)\, dt,$$

or

$$\ln R(t) = -\int_0^t \lambda(t)\, dt, \quad \text{since} \quad R(0) = 1 \text{ and } \ln(1) = 0.$$

This equation can now be solved for $R(t)$, giving*

Equation 13-4
$$R(t) = e^{-\int_0^t \lambda(t)\, dt}.$$

$R(t)$, the theoretical probability that a component will operate for t or more hours without failure, could also be approximated by the fraction of survivors at time t.

Equation 13-5
$$R(t) \simeq \frac{N_t}{N_0}. \qquad = RELIABILITY @ t$$

1304 SPECIAL FAILURE PROBABILITY DISTRIBUTIONS

Experience has shown that *electronic* parts and systems, once the weak and defective parts have been weeded out in the initial or debugging stage (through quality control or other such techniques), fail randomly in time. The reliability curve will take the general form shown in Figure 13-3.

*This relationship can also be found using a development similar to that used for the continuous looking model in Section 404.

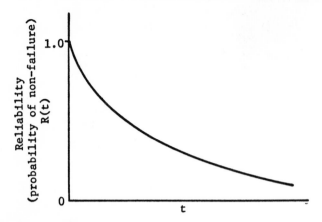

Typical reliability curve for random failures.

Figure 13-3.

To illustrate this, let N_0 be the number of similar vacuum tubes in a sample. Let N_t be the number of tubes which survive to the end of time t. It has been determined through experimentation that chance failures are equally likely to occur during equal time intervals which implies that $\lambda(t) = \lambda$, a constant rate. Figure 13-4, where the ordinate is a log scale, shows a plot of the fraction of survivors as a function of time. These are actual data for a sample of 900 vacuum tubes. The significant fact here is that $\lambda(t)$ is a constant. This is typical of electronic parts and systems. Thus, chance failures not only occur at any time during the life of the sample (assembly), but are equally likely to occur during equal time intervals throughout the life of the sample.

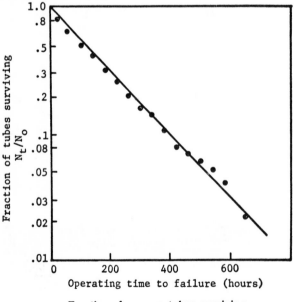

Fraction of vacuum tubes surviving.

Figure 13-4.

Since $\lambda(t)$ is a constant, it can be written simply as λ. The reliability, from Equation 13-4, then becomes

Equation 13-6
$$R(t) = e^{-\lambda t}.$$

From Equation 13-5,

$$R(t) = \frac{N_t}{N_0} = e^{-\lambda t}.$$

Then:

Equation 13-7
$$N_t = N_0 e^{-\lambda t},$$

and

Equation 13-8
$$\lambda = -\frac{1}{t}\ln\left(\frac{N_t}{N_0}\right).$$

$\lambda = -\frac{1}{600}\ln\left(\frac{N_t}{N_0}\right)$

$= -\frac{1}{600}\ln(.02)$

$= \# \text{Failures}/\text{unit time}$

This gives a direct method of computing λ from recorded data. From Figure 13-4 and by means of Equation 13-8, λ can be determined to be 0.0058 failure per tube hour for these tubes.

The histogram in Figure 13-5 is an actual plot of the number of failures for 20-hour intervals of time for this same sample of vacuum tubes. By using the value of λ found from Equation 13-8 and noting that for $t \geq 10$ the number of failures in any

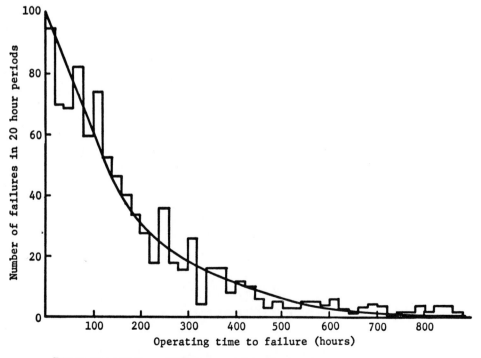

Distribution of failure of 900 vacuum tubes showing chance-failure behavior.

Figure 13-5.

20-hour time interval centered at t is $N_{t-10} - N_{t+10}$, the smooth curve is obtained theoretically as follows:

$$N_{t-10} - N_{t+10} = N_o \left[\frac{N_{t-10}}{N_o} - \frac{N_{t+10}}{N_o} \right]$$

$$= N_o [e^{-\lambda(t-10)} - e^{-\lambda(t+10)}].$$

After substituting $N_o = 900$ and $\lambda = .0058$ and simplifying

$$N_{t-10} - N_{t+10} = 106 e^{-.0058t}.$$

These quantities when plotted as the smooth curve in Figure 13-5 are seen to give a close approximation to the histogram and hence provide an additional check on the model. The fact that the instantaneous failure rate is constant over all time implies that replacement of any or all surviving units with new, unused units will not affect the failure rate of the aggregate. *Thus, replacement of units with these characteristics as a form of preventive maintenance is useless.* This consideration is always true of components whose failure resistance remains constant with use, and is essentially the case if failures occur long before the expected wear-out time of the particular component.

The mean (expected) time to failure or *mean time between failures* (MTBF) can be found from the expression

$$E(T) = \int_0^\infty t \cdot f(t) \, dt,$$

where T is the time at which failure occurs and $f(t)$ is the probability density function for T. To find $f(t)$, note that

$$R(t) = P(T > t)$$
$$= 1 - P(T \leq t)$$
$$= 1 - F(t).$$

$F(t)$, the cumulative distribution function, can be written as

Equation 13-9
$$F(t) = 1 - R(t)$$
$$= 1 - e^{-\int_0^t \lambda(t) \, dt}.$$

$f(t)$ is found by differentiating:

$$f(t) = \frac{dF(t)}{dt}.$$

Thus:

Equation 13-10
$$f(t) = \lambda(t) e^{-\int_0^t \lambda(t) \, dt}.$$

For chance failures, λ is a constant, so that

Equation 13-11
$$f(t) = \lambda e^{-\lambda t},$$

which is the familiar *exponential* probability distribution, and the expected time to failure is

Equation 13-12
$$E(T) = \int_0^\infty t \lambda e^{-\lambda t} = \frac{1}{\lambda}$$

from a table of integrals or integrating by parts. Thus, $1/\lambda$ *is the mean time until failure or mean time between failures* when the failure rate is constant.

The exponential distribution has been seen to describe the time-to-failure of equipment subject to chance failure, such as electronic equipment. The *normal* distribution and the *log normal* distribution best describe *wear-out* types of failures.

An example of the normal distribution of time-to-failure can be shown in the case of flashlight cells. A group of cells of similar manufacture can be expected to develop a prescribed power for approximately the same length of time before failing. The density of failure of a sample of 100 dry cells is shown in Figure 13-6. Although failures were observed during almost every 10-minute interval between 630 and 850 minutes, approximately four-fifths of the cells failed between 700 and 800 minutes. This clustering of the lifetimes about a mean value permits anticipation of wear-out failures. Thus by preventive maintenance it is possible to forestall wear-out failure during operation.

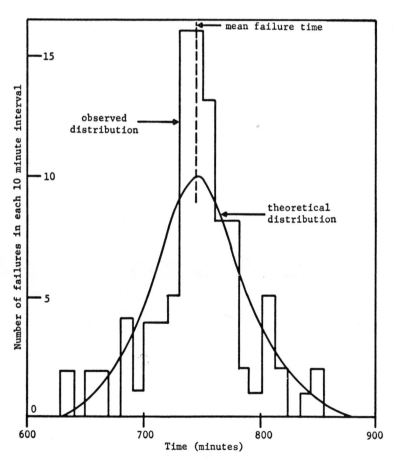

Distribution of flashlight battery failures showing wear-out failure behavior.

Figure 13-6.

1305   RELIABILITY OF COMPLEX SYSTEMS

The subcomponents of a system can be linked for reliability considerations in two ways, *series* or *parallel*. Series linkage implies that the simultaneous operation of all links is necessary for proper operation of the system. Parallel linkage implies that operation of any one of the paralleled members will permit proper operation of the overall system. Notice that this is *not* the same definition of series and parallel used in electrical circuits. An electrical system consisting of several components put together in a complicated combination of series and parallel circuits may still be considered, for reliability purposes, to be a simple series linkage of the components *if* each component is essential to the proper operation of the system.

The addition of parallel-linked components usually constitutes an increase in reliability because it decreases the fraction of task-performing components vital to operation. On the other hand, the addition of series-linked components usually constitutes a decrease in reliability.

For a series-linked assemblage of components whose separate reliabilities are R_1, R_2, R_3, ..., the reliability of the assemblage, R_{TOTAL}, is

Equation 13-13 $$R_{TOTAL} = R_1 \times R_2 \times R_3 \cdots .$$

If the components have constant chance failure rates $\lambda_1, \lambda_2, \lambda_3, \ldots$, then the overall reliability becomes

$$
\begin{aligned}
R_{TOTAL} &= e^{-\lambda_1 t} \times e^{-\lambda_2 t} \times e^{-\lambda_3 t} \cdots \\
&= e^{-(\lambda_1 + \lambda_2 + \lambda_3 \cdots)t} \\
&= e^{-\lambda_{TOTAL} t},
\end{aligned}
$$

where the total instantaneous failure rate for chance failure of a series-linked system is

$$\lambda_{TOTAL} = \lambda_1 + \lambda_2 + \lambda_3 \cdots .$$

The mean time between failures for the system is then

$$\text{MTBF} = \frac{1}{\lambda_{TOTAL}} = \frac{1}{\lambda_1 + \lambda_2 + \lambda_3 + \cdots}.$$

The instantaneous failure rate increases as the number of components increase. In general, *doubling* the number of components (of same life expectancy) *halves* the mean time between failures. To maintain a given reliability, the average component life must be increased in proportion to the increase in the number of components.

For a parallel-linked assemblage of units whose separate reliabilities are R_1, R_2, R_3, ..., the reliability of the assemblage, R_{TOTAL}, is

Equation 13-14 $$R_{TOTAL} = 1 - [(1 - R_1)(1 - R_2)(1 - R_3) \cdots],$$

and when $R_1 = R_2 = \cdots = R_n$,   then

$$R_{TOTAL} = 1 - (1 - R)^n.$$

1306   ANALYSIS AND PREDICTION OF RELIABILITY

The failure of three different types of airborne radar and some of their components such as RF heads, indicators and power supplies have been gathered for analysis. For the cases under study, the distribution of failures with time was of a chance failure

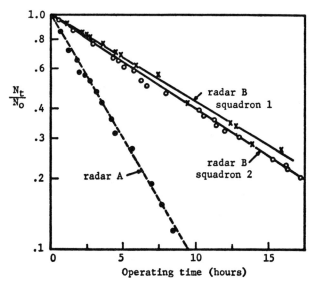

Fraction of sets without part replacement (on semi-log scale).

Figure 13-7.

type. Figure 13-7 shows the fraction of radar A and radar B sets that operated for time t without a failure, which required a replacement of some part. The linear relationship between the logarithm of the fraction surviving and time indicates a constant instantaneous failure rate.

The close agreement of the data from two different squadrons in widely separated parts of the world should be noted. Squadron one was deployed to a forward area flying actual combat missions, while squadron two was stationed in the United States flying training missions. This close correlation of failures indicates that the failure rate is more characteristic of the equipment and its immediate environment than of the operational situation in which it is used.

These statistics verify the fact that consideration of the operating environment is vital in any reliability study. For comparison, tubes of similar design and construction to the ones used in radar have exhibited lifetimes as high as 85,000 hours when used in static installations such as computers. It is apparent that the constants developed for a particular type of tube or part must not be used indiscriminately wherever that component is employed, but rather that constants must be developed for each environment.

It is assumed that all of the components in a radar are essential to its proper functioning. Since vacuum tubes fail appreciably faster than other parts, the total failure rate of the set can be considered to be made up of two failure rates, one proportional to the number of vacuum tubes and the other proportional to the number of other electrical parts. That is,

Equation 13-15 $$\lambda_{\text{TOTAL}} = \lambda_t T + \lambda_p P,$$

where λ_t and λ_p are the average failure rate constants for vacuum tubes and other parts, and T and P are the number of tubes and other parts, respectively.

Unit	Number of tubes T	Number of other electrical parts P	Measured average hours between failure 1/λ
Radar A	66	882	4.5
Transmitter–converter	19	292	15
Power unit	11	73	45
Receiver amplifier	28	307	12
Modulator	7	84	45
Indicator	1	27	160
Control unit	0	11	450
Scanner	0	88	55
Radar B	50	470	8.1
Receiver-transmitter	26	269	15
Synchronizer	24	116	25
Antenna	0	43	115
Control box	0	42	120
Radar C	57	578	6.7
High-voltage rectifier	2	22	170
Indicators	6	36	90
Modulators	3	54	75
Control box	0	33	150
Low-voltage rectifier	10	59	50
Synchronizer	28	293	15
RF head	8	91	40

Data on units that were studied (radar C not shown in Figure 13-7).

Figure 13-8.

Failure rate constants were computed from the data in Figure 13-8 by taking any two subassemblies and writing Equation 13-15 for both, then solving the two equations simultaneously. Using all combinations of two subassemblies for each radar, the average component failure rates are:

$$\lambda_t = 0.0007 \text{ per hour,}$$
$$\lambda_p = 0.0002 \text{ per hour.}$$

The average component lives, which are the reciprocals of these values, are:

$$t_t = 1,400 \text{ hours,}$$
$$t_p = 5,000 \text{ hours.}$$

Determining the failure rate constants for equipment that has been in use long enough to generate sufficient data can be of considerable value in evaluating new and untried equipment.

Where failure rate constants for airborne radar in current use have been determined, they may be used to predict reliabilities of other radar if:

a. The radars are homologous. They must be constructed from similar components, and their circuitry must be similar to the ones whose failure rates are known.

b. The reliability study is made within a single set of environmental conditions. Since failure rates vary with environment, the use of one set of constants to predict the reliability in a different environment will lead to error.

Consider two new radars being designed whose performance would be a significant improvement over the performance of radars A, B and C. Both of these new radars have circuitry and components similar to the old radar. The use of the failure rates obtained from the operational data on radars A, B and C should produce no significant error, and can aid in predicting the reliability of the new radar.

Radar D has 360 tubes and 2,200 other parts; radar E has 122 tubes and 1,150 other parts. The reliability of this radar then decreases over time according to

$$R_{\text{TOTAL}} = e^{-[\lambda_p P + \lambda_t T]t}.$$

For radar D then,

$$R_{\text{TOTAL}} = e^{-[.0002(2200) + .0007(360)]t} = e^{-.692t}.$$

For radar E,

$$R_{\text{TOTAL}} = e^{-[.0002(1150) + .0007(122)]t} = e^{-.314t}.$$

The reliability of the two new radars and radar C are plotted versus mission length in hours in Figure 13-9. The less complex radar C has a 58 percent chance of surviving a 4-hour mission, while the more complex newer radar D has a 7 percent chance for the same period. Radar E has a reliability of approximately 30 percent for the same period.

Reliabilities may be used to predict force requirements or allowances for a particular item. It can be seen that if the operational requirements demand a specific

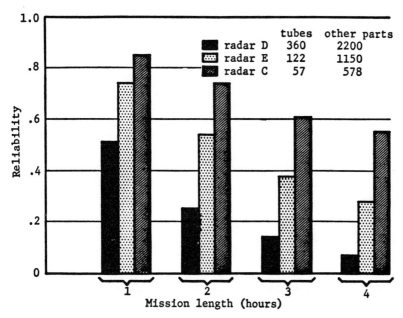

Reliability of airborne radar versus mission length.

Figure 13-9.

reliability in order to be satisfactory, and analysis shows that the equipment in use has a very small chance of providing this reliability, then additional redundant (parallel) units may be assigned.

The number, N, of redundant units needed to obtain a desired reliability, $R_{TOTAL}(t)$, utilizing units of reliability $R(t)$, is given by

Equation 13-16

$$R_{TOTAL}(t) = 1 - [1 - R(t)]^N.$$

In summary, when failure is due to *wear-out,* system performance can be increased by a statistical study of the mean time to failure and replacing units before they fail. Where failure is due to externally induced *chance,* no benefit can be derived from such preventive maintenance.

Increases in the reliability of equipment whose failures are caused by *chance* can be achieved by adding parallel-linked components or by increasing the failure resistance of the parts. In some cases, as in the radar example, lessening the demands of the environment can produce an increase in reliability due to the increased longevity of the parts.

When one is developing new equipment, the improved operational characteristics, which generally entail greater complexity, should be carefully weighed against an *attendant loss of reliability.*

1307   MAINTAINABILITY CONSIDERATIONS

Gear may be designed in a manner that utilizes redundancy of components, in order to optimize its overall *reliability.* However, the time to return a failed system to service is also significant in determining the effectiveness of a weapons system. Figure 13-10 shows a system with a *higher* reliability (longer times between system failure) but with a *lesser* ratio of time available to time needed, because of longer times required to return the system to service (*maintainability*).

If *Operational Availability* is measured, with supply effectiveness constant for two systems, then reliability may have to be traded off in view of the maintainability comparisons. *Maintainability* of equipment and systems is the speed and ease with which malfunctions may be detected, localized and repaired, and normal operation restored. There are in this definition five key words or phrases: *speed and ease, detect, localize, repair* and *restore* to normal operation. Each has important human engineering as well as engineering aspects. Therefore, it is necessary to analyze not only the reliability of the system but also its maintainability, if a selection can be made between alternative systems during initial procurement. Some items to consider in appraising the maintainability of a system will be listed.

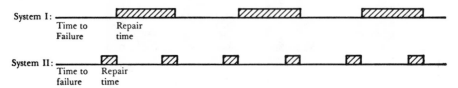

Figure 13-10. System I has longer MTBF but much longer MTBR (mean time between repair) than System II.

In an immediate operational situation, the maintainability of a given redundant system may have been estimated, and decisions must be made as to which gear to continue depending on, and which gear to perform *preventive* maintenance on. Here the estimated parameters of maintainability are inputs to optimizing the expected outcome. An example of such an operational decision is included in this section.

Detection of Malfunctions

There are two general kinds of malfunction: (1) catastrophic failure which provides immediate indication of malfunction, e.g., equipment won't operate, and so forth, and (2) those malfunctions that degrade performance, such as loss of sensitivity in a radar set. The first category is usually readily detected; with the second, it is more difficult to detect the fact that equipment is performing improperly.

Degraded performance in some systems may continue for considerable periods of time before the operator becomes aware of the difficulty. One can hardly correct a difficulty that is not known. Often equipment designers state performance characteristics without ensuring that degraded operation will be found by the operators. From an operational point of view, such procedures as routine checks are expected to detect degraded performance. The detection of degraded performance remains a problem, and preventive maintenance systems (PMS) are an important aspect of the naval maintenance concept.

7-31

Localization of Malfunctions

Once a malfunction has been detected, the problem for maintainability is to localize the source (subsystem, module and component) of the difficulty and effect correction. In some systems, localizing the malfunction may cause up to 80 percent of the down time. (Down time is the length of time that an equipment is inoperable because of malfunction.)

Items to Consider in Estimating Maintainability

1. Maintenance openings are large enough to insert hands and the tools or instruments that may be required.
2. Only the number of fasteners required for security is used.
3. The fasteners employed are easy to open.
4. Components are mounted in an array, not stacked on each other.
5. Component arrays fold out or may be pulled out in drawers.
6. No blind adjustments are required.
7. Parts are keyed or coded to prevent wrong insertion or installation.
8. Adequate space is available for using test equipment.
9. Access doors are hinged at the bottom.
10. Replaceable components are of the plug-in type.
11. Test points, meter jacks, probe points, and so on, are conveniently located and labeled.
12. Quick-disconnect plugs are used where possible.
13. Cable connectors incorporate aligning pins.
14. Cable connectors are designed to prevent wrong connections.
15. Desired signal and tolerance limits of test points are specified.
16. The layouts of components, controls and displays are according to function or sequential grouping.

17. Functional groups are outlined by a line inscribed on the panel or chassis.
18. The number of tools and test equipments of different kinds is held to a minimum consistent with requirements.
19. Where practical, built-in meters and test instruments are employed.
20. Special illumination facilities are provided where required.
21. Standard components and hardware have been used to the extent practicable.

Problem

The following operational decision problem takes into consideration the maintainability of the system gear (time to repair = 5 hours):

In the CIC spaces of a ship, there are three radar repeaters, each of which has the following failure rate function:

$$\lambda = .0003, \qquad \text{during the first 500 hours of the repeater operation;}$$
$$\lambda(t) = .0003 + .005t, \quad \text{during the wear-out phase of the radar after the initial 500 hours of operation.}$$

All three repeaters have just completed the first 500 hours of operation and are in the wear-out phase of component life. At this time, an exercise commences which is to last 30 hours, during which time it is necessary to have an operating radar. You have sufficient personnel on board to repair (renew) two repeaters at once, which would necessitate operating on only one repeater for 5 hours. Which is the best choice:

1. Operate with the three old repeaters for the duration of the exercise; or,
2. Operate on a single old repeater for the first 5 hours while repairing the two repeaters and then use two new and one old repeater for the remaining 25 hours of the exercise; or,
3. Operate on two old repeaters for the first 5 hours while repairing a repeater and then operate on one new and one old repeater while you repair a second repeater during the second 5 hours of the exercise and then operate on one old and two renewed repeaters for the remaining 20 hours of the exercise?

Solution

$$R_O = \text{Reliability of an old repeater}$$
$$R_N = \text{Reliability of a new repeater}$$
$$R_1 = \text{System reliability for alternative 1}$$
$$R_2 = \text{System reliability for alternative 2}$$
$$R_3 = \text{System reliability for alternative 3}$$

Alternative 1:

$$R_1 = 1 - (1 - R_O(0,30))^3.$$
$$R_O(0,30) = e^{-\int_0^{30} (.0003 + .005t)\, dt} \quad =\sim\int_o^{30} .0003t + \frac{.005t^2}{2} = e^{-[.009 + (4.5/2)]}$$
$$= e^{-2.259}$$
$$= .104.$$
$$R_1 = 1 - (1 - .104)^3 = 1 - (.896)^3 = 1 - .719 = .281.$$

Alternative 2:

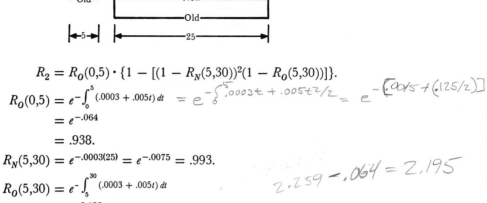

$$R_2 = R_O(0,5) \cdot \{1 - [(1 - R_N(5,30))^2(1 - R_O(5,30))]\}.$$

$$R_O(0,5) = e^{-\int_0^5 (.0003 + .005t)\, dt} \quad = e^{-\int_0^5 .0003t + .005t^2/2} = e^{-[.0015 + (.125/2)]}$$

$$= e^{-.064}$$

$$= .938.$$

$$R_N(5,30) = e^{-.0003(25)} = e^{-.0075} = .993.$$

$$R_O(5,30) = e^{-\int_5^{30} (.0003 + .005t)\, dt}$$

$$2.259 - .064 = 2.195$$

$$= e^{-2.195}$$

$$= .111.$$

$$R_2 = (.938)\{1 - [(.007)^2(.889)]\}$$

$$= (.938)(.999) = .937.$$

Alternative 3:

$$R_3 = \{1 - [(1 - R_O(0,5))^2]\}\{1 - [(1 - R_O(5,10))(1 - R_N(5,10))]\}$$
$$\{1 - [(1 - R_O(10,30))(1 - R_N(10,30))^2]\}.$$

$$R_O(0,5) = .938.$$

$$R_O(5,10) = e^{-\int_5^{10} (.0003 + .005t)\, dt}$$

$$.253 - .064 = .189$$

$$= e^{-.189}$$

$$= .828.$$

$$R_N(5,10) = e^{-.0003(5)} = .999.$$

$$R_N(10,30) = e^{-.0003(20)} = e^{-.006} = .994.$$

$$R_O(10,30) = e^{-\int_{10}^{30} (.0003 + .005t)\, dt}$$

$$2.259 - .253 = 2.006$$

$$= e^{-2.006}$$

$$= .135.$$

$$R_3 = (.996)(1.0)(1.0) = .996.$$
$$R_2 = .937.$$
$$R_1 = .281.$$

$\left.\begin{array}{c}\\ \\ \\ \end{array}\right\}$ Choose R_3.

1308 INVENTORY CONTROL

Inventory is defined as the physical stock of goods. These goods may be those items used within the organization, such as administrative supplies, or items demanded by consumers external to the organization. The military organizations are large consumers of food, clothing, petroleum, and so on.

The primary goal of inventory control is to provide the decision-maker the means of managing an efficient inventory system at minimal cost. The costs associated with maintaining an inventory are normally grouped into three categories:

a. Ordering or production costs. These are the costs associated with acquiring goods. Administrative or "set-up" costs are sometimes included.

b. Holding costs. Included are costs for storage, insurance and spoilage.

c. Penalty or shortage cost. This is the cost of losing a sale or having to place a special order if the inventory drops to zero and demand still exists for the goods.

Besides attempting to minimize total costs, most inventory control models establish decision rules that indicate:

a. When to order or produce goods, and

b. How much to order or produce.

Many inventory control models have been developed; three of the more familiar models are:

a. Economic Order Quantity model (Wilson Lot Size),

b. Single decision static model,

c. Stochastic demand model.

The Economic Order Quantity model in its simplest form assumes constant and known demand and instantaneous reordering capability, and does not permit shortages. A graphical illustration of the model is given by Figure 13-11. Terms employed in this model include:

Q = Amount of goods ordered

t = Cycle time (time between orders, $t = Q/D$)

K = Set up cost

c = Unit purchase cost

D = Demand rate per unit time

h = Holding cost per unit item per unit time.

To minimize storage or holding costs, orders should not be placed until the inventory reaches 0. The optimal amount to order, Q^*, is that amount which minimizes total cost (set up, purchase, holding, etc.):

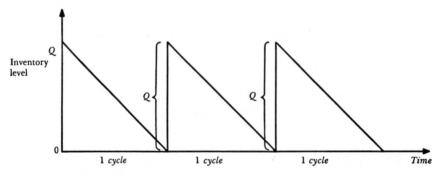

Figure 13-11. Economic Order Quantity model.

The total cost function per order cycle, t, is the set up cost plus order cost plus holding cost:

Equation 13-17

$$\text{Total cost} = K + cQ + h\frac{Q^2}{2D},$$

and:

Equation 13-18   Total cost per unit time $= \dfrac{K + cQ + \dfrac{hQ^2}{2D}}{Q/D}.$

(The average inventory level per cycle is $Q/2$ and the holding cost is thus $h\,Q/2$ per unit of time. Since each cycle is of length Q/D, the holding cost per cycle is $h\,Q^2/2D$.)

The optimal amount to order, $Q^* = \sqrt{2DK/h}$ when Equation 13-18 is minimized using standard calculus techniques. The length of each cycle can now be found as $Q^*/D = \sqrt{2K/Dh}$.

If a lag time of, say, t' exists between order placement time and time received, then Q^* items should be ordered t' before the end of each cycle.

An important assumption of the EOQ model is that the demand rate is known and constant. Stochastic models have been developed for those cases where demand is not constant but has a known probability distribution. If demand is not known (usually the case), then it must be estimated from past data. Common techniques used to *forecast* demand are moving averages, exponential smoothing, least squares regression and harmonic functions. Trends and seasonal variations in demand must be accounted for to keep forecast errors small.

Other EOQ and more involved inventory models have been developed which take into consideration allowances for shortages, penalties for shortages, single period orders, quantity discounts, safety stock, and so on. Many organizations utilize a service-level policy which determines the amount of safety stock necessary to meet all demands with a certain probability, say 80 or 90 percent.

PROBLEMS

1. Field observations of a radar system show that 114 failures occur in 1,256 total hours of operation.

   a. What is the approximate mean time between failures? $\frac{1256}{114} = 11.01$
   b. If the failure rate of the system is constant over the 1,256 hours of operation, what is the estimated failure rate? $\frac{114}{1256} = .09$

2. Show that for a number of components exhibiting chance failures each with instantaneous failure rate λ:

   a. The fraction of components operating at time t which fail during the next 10 hours, i.e., $(N_t - N_{t+10})/N_t$, is constant for all t.
   b. The fraction of components operating at time t which survive the next h hours is constant for all t.

3. The following data were obtained from a test of 1,000 vacuum tubes on board ship:

Operating time (hours)	Number of failures	R(x)
10	600	.4
20	240	.16
30	96	.064
40	38	.026
50	16	.010

990

a. Tabulate the reliability for the times given.
b. What type of failure is exhibited by the tubes in this test? *Chance* p 264
c. What is the number of failures per tube hour? $\lambda = -\frac{1}{50} \ln\left(\frac{12}{1000}\right) = .0921$
d. What is the mean time between failures? $1/\lambda = 1/.0921 = 10.85$
e. The communications officer of the ship decides to replace each tube as soon as it has operated for the time obtained in part d less one hour to avoid any failures of equipment during critical operations. Do you concur with his decision? Explain. *Chance type failures cannot be avoided by replacement*

4. The failure rate of an X-80 tube in a laboratory computer is 5.84×10^{-6} per tube hour. $= \lambda$

   a. What is the reliability of this tube for 100,000 hours of operation in the laboratory? $R(1 \times 10^5) = e^{-5.84 \times 10^{-6} \cdot 1 \times 10^5} = e^{-.584} = .558$
   b. What is the probability that this tube will not survive 100,000 hours of operation in the laboratory? $1 - .584 = .442$
   c. When it is installed on board a ship, do you estimate the reliability of this tube to be higher than, lower than or the same as the reliability when installed in the laboratory computer? *lower*

5. A certain electronic device exhibits a constant instantaneous failure rate in the laboratory of .02 failure per hour of operation.

   a. What is its probability of its surviving 10 hours and then failing during the eleventh hour?
   b. What is its probability of its surviving 10 hours and then failing during the next half hour?
   c. Suppose the device is operated for 100 hours:
      (1) What is the probability of its failing during the first 10 hours of operation?
      (2) What is the conditional probability of failure during a 10-hour period between the 63rd and 73rd hour of operation, given that it survives to the 63rd hour?
      (3) What is the probability of its failing during the last 10 hours of operation, given that it lasts 90 hours?
      (4) What is the probability of the device's operating for 63 hours without failure and then failing between the 63rd and 73rd hours? $.051$
      (5) What is the probability of the device's operating for 90 hours without failure and then failing during the time $t > 90$ hours?
   d. Given that the device has survived the sixth hour of operation, what is the probability that it will fail in the next half hour?
   e. Given that the device has survived the thirteenth hour, what is the probability that it will fail in the next half hour?

6. For a component which exhibits chance failure, prove that

$$P(T \geq t + h \mid T > t) = P(T > h).$$

7. You are given the task of studying two different types of light bulbs to determine the failure characteristics of each. These light bulbs are to be used in aircraft where they are vital to safe night flying.

Bulb A

Hours of operation	Cumulative failures
0–40	0
50	2
60	10
70	34
80	66
90	90
100	98
110	99
120	100

Bulb B

Hours of operation	Cumulative failures
0–60	1
70	5
80	30
90	70
100	95
110	99
120	100

a. What type of failure is exhibited by these bulbs? (Hint: Plot number of failures in each 10-hour interval versus operating time.)
b. Estimate the mean failure time and standard deviation of each type of bulb.
c. Which bulb would you choose for installation? Explain.
d. Would the capacity to replace the bulb in flight have an effect on your decision?

8. Using the data in Problem seven for bulb A:

a. Plot the reliability as a function of time.
b. Assuming that the time to failure, T, has a normal distribution, write the equation for the reliability function.
c. Sketch the shape of the corresponding instantaneous failure rate curve as a function of time.
d. Express the normal instantaneous failure rate as a function of the normal density function, $f(t)$, and the normal cumulative distribution function, $F(t)$. (Hint: Start with Equation 13-3.)

9. A certain piece of equipment fails according to the Weibull probability law, where $T =$ time to failure and the probability that the equipment will fail prior to time t is given by

$$P(T \le t) = 1 - e^{-(kt^2/2)}, 0 \le t,$$
$$= 0 \qquad , t < 0.$$

a. What is the failure rate $\lambda(t)$ for this equipment?

b. What is the density function, $f(t)$, associated with this cumulative distribution function?

c. What is the mean time between failures for this equipment?

$$\text{Note that} \int_0^\infty x^2 e^{-x^2} \, dx = \frac{\sqrt{\pi}}{4}.$$

10. Assume that the following data apply to the radar of an active homing surface to air missile:

Subassembly	Number of tubes	Number of other parts	Time (in minutes) between failures
Transmitter	20	150	40
Receiver	15	50	80
Power unit	10	50	100
Data converter	20	100	50

a. Determine the average time between failures of the radar.

b. Determine the failure rate of the radar.

c. What is the reliability of this radar for a mission of two minutes?

d. Determine the average failure rate of tubes, λ_t, and other parts, λ_p.

11. Compute the reliability of the various electronic systems, R_{TOTAL}, made up of components A, B and C, whose reliabilities are

$$R_A = .3, \ R_B = .4, \ R_C = .8.$$

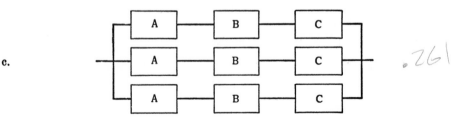

a.   A .3 — B .4 — C .8   .096

b.   A₁ .3 / A₂ .3 / A₃ .3 — B .4 — C .8   .210

c.   [A B C / A B C / A B C]   .261

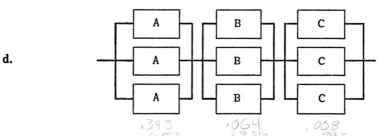

.343   .064   .008
.657   .936   .992

12. It has been decided that the reliability of the missile radar described in Problem ten is not sufficient, and the performance capability (in acquisition, discrimination, and so on) is greater than necessary. Therefore, a similar radar with acceptable performance characteristics has been designed. The new radar has 50 tubes and 250 other parts.

a. What is the predicted reliability of the new radar for a 2-minute mission?
b. How many missiles equipped with the new radar would have to be fired to ensure a radar reliability of .99 for this mission?
c. How many missiles equipped with the old radar (with a reliability of .87) would have to be fired to ensure a radar reliability of .99 for this mission?

13. The reliability of a tracking radar is $R(t) = e^{-0.0834t}$. This could be increased either by using two radars in parallel or by reducing the failure rate. If the failure rate could be halved, how would the improvement in reliability compare to the improvement gained by having an extra radar for a mission length of:

a. $t =$ one hour.
b. $t = 24$ hours.

14. In the cic spaces in a ship, there are two radar repeaters which have the following failure rates:

$$\lambda(t) = \begin{cases} .0002 & , \quad t \leq t_w \\ .0002 + .004(t - t_w), & \quad t > t_w \end{cases}$$

Both sets have just reached the wear-out phase (time now is t_w), and you are prepared to replace one of them with a new repeater identical to the old one. At this time an exercise commences which is expected to last for 24 hours, during which time it is necessary to have an operating repeater. You have sufficient personnel on hand to install the new repeater, but this would necessitate operating on only one repeater for about 6 hours. Assume that if a repeater fails it cannot be repaired during the exercise.
    Which is better:

a. To operate with both old repeaters for the duration of the exercise?
b. To operate on a single old repeater for the first 6 hours while installing the new repeater, and then use one new and one old repeater for the remaining 18 hours of the exercise?

15. A system consists of two components, A and B, which perform the same function, so that if either is operating the system is operative. Each exhibits chance failures with failure rates λ_A and λ_B, respectively.

    a. Find the mean time to failure, $E(T)$, for the system. Hint: remember that

    $$E(t) = \int_0^\infty t \cdot f(t) \, dt, \text{ and that } \int_0^\infty kte^{-kt} = \frac{1}{k}.$$

    b. Is the instantaneous failure rate for the system constant?

16. Your ship burns 40 barrels of ND a day during normal operations and has a maximum storage capacity of 300 barrels. The cost associated with refueling is estimated at $150 and the unit purchase price is $10 per barrel. The unit holding cost is $.30 per barrel.

    a. How much fuel should be purchased, and how often will the ship refuel?
    b. Suppose the fleet policy is to refuel before the amount of fuel on board reaches 30 percent of capacity. How much fuel is purchased, and how often will the ship refuel?

14 Modern Techniques of OA

This text has presented only the most elementary of the variety of mathematical tools available to the operations analyst at the present time. Many more, of varying degrees of sophistication, do exist and are currently employed in analysis. Some of these will be discussed in this chapter. Historically, some of these techniques were developed in connection with solutions to problems in economics, industry and management, and it is important to note that practically all of them are readily transferable to the study of problems connected with naval operations. They include: *linear programming, queueing theory, information theory, dynamic programming, simulation, Monte Carlo models, operational gaming models* and *Program Evaluation and Review Techniques* (PERT).

This chapter provides a brief introduction to the OA techniques listed.

1401 LINEAR PROGRAMMING

In recent years, a new class of optimization problems has grown out of the complex organizational structures that permeate modern society. These problems are problems of allocation, dealing with many variables and subject to a host of restraining conditions. Problems of allocation arise whenever there are a number of activities to be performed but limitations on either the amount of resources or the manner in which they may be allocated prevent accomplishment of each separate activity in the most effective way conceivable. In such a situation, the available resources must be allocated to the activities in a way that will optimize the total effectiveness of the organization.

A powerful technique that has been developed to solve such problems is called *mathematical programming*. When the problem can be formulated within a mathematical framework in such a way that it becomes one of maximizing or minimizing a linear expression subject to certain linear constraints, the technique is known as *linear programming*.

Historically, the linear programming model was first formulated by G. B. Dantzig in 1947, while working for the U. S. Air Force. He was involved in a study of the feasibility of applying scientific and mathematical methods to the problem of allocating and programming national resources for the purpose of optimizing the national defense structure. The broad applicability of this model to modern-day problems has resulted in the rapidly rising significance of linear programming in recent years. This section will give a brief introduction to the mathematical formulation of the problem and an elementary example of the specific problem-solving technique.

There are three broad classes of linear programming problems. In order of increasing complexity, they are: *assignment problem, transportation problem* and *generalized allocation problem.*

a. The assignment problem is the simplest of the linear programming problems. It is one in which n tasks are to be distributed among n units, one task to each unit. Each pairing of the ith task with the jth unit results in an individual return. The problem is that of distributing the tasks in such a way that the overall return is maximized.

b. The transportation problem can be thought of as a generalization of the assignment problem. Simply stated, it consists of moving a given amount of material from m warehouses to n retail outlets. The total amount required at the outlets equals the total amount stored among the warehouses. The specific amount stored at each warehouse is known; the specific amount required at each outlet is known; and cost of moving one unit of the material from warehouse i to outlet j is known. The problem is that of programming the shipments in such a way as to minimize the overall transportation cost.

c. The generalized allocation problem encompasses both of the other classes, in that it includes all problems which can be formulated in terms of maximizing or minimizing a linear mathematical expression which is subject to linear constraints.

There are various mathematical techniques tailored specifically to solving each of these classes of linear programming problems. Only two techniques will be considered here, both of which are applicable to the more complicated generalized allocation problem. These are the *graphical method* and the *simplex method.* The simplex method is by far the most powerful and versatile technique used in the solution of linear programming problems. For visualization, the graphical method will be demonstrated by the following example.

A defense contractor is geared to build two types of missiles, type A with a 2-kiloton warhead and type B with a 3-kiloton warhead. In its manufacture, missile A requires three critical guidance units and four booster units. Missile B requires four guidance units and eight booster units. Because of the limited supply of the components involved, the total number of the guidance units available to the contractor is 120 per week. The total availability of the booster units is limited to 200 units per week. If no other constraints are present, how should the project director program the weekly production of missiles in order to maximize the killpower of the missile stockpile?

The first step in any approach to solving linear programming problems is its formulation in mathematical language. For this particular example, let

$$x_1 = \text{number of type } A \text{ missiles constructed,}$$
$$x_2 = \text{number of type } B \text{ missiles constructed,}$$
$$M = \text{total killpower in kilotons resulting from the}$$
$$\text{missiles produced during the week.}$$

Then the problem can be stated as follows:

maximize the expression

Equation 14-1 $M = 2x_1 + 3x_2,$ also called objective Fu   7-45

subject to the following constraints:

Equation 14-2 $x_1 \geq 0,$

Equation 14-3 $x_2 \geq 0,$

Equation 14-4   Guidance $3x_1 + 4x_2 \leq 120,$ Line CD

Equation 14-5   Boosters $4x_1 + 8x_2 \leq 200.$ Line AB

The graphic solution consists of first plotting the constraint relationships using each of the variables as an axis of the graph. (Figure 14-1).

In Figure 14-1, it can be seen that Equations 14-2 and 14-3 restrict the solution to the region above the x_1 axis and to the right of the x_2 axis. Equation 14-4 restricts the solution to the region below line *CD*. Equation 14-5 restricts the solution to the region below line *AB*. The resultant solution must therefore be contained on or within the boundaries of the convex polygon *OAED*.

The next step is to consider Equation 14-1, $M = 2x_1 + 3x_2$, which is the expression to be maximized and is called the *objective function*. As can be seen from Figure 14-2, the expression $M = 2x_1 + 3x_2$ is a one-parameter family of parallel straight lines with a slope of $-2/3$. It can also be seen from Figure 14-2 that the value of M increases as the line is displaced farther from the origin.

The problem then is to determine from among the infinity of points within the polygon *OAED* the one or more points that will maximize the expression $M = 2x_1 + 3x_2$. This maximum will be the particular line segment of the family $M = 2x_1 + 3x_2$ which is farthest from the origin but still contains at least one point of the polygon *OAED*. The optimum solution, as shown from Figure 14-3, is the point

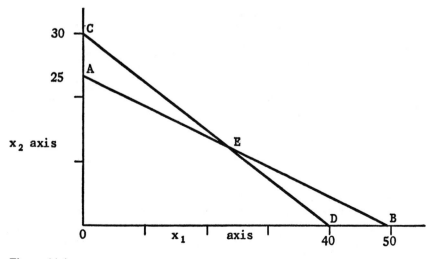

Figure 14-1.

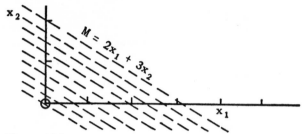

Figure 14-2.

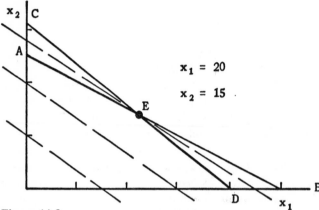

Figure 14-3.

$x_1 = 20$, $x_2 = 15$. In other words, the contractor should produce 20 type A missiles and 15 type B missiles. The maximized killpower thus produced will be

$$M = (2)(20) + (3)(15) = 85 \text{ kilotons.}$$

The reader is cautioned against inferring that the solution is always the intersection of two such obvious constraints. If the slope of Equation 14-1 had been shallower or steeper, the solution could have been at point A or D.

The graphical method is effective for solving linear programming problems involving only two variables even though there may be many linear constraints on these two variables. This method, however, becomes exceedingly cumbersome for a three-variable problem, and essentially impossible when four or more variables are involved. An algebraic method of solution (an algorithm) is an obvious necessity. One such algorithm, discovered by Dantzig, is called the *simplex method,* and it ranks high among the achievements of twentieth-century applied mathematics. Contrary to its name, the simplex method, which is based upon the Gauss-Jordan elimination procedure for solving systems of linear equations, is anything but simple in theory. The mechanical application of the method, however, breaks down into a relatively simple, though tedious, iterative process. Because this process can be programmed for a high-speed digital computer, it becomes a particularly powerful tool for solving a wide range of multivariable problems.

No attempt will be made to develop the theory underlying the method. Suffice it to say that it can be demonstrated that the solution to the linear programming problem lies at one of the vertices of the convex polygon (see Figure 14-3) or else consists of all points on the line connecting two vertices. The simplex method is an algebraic scheme for systematically checking each vertex of the polygon to determine the one where the objective function takes on its maximum value.

An illustration of the use of linear programming in a more complex situation is given by this example.

Two types of attack aircraft are available on a particular aircraft carrier. Their mission has been defined as the destruction of any one of three bridges which enemy tanks must cross (in series) to reach the front line. There is an acute shortage of fuel which limits the total fuel supply to 3,000 gallons for this mission. Any plane sent to any target must have at least enough fuel for the round trip flight plus a reserve of 50 gallons. The number of available planes plus other pertinent data is as follows:

Plane type	Description	Fuel consumption miles/gallon	Number of planes available
1	dive bomber	4	20
2	low-level bomber	5	12

Information about the location of the bridges and the various individual probabilities of success is as follows:

Bridge	Distance from carrier in miles	Probability of destruction by a dive bomber	Probability of destruction by a low-level bomber
1	160	.12	.10
2	210	.22	.20
3	175	.16	.16

The problem can be stated: *how many of each type of plane should be sent,* and *how should they be assigned to the various targets so that the probability of success of the mission is maximized?*

The problem can be stated mathematically in the following manner:

Let n_{ij} be number of planes of type i sent to bridge j ($i = 1, 2; j = 1, 2, 3$). The requirement is to maximize the probability of destroying at least one bridge. This is the same as minimizing the probability of not destroying at least one bridge. Let P denote this probability. Assuming independence between attacks,

$$P = (1 - .12)^{n_{11}}(1 - .22)^{n_{12}}(1 - .16)^{n_{13}}(1 - .10)^{n_{21}}(1 - .20)^{n_{22}}(1 - .16)^{n_{23}}.$$

The restrictions on the n_{ij} because of fuel and aircraft limitations are given by:

$$\frac{(2 \times 160)}{4} n_{11} + \frac{(2 \times 210)}{4} n_{12} + \frac{(2 \times 175)}{4} n_{13} + \frac{(2 \times 160)}{5} n_{21} + \frac{(2 \times 110)}{5} n_{22}$$

$$+ \frac{(2 \times 175)}{5} n_{23} + 50 (n_{11} + n_{12} + n_{13} + n_{21} + n_{22} + n_{23}) \leq 3000,$$

$$n_{11} + n_{12} + n_{13} \leq 20,$$
$$n_{21} + n_{22} + n_{23} \leq 12.$$

Everything in the problem is linear except the function P. However, P can be minimized by maximizing log 1/P which equals $-\log P$. Thus, the following equation is obtained:

$$\log 1/P = .056n_{11} + .108n_{12} + .076n_{13} + .046n_{21} + .097n_{22} + .076n_{23},$$

which is to be maximized subject to the given linear constraints.

The matrix of coefficients (sometimes called a tableaux) for this problem is:

n_{11}	n_{12}	n_{13}	n_{21}	n_{22}	n_{23}	u	v	w	M	numbers
13	15.5	13.75	11.4	9.4	12	1	0	0	0	300
1	1	1	0	0	0	0	1	0	0	20
0	0	0	1	1	1	0	0	1	0	12
−.056	−.108	−.076	−.046	−.097	−.076	0	0	0	1	0

The optimal solution can be found by the simplex technique previously mentioned.

1402 QUEUEING THEORY

Queueing theory is a mathematical technique for analyzing those situations involving units arriving at a servicing facility and having to wait before being serviced. Examples of these situations are aircraft arrivals at airports, customer servicing at barbershops, operation of supermarket counters and loading and unloading of ships. Many factors must be considered when one is analyzing waiting-line problems. Among these are: *the probability distribution underlying arrival times, the probability distribution underlying servicing times, the number of waiting lines, the number of servicing facilities* and *the queue discipline.*

Having a knowledge of these factors, the analyst can in many cases predict such important results as the average length of the waiting line and the average idle time for a service facility during any specified period of time. Coupling these results with the *costs* associated with the waiting lines, he can then make meaningful recommendations to the decision-maker for optimizing the service operations.

An illustration of the usefulness of the theory is given by this example.

Messages arrive randomly at a communications center on a large ship with an average time of 10 minutes between one arrival and the next. The service time for sending these messages is assumed to be distributed exponentially with a mean of 3 minutes. The questions to be answered are:

a. What is the average number of messages in the system?
b. What is the average length of the queue of messages that forms from time to time?
c. Another radioman will be put on watch when the average waiting time for a message to be sent exceeds 3 minutes. What rate of arrivals will require another radioman put on watch?

As a first step in working this problem, define the following terms:

λ = rate at which messages arrive = 1/10 per minute
$1/\lambda$ = average interval between arrival of messages = 10 minutes
μ = mean service rate = 1/3 per minute
$1/\mu$ = average service time = 3 minutes
$\rho = \lambda/\mu$ = the ratio of arrival rate to mean service rate = load factor
$\rho = 3/10 = .3$.

For this particular type of queue, which has arrivals distributed in accordance with the Poisson distribution and service times distributed exponentially, the following relationships can be derived by means of queueing theory:

$\lambda^2/\mu(\mu - \lambda)$ = average queue length

$\mu/(\mu - \lambda)$ = average length of nonempty queues

$\lambda/(\mu - \lambda)$ = average number of messages in system

$\lambda/\mu(\mu - \lambda)$ = average waiting time of a message

$1/(\mu - \lambda)$ = average waiting time of a message which must wait.

Solution:

$$\lambda = 0.1 \text{ arrival/minute} = \text{arrival rate}$$
$$\mu = 0.33 \text{ message serviced/minute} = \text{service rate}$$

Therefore, the answers to the questions are

a. $\lambda/(\mu - \lambda) = 0.1/.23 = .43$ message

b. $\lambda^2/\mu(\mu - \lambda) = .01/.33(.23) = .132$ message

c. Let λ' be the maximum allowable arrival rate before another radioman is put on watch. Then $\lambda'/.33 \ (.33 - \lambda') = 3$, and $\lambda' = .16$ message arrival per minute.

1403 INFORMATION THEORY

Information theory is a relatively new subject, having been developed in its present form by C. E. Shannon in 1948. Simply stated, it is an analysis of the problem of transmission of information from a systems standpoint as opposed to the more conventional studies related to equipment capabilities, circuitry, etc.

Among other things, information theory introduces the notion of a quantitative measure of information by attaching a numerical measure to the information *bits* in a message. The theory is highly mathematical in nature, but a general idea can be obtained by considering a typical communications system as a block diagram. Information theory, in effect, replaces each box of the diagram by a mathematical model intended to duplicate the behavior of the box. It then studies the interplay of these mathematical models and, by analyzing their interdependence, arrives at general theorems applicable to communications systems.

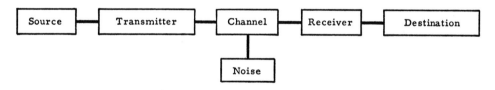

1404 DYNAMIC PROGRAMMING

When the assumptions of linearity required by Section 1401 are not met, for example, because of a time-sequential effect of the elements in the objectives on each other, alternative models may be more useful. If the objective of the bomber allocation example were to destroy at least two bridges, and the probabilities of destroying a bridge increased when one was already destroyed, the *dynamic* aspect of this situation would suggest a *dynamic programming* technique.

Dynamic programming models are also often used for situations that are *not* essentially dynamic in time, such as product allocation among outlets which have nonlinear profit return functions, as well as *sequentially dependent* situations such as equipment replacement and production scheduling.

The following discussion illustrates the dynamic programming *shortest-route* algorithm applied to optimal (shortest time) ship routing. [1]

The goal of optimal ship routing is to select a route for a particular voyage which achieves an objective such as minimizing time, minimizing cost or avoiding risk to vessel and crew. Great circle routes, which achieve shortest *distances,* are not always optimal. For example, it may be preferable to take a longer route to avoid a part of the ocean where waves are high because of storm conditions. Experiments have shown that optimal routing can save substantial amounts of time over great circle routing; for example, Nagle [2] has estimated that during the winter months (January and February) on an Atlantic voyage from Gibraltar to Norfolk by a 15-knot vessel, an average of 13 to 15 hours can be saved. The potential savings for Pacific voyages are even greater.

Ship routing based on navigational experience has been practiced ever since ocean voyages have been made. Only recently, however, have the mathematical sciences been applied in an attempt to *optimize* ship routing. Optimal ship routing (osr) can be considered as a problem in operations analysis by developing a mathematical model which relates the controllable decision variables (choice of route) and the uncontrollable variables (weather and wave conditions) to the objective of the optimization (such as minimizing cost or time). For this introductory discussion of osr the following assumptions are made:

Assumption 1. The point of origin P_0 and the destination P_d are known; the ship type and the departure date are known; the objective of the optimization is to *minimize the time* required to go from P_0 to P_d. Assumption 1 provides the context for the osr analysis.

Assumption 2. At any point in the ocean, the speed at which the vessel can move is determined by two factors: (a) the height of the waves, and (b) the direction of the waves relative to the ship's course.

The relationship of assumption 2 giving ship velocity as a function of wave height and wave direction is discussed by Bleick and Faulkner [3]:

> A basic ingredient of the theory is the polar diagram of Figure 14-4, giving the ship velocity v as a function of the angle θ between the ship's heading and the wave direction. A diagram of this kind must be specified for each wave height H (and for each type of ship). The vectors OL, OM, ON on the diagram correspond to the ship speed v_h in head waves, v_b in beam waves, and v_f in following waves. Empirical curves for these three speeds as functions of wave height H are available in the pioneer work of James [1957].

The vector OK then gives the ship's velocity v when the ship's heading makes an angle of θ with the wave direction. Since distance = velocity $\times$ time, we can also interpret the polar diagram as showing the distance the ship can travel in any direction through a given wave field in one unit of time (assuming the velocity remains constant, or equivalently, assuming that the wave conditions do not change during this time unit).

Bleick and Faulkner continue to show how the polar velocity diagram can be represented by a mathematical formula, but the details of such a formula would lead us too far from our major interest—route optimization—so we will merely suppose that the diagrams (or the corresponding formulas) are available for use in the analysis that follows.

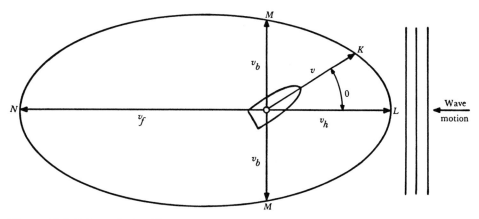

Figure 14-4. Polar velocity diagram.

Assumption 3. The height and direction of the wave field can be predicted for any point in the ocean for as far into the future as is necessary to complete the voyage.

Assumption 3 requires that the wave conditions can be forecast for at least several days into the future. To plan routes which take advantage of favorable wave conditions requires that forecasts of these conditions be available to the planner. Such forecasts can be obtained from the Navy's Fleet Numerical Weather Central. The accuracy and reliability of wave forecasts are being continually improved, but much work remains to be done in this difficult area of oceanographic and meteorological research. The optimization techniques which follow are only as good as the forecasts on which they are based.

A Graphic Route Optimization Technique

The polar velocity diagrams can be used in a graphic approach to osr. Choose a time step size Δt (say $\Delta t = 6$ hours) and assume that course changes will only be made at intervals of Δt hours. Let point P_0 be the origin point for the voyage. Draw the polar velocity diagram at P_0 (at time $= 0 =$ start time), increasing it radially by a factor of Δt. The resulting curve C_1 represents all the points that can be reached in time Δt from P_0, in Figure 14-5.

To find all the points that can be reached in time $2 \times \Delta t$, repeat this process from every point on the curve C_1. In practice we choose a few points $P_{11}, P_{12}, \ldots, P_{1n}$ on C_1 and draw the polar diagram (increased by the factor Δt) at each of these points for the time Δt. Note that to do this requires a forecast of wave conditions Δt hours into the future. The resulting curves $C_{11}, C_{12}, \ldots, C_{1n}$ in Figure 14-5 represent the points where the ship would be at time $2 \times \Delta t$ if it took one heading in the first time period and another in the second period. The envelope of these curves (call it C_2) can be sketched in and represents the farthest distance that the ship could be from P_0 after $2 \times \Delta t$ time units.

Now choose several points $P_{21}, P_{22}, \ldots, P_{2n}$ on curve C_2 and repeat the process of the previous paragraph to construct a curve C_3. This process is repeated until the resulting curve C_N at stage N encloses the destination point P_d. Then the shortest time to go from P_0 to P_d is between $(N-1) \times \Delta t$ and $N \times \Delta t$; one interpolates to get the actual time. The optimal route is constructed by interpolating backwards from P_d to

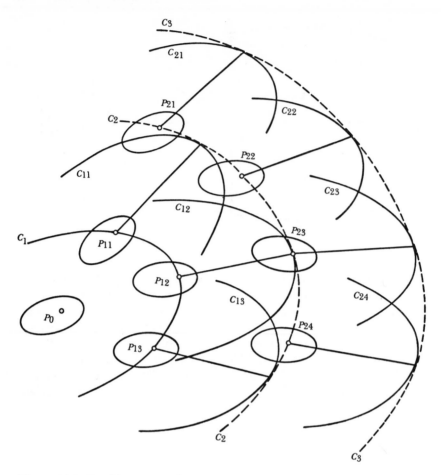

Figure 14-5. Graphic construction.

P_0. Figure 14-6 shows the last two segments of the route obtained from this backwards interpolation.

The curves $C_j (j = 1, 2, \ldots, N)$ generated in this way are called isochrones (equal time) or time fronts, since each point on the curve C_j can be reached in the same $j \times \Delta t$ time units. The method of isochrones has been extensively used in the Navy as a manual method for graphically generating approximate optimal routes. It should be clear that as the size of the time step Δt decreases (allowing course changes more frequently), the approximation to optimality improves, but the amount of graphing required also increases.

Dynamic Programming for OSR

The development of the digital computer has inspired research on mathematical (as opposed to graphical) approaches to OSR. One technique currently being used applies dynamic programming. The resulting OSR method is described here.

Begin by selecting a grid of points in the ocean between the origin, P_0, and the destination, P_d. As an example see Figure 14-7, although in practice the grid would have many more points. The points are labeled P_{ij}, where the first subscript i indicates

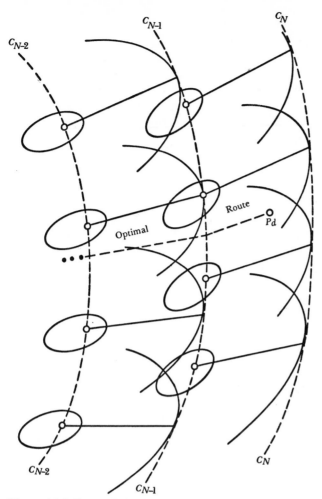

Figure 14-6. Interpolating backwards to find optimal route.

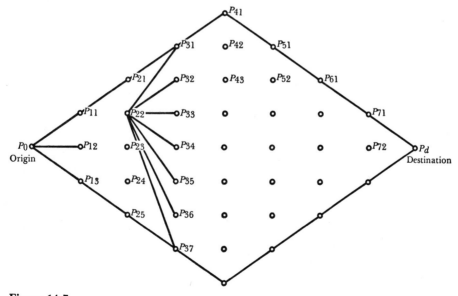

Figure 14-7.

the column in which the point appears and the second subscript j indicates which point in column i we are considering. The grid is chosen to cover the portion of the ocean that is likely to contain the optimal route. In computing the optimal route, we consider the paths from each point in column i to every point in the next column, $i + 1$. For example, the possible route segments leaving the point P_{22} are shown in Figure 14-7 as the seven straight lines leading to $P_{31}, P_{32}, \ldots, P_{37}$.

Suppose the vessel leaves the origin P_0 at time $t = 0$. Its three possible courses lead to P_{11}, P_{12} and P_{13}. If the wave conditions at P_0 are known, then the ship velocity for each of these three headings can be computed from the formula that represents the polar velocity diagram. Assuming constant velocity, we can then compute the earliest time t_{11}, t_{12}, t_{13} at which the ship could arrive at the points P_{11}, P_{12}, P_{13} in the first column.

Define t_{ij} as the earliest time that the ship could arrive at point P_{ij}. Now consider the 15 possible route segments from each point in column 1 to each point in column 2. Knowing the times of arrival t_{1j} at each point P_{1j}, we can predict the wave conditions and hence the velocities for each of these 15 possible route segments. Knowing the velocity and distance, we can compute the time $T(P_{1j}, P_{2k}) j = 1, \ldots, 3, k = 1, \ldots, 5$ required to cover each of the 15 possible route segments. Finally, the earliest possible arrival time for each point P_{2k} in column 2 can be computed as:

Equation 14-6
$$t_{2k} = \min_{j = 1, \ldots, 3} [t_{1j} + T(P_{1j}, P_{2k})].$$

That is, the earliest time to get to P_{2k} is the minimum over all possible predecessor points P_{1j} of the sum of (1) the earliest time t_{1j} to get to P_{1j}, plus (2) the time to go from P_{1j} to P_{2k}. In computing t_{2k}, the j that gives the minimum indicates the point in column 1 which is before P_{2k} on the shortest route to P_{2k}. We record this route segment (P_{1j}, P_{2k}) for use later in reconstructing the overall optimal route.

Having computed t_{2k} $k = 1, \ldots, 5$, we can proceed to consider the 35 possible route segments from each point in column 2 to each point in column 3. Repeating the above procedures, we eventually compute the earliest time

Equation 14-7
$$t_{3k} = \min_{j = 1, \ldots, 5} [t_{2j} + T(P_{2j}, P_{3k})]$$

and the route segments (P_{2j}, P_{3k}) for each of the seven points P_{3k} $k = 1, \ldots, 7$. We continue in this fashion until at the last stage we compute the earliest time the ship can arrive at the destination as

Equation 14-8
$$t_d = \min_{j = 1, 2, 3} [t_{7j} + T(P_{7j}, P_d)].$$

Then the optimal route which achieves this minimal time can be found by working backwards through the network of points using the pairs (P_{ij}, P_{i+1}, k) that we recorded at each stage.

Example. Consider the simple grid of Figure 14-8, where all the possible route segments are labeled with their transit times. [For example, $T(P_0, P_{11}) = 4$; $T(P_{11}, P_{22}) = 5$.] Then the computations are (in order of calculation):

$$t_{11} = T(P_0, P_{11}) = 4 \text{ and record } (P_0, P_{11})$$
$$t_{12} = T(P_0, P_{12}) = 7 \text{ and record } (P_0, P_{12})$$

$$t_{21} = \min_{j=1,2} [t_{1j} + T(P_{1j}, P_{21})]$$
$$= \min [4 + 7, 7 + 3]$$
$$= 10 \text{ and record } (P_{12}, P_{21})$$
$$t_{22} = \min_{j=1,2} [t_{1j} + T(P_{1j}, P_{22})]$$
$$= \min [4 + 5, 7 + 4]$$
$$= 9 \text{ and record } (P_{11}, P_{22})$$
$$t_d = \min_{j=1,2} [t_{2j} + T(P_{2j}, P_d)]$$
$$= \min [10 + 5, 9 + 5]$$
$$= 14 \text{ and record } (P_{22}, P_d).$$

Then the shortest time to go from P_0 to P_d is 14, and we construct the shortest route from P_d back to P_0 using the recorded pairs

$$(P_0, P_{11}) \leftarrow (P_{11}, P_{22}) \leftarrow (P_{22}, P_d). \qquad 7\text{-}56$$

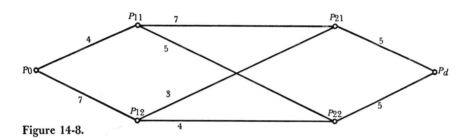

Figure 14-8.

This dynamic programming computation is ideally suited for computer implementation, and extremely large grids can be routinely computed. The limiting factor for the method is the accuracy of the currently available wave forecasts. It should be noted that it is easy to bypass land masses using this method by simply omitting any grid points on land and any route segment which crosses over land. $7\text{-}57$

1405 PROGRAM EVALUATION AND REVIEW TECHNIQUE

Program Evaluation and Review Technique (PERT) is a rather formal planning tool designed to measure, review and control progress in a complex project that is made up of several interdependent tasks. The main feature of PERT is the use of a flow diagram or graphical network which visually portrays, in a logical order, the interrelationships among the various tasks making up the overall project. This technique can lead to a substantial reduction in the overall cost and completion time for such projects by providing closer coordination of the simultaneous execution of the individual tasks. $7\text{-}58$

The Navy, as a result of a concentrated search for new ideas on scientific management control, was the first organization to introduce the use of PERT techniques. This was in connection with the management of the Polaris Missile program. The Army and Air Force soon saw that this technique had wide applicability, and it has also grown heavily in use of industry, sometimes being referred to as Critical Path Monitoring (CPM) or Critical Path Scheduling (CPS). Judiciously applied, this technique can be a powerful managerial tool in implementing plans leading to goals, in

Table 14-1. Preparing a naval air squadron for overseas deployment

Task code	Task name	Duration (work days)	Predecessors
A	ECP-32 Installation Training	5	Start
B	VD Education	3	Start
C	Drug Education	3	Start
D	ECP-32 Field Testing	2	A
E	ECP-32 Installation	6	D,G
F	ECP-32 Operation Training	5	B,E
G	Predeployment Leave	7	C
H	Tool Inventory	3	B,E
I	Inspection of All Equipment	2	D,G
J	Repair/Replace Faulty Equipment	2	F,I
K	UNREP Qualification	3	B,E
	Project Completion		H,J,K

measuring progress towards those goals, and in indicating problem areas involved in achieving those goals.

A graphical network is constructed, representing the precedence relationships of the tasks composing a project. The network also contains information on the time required to do each task. In more advanced applications, information about the reliability of the time estimates and data about resources required to conduct the project may be included on the network.

The following example illustrates the construction of a PERT network for a project and the method used to compute the time required to complete the project. The project is the preparation of a Naval Air Squadron for overseas deployment. Table 14-1 lists the tasks in the project, the estimated times to conduct each task, and the other tasks that must be completed *before* the start of each task.

In using PERT for project planning, it is necessary to carry out three steps to build a table like Table 14-1: (1) Break down (or decompose) the project into individual tasks and list the tasks; (2) obtain time estimates for each task; (3) identify the other tasks that immediately precede each task. This systematic method for project planning offers the advantage that the estimates of the time needed to complete each task are obtained from personnel most expert in that particular activity. (Much better project time estimates are obtained by breaking the project into parts and obtaining estimates of the time to do each task from the most knowledgeable people and the people responsible for each task, than by trying to estimate whole-project time.) Then the time to complete the entire project is computed, using the methodology presented below.

After information has been collected and organized in the form of Table 14-1, a network is constructed which displays a graphical representation of the relationships between tasks. The tasks are represented by progress-directed arcs connecting nodes that signify the completion or beginning of a task. Nodes in PERT terminology are called *events*. The following rules are used in the network construction:

(1) Each task is represented by only *one* arc.

(2) If the nodes (events) are numbered 1, 2, ... *n*, then it must be possible to uniquely identify each task by specifying the starting and completion events. To satisfy this rule, sometimes it is necessary to add dummy or artificial tasks. This rule is required by the algorithm used to compute the total project time.

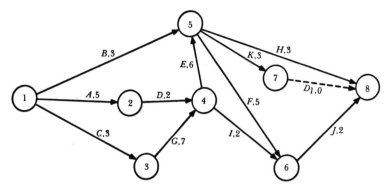

Figure 14-9.

The network representing predeployment plans is shown in Figure 14-9. The times to complete each task are also included.

Notice that a dummy task, labeled D_1, was added so that tasks H and K did not have the same starting and ending events. The duration time of D_1 is 0 days (all dummy tasks have zero duration). The events have been numbered so that if i is the starting event and j the terminal event of a task, then $i < j$. Numbering of the events in this fashion is necessary in order to use the algorithm for computing the duration time of the project; this is done by numbering the starting event as node 1 and then checking off its outgoing arcs. Then number any node with only *unchecked* outgoing arcs with the next higher number, check off its arcs and continue until all nodes are numbered.

The time to complete a project is computed by finding the length of the *longest* path to each event from the starting event, where the length of each arc is the time to complete the corresponding task. The longest path from the start of the project to its completion is called the *critical path.*

The longest-path algorithm for a PERT network:

1. Let $n = 1$.
2. Label node 1 with the number 0. (On our network a node will be labeled by putting the required number in a box next to the node.)
3. If n is the terminal event, stop; otherwise replace n by $n + 1$.
4. Label node n with the *largest* sum of the time on each incoming arc plus the node label preceding that arc. Return to step (3).

Assuming the task time estimates are accurate, the node labels indicate the *earliest* time possible that an event could occur; this is also the earliest time that tasks beginning with that event could be initiated.

Figure 14-10 shows the aircraft squadron predeployment project network after all the node labels have been computed.

The predeployment project will take 23 days to complete the critical path 1, 3, 4, 5, 6, 8 or tasks C, G, E, F, J. If any of these tasks is *delayed,* the completion of the project will be delayed.

More can be done in analyzing the PERT network. The amount of time each task *not* on the critical path can be delayed without affecting the project completion time can easily be computed. This information then can be used by the project manager

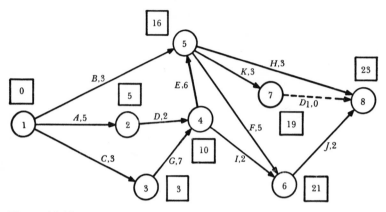

Figure 14-10.

when allocating resources to the tasks and can be used to manage the progress of the project.

Practical techniques have also been developed for dealing with the duration of tasks as random variables rather than deterministic estimates. As the actual progress is monitored, the network can be re-evaluated anytime an estimate is revised or a task completed.

1406   NAVIGATIONAL ERROR AND POSITIONAL UNCERTAINTY [4]

This section discusses the effect of navigational error on positional uncertainty. The discussion applies probability theory to a topic of interest in the analysis of tactics and related activities.

The various sources of navigational error are not treated in this text. However, it is assumed that navigational error consists of a systematic (deterministic) component added to a random (probabilistic) component whose average or mean value is zero. The systematic component of navigational error is that component which can be specified and, hence, accounted for. The index error of a sextant is an example of systematic error. The random component of navigational error is that component which can be described in terms of probabilities. A chronometer's error, for example, can be assumed to consist of a systematic component plus a random component.

This section deals only with positions which are determined by the intersection of two lines of position. Lines of position may be determined by various means. For example, a bearing line is a line of position, the circle determined by a radar range is a line of position, and the spherical hyperbolas determined by LORAN are lines of position.

The section consists of two parts. In the first part, the lines of position determine a position which is the same as the position determined by advancing a known position along a course line. Determining a position in this manner is called dead reckoning (DR). A position determined by dead reckoning is called an estimated position (EP). In the second part, each line of position is determined by an observation with a navigational system. A position determined by the intersection of two lines of position determined in this manner is called a fix.

Part 1. Positions Determined by Dead Reckoning

A craft is to proceed from a known position with a specified course and speed; this information determines a DR line. For any given time, a DR range circle is also determined. The intersection of the DR line with the DR range circle determines a position, which is the EP. The course error and speed error are assumed to be independent random variables. (Systematic errors such as that introduced by current are assumed to have been accounted for in establishing the EP.) Two cases are considered:

Case I. The probability that the course error will lie within some given interval and the probability that the speed error will lie within some given interval are assumed to be known. When this is the case, a probability statement can be made about the location of the true position with respect to the EP at a specified time. To illustrate this, consider the following example: A ship is to proceed from a known position at a speed of 10 knots on a specified course. The probability that the error in course will be between ±2.5° is .5, and the probability that the error in speed will be between ±10 percent is .8. Then, the probability that the ship's true position will be within the fan-shaped region shown in Figure 14-11 ten hours from the known position is (.5)(.8) = .4. The probability that the ship's true position will be outside the fan-shaped region is 1 − .4 = .6.

Case II. The course error and the speed error are assumed to be independent normally distributed random variables, each with a mean of zero. In addition, it is assumed that a region can be established like that shown in Figure 14-11 that includes the true position and is effectively rectangular (even for cases where the probability of including the true position is essentially one). With this assumption, the DR range circle arc which intersects the DR course line can be considered to be a straight line perpendicular to the DR course line, and a rectangular coordinate system can be defined as follows: Let the DR course line be the x-axis and the DR range circle arc by the y-axis. The EP is then the origin of the system. The location of the true position with respect to the estimated position can be described in terms of the coordinates of this system. Because of the above assumptions, the x and y coordinates of the true position can be taken to be independent normally distributed random variables, each with a mean of zero. And the joint distribution of x and y is a bivariate normal distribution. Two additional values will specify this distribution, the standard deviations of x and y. These values can be determined for a specified time as follows: Let s be the speed and t be the time the ship or aircraft is to proceed from its last known position. Let σ_s be the standard deviation of the speed error and σ_θ be the standard deviation of the course error in

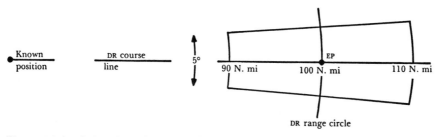

Figure 14-11. A fan-shaped probability region.

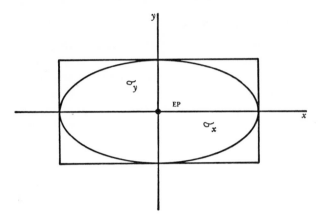

Figure 14-12. A $2\sigma_x$ by $2\sigma_y$ rectangle and inscribed ellipse.

radians. Then $\sigma_x = \sigma_s t$ and $\sigma_y = \sigma_\theta st$. The probability that the true position will be within an ellipse centered on the EP with semiaxis $k\sigma_x$ and $k\sigma_y$ is $1 - \exp(-k^2/2)$. This result can be found by integrating the bivariate normal density function over the elliptical region. For example, the probability is .39 for $k = 1$ and .86 for $k = 2$. The probability the true position will be in the rectangle shown in Figure 14-12 of sides $2\sigma_x$ and $2\sigma_y$ centered on the EP is $(.68)(.68) = .47$, since the probability that either coordinate of the true position will be between plus and minus one standard deviation is .68 and these events are independent. The probability for the inscribed ellipse is .39, since $k = 1$.

Part 2. Positions Established by Two Determined Lines of Position

A determined (estimated) line of position and the true line of position (the determined line of position when the random error is zero) are assumed to be essentially straight and parallel in the region containing the true position and the fix. The degree of approximation involved in these assumptions will depend on the method used to establish a line of position. The distance between the true line of position and a determined line of position will be referred to here as the line of position error. Line of position errors are assumed to be independent random variables. Two cases will be considered.

Case I. The probability that the line of position error will lie within a given interval is assumed to be known. When this is the case, a probability statement can be made about the location of a fix with respect to the true position. To illustrate this, consider the following example: Suppose two lines of position are to be determined and suppose the probability that the line of position error of the first will be less than 5 N.mi. is .7 and the probability that the line of position error of the second will be less than 3 N.mi. is .8. Then the probability that the fix will be within the parallelogram which is centered on the true position as shown in Figure 14-13 is $(.7)(.8) = .56$. The probability that the fix will lie outside the parallelogram is $1 - .56 = .44$.

Case II. The line of position errors are assumed to be independent normally distributed random variables, each with a mean of zero and a known standard deviation. A result of this assumption is that the probability that a line of position error will lie

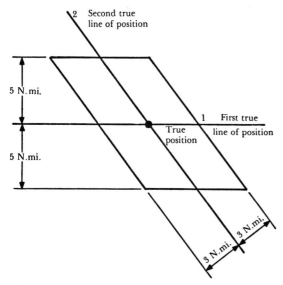

Figure 14-13. The true position with an associated parallelogram.

within any specified interval can be determined. For example, assume the standard deviation associated with the first line of position error, σ_1, is 5 N.mi. and that with the second, σ_2, is 3 N.mi. Then, if the intersection of the true lines of position were to be as shown in Figure 14-13, the probability that the fix would lie within the parallelogram would be $(.68)(.68) = .47$, by the same argument used in Case II of Part 1. An elliptical region can also be developed in this case, but the development is more complex than that in Case II of Part 1. However, if the lines of position intersect at $90°$, the two cases are equivalent and Figure 14-12 can be used to represent this situation if "x" is replaced by "1" and "y" by "2", "σ_x" by "σ_2" and "σ_y" by "σ_1".

A question which is of interest in the practice of navigation can be stated as follows: A craft has proceeded for a time corresponding to an EP, or a fix has been determined. What can be said about the location of the true position? The notion of a confidence region can be used to give an answer to this question.

The regions discussed in Part I can be interpreted directly as confidence regions. For example, for the situation described in Case I of Part 1, the fan-shaped region shown in Figure 14-11 is a .4 confidence region for the true position.

Because of the assumptions made in Part 2, the regions discussed there can be easily converted to confidence regions. For example, in the situation described in Case I of Part 2 the probability is .56 that a fix will be determined within the described parallelogram shown in Figure 14-13. Because of the assumptions made in Part 2, this is equivalent to saying that, for the given true position, in 56 percent of the determinations of a fix the true position will be included within a parallelogram which is identical to the one shown in Figure 14-13 except that its center will be located on the fix. This implies that if the center of the parallelogram of Figure 14-13 were the fix and the two axes were the determined lines of position, then the parallelogram would bound a .56 confidence region for the true position.

If more than two lines of position are involved, the definition of a fix is not immediately evident. In the case of three lines of position, the estimated lines will in general intersect at three different points. One way to define a fix in this case is to designate it to be the centroid of the triangle formed by the three lines. With sufficient assumptions, probability statements dealing with the relation between the true position and a fix can be made and confidence intervals can be defined; but, in general, when more than two lines of position are involved, the analysis is significantly more difficult.

1407 SIMULATION; MONTE CARLO MODELS; OPERATIONAL GAMING MODELS

Ideally, the analyst hopes to solve complex operational problems by means of a step-by-step application of the scientific method. This might include the following steps:

a. Develop an analytical model which completely describes the real world situation under study.
b. Make pertinent predictions based upon the theory.
c. Test the validity of the predictions by means of controlled experimentation.

Unfortunately, many problems are not amenable to this type of solution. For example, the operation under study may be so complex that the development of a numerical relationship to explain it is not possible. Or, the physical size of the operation may be so large as to preclude the experimental testing of mathematical theories related to the operation. In situations of this type, a powerful tool available to the analyst is the method of *simulation*.

Simulation can be broadly defined as a method of duplicating a real-world operation by other than formal analytic techniques. In general usage today are two other terms which describe some special types of simulation. The term *Monte Carlo* model generally refers to a simulation model that includes the use of an assumed probability distribution in its makeup. The rolling of a die and the use of a table of random numbers are two examples of distributions used in Monte Carlo models.

Operational gaming refers to simulation models that include decision-making by two or more *opponents* as part of the *play*. The game of *Monopoly* is a simple example of this type of simulation. The traditional war game is another example. Simulation, as referred to previously, can be performed manually, but the modern trend is towards the use of high-speed digital computers wherever possible. Computers are particularly useful in Monte Carlo models where a large number of replications are necessary in order to gather sufficient statistical data.

1408 EXERCISE DESIGN [5]

This final section presents a basic logical approach to the design of an exercise. It is hoped that the acquaintance with basic Naval Operations Analysis thus far gained from this text will provide one with more understanding of this topic than a previous vague knowledge would have allowed.

The purpose of any exercise is to gain experience. Analysis translates the experience into knowledge. If an exercise is to yield knowledge, then that exercise must be designed to accommodate the methods that will be used for analysis.

The analyst begins structuring the exercise by *translating* the exercise *objectives* into questions to be answered. Next, he *arranges* the questions in order of *importance*. Then he must *select* the applicable *measures* to be used in the analysis. Also for each measure, he must *identify* the required *data* and *determine* how the data will be *collected*. The resources available must be budgeted for the analysis to produce optimum results. Simulation techniques can be occasionally used by the analyst prior to the exercise to weed out less effective tactics. That way, at-sea time can be devoted to exercising the most promising tactics.

There exists another operational and administrative facet to exercise design. It is the aspect of interpreting requirements and providing directions to the participants of the exercise. It includes communications, command and control, logistics, scheduling, safety, geographical location, administrative requirements and operational constraints. This aspect of exercise design is not treated here. It is mentioned to emphasize that the two facets of exercise design must be integrated. Consideration of both assures more successful conduct of the exercise, useful data collection and meaningful analysis of results. The analyst, in designing the exercise, must be aware of the second facet as well as be directly concerned with answering the questions posed by the exercise objectives.

The analyst will provide specific information to the exercise designer to factor into the overall exercise design. The designer, in turn, will provide information to the analyst to use in designing the exercise analysis and data collection plans. In many cases, the exercise designer and the analyst will be one person. If so, that person should be aware of the two distinct functions he is performing.

Selection of Exercise Objectives

The initial phase of the design of at-sea exercises is the establishment of the objectives. Exercises can generally be assigned to one or more of four categories, according to objectives:

- Combat role effectiveness
- Tactical development
- Force training
- Performance characteristic assessment

The objectives that deal with *combat role effectiveness* are the *broadest*. Combat role effectiveness objectives are extensive data collections. They support the development, evaluation, validation or refinement of overall combat role measures of effectiveness. On the other hand, the objectives of *performance characteristic assessment* are *narrow* in scope. Usually, a characteristic is specified, such as probability of detection as a function of range. The objectives in both these categories require data collection. In pursuing the objectives in both these categories, training of personnel takes place, but only as a consequence of at-sea operations. Another category of exercises, force training, has the specific purpose of increasing the proficiency of personnel in procedures by actual experience. There is usually less emphasis on data collection. Generally, an exercise will incorporate objectives from *all four* categories.

The exercise planner currently has four *primary sources* for selection of objectives. These sources are:

- War plans
- Directives from higher authority
- Annual project programs
- Previous exercise reports

The current war plans can provide the basic concepts as to which operations should be exercised. Directives from higher authority generally provide the planner with broad overall objectives. Guidance concerning the priority of the objectives available here may be associated with, or in addition to, the concepts considered in the war plans. The Annual Project programs coordinated with type and fleet commanders will contain those basic objectives which are to be addressed during that particular year. The exercise reports on topics similar to those being considered should contain those objectives which have been addressed, the extent to which the objectives have been met and gaps which may exist in the objectives addressed.

Once the tentative exercise objectives have been selected, the planner should then *rank* them according to the *importance* of the objective to the specific exercise. This ranking will achieve several purposes. First, it will provide a basis for rejecting or altering objectives in the event of conflicting requirements or inadequate resources in time and forces. The planner must ensure that sufficient data will be collected from which to draw reasonable statistical inferences. If reasonable inferences cannot be made for all the objectives, then a selection process to eliminate or alter the objectives according to rank of importance must be undertaken. Second, in the event that the number and types of objectives might reasonably be fulfilled in a single exercise, the ranking provides a basis for selecting the accuracy and confidence limit level for each objective. Thus, the exercise might be designed such that lower-priority objectives are met with low accuracy and confidence level, while the major objectives will be met with high confidence and accuracy. For any given exercise, the planner should conduct a trade-off analysis of each objective with respect to the time, equipment and level of effort required to achieve acceptable accuracy and confidence levels. This analysis may reveal that there are sufficient resources to accommodate additional objectives in the exercise. In this case, additional and noninterfering objectives could be added to the test plan. An additional perspective to the selection of objectives may be achieved if the planner also designates which objectives are noninterfering. A noninterfering objective is one which can be fulfilled without degradation of the primary objectives.

Design of the Analysis Plan

Once the objectives of the exercise have been selected and ranked according to priority, the planner should direct his attention to the analysis plan. An analysis plan is simply a logical development of the data to be collected and the methodology to be used in statistical measurement. The analysis plan should:

1. Specify the objectives of the analysis in detail. They should correspond to the exercise objectives.

2. Specify the analytical procedures that will be employed. If the methodology and statistical models have previously been developed, they should be specified. If new techniques are to be employed, a brief description of the techniques and reference to the development sources should be made. State the assumptions used in the methodology.

3. List the specific parameters that will be measured or investigated.

4. State how the data will be treated. Are the data to be separated according to the parameter being investigated? Are they to be aggregated, and under what conditions? Are they valid for aggregation in a larger data base? Will they be used to develop, validate or modify a particular model?

In the formulation of the analysis plan, several preliminary steps may assist in the development of the data requirements. The first step should be tabulation of the *measure of effectiveness* and of *performance measures* applicable to the exercise being designed.

The second logical step is the consideration of the *parameters that may control* the resultant data. For example, those parameters which could be considered in a submarine exercise include:

Environment	*Target*	*Own ship*
Ocean area	Type	Speed
Depth of water	Operating mode	Search mode
Sea state	Speed	Search tactic
Layer depth		
Boundary configuration		

When the basic parameters have been specified, additional parameters to be investigated should be listed. For example, assume that an objective of the exercise is to measure the ability of a submarine to close the target as a function of target speed. The speed parameter is included in the basic list, but angle on the bow at time of detection should be specified as an additional parameter.

The use of the data and the statistical inferences to be drawn can now be specified in accord with the performance measures and parameters developed. This step should address the *specific treatment of the data*. For instance, if a variety of target types are planned, the detection and classification data would be segregated. From the example above, however, the data which test ability to close the target as a function of target speed and angle on the bow could be combined. Where appropriate, the planner should determine the desired confidence level and accuracy. He should obtain an estimate of the sample statistic and required sample size.

Design of the Data Collection Plan

Careful attention must be given in the exercise design phase to the scope, content and amount of data to be recorded at sea. In general, the exercise designer should plan to collect as large an amount of data as possible. He is bounded by the operational and safety limitations of the exercise participants. The elimination of unnecessary data during reconstruction is more desirable than the extrapolation of data which were not recorded during the exercise.

The first step in design of the data collection plan is the *preparation of a reconstructed data chart*. The designer should review each objective of the analysis plan to determine specifically what data are required to support the analysis. A summary of the data should then be listed on the data chart. When all objectives have been reviewed, the data chart should be a summary of the data requirements for the exercise. An example of a reconstructed data chart used in submarine exercises is presented in Figure 14-14.

The second step in data collection design is to prepare a *list* of data requirements for *the exercise participants*. This listing should specify the data form number referred to in the appropriate data collection guide.

If nonstandard data are required in support of the analysis plan, the designer should provide additional instructions and formats to the exercise participants.

An example of a data collection plan to support the analysis plan would incorporate the data chart in Figure 14-14 and the submarine exercise data collection requirements in the following list:

RECONSTRUCTED DATA

Exercise _____
Time Period _____
Water Depth _____

Environment and Geometry	RUN AND ENCOUNTER IDENTIFICATION
	SEA STATE (0-9)
	LAYER DEPTH (Ft)
	SEARCH AREA SIZE (Mi²)
	TARGET AREA SIZE (Mi²)
Exercise Ship Data	SPEED (Kts)
	DEPTH (Ft)
	LAYER (In or Below)
	TIME OF DETECTION
	RANGE
	OWN COURSE
	SENSOR
	MODE
	CPA IF NO DETECTION
	RELATIVE BEARING
	SEARCH TIME
	TIME OF CLASSIFICATION
	RANGE AT CLASSIFICATION
	TIME CONTACT HELD
	LOST CONTACT RANGE
	LOST CONTACT REL. BEAR.
	FIRM/INTERMITTENT RATIO
	NUMBER FALSE DETECTIONS
	NUMBER FALSE CLASSIFICATIONS
	NUMBER NON-EXERCISE CONTACTS
Target Ship Data	SPEED (Kts)
	DEPTH (Ft)
	LAYER (In or Below)
	TIME OF COUNTERDETECTION
	RANGE OF COUNTERDETECTION
	SENSOR
	RELATIVE BEARING
	EVASION ATTEMPTED?
	NUMBER OF ATTEMPTS
	NUMBER FALSE COUNTERDETECTIONS
	NUMBER FALSE CLASSIFICATIONS
	NON-EXERCISE CONTACTS

Figure 14-14. Sample reconstructed data chart.

- The Commanding Officer's Narrative, OPNAV Form 3360/28
- Sonar Contact Record, OPNAV Form 3360/32
- Sonar Operation Chronology, OPNAV Form 3360/33
- Navigation Position and DRAI/DRT Reset Log, OPNAV Form 3360/41D (Duplicate Ship's Position Log)
- Submarine Vehicle Data Form OPNAV 3360/9
- Track charts
- Passive Ranging and Strip Plots
- Sound Velocity Profiles prior to COMEX and at FINEX
- BTR traces
- Magnetic tape recordings of contacts
- Duplicate Quartermaster Notebook, NAVPERS Form 3100/5
- Navigation data
  - SINS Type 33 Printouts
  - SINS Reset Sheets
  - Absolute Monitor Plot
- UQC Log
- Ship Weather Observation Sheet, OPNAV Form 3144/1

Additional data from searcher:

- Active Sonar Log; mode, pulse, pattern, interval
- $(L_N - N_{DI})$ versus speed for the equipment prior to COMEX and at FINEX

Additional data from target ship:

- Estimates of the following:
  - Whether target is tracking searcher (document holding time)
  - Bearing and range to searcher
  - Target track
  - Target search mode
  - Target search pattern
  - Size and relative position of target's patrol area

Use of Prediction/Simulation in Exercise Design

The use of prediction techniques is important in the design of an exercise plan. Although prediction/simulation methods have wide application in areas such as force level studies and resource allocation studies, this discussion is limited to their application in exercise design. Specifically, the exercise planner may find prediction/simulation methods useful in:

- Obtaining reasonable geographical, operational and tactical bounds on the exercise. This helps achieve a desired number of valid exercise opportunities.
- Estimating the sample-size requirements.
- Assisting in the selection of the types and values of parameters for which the results should be investigated.
- Estimating the time requirements for the exercise.
- Estimating the measurement errors in the data collection and reconstruction and the effects of these errors on the analysis results.
- Preliminary evaluation of tactics.
- Providing insight into key parameters that significantly affect the results.

The inputs for prediction/simulation may be obtained from many sources, including:

- Results of previous exercises conducted under comparable conditions.
- Acoustical and environmental measurements.
- Technical publications and specifications for equipment or system.
- Mathematical model derivations.

Sample-Size Requirements

One important factor in exercise design is the estimation of sample size (i.e., number of firings, number of runs, number of trials, and so forth) required for making valid statistical inferences. Larger samples increase the user's confidence that the results are representative of the conditions being tested. But larger samples also mean higher costs in terms of exercise time. Therefore, the designer must compromise between large samples (for increased confidence) and small samples (for minimum cost).

Guidelines for Factorial Design

So far, the test designer has been provided most of the tools he requires to obtain *single estimates* of ASW effectiveness and/or performance measures. In addition, the test designer has some techniques for planning experiments intended to *compare two* sample estimates of the desired measures. As a simple example, he can plan an experiment to compare two different search tactics based on the mean detection range. The most suitable technique for estimating sample-size requirements would be the one for comparing two sample means.

In this simple example, the parameter of interest is "type of search tactic"; and the experiment is intended to investigate only *two* different types of search tactic. All other parameters affecting the detection performance of a system must be the same for each tactic, or the conclusions will be invalid. Since it is impossible to stipulate that certain parameters remain constant (e.g., weather), it is usual to make a test for a mix of conditions and to make comparisons only when the mixes are equivalent.

In a realistic at-sea exercise, the test designer is usually interested in investigating *more than one parameter;* and further, he may be interested in studying *more than two values of each parameter.* If "type of search tactic" is the parameter of interest, the analyst may wish to design an experiment that will use three (or more) different search maneuvers. Further, he may specify another parameter of interest, such as "type of sonar." A second parameter may have three values associated with it, in this case each corresponding to the different types of sonar on board the detecting unit. This type of experiment, in which the analyst investigates two or more sample estimates of the desired effectiveness and/or performance measures, is a *factorial experiment.* The simple experiment designed to study only *two* types of search tactics should be handled as a factorial experiment to ensure that a proper (i.e., same) mix of other parameters (e.g., environment, operational, human factors) is included in the sample for each of the two tactics. Thus, any difference in the detection performance should be due to the search tactics and not due to the other parameters.

In summary, all realistic at-sea experiments are factorial experiments, even if the ultimate objective of the analysis plan is to compare two sample estimates or to obtain a single estimate of the desired effectiveness and/or performance measure(s).

BIBLIOGRAPHY

[1] Prepared by Associate Professor J. K. Hartman, Naval Postgraduate School.
[2] F. W. Nagle, *A Numerical Study in Optimum Track Ship Routing Climatology*, Environmental Prediction Research Facility, Monterey, Calif. (AD-761620), September 1972.
[3] W. E. Bleick and F. D. Faulkner, *Minimal-Time Ship Routing*, Naval Postgraduate School, Monterey, Calif. (AD-604353), August 1964.
[4] Prepared by Associate Professor R. N. Forrest, Naval Postgraduate School.
[5] This section extracted and revised from "Submarine Analysis Notebook," COMSUBDEVGRU TWO, 1973.

PROBLEMS

1. A small firm manufactures two types of electronic tubes (*A* and *B*) and sells them at a profit of 50 cents on type *A* and 40 cents on type *B*. Each type is processed on two machines, an automatic production machine and a finishing machine. Tube *A* requires 2 minutes of processing time on the automatic production machine and 5 minutes of processing time on the finishing machine. Tube *B* requires 3 minutes on the automatic production machine and 2 minutes on the finishing machine. Each machine is available for not more than 60 hours during any working week.

    a. Using the graphical method, determine how many of each type of tube the firm should produce each week in order to make a maximum profit.
    b. What is the maximum profit?

2. An early warning radar installation is under construction. In this particular installation, all the radar units will be operating in parallel because of the critical importance of the area being defended. A maximum of 1,000,000 dollars has been set aside for the radar units to be used in the installation. Two radar types are under consideration: type *A* which costs 50,000 dollars per unit and type *B* which costs 75,000 dollars per unit. Each type *A* radar console requires 16 square feet of floor space and each type *B* console requires 8 square feet of floor space. The total floor space available for the installation of radar consoles is 160 square feet. Operational tests have shown that the mean time between failures for radar *A* during its operational lifetime in this particular environment is 100 hours. For radar *B* this mean time is 120 hours.

    a. Graphically determine how many radars of type *A* and how many radars of type *B* should be installed in the early warning installation in order to maximize the overall reliability of the radar complex for a 120-hour period.
    b. What is the numerical value of this reliability?
    c. Set up the simplex tableaux for this problem.

3. A 5-hour random search is to be conducted in an area 500 N.mi. by 500 N.mi. A total of 9,000 gallons of aviation fuel is available for the search. Three types of aircraft are available for use in the search. The operational characteristics of these aircraft are listed in this table:

Type aircraft	Sweep width nautical miles	Fuel consumption (gallons/nautical mile)	Search speed (knots)	Number aircraft available
A	20	2.5	200	5
B	25	2.0	175	7
C	30	1.7	120	10

Formulate as a linear program the problem of determining the optimum number of each type of aircraft to use in the random search in order to maximize the overall probability of detection.

4. A radar manufacturer is capable of building four types of radar set. In this particular company's production set-up, there are three distinct phases in the production of each radar set. Production line data, as well as profit information on each type of set, are given in the following table:

Man-hours required per set

Radar model	Phase I	Phase II	Phase III	Profit per set
A	100	60	45	900 dollars
B	50	60	180	700 dollars
C	20	20	15	600 dollars
D	10	20	60	400 dollars
Maximum man-hours available per week	500	360	810	

Formulate as a linear program the problem of determining the number of each type of radar the firm should manufacture each week in order to maximize profits.

5. The queueing theory formulas given in this chapter have been derived mathematically. Accepting their validity, draw the graph of the relation representing L, the average length of the nonempty queues which form, as a function of the load factor, ρ. Use this graph to find the value of L, for a service rate of 0.33 when the arrival rate increases to:

a. 0.2 arrival/minute.
b. 0.3 arrival/minute.
c. 0.33 arrival/minute.

6. Number the nodes of the following PERT network so that each task can be identified by a pair of node numbers (i, j) where i is starting node and j the ending node of the task with $i < j$.

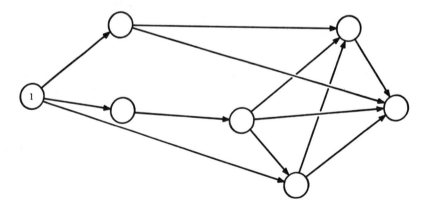

7. The following network is intended to be a PERT network but is not, since some of

the tasks are not uniquely identifiable by a pair of node numbers. Make it a PERT network by adding nodes and dummy activities connecting them, and then number the nodes as in Problem six.

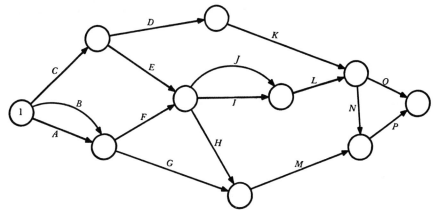

8. The following table describes a project in terms of its individual tasks, their duration times and the task which must be complete before the task can begin.

Task label	Duration time (days)	Predecessors
A	3	Start
B	4	Start
C	2	Start
D	1	A
E	2	A
F	5	D, E
G	4	C
H	2	B, E
J	4	C
K	5	I
End of project	—	F, G, H, K

The following network is supposed to represent the project, but does not. There is an error in representing the precedence relationships. Redraw the network correctly, and number the nodes as required in Problem six.

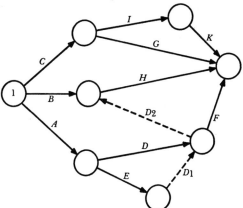

9. For the following PERT network determine the critical path and compute the time it will take to do the project. The task times are measured in days.

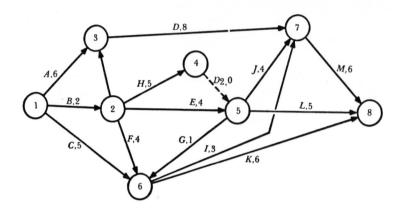

10. The following table describes a project in terms of its individual tasks, their times and the tasks which must be completed previously. Draw the PERT network representing this project. Number the nodes in the manner specified in Problem six. Determine the critical path and the time required to complete the entire project.

Task label	Duration time (weeks)	Predecessors
A	2	Start
B	1	Start
C	3	A
D	2	A
E	3	B
F	4	C, E, G
G	1	D
H	2	D
I	3	C, E, G
J	2	F
K	1	F, J
L	3	G, H
M	1	K, L, N
Project Completion		J, M

11. You are planning an operation that will require heavy use of EMCON (emission control). To avoid precise location of an aircraft carrier by the enemy, aircraft approaches to the carrier will be made without use of radar, navaids or voice communications. Night approaches will commence EMCON with the aircraft 4 N.mi. astern of the carrier and closing at a relative speed of 120 knots. At the end of the approach, if the fantail lights are not in sight, the pilot must immediately execute missed approach procedures (climbout, etc.) to avoid possible collision with the carrier's island. Since descent is required during the approach, the pilot's only real chance to look for the lights is at the end of the approach.

It has been suggested that the brightness of the fantail lights also threatens precise carrier localization by the enemy and recommended that their intensity be reduced. Data collected on such "blind approaches" show that the cumulated course and airspeed adjustments applied by the pilots have independent normal distributions with standard deviations, $\sigma_\theta = 1°$ (.0175 radian) and $\sigma_s = 2$ knots.

What would be the minimum lights visibility symmetric ahead and behind and the minimum lights visibility symmetric to either side, just to ensure a 0.47 probability of the pilot's seeing the light at the end of an approach? (Consider any miss to be equally likely from either axis.)

Appendix I
PROBABILITY—
THE MATHEMATICS
OF UNCERTAINTY

The key phrase appearing in many definitions of Operations Analysis is *quantitative basis for decision-making*. It is therefore not surprising to find that solving a problem by the OA method usually involves the judicious application of some aspect of mathematics. This is true of both theoretical and empirical models for problem solving, and one finds both classical and modern mathematics being applied extensively in the discipline.

The single most useful field of mathematics in the analysis of naval operational problems is mathematical *probability theory*. In fact, the concepts of probability are indispensable to objective, analytical treatment of those problems. For diverse as is the field of naval operations, there is one factor common throughout. That one factor is *uncertainty*. Not every missile leaves the launcher when the firing key is pressed. Not every attack pilot is able to find the target and deliver his load of bombs. Not every enemy aircraft within theoretical range of the air search radar produces a blip on the scope on each sweep of the radar antenna. The list of cases is practically boundless. Whatever the area of naval operations, *uncertainty* is the one quality invariably present. One may deal analytically with these essentially random events thanks to that way of thinking called probability theory.

Accordingly, this appendix is devoted to a coverage of the fundamental concepts of probability theory with particular emphasis given to those aspects which will prove most useful to the study of the methods of Naval Operations Analysis.

I-1 CALCULATION OF SIMPLE PROBABILITIES

It is possible to approximate the probability of a simple event, say the probability of a coin turning up *heads*, by counting the number of *heads* which occur in n tosses and dividing by the total number of tosses. As the number of tosses becomes larger and larger, this ratio approaches closer and closer to the precise value of the desired probability. In a similar manner, it would be possible to calculate the probabilities associated with the faces of a die, the probability of a newborn baby being a boy, and so on. Symbolically, the true probability of a simple event is defined as follows:

Equation I-1

$$P(\text{event}) = \lim_{n \to \infty} \left(\frac{\text{number of occurrences of the event in } n \text{ trials}}{\text{total number of trials, } n} \right).$$

In the special case where all the *possible outcomes* of a trial are equally likely, the probability of a simple event may be expressed as

Equation I-2

$$P(\text{event}) = \frac{\text{number of possible outcomes which constitute the event}}{\text{total number of possible outcomes}}.$$

The simplification represented by Equation I-2 applies to all simple chance devices such as fair coins, fair dice, and so forth, and to many of the more common probabilistic situations. For example, consider the probability of a three turning up when a die is tossed:

$$P(3) = \frac{\text{number of possible outcomes which constitute a three (one)}}{\text{total number of possible outcomes (six in this instance)}}$$
$$= 1/6.$$

This expression, Equation I-2, is particularly useful in developing the so-called *laws of probability* which are simply rules for calculating the probabilities of *compound events* in terms of known probabilities of the *simple events* involved. In terms of the die example, we might refer to the rolling of a three as a simple event, say event A. Similarly, we might refer to the rolling of a four as a simple event, say event B. However, dealing with two dice we would generally refer to the rolling of a seven as a compound event, C, involving two simple events, A and B. It is possible to derive the probabilistic expression for this particular compound event, as well as for other types of compound events, in terms of the simple probabilities, $P(A)$ and $P(B)$.

The statements made concerning probability have been to a large extent intuitive. It is possible, however, to develop the theory in a completely abstract manner by invoking the mathematics of *set theory*. The set theoretic development, first formulated by the Russian probabilist Kolmogorov in 1933, has the advantage of being mathematically streamlined and rigorous, but it has the disadvantage of being somewhat devoid of intuitive appeal. The set theorist first presents probability as an example of a particular type of set function and then relates this set function to the intuitive notion of probability. The intuitive approach to probability will be used here, invoking the language and trappings of set theory only when such a procedure appears to offer a convenient framework for visualizing probabilistic notions.

I-2 SETS AND SUBSETS

In order to discuss set theoretical concepts, the following basic definitions are necessary:

a. Set—A set is a well defined collection of entities or *elements*.
b. Subset—A subset is a set containing *some* of the elements of another set.

c. Venn diagram—A Venn diagram is a convenient graphical method for representing various sets and subsets. As an example of its use, consider the following simple Venn diagram which represents a set of nine elements, and two overlapping subsets, A and B, each containing two of these elements.

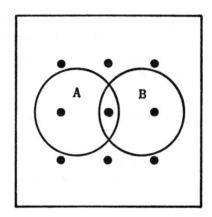

This diagram is also useful for illustrating some of the basic types of sets and subsets:

a. Universal set—The universal set is the set containing *all* of the elements and is represented symbolically by the letter S.

b. Null set—The null set is the set containing *no* elements at all and is usually represented by the symbol ϕ.

c. Intersection—The intersection of two subsets, A and B, is defined as the set of those elements which are common to *both A and B*. The symbol used to represent the intersection of two subsets is $\cap$; i.e., $A \cap B$ represents the intersection of A and B, the set of those elements in both A and B. In the example, there is one element in the intersection of A and B. Note that $A \cap \phi = \phi$ and $A \cap S = A$.

d. Union—The union of two subsets, A and B, is defined as the set of those elements which are in *either A or B*. The symbol used to represent the union of two subsets is $\cup$; i.e., $A \cup B$ represents the union of A and B, the set of those elements in either A or B. In the example, there are three elements in the union of A and B. Note that $A \cup S = S$ and $A \cup \phi = A$.

e. Complement—The complement of a subset A is defined as the set of all elements *not* in the subset A. The symbol for the complement is $^{-}$; i.e., $\overline{A}$ represents the set of elements *not* in the subset A. In the example there are seven elements in the complement of A. The complement of S is ϕ.

f. Disjoint sets—Two subsets, A and B, are said to be disjoint if they have no elements in common, i.e., if $A \cap B = \phi$.

I-3 PROBABILITY SAMPLE SPACE

A sample space is the collection of all possible outcomes of an experiment. Thus the sample space is a universal set S and each subset of S is an event. The term *sample points* is used to represent the individual outcomes in the sample space. When an event is thought of as a set of possible outcomes in this manner, it then becomes quite easy to express its probability. For example, consider again the probability of a three turning up when a die is tossed. The sample space contains six outcomes, each assumed equally likely, i.e., $S = \{1,2,3,4,5,6\}$. Let A be the event that a three is tossed, i.e., $A = \{3\}$, a subset of S. Let $P(A)$ represent the probability that the event A occurs and $n(A)$ represent the number of outcomes in the event A. The possible outcomes can be represented by the Venn diagram:

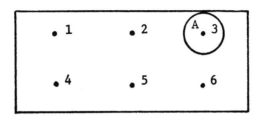

The probability of a three is then:

$$P(3) = P(A)$$

$$= \frac{\text{number of outcomes in } A}{\text{total number of outcomes}}$$

$$= \frac{n(A)}{n(S)}$$

$$= \frac{1}{6}.$$

Using the concepts and definitions discussed thus far, the following basic relationships can be derived for any two events A and B:

$$0 \leq P(A) \leq 1$$
$$P(\overline{A}) = 1 - P(A)$$
$$P(A \cap \overline{A}) = P(\phi) = 0$$
$$P(A \cup \overline{A}) = P(S) = 1$$
$$P(A \cup B) = P(A) + P(B) - P(A \cap B)$$
$$P(A \cup B) = 1 - P(\overline{A} \cap \overline{B})$$
$$P(\overline{A \cup B}) = P(\overline{A} \cap \overline{B})$$
$$P(\overline{A} \cup \overline{B}) = P(\overline{A \cap B})$$
$$P(A) = P(A \cap B) + P(A \cap \overline{B})$$

If $A \subset B$, then $P(A \cap B) = P(A)$, and $P(A \cup B) = P(B)$.

(The symbol $\subset$ is read: is a subset of.)

In addition to the relationship previously listed, there are three theorems concerning set operations which will be stated here without proof.

a. Commutative law

$$P(A \cap B) = P(B \cap A)$$
$$P(A \cup B) = P(B \cup A)$$

b. Distributive law

$$P[A \cap (B \cup C)] = P[(A \cap B) \cup (A \cap C)]$$
$$P[A \cup (B \cap C)] = P[(A \cup B) \cap (A \cup C)]$$

c. Associative law

$$P[A \cup (B \cup C)] = P[(A \cup B) \cup C]$$
$$P[A \cap (B \cap C)] = P[(A \cap B) \cap C]$$

I-4   ADDITION LAW

One relationship is commonly referred to as the *addition law* of probability. It provides a rule for calculating the probability of the union of two events, A and B, in terms of the individual probabilities, $P(A)$ and $P(B)$. The result is significant enough to warrant repeating.

Equation I-3 $P(A \cup B) = P(A) + P(B) - P(A \cap B)$

Suppose for example that two aircraft are searching for a target. If A is the event that the first aircraft detects the target and B is the event that the second aircraft detects the target, then the event that the target is detected, i.e., by at least one of the aircraft, is represented by $A \cup B$. The addition law provides a method of computing this probability in terms of the simple event probabilities.

In the case where the events A and B cannot occur simultaneously, then $A \cap B = \phi$ and $P(A \cap B) = 0$. We say in this case that A and B are *mutually exclusive* events (or that A and B are *disjoint* sets). The addition law then becomes simply

$$P(A \cup B) = P(A) + P(B).$$

For example let A be the event that an even number is rolled on a die, and B the event that an odd number less than four is rolled. Then

$$P(A) = P\{2,4,6\} = 3/6,$$
$$P(B) = P\{1,3\} = 2/6,$$
$$P(A \cap B) = P(\phi) = 0, \text{ and}$$
$$P(A \cup B) = P(A) + P(B) = 5/6$$

I-5   CONDITIONAL PROBABILITY AND MULTIPLICATION LAW

An expression was developed in Section I-4 for the probability of the *union* of two events. In this section an expression will be developed for the probability of the *intersection* of two events (the probability that *both A and B* occur). First, however, the notion of conditional probability will be discussed.

The conditional probability of one event, B, occurring given that another event, A, has occurred is denoted by $P(B|A)$. As an aid in visualizing this conditional event consider again the Venn diagram:

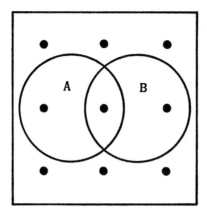

In any experiment, only one of the possible outcomes may result. In this diagram depicting nine possible outcomes, it can be seen that if the event A has occurred, the outcome must be one of the two outcomes included in A. Now what is the probability that B occurs? If each outcome is equally likely, this probability would be one-half, computed from $n(A \cap B)/n(A)$, so that

Equation I-4 $P(B|A) = \dfrac{n(A \cap B)}{n(A)}$ where $n(A) > 0$.

By dividing the numerator and the denominator of the right-hand side of Equation I-4 by the total number of outcomes in the entire sample space (nine in the example) the conditional probability of B given A becomes

Equation I-5 $P(B|A) = \dfrac{\dfrac{n(A \cap B)}{n(S)}}{\dfrac{n(A)}{n(S)}} = \dfrac{P(A \cap B)}{P(A)}$.

Equation I-5 expresses mathematically the conditional probability of B given A, whether or not the outcomes are equally likely. An expression can then be found for the probability of the intersection of two events, A and B, by rearranging Equation I-5 as follows:

Equation I-6 $P(A \cap B) = P(A)P(B|A)$.

This expression is known as the *multiplication law* of probability.

I-6 STATISTICAL INDEPENDENCE

Consider two events having non-zero probabilities, $P(A)$ and $P(B)$. If it so happens that the *conditional* probability of event B given event A equals the *unconditional* probability of event B, i.e., if $P(B|A) = P(B)$, then the multiplication law simplifies to

$$P(A \cap B) = P(A)P(B).$$

(The student should verify this.) When this mathematical relationship holds, the events A and B are said to be *statistically independent* of one another. Students frequently find that this mathematical definition of independence is difficult to reconcile with their own intuitive notion of independence. In determining whether two events are independent then, it is wise to make the mathematical test where possible, and rule out the use of intuition.

Consider a simple experiment in which the probability sample space can be represented by the following Venn diagram depicting three equally likely outcomes:

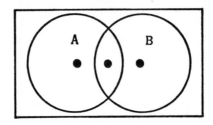

$$P(A|B) = \frac{n(A \cap B)}{n(B)} = \frac{1}{2},$$

$$P(A) = \frac{n(A)}{n(S)} = \frac{2}{3},$$

$$P(A|B) \neq P(A).$$

Therefore, A and B are not statistically independent. Consider however, the following slight modification to this probability sample space:

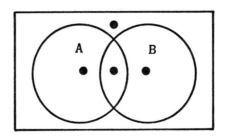

$$P(A|B) = \frac{n(A \cap B)}{n(B)} = \frac{1}{2},$$

$$P(A) = \frac{n(A)}{n(S)} = \frac{2}{4} = \frac{1}{2}$$

$$P(A|B) = P(A).$$

Therefore, A and B are statistically independent in this case.

The purpose of these examples is to emphasize the mathematical requirements that must be met before any statements can be made regarding the statistical independence of events. In some practical situations, however, the only information known about the events A and B is their probabilities of occurrence, $P(A)$ and $P(B)$. With this information only, it is impossible to find $P(A \cap B)$ or $P(A \cup B)$ unless some assumptions are made. If, for example, it can be reasoned that knowledge of the occurrence of the event A on a particular trial would be of no value in determining whether B did or will occur, then this is equivalent to reasoning that $P(B\,|\,A)$ is the same as $P(B)$, and hence, that A and B are *causally* independent.

In practical problems when additional information is lacking, statistical independence is frequently assumed on the basis of this intuitive (causal) justification, in order to make further computations possible.

I-7 COMPOUND PROBABILITIES INVOLVING THREE OR MORE EVENTS

Using the simple method of counting sample points in conjunction with a Venn diagram, it is fairly easy to generalize the *addition law* so as to include three events

$$P(A \cup B \cup C) = P(A) + P(B) + P(C) - P(A \cap B) - P(A \cap C)$$
$$-P(B \cap C) + P(A \cap B \cap C).$$

The expression for the probability of the union of more than three events becomes quite cumbersome in the general case. It becomes useful therefore to consider another approach. The probability of the union of several events $E_1, E_2, \cdots, E_n$, represents the probability that *at least one* of these events occurs. The only other possible outcome is for *none* of the events to occur, i.e., each of the events fail to occur. DeMorgan's law states this fact as

$$\overline{E_1 \cup E_2 \cup \cdots \cup E_n} = \overline{E}_1 \cap \overline{E}_2 \cap \cdots \cap \overline{E}_n.$$

From this, the probability of the union of several events can be written as

Equation I-7 $P(E_1 \cup E_2 \cup \cdots \cup E_n) = 1 - P(\overline{E}_1 \cap \overline{E}_2 \cap \cdots \cap \overline{E}_n).$

In the special case of *mutually exclusive* events, the probability of this union can be generalized to include an arbitrarily large number of events

$$P(E_1 \cup E_2 \cup \cdots \cup E_n) = P(E_1) + P(E_2) + \cdots + P(E_n).$$

It is often necessary, as in Equation I-7, to find the probability of the *intersection* of several events. To do this, Equation I-6 can be extended by induction to

Equation I-8
$$P(E_1 \cap E_2 \cap \cdots \cap E_n)$$
$$= P(E_1)P(E_2\,|\,E_1)P(E_3\,|\,E_1 \cap E_2) \cdots P(E_n\,|\,E_1 \cap E_2 \cap \cdots \cap E_{n-1}).$$

If these events are *independent*, then the multiplication law simplifies to

$$P(E_1 \cap E_2 \cap \cdots \cap E_n) = P(E_1)P(E_2) \cdots P(E_n).$$

I-8 BAYES THEOREM

Suppose in some experiment the event B can occur only in conjunction with *one* of several mutually exclusive events $A_1, A_2, \cdots, A_n$. Then,

$$B \subset (A_1 \cup A_2 \cup \cdots \cup A_n),$$

and

$$B = B \cap (A_1 \cup A_2 \cup \cdots \cup A_n)$$
$$= (B \cap A_1) \cup (B \cap A_2) \cup \cdots \cup (B \cap A_n),$$

so that

$$P(B) = P(B \cap A_1) + P(B \cap A_2) + \cdots + P(B \cap A_n),$$

since these events are mutually exclusive.

If an experiment is conducted and B is noted to occur, what is the probability that the simultaneous event which occurred was A_i? That is, what is $P(A_i|B)$? From the definition of conditional probability,

$$P(A_i|B) = \frac{P(B \cap A_i)}{P(B)}$$

$$= \frac{P(B \cap A_i)}{P(B \cap A_1) + P(B \cap A_2) + \cdots + P(B \cap A_n)},$$

and finally

$$P(A_i|B) = \frac{P(B|A_i)P(A_i)}{P(B|A_1)P(A_1) + P(B|A_2)P(A_2) + \cdots + P(B|A_n)P(A_n)}.$$

This result is referred to as *Bayes theorem.*

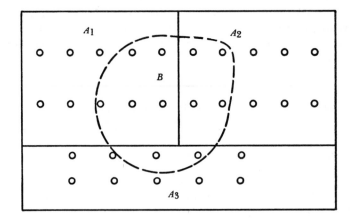

As an example of its applicability, consider three identical boxes each containing 10 parts. There are five, six and eight good parts in boxes one, two and three, respectively. The remaining parts are defective. First, a box is chosen at random and then a part is drawn from it. If the part drawn is defective, what is the probability that the first box was chosen?

To solve, let A_1 denote the event the first box was chosen, A_2 the event the second box was chosen, A_3 the event the third box was chosen, and B the event that a defective part was drawn. Then the desired probability is

$$P(A_1|B) = \frac{P(B|A_1)P(A_1)}{P(B|A_1)P(A_1) + P(B|A_2)P(A_2) + P(B|A_3)P(A_3)}$$

$$= \frac{(5/10)(1/3)}{(5/10)(1/3) + (4/10)(1/3) + (2/10)(1/3)}$$

$$= 5/11.$$

I-9 COMBINATORIAL FORMULAS—STREAMLINED METHODS OF COUNTING

In the simple case where all possible outcomes of an experiment are equally likely, the probability of an event, A, was given by the following expression:

$$P(A) = \frac{\text{number of outcomes corresponding to event } A}{\text{total number of possible outcomes}}.$$

This expression is sometimes referred to as the *classical* definition of probability because it was the original definition adopted in the seventeenth century by the mathematicians investigating simple games of chance. In probabilistic situations such as simple games of chance, it is easy to visualize and to list all of the possible outcomes of an experiment as well as those outcomes corresponding to a particular event of interest. For example, it is easy to list the six possible outcomes resulting when a single die is tossed. It is not particularly difficult to list the 36 possible outcomes resulting when two dice are tossed. But it becomes a considerable chore to list the 216 possible outcomes resulting when three dice are tossed, and it becomes a time-consuming task to list the 1,296 possible outcomes resulting when four dice are tossed. Fortunately, in calculating probabilities it is not necessary to list all of the outcomes but simply to be able to *count* all of the outcomes. As will be seen in the next two sections, formulas can be developed without too much difficulty which provide a streamlined method for counting outcomes without having to visualize each individual outcome. These formulas are referred to as *combinatorial* formulas, and they are all based upon one simple, fundamental principle: *if A can be accomplished in n separate and distinct ways and B can be accomplished in m separate and distinct ways, then A and B together can be accomplished in m × n ways.*

I-10 PERMUTATIONS

The first formula to be considered is one for counting the number of *k object arrangements* which can be made from *n* distinct objects. As an aid in visualizing the development of this formula, consider the simple problem of determining the number of two-letter arrangements which can be made from the letters *a, b, c*. A convenient method of visualizing the situation is to consider filling two squares with letters drawn from the set *a, b, c* by placing the first one drawn in the left square and the second one drawn in the right square.

$$\square \qquad \square$$

There are three letters to choose from in filling the first square, i.e., there are three ways of filling the first square. With the first square filled, there are now only two letters left to fill the second square. Therefore, in accordance with the fundamental combinatorial principle, there are a total of 3 × 2, or six distinct ways of filling the two squares. In other words, there are six possible two-letter arrangements which can be made up from the letters *a, b, c*. Specifically, these arrangements are: *ab, ba, ac, ca, bc,* and *cb*. The number of arrangements, or *permutations,* is often represented by the symbol $_nP_k$ ($_3P_2$ in the case of the example). In general, when forming *k* object arrangements from *n* objects, there are *n* ways of choosing the first object, $(n-1)$ ways of choosing the second object, etc., until finally there are $(n-k+1)$ ways of choosing the kth object. Therefore, there are $(n)(n-1)(n-2)\cdots(n-k+1)$ ways of forming *k* object arrangements. Symbolically,

$$_nP_k = (n)(n-1)(n-2)\cdots(n-k+1).$$

Using the factorial notation where $n! = (n)(n-1)(n-2) \cdots (1)$, this expression can be written in a more compact manner as

Equation I-9
$$_nP_k = \frac{(n!)}{(n-k)!},$$

where it is necessary to define $0!$ to be equal to *one*.

Consider, however, the calculation of the number of four-letter arrangements possible from the set a, a, b, b. It is intuitively clear that there would be a smaller number of distinct arrangements possible from a set of this kind, where some of the elements are identical. By an extension of the reasoning that led to Equation I-9, it is fairly easy to develop a formula for determining this number of n object arrangements possible from n objects, when some of the objects are alike. Without going through the explicit development of the formula, suffice it to say that if there are r *distinct types* of objects contained in the set of n, the total number of n object arrangements is given by

Equation I-10
$$_nP_{nr} = \frac{n!}{(n_1!)(n_2!)(n_3!) \cdots (n_r!)}$$

where n_i is the number of identical objects in each of the r types.

In the example, the number of four-letter arrangements possible from the a, a, b, b is

$$\frac{4!}{2! \, 2!} = \frac{24}{4} = 6.$$

This six possible arrangements are:

$$a, a, b, b \qquad a, b, a, b \qquad a, b, b, a$$
$$b, b, a, a \qquad b, a, b, a \qquad b, a, a, b$$

I-11 COMBINATIONS

A similar but distinct problem is that of determining the number of k *object groupings* possible from n objects *in which no two groups contain exactly the same objects*. Such groupings are generally referred to as k *object combinations*. The symbol $_nC_k$ is often used to represent the formation of these combinations, but the more commonly used symbol is $\binom{n}{k}$. The difference between combinations and permutations is that in combinations the order in which the objects are arranged in a particular grouping has no significance. For example, consider the a, b, c example. In forming the two-letter *permutations*, ab and ba are considered as two distinct arrangements and would be counted as such. However, since ab and ba contain exactly the same letters with only the order changed, they would not be counted as two distinct groupings when forming the two-letter *combinations*. This point is important enough to be re-emphasized. In permutations *order counts*. In combinations *order does not count*. On the other hand, ab and ac would be counted as two distinct groupings since they contain different letters. It is fairly obvious from this that the number of k object combinations possible from n objects will always be smaller than the number of k object permutations for $k > 1$.

To derive an expression for the number of combinations, $\binom{n}{k}$, of n objects taken k at a time, consider again the formation of all possible two-letter permutations from the letters a, b, c. A method, not previously considered, for determining the total number of these permutations (six) would be to form all possible two-letter combinations and then permute each of these combinations, i.e.,

$$a \; b \cdots \begin{cases} a & b \\ b & a \end{cases}$$

$$a \; c \cdots \begin{cases} a & c \\ c & a \end{cases}$$

$$b \; c \cdots \begin{cases} b & c \\ c & b \end{cases}$$

As can be seen, there are three ways of forming the two-letter combinations and two ways of permuting (arranging) each combination. There are, therefore, a total of six ways of forming the two-letter permutations by means of this two-step process. In general, there are $\binom{n}{k}$ ways of forming the k object combinations from n objects, and there are $_kP_k = k!$ ways of permuting each of these combinations. There are, therefore, $\binom{n}{k} \times k!$ ways of forming the k object permutations from n objects. Combining this with Equation I-9 gives

$$_nP_k = \frac{n!}{(n-k)!} = \binom{n}{k} \cdot k!,$$

from which follows

Equation I-11
$$\binom{n}{k} = \frac{n!}{k!(n-k)!},$$

which is the desired formula for determining the k object combinations possible from n objects.

As it turns out, the formula for combinations is used much more frequently in probability calculations than is the permutation formula. An example of the use of combinations in calculating probabilities is:

A bridge hand consisting of 13 cards is chosen from an ordinary deck. What is the probability that such a hand will contain exactly five hearts?

Since a bridge hand is not affected by the order in which the various cards are obtained, the total number of possible bridge hands is equal to the number of 13 object combinations possible from 52 objects, which is simply $\binom{52}{13}$. This is the total number of sample points in the sample space. The number of hands containing exactly five hearts is equal to the number of ways of choosing five hearts from the 13 hearts in the deck or $\binom{13}{5}$, multiplied by the number of ways of choosing eight non-hearts from 39 non-hearts, or $\binom{39}{8}$. Hence, the desired probability is given by

$$P(\text{five hearts}) = \frac{\binom{13}{5}\binom{39}{8}}{\binom{52}{13}} = \frac{(13!)(39!)(13!)(39!)}{(5!)(8!)(8!)(31!)(52!)}.$$

Thus far, only those probabilistic situations having a finite number of possible outcomes have been considered. The next logical step is to consider those situations having an infinite number of outcomes. As an example of such a situation, consider the spinning of a simple pointer. There are an *infinite* number of points between zero and 360 degrees at which the pointer might stop. This continuum of possible outcomes is referred to as a *continuous probability sample space* as opposed to the *discrete probability sample space* associated with a finite or countably infinite number of outcomes.

I-12   RANDOM VARIABLE

A definition fundamental to all that follows is that of a *random variable*. A random variable is a transformation which associates with each point or collection of points in the sample space some real number. The precise verbal description of the random variable to be used in a particular probabilistic situation will usually be apparent from the nature of the situation itself. For example, in the case of two dice being tossed simultaneously, the outcomes could be represented very conveniently by a random variable such as

Let $X =$ the *sum* of the spots on the dice.

In terms of this random variable, the outcomes would be represented as follows:

Specific outcomes	*Value of the random variable, X*
(1,1)	2
(1,2), (2,1)	3
$\vdots$	$\vdots$
(1,6), (2,5), (3,4), (4,3), (5,2), (6,1)	7
$\vdots$	$\vdots$
(5,6), (6,5)	11
(6,6)	12

To say that $X = 3$ then, is to say that one of the two outcomes has occurred which results in a sum of three.

It should be noted that there are other ways of defining the random variable X in this experiment. Instead of the *sum* of the spots, it might be of interest to define X as the *difference* between the spots on the two dice, the *greater of the two numbers* of spots showing, or the *number of ones* showing. In each case, the random variable specifies a *number* to be associated with each possible outcome of the experiment. A random variable is said to be discrete if it can take on only a finite or countably infinite number of values. Otherwise it is said to be continuous and usually takes on as values all the real numbers in some continuous interval.

I-13   DISCRETE PROBABILITY FUNCTIONS

When discussing probabilities in terms of random variables, it is convenient to employ the use of certain probability functions. In the discrete case the *probability function*, denoted $p(x)$, is of particular interest. For any real number x, this probability function yields the probability that on a particular outcome of the experiment the value of the random variable is x. Symbolically, this is

Equation I-12 $$p(x) = P(X = x).$$

In the previous example where X represents the sum of spots on a throw of two dice, each of the 36 possible outcomes is equally likely. Then

$$p(3) = P(X = 3)$$
$$= \frac{2 \text{ outcomes for which } X = 3}{36 \text{ possible outcomes}}$$
$$= \frac{1}{18}.$$

The other function of interest for a discrete random variable is the *cumulative distribution function,* denoted by $F(x)$. For any real number x, this function gives the probability that on a particular outcome of the experiment the value of the random variable is *less than or equal* to x. Symbolically, this is

Equation I-13 $F(x) = P(X \le x)$.

In terms of the dice example:

$$F(3) = P(X \le 3)$$
$$= P(\text{sum of spots is less than or equal to 3})$$
$$= P[X = 2] + P[X = 3]$$
$$= p(2) + p(3)$$
$$= 1/36 + 2/36$$
$$= 3/36.$$

It should be noted that for the sake of completeness, these two functions, $p(x)$ and $F(x)$, are defined when x is any real number. The reader should verify that in the dice example, the real numbers, x, in the following table are the correct values of $p(x)$ and $F(x)$.

x	$p(x)$	$F(x)$
-3	0	0
0	0	0
2.69	0	1/36
π	0	3/36
11	2/36	35/36
13.2	0	1

For example, $F(\pi)$, from its definition, represents the probability that the sum of the spots is a number less than or equal to 3.1416. This event occurs if and only if the sum is a two or a three, hence

$$F(\pi) = P(X \le \pi) = p(2) + p(3) = 3/36.$$

In general, if the possible values for the random variable X are denoted by $x_1, x_2, \cdots, x_n$, then

Equation I-14 $F(x) = P[X \le x] = \sum_{\text{all } x_i \le x} p(x_i)$

and also

$$\sum_{\text{all } x_i} p(x_i) = 1.$$

As another example of a discrete random variable, consider an experiment in which two coins are tossed. The sample space, S, contains the four outcomes *HH, HT,*

TH, TT (each equally likely). Let the random variable *X* denote the number of heads appearing. Then *X* can take on the values *zero, one* and *two*. The probability function $p(x)$ could be graphed as follows:

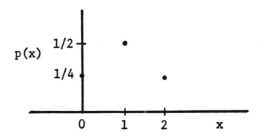

or written analytically as

$$p(x) = \begin{cases} 1/4, & \text{if } x = 0 \\ 1/2, & \text{if } x = 1 \\ 1/4, & \text{if } x = 2 \\ 0, & \text{if } x \text{ is any other real number.} \end{cases}$$

Likewise the cumulative distribution function would have as a graph:

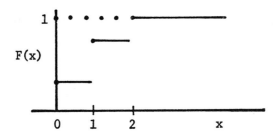

The mathematical notation which expresses this situation is

$$F(x) = \begin{cases} 0, & x < 0 \\ 1/4, & 0 \le x < 1 \\ 3/4, & 1 \le x < 2 \\ 1, & x \ge 2 \end{cases}$$

I-14   CONTINUOUS PROBABILITY FUNCTIONS

Thus far the random variable has only been considered to have a finite or countably infinite number of values. A logical extension of this concept is to let the random variable take on *all* values $(-\infty \text{ to } \infty)$. The probability associated with a continuous random variable is characterized by a function $f(x)$ called a density function. The area under this function represents probability and hence has a total area of 1. The area $f(x)\Delta x$ can be defined as a *probability element* which gives the approximate probability that the value of the random variable *X* will occur in that interval Δx. If Δx is considered to be bounded by $x - (\Delta x)/2$ and $x + (\Delta x)/2$, and $f(x)$ describes the average height of the curve between these two points, then the probability element is

$$f(x)\Delta x \cong P\left(x - \frac{\Delta x}{2} \le X \le x + \frac{\Delta x}{2}\right).$$

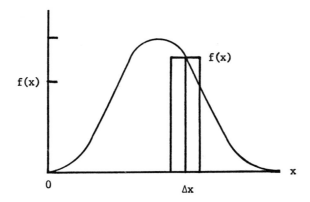

By letting Δx become small and imposing the notion that integration is just the limiting form of summation of a large number of small probability elements, the probability that the value of a random variable will fall in an interval (x_1, x_2) is just

Equation I-15 $$P(x_1 \leq X \leq x_2) = \int_{x_1}^{x_2} f(x)\, dx.$$

Graphically this is represented as:

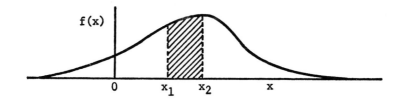

The probability density function is further defined by

$$f(x) \geq 0, \quad \text{for all } x,$$

and since

$$P(-\infty \leq X \leq \infty) = 1,$$

it follows that

$$\int_{-\infty}^{\infty} f(x)\, dx = 1,$$

i.e., the total area under the curve must be equal to one.

The *cumulative distribution function*, $F(x)$, is defined for a continuous random variable exactly as it was for the discrete case,

$$F(x) = P(X \leq x).$$

This is equivalent to writing

$$F(x) = P(-\infty \leq X \leq x),$$

which can be evaluated using the definition of the *probability density function* by

Equation I-16
$$F(x) = \int_{-\infty}^{x} f(x)\,dx. *$$

This is the area to the left of x under the curve defined by the probability density function.

From these definitions, it follows that $F(\infty) = 1$, $F(-\infty) = 0$ and that

$$P[x_1 \leq X \leq x_2] = \int_{x_1}^{x_2} f(x)\,dx$$

$$= \int_{-\infty}^{x_2} f(x)\,dx - \int_{-\infty}^{x_1} f(x)\,dx$$

$$= F(x_2) - F(x_1)$$

Using the Leibnitz theorem for differentiation of an integral, the probability density function can also be defined as

$$f(x) = \frac{dF(x)}{dx}.$$

As an example of a continuous random variable consider observing the ship traffic down a channel 1,000 yards wide from a position on one side of the channel. The random variable of interest is the distance (in yards) from the observer to a ship as it passes his position. The probability density function for such a situation would perhaps be something like that shown in this graph.

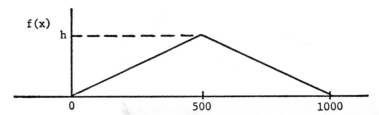

The height h must be chosen so that the area under the curve is one. In this case, it would require that h be .002.

The probability that a particular ship passes in the middle 500 yards of the channel would then be

$$P(250 \leq X \leq 750) = \int_{250}^{750} f(x)\,dx.$$

The *probability density function*, $f(x)$, can be expressed analytically as follows:

$$f(x) = \begin{cases} \dfrac{.002}{500}\,x \quad, & \text{for } x \text{ between 0 and 500} \\[2ex] .004 - \dfrac{.002}{500}\,x, & \text{for } x \text{ between 500 and 1,000} \\[2ex] 0 \quad, & \text{for all other } x. \end{cases}$$

*Rather than introduce additional notation at this time, it should be noted that the x in $f(x)$ and dx is a *dummy variable* and not a specific value of the random variable X. The x of the upper limit is, however, the *value* of interest for the random variable X.

Since $f(x)$ cannot be expressed as a single equation, each portion of $f(x)$ must be integrated separately:

$$P(250 \leq x \leq 750) = \int_{250}^{750} f(x)\, dx$$

$$= \int_{250}^{500} \frac{.002}{500} x\, dx + \int_{500}^{750} \left(.004 - \frac{.002}{500} x\right) dx$$

$$= \frac{.002x^2}{1000} \Big|_{250}^{500} + \left(.004x - \frac{.002x^2}{1000}\right) \Big|_{500}^{750}$$

$$= .75$$

Note that this probability could be determined fairly easily using graphical techniques from the above graph of $f(x)$.

The general term *probability distribution* is used to denote the particular probability functions applicable to a given random variable. In the discrete case, the probability distribution may be specified by stating either the probability function or the cumulative distribution function. The discrete probability distributions encountered most frequently in this text are the *binomial distribution,* the *Poisson distribution* and the *geometric distribution,* each of which is discussed separately in this appendix.

A continuous probability distribution may be specified by identifying either its probability density function or its cumulative distribution function. The most common of these continuous probability distributions are the *uniform, normal* and *exponential.* These are also discussed in this appendix.

Before introducing specific probability distributions, two quantities will be presented which are most important in summarizing the characteristics of all probability distributions. These quantities are the mean or *expected value* and the *variance* of a random variable.

I-15 EXPECTED VALUE

As the name implies, the *mean value* or *expected value* of a random variable is a measure of *central tendency* of the probability distribution. It is somewhat analogous to the center of gravity used in physics. The symbols commonly used to represent this expected value of a random variable X are $E(X)$ and μ. In the discrete case, the mean is calculated by taking the weighted average of all the possible values of the random variable, i.e., by multiplying each value by its respective probability of occurrence and then summing all of the resulting products. Symbolically,

Equation I-17 $$E(X) = \mu = \sum_{\text{all } x_i} x_i p(x_i).$$

As an example of the mean value of a discrete probability distribution, consider the probability sample space associated with the rolling of a single die. Let the random variable X be the number of spots showing on the die. What is the mean or expected value of X?

$$E(X) = \sum_{\text{all } x_i} x_i p(x_i)$$

$$= (1)\tfrac{1}{6} + (2)\tfrac{1}{6} + (3)\tfrac{1}{6} + (4)\tfrac{1}{6} + (5)\tfrac{1}{6} + (6)\tfrac{1}{6}$$

$$= 3.50.$$

Note that in this example, where all values of the discrete random variable are equally likely, the calculation of the mean simply consists of taking the arithmetic mean of all the values of the random variable. Note also that the mean is not necessarily one of the possible values of the random variable.

Let the random variable X be the sum of spots showing when two dice are rolled. Then the calculation of the mean value of X is done in a similar manner, although in this case the values of the random variable are not equally likely. The results are

$$E(X) = \sum_{\text{all } x_i} x_i p(x_i)$$

$$= (1)(0) + (2)\frac{1}{36} + (3)\frac{2}{36} + (4)\frac{3}{36} + \cdots + (11)\frac{2}{36} + (12)\frac{1}{36}$$

$$= \frac{252}{36} = 7.$$

The extension of the concept of mean value to the continuous case follows directly in a manner completely analogous to the discrete case. The mean is calculated by taking the limit of the weighted sum of all possible values of the random variable, i.e., by multiplying each value by its associated probability element and then taking the limit of the sum of the resulting products. In this case $f(x)\,\Delta x$ is the approximate probability that the random variable lies between x and $x + \Delta x$, hence

$$E(X) = \mu = \lim_{\Delta x \to 0} \sum_{\text{all } x_i} x_i[f(x_i)\Delta x],$$

or

Equation I-18
$$E(X) = \mu = \int_{-\infty}^{\infty} xf(x)\,dx.$$

As an example of the expected value of a continuous probability distribution, consider the probability distribution represented by the following function:

$$f(x) = \frac{1}{18}x^2, \qquad -3 \le x \le 3$$

$$= 0 \quad , \qquad \text{elsewhere.}$$

$$E(X) = \int_{-\infty}^{+\infty} xf(x)\,dx$$

$$= \int_{-\infty}^{-3} 0 \times dx + \int_{-3}^{+3} x\left(\frac{x^2}{18}\right) dx + \int_{+3}^{+\infty} 0 \times dx = \frac{x^4}{4(18)}\Bigg]_{-3}^{3} = 0.$$

The mean of this probability distribution occurring at zero is not surprising when one plots the graph of its probability density function.

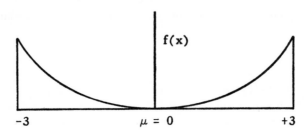

It is possible in a similar manner to compute the expected (or average) value of *any* function of a random variable X, denoted $g(X)$. For a continuous random variable

Equation I-19
$$E[g(X)] = \int_{-\infty}^{\infty} g(x) \cdot f(x)\, dx,$$

and for a discrete random variable

Equation I-20
$$E[g(X)] = \sum_{\text{all } x_i} g(x_i) p(x_i).$$

In computing the expected value of some functions, use can be made of the property that the expected value of a constant is a constant. For example, if $g(X)$ equals $aX + b$, where a and b are constants, then when X is continuous:

$$E(aX + b) = \int_{-\infty}^{\infty} (ax + b) f(x)\, dx$$

$$= a \int_{-\infty}^{\infty} x f(x)\, dx + b \int_{-\infty}^{\infty} f(x)\, dx$$

$$= a[E(X)] + b$$

since $\int_{-\infty}^{\infty} f(x)\, dx = 1$.

This property is also true when X is discrete. To summarize:

$$E(a) = a,$$
$$E(aX) = aE(X),$$

and

$$E(aX + b) = aE(X) + b.$$

I-16 VARIANCE AND STANDARD DEVIATION

As mentioned in the previous section, the mean value might be thought of as the center of gravity of the probability distribution. For many readers, this probably brings to mind the more general notions (which are encountered in the study of mechanics) of the moments of a distribution (of mass) about a particular point. To be specific, the kth *moment* of a probability distribution about a point, a, is represented by the symbol μ_a^k, and is defined as

$$\mu_a^k = E[(X - a)^k],$$

which can be computed from

$$E[(X - a)^k] = \sum_{\text{all } x_i} (x_i - a)^k p(x_i)$$

for a discrete probability distribution, and by

$$E[(X - a)^k] = \int_{-\infty}^{\infty} (x - a)^k f(x)\, dx$$

for a continuous probability distribution. In terms of this general expression for moments, the *mean* of a probability distribution is simply the *first moment* about the *origin*. Using this notation, the mean should more properly be represented by the symbol, μ_0^1. However, owing to the fact that the mean is such a commonly used measure, the superscript and the subscript are normally dropped, and it is represented by the symbol μ.

The concept of moments of a distribution serves as a convenient device for the introduction of the second of the two most useful parameters for describing a probability distribution, the *variance*. Whereas the mean is a measure of the *central tendency* of a probability distribution, the variance is a measure of the *dispersion* of the distribution about this central point. In terms of the general expression for moments, the variance is defined as the *second moment* about the *mean*. The symbol commonly used to represent the variance is σ^2. Symbolically, the variance is given by

Equation I-21
$$\sigma^2 = \mu_\mu^2 = \mathrm{E}[(X - \mu)^2].$$

The variance of a probability distribution is analogous to the moment of inertia of mechanics.

To illustrate the usefulness of the variance as a measure of dispersion, it is convenient to introduce a unit or measure called the *standard deviation*, σ, which is defined as the square root of the variance. It can be shown that for any symmetric probability distribution, the great majority of the distribution falls within the three standard deviation units on either side of the mean, i.e., within the interval $\pm 3\sigma$ from the mean. Therefore, a probability distribution having a small σ^2 and hence a small σ

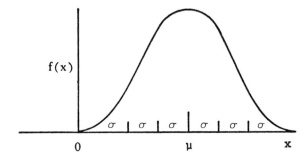

would be concentrated tightly about the mean. On the other hand, a probability distribution having a large σ^2 would be dispersed more widely about the mean.

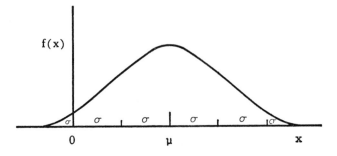

By employing the linear operator characteristics of the expectation function $\mathrm{E}(\cdot)$, an alternate expression for the variance can be derived.

$$\sigma^2 = E[(X - \mu)^2]$$
$$= E[X^2 - 2\mu X + \mu^2]$$
$$= E[X^2] - 2\mu E(X) + \mu^2$$
$$= E(X^2) - 2\mu^2 + \mu^2$$
$$= E(X^2) - \mu^2, \text{ or}$$
$$\sigma^2 = E(X^2) - [E(X)]^2.$$

As a numerical example of the computation of the variance in the continuous case, recall the density function

$$f(x) = \frac{1}{18}x^2, \quad -3 \leq x \leq +3$$

$$= 0 \quad , \quad \text{elsewhere.}$$

Since the mean for this particular distribution equals zero, we have

$$\sigma^2 = E(X^2) - [E(X)]^2$$
$$= E(X^2) - 0$$
$$= \int_{-3}^{+3} x^2 \left(\frac{1}{18}x^2\right) dx$$
$$= \int_{-3}^{+3} \frac{x^4}{18} dx = \frac{486}{90}.$$

Higher moments are used (although rarely) to give further information about the probability distribution. For example, the third moment can be used to give a measure of the *skewness* of a non-symmetric probability distribution. The fourth moment is sometimes used as a measure of the *sharpness* or the *peakedness* of the density function. By far the most frequently used descriptive measures are the first and second moments, or the mean and variance.

Up to this point, the primary emphasis has been upon the general mathematical properties of *all* probability distributions. As a consequence, some of the numerical examples used to illustrate the principles have been arbitrary and not necessarily representative of any real-world phenomena. The next step will be to look at those probability distributions which *are* representative of real-world phenomena. Although there are a number of such distributions, each applying to different situations, only six of the most widely applicable will be presented here. These are the binomial, Poisson, geometric, uniform, normal and exponential distributions. The first three are *discrete distributions* while the others deal with *continuous random variables*.

I-17   THE BINOMIAL DISTRIBUTION

Many situations occur in the real-world in the form of a series of simple independent trials in which the occurrence or the nonoccurrence of an event is the only item of interest. If, in such a series of trials, the individual probability of the event's occurring on any one trial remains constant through the series, then these trials are sometimes referred to as *Bernoulli* trials. A good example of Bernoulli trials is a series of coin tosses for which the probability of a *head* on a single toss is p and the probability of a tail is $q = (1 - p)$. Another example might be provided by considering defects in a series of items being produced on an assembly line in which the probability of an individual item being defective is a constant, p. In situations such as these, it is desirable to know the probability of a specified number of occurrences of the event in a given number of trials. An occurrence of the event is sometimes referred to as a *success,* and a nonoccurrence as a *failure.* The *binomial distribution* provides the means of predicting the probability of exactly x occurrences of an event in n independent trials.

The development of the binomial distribution may be visualized by means of the coin-tossing example. Assume that for a particular coin the probability of a head on a single toss is $\frac{1}{3}$, and the probability of a tail is $\frac{2}{3}$. Let the random variable X, be the number of heads occurring in five tosses, and find $P(X = 2)$ or $p(2)$. A logical approach to such a problem is to consider all of the ways in which two heads might occur. Determine probabilities for each of these mutually exclusive occurrences, and then sum the resulting probabilities. One way for the two heads to occur in five tosses is

$$H \quad H \quad T \quad T \quad T$$

and its probability is given by

$$(p)(p)(q)(q)(q) = p^2q^3 = (1/3)^2(2/3)^3.$$

To determine the total number of ways of getting exactly two heads in five tosses, the total number of possible arrangements, or permutations, of this array must be found. Note that this is a special type of permutation, namely an n object permutation where there are two distinct types of objects. From Equation I-10, the total number of such arrangements is given by

$$\frac{n!}{n_1!n_2!} = \frac{5!}{2!3!} = 10.$$

The 10 arrangements which yield exactly two heads are

H	H	T	T	T		T	H	H	T	T		T	T	H	H	T
H	T	H	T	T		T	H	T	H	T		T	T	H	T	H
H	T	T	H	T		T	H	T	T	H		T	T	T	H	H
H	T	T	T	H											

Recall that $\dfrac{5!}{2!3!}$ can also be represented by the symbol $\binom{5}{2}$ which is frequently used to simplify the notation. Since the probability associated with each of these arrangements is the same, namely $(\frac{1}{3})^2(\frac{2}{3})^3$, the overall probability of exactly two heads in five tosses is given by

$$P(X = 2) = p(2) = \frac{5!}{2!3!}(1/3)^2(2/3)^3 = \binom{5}{2}(1/3)^2(2/3)^3 = .31$$

In general, the probability of exactly x successes in n trials is given by the following expression:

Equation I-22 $\quad P(X = x) = p(x) = \binom{n}{x}p^xq^{n-x}, \quad \text{for } x = 0,1,2 \cdots, n,$

which is also the general expression for the probability function of the binomial distribution.

As verification that the previous expression is a probability function, it must be shown that

$$\sum_{\text{all } x_i} p(x_i) = 1.$$

By its very definition, the particular random variable associated with the binomial distribution can take on all integer values from zero to n. Therefore,

$$\sum_{\text{all } x_i} p(x_i) = \sum_{x=0}^{n} \frac{n!}{x!(n-x)!} p^x q^{n-x}$$

$$= \frac{n!}{0!n!} p^0 q^n + \frac{n!}{1!(n-1)!} p^1 q^{n-1} + \frac{n!}{2!(n-2)!} p^2 q^{n-2} + \cdots$$

$$+ \frac{n!}{n!(n-n)!} p^n q^0$$

$$= q^n + nq^{n-1}p + \frac{n(n-1)}{2!} q^{n-2}p^2 + \cdots + p^n.$$

A bit of scrutiny of this expression will reveal that it is nothing more than the binomial expansion of $(q + p)^n$. Therefore,

$$\sum_{\text{all } x_i} p(x_i) = (q + p)^n = 1^n = 1,$$

and the mathematical requirement that the probability function sum to one is met.

To determine the mean of the binomial distribution, the general definition for expected value is used as follows:

$$E(X) = \mu = \sum_{\text{all } x_i} x_i p(x_i) = \sum_{x=0}^{n} x \binom{n}{x} p^x q^{n-x}.$$

Since a zero value of x does not contribute to the summation, the lower limit of the summation can be changed to $x = 1$:

$$\mu = \sum_{x=1}^{n} x \frac{n!}{x!(n-x)!} p^x q^{n-x}.$$

Dividing through by x, gives

$$\mu = \sum_{x=1}^{n} \frac{n!}{(x-1)!(n-x)!} p^x q^{n-x},$$

and by factoring out an n and a p, this expression becomes

$$\mu = np \sum_{x=1}^{n} \frac{(n-1)!}{(x-1)!(n-x)!} p^{x-1} q^{n-x}.$$

If $x - 1$ is replaced by the dummy variable y, and $n - 1$ is replaced by m, the expression in terms of y and m becomes

$$\mu = np \sum_{y=0}^{m} \frac{m!}{y!(m-y)!} p^y q^{m-y}.$$

Since the quantity being summed here is simply the expression for exactly y successes in m trials, and further, since it is summed over all possible values of y, the sum must equal one. Therefore,

Equation I-23 $$\mu = np(1) = np,$$

which is the expression for the mean of the binomial distribution.

By a similar bit of mathematical manipulation, and by use of the relation $x^2 = x(x - 1) + x$, the *variance* of the binomial distribution can be found to be

Equation I-24 $$\sigma^2 = npq.$$

As an application of the binomial distribution, consider the following hypothetical situation. Merchant vessel losses to enemy submarines are being studied. Statistics on past sinkings indicate that the probability that an individual merchant vessel is sunk on a single crossing is $1/10$. What is the probability that exactly two merchant vessels are sunk in a total of 10 attempted crossings? Also, what is the mean number of sinkings in 10 attempted crossings?

Let $X =$ the number of merchant vessel sinkings. Then

$$n = 10, \ p = 1/10, \ q = 9/10,$$

$$P(X = 2) = p(2) = \binom{10}{2}(1/10)^2(9/10)^8 = .19,$$

and

$$\mu = np = (10)(1/10) = 1.$$

Because of the frequent appearance of the binomial distribution in applications of probability theory, standard binomial tables have been compiled in mathematical handbooks giving the probabilities for various values of x, n and p.

The binomial distribution is used most frequently in this text to answer the question: *What is the probability that at least one success occurs in n trials?* This is computed as follows:

$$P(\text{at least one success}) = P(X \geq 1)$$
$$= p(1) + p(2) + \cdots + p(n)$$
$$= \sum_{x=1}^{n} \binom{n}{x} p^x q^{n-x}.$$

This may be difficult to evaluate without tables, but may be made much easier by noting that

$$P(X \geq 1) = 1 - P(X = 0)$$
$$= 1 - p(0)$$
$$= 1 - \binom{n}{0} p^0 q^n$$
$$= 1 - q^n,$$

where one term instead of n terms must be computed. For other required probabilities, the computational effort required can often be reduced by a similar approach.

I-18   THE POISSON DISTRIBUTION

Another extremely useful probability distribution is the Poisson, which applies in certain situations in which an event occurs repeatedly in a completely random or haphazard manner. In order for the Poisson distribution to hold, the situation in question must fulfill certain requirements which will be specified in more detail in the following paragraph. Typical examples of situations which *do* meet the necessary requirements are those involving alpha-particle emissions from radioactive material, arrivals of automobiles at freeway toll booths, arrivals of telephone calls at switchboards, random failures of electronic equipment and random arrivals of merchant vessels at cargo-unloading points. For such situations, the Poisson distribution yields the probability of a specified number of occurrences of the event in a given interval of interest. Owing to the fact that the interval in question is usually (but not always) an interval of time, we use the symbol t to represent the interval of interest. The random variable for the Poisson distribution is defined as

X = the number of occurrences of the event during the interval t.

The general criteria which must be met in order for the Poisson distribution to hold are:

a. The event must occur repeatedly, but in a completely random manner.
b. The probability of the event occurring during any small subinterval, Δt, must be proportional to the magnitude of the subinterval.
c. The probability of the event occurring during a small subinterval, Δt, must be completely independent of whether the event has occurred in the previous subinterval.
d. The probability that the event will occur more than once during a small subinterval, Δt, must be negligible.

We will not, however, go into a detailed derivation of the Poisson distribution. Instead, suffice to say that when these requirements are translated into mathematical language they lead to a group of differential equations from which the Poisson probability function is found to be

Equation I-25 $$P(X = x) = p(x) = \begin{cases} \dfrac{e^{-\lambda t}(\lambda t)^x}{x!}, & x = 0,1,2, \cdots \\ 0, & \text{elsewhere} \end{cases}$$

where x = the exact number of occurrences of the event in an interval t, and λ = the average *rate* of occurrences during the interval. If λ is known, then the average *number* of occurrences during the interval t is $\lambda t = \mu$.

It can be seen that if the occurrence of a particular event conforms to the Poisson distribution, all that is needed is the average number of occurrences during any interval of interest in order to make predictions concerning specified numbers of occurrences during that interval. The beauty of the Poisson distribution is that it is often quite easy to determine the average rate of occurrence of the event, λ, (from which the average number of occurrences for a specified time interval follows directly) by simply summing the number of occurrences in any series of randomly chosen intervals and then dividing this sum by the sum of the lengths of the intervals.

As a numerical example of the Poisson distribution, consider a situation where emissions from a radioactive material are being studied. It has been determined by physically counting these emissions that they are occurring at an average rate of 20 per hour. What is the probability of exactly five emissions in one-half hour?

Let X = the number of radioactive emissions in one half hour.

$$\lambda = 20; \quad \mu = \lambda t = 20(1/2) = 10.$$

Therefore:

$$P(X = 5) = p(5) = \frac{e^{-10}(10)^5}{5!} = .038.$$

The *mean* of the Poisson distribution was introduced as part of the definition of the distribution itself. It may be shown without undue difficulty that the *variance* of the Poisson distribution is identically equal to the mean, i.e., $\sigma^2 = \mu = \lambda t$.

I-19   THE POISSON AS AN APPROXIMATION TO THE BINOMIAL

In addition to having many applications in its own right, the Poisson distribution can also be used, under certain circumstances, as a good approximation to the binomial distribution. As will be seen, the use of this approximation is most convenient for those situations in which calculations with the binomial formula would be quite tedious.

Recall that the binomial distribution yields the probability of x occurrences of an event in n independent trials when p, the probability of occurrence on one trial, remains constant. In those instances where n is large and p is small, the binomial distribution can be approximated by the Poisson distribution. In making this approximation, substitute the mean of the binomial $(\mu = np)$ for the mean appearing in the Poisson density function, i.e.,

Equation I-26 $$p(x) = \frac{e^{-(np)}(np)^x}{x!}.$$

The particular values of n and p for which the Poisson yields a good approximation of the binomial depend upon one's definition of the term good. In most cases the approximation is quite accurate for all values of $n \geq 100$ *and* $p \leq .05$. In many other cases the approximation is sufficiently accurate for even smaller values of n and larger values of p.

As mentioned earlier, the value of the Poisson approximation lies in the fact that through its use one is able to eliminate much of the tedious arithmetic associated with the combinatorial calculations required for the binomial. Whereas the raising of fractions to large powers can be performed conveniently on a slide rule or a hand calculator or by use of tables of logarithms, the calculation of combinatorials is usually a long and laborious process. The following numerical example will illustrate the savings in effort which can be realized by using the Poisson approximation.

Assume that the occurrences of a particular event conform to a binomial distribution with $p = 1/100$. What is the probability of exactly six occurrences of the event in 300 independent trials? The result, using the binomial probability function is

$$p(6) = \binom{300}{6} (1/100)^6 (99/100)^{294}$$

$$= \frac{(300)(299)(298)(297)(296)(295)}{(6)(5)(4)(3)(2)(1)} (10^{-12})(.052) = .0502$$

The calculation of this expression is quite tedious. However, if the Poisson approximation is used with $\mu = (300)(1/100) = 3$, the result is

$$p(6) = \frac{e^{-3}(3)^6}{6!} = \frac{(.05)(729)}{(720)} = .0504.$$

I-20 THE GEOMETRIC DISTRIBUTION

It has been seen that the binomial distribution applies to situations where the random variable is the number of successes in n independent Bernoulli trials with a constant probability, p, of success on each trial. An associated random variable is the number of independent Bernoulli trials until the first success occurs.

Let N be a random variable defined as the number of the trial on which the first success occurs. The probability function can be stated as:

$$\begin{aligned}
p(1) &= P(N = 1) \\
&= P(\text{number of trials for one success} = 1) \\
&= P(\text{success occurs on the first trial}) \\
&= p \\
p(2) &= P(N = 2) \\
&= P(\text{number of trials for one success} = 2) \\
&= P(\text{failure occurs on the first trial} \cap \text{success on second trial}) \\
&= (1 - p)p, \text{ assuming independence.}
\end{aligned}$$

For n trials,

$$\begin{aligned}
p(n) &= P(N = n) \\
&= P(\text{number of trials for one success} = n) \\
&= P(\text{failure on first } n - 1 \text{ trials} \cap \text{success on } n^{\text{th}} \text{ trial}) \\
&= (1 - p)^{n-1}p.
\end{aligned}$$

This probability distribution is therefore:

$$p(n) = \begin{cases} (1 - p)^{n-1}p, & \text{for } n = 1,2,3, \ldots \\ 0 & , \text{ elsewhere.} \end{cases}$$

The name of this distribution comes from its resemblance to a *geometric series* where the sum of the first n terms is

$$a + ar + ar^2 + \cdots + ar^{n-1} = a\frac{(1 - r^n)}{1 - r}.$$

In this series if r is between minus one and one, then the sum as n approaches infinity becomes

Equation I-27
$$a + ar + ar^2 + \cdots = \frac{a}{1 - r}.$$

Use of this fact makes it easy to show that the probability function does in fact sum to one, i.e.,

$$\sum_{n=1}^{\infty} p(n) = p + p(1 - p) + p(1 - p)^2 + \cdots = 1,$$

since it is a geometric series with $a = p, r = 1 - p$, and the sum from Equation I-27 is

$$\frac{a}{1 - r} = \frac{p}{p} = 1.$$

The mean number of trials required for one success is

$$E(N) = \sum_{\text{all } n} n(1 - p)^{n-1}p$$

$$= \sum_{n=1}^{\infty} n(1 - p)^{n-1}p$$

$$= p + 2p(1 - p) + 3p(1 - p)^2 + \cdots,$$

which can be evaluated after noting that the derivative with respect to r of both sides of Equation I-27 gives

$$a + 2ar + 3ar^2 + \cdots = \frac{a}{(1 - r)^2};$$

using $a = p$ and $r = 1 - p$, this becomes

$$p + 2p(1 - p) + 3p(1 - p)^2 + \cdots = \frac{p}{p^2} = \frac{1}{p},$$

and the expected value of N then becomes

Equation I-28 $$E(N) = \mu = \frac{1}{p}.$$

The variance of N is $(1 - p)/p^2$. This can also be computed with slight additional difficulty, using the second derivative of the infinite geometric series and the additional fact that $x^2 = x(x - 1) + x$. This computation will be left as an exercise for the interested reader.

I-21   THE UNIFORM DISTRIBUTION

The first continuous probability distribution to be discussed is the uniform distribution. It is simply the continuous analogue of the discrete distribution in which each outcome is equally likely. The set of outcomes resulting from the toss of a single die has been used as an example of such a discrete distribution where, if X represents the number of spots showing, then $p(x) = P(X = x)$ would be constant for all possible values of x. This constant probability is the distinguishing characteristic of an equally likely distribution. As a continuous analogue to this, consider spinning a pointer which might stop with equal likelihood anywhere between two numbers, say a and b. In complete analogy to the die example, the probability density function associated with the stopping point of the spinner would likewise have a constant value, $f(x) = k$, over the entire range of possible values of the random variable.

The graph of the probability function for the discrete case would have a constant height for each possible outcome.

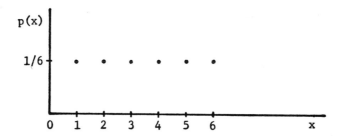

The graph of the probability density function for the continuous case would be a smooth curve of constant height $f(x) = k$.

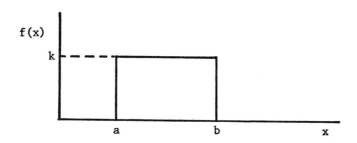

Because of its characteristic appearance, the uniform distribution is sometimes referred to as the rectangular distribution. To determine the mathematical expression for the uniform probability density function, recall the fact that the area under the density function must always sum to one. Specifically, in the case of the uniform distribution

$$\int_{-\infty}^{\infty} f(x)\, dx = 1,$$

where

$$f(x) = \begin{cases} k, & a \le x \le b \\ 0, & \text{otherwise.} \end{cases}$$

Then

$$\int_{-\infty}^{\infty} k\, dx = \int_{-\infty}^{a} 0 \cdot dx + \int_{a}^{b} k\, dx + \int_{b}^{\infty} 0 \cdot dx = 1,$$

or

$$\int_{a}^{b} k\, dx = 1,$$

from which

$$k = \frac{1}{b-a},$$

and

Equation I-29
$$f(x) = \begin{cases} \dfrac{1}{b-a}, & a \le x \le b \\ 0, & \text{otherwise.} \end{cases}$$

The general form of the cumulative distribution function is

$$F(x) = \begin{cases} 0 & , \ x < a \\ \displaystyle\int_a^x \frac{1}{b-a}\, dx = \frac{x-a}{b-a}, & a \le x \le b \\ 1 & , \ x > b. \end{cases}$$

And

$$P(x_1 \le X \le x_2) = \int_{x_1}^{x_2} f(x)\, dx = \frac{x_2 - x_1}{b-a}, \quad a \le x_1 \le x_2 \le b.$$

The mean of the uniform distribution is determined by applying the general definition for the mean.

$$E(X) = \mu = \int_{-\infty}^{\infty} x f(x)\, dx$$

$$= \frac{1}{b-a} \int_a^b x\, dx$$

or

Equation I-30
$$\mu = \frac{b+a}{2}.$$

In a similar manner, it can easily be shown that the *variance* of the uniform distribution is

Equation I-31
$$\sigma^2 = \frac{(b-a)^2}{12}.$$

I-22 EXPONENTIAL DISTRIBUTION

The negative exponential or simply the *exponential* distribution is one of the continuous distributions which arises most frequently to describe real-life situations. It is the continuous analog of the geometric distribution in the following sense. In an experiment where the binomial describes the *number of successes in n trials,* the geometric describes the *number of trials necessary for one success.* In an experiment where the Poisson describes the *number of random occurrences of some event in an interval, t,* of time, distance, area, volume, etc., the exponential describes the *interval required for one such random occurrence.*

Let the random variable X represent the number of random occurrences in time t and let the random variable T represent the time of the first random occurrence. From the Poisson distribution

$$p(x) = P(X = x) = \frac{e^{-\mu}\mu^x}{x!}, \quad x = 0, 1, 2, \cdots,$$

where $\mu = \lambda t$ and λ is constant.

The number of occurrences in time t is zero *if and only if* the time to first occurrence is greater than t. Symbolically

$$P(X = 0) = P(T > t)$$
$$= 1 - P(T \le t),$$

but $P(T \leq t)$ is the cumulative distribution function, $F(t)$, for the random variable T. Solving for this function gives:

$$F(t) = P(T \leq t) = 1 - P(T > t)$$
$$= 1 - P(X = 0)$$
$$= 1 - p(0)$$
$$= 1 - \frac{e^{-\mu}\mu^0}{0!}$$
$$= 1 - e^{-\mu}$$
$$= 1 - e^{-\lambda t} \quad \text{for } t > 0.$$

The probability density function, $f(t)$, can then be found by taking the derivative of $F(t)$

$$f(t) = \frac{dF(t)}{dt} = \frac{d(1 - e^{-\lambda t})}{dt}$$
$$= \lambda e^{-\lambda t},$$

so that

Equation I-32
$$f(t) = \begin{cases} \lambda e^{-\lambda t}, & t > 0 \\ 0, & t \leq 0. \end{cases}$$

The mean time to an occurrence can be found using integration by parts by partitioning $t\lambda e^{-\lambda t}\, dt$ into t and $\lambda e^{-\lambda t}\, dt$. Thus:

Equation I-33
$$E(T) = \int_0^\infty t\lambda e^{-\lambda t}\, dt$$
$$= te^{-\lambda t}\Big]_0^\infty - \int_0^\infty - e^{-\lambda t}\, dt$$
$$= 0 - \frac{1}{\lambda}e^{-\lambda t}\Big]_0^\infty$$
$$= \frac{1}{\lambda}.$$

In a similar manner it can be shown that the variance of T is $1/\lambda^2$.

I-23 THE NORMAL DISTRIBUTION

The occurrence of many real-world phenomena can be conveniently explained in terms of a well-known continuous probability distribution called the *normal distribution*. In general, the normal distribution can be said to apply to most situations involving measurements whose values fall within symmetric patterns about a central value.

For example, consider the values which might be obtained when taking any of the following measurements:

a. The heights of all men, age 21 or older, in a large city.
b. The grades received on the graduate record examination by all college seniors throughout the country.

c. The circumferences of all the full-grown trees in a large forest.

d. The thicknesses of all the metal discs produced by an automatic machine in a 24-hour period.

The measurements in all of these situations would fall into the same general pattern. To emphasize the underlying similarities involved, consider the so-called relative frequency diagrams associated with these measurements. A relative frequency diagram for any of these situations would be constructed by first grouping the measurements into arbitrary intervals of equal length and then counting the number of measurements falling into each interval and dividing these tallies by the total number of measurements. By the relative frequency definition of probability, these ratios would yield the approximate probability that any one random measurement will fall into any particular interval. Finally, to complete the relative frequency diagram, the results for all of the intervals can be plotted in the form of a bar graph. The similarities underlying all of the situations would be evidenced by the fact that in all cases the relative frequency diagrams would have the following general shape:

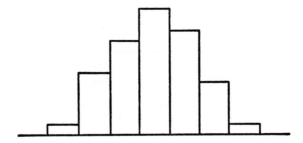

Note that all of the measurements are grouped in a roughly symmetrical fashion about a central value, and that the relative frequencies drop off rather sharply as the distance from that central value increases.

It would seem reasonable to assume that if more and more measurements were tabulated, and if the measuring instruments were sufficiently accurate so as to allow the data to be grouped into finer and finer subintervals, then the bar graph would approach the form of a smooth bell-shaped curve:

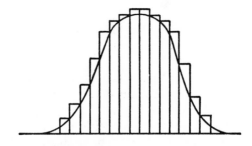

It would also seem reasonable to assume that, whereas the bar graph represents a rough approximation of probabilities in the form of a relative frequency diagram, the smooth curve would yield a precise representation of probabilities in the form of a smooth probability density curve. It is by this reasoning process that one arrives logically at the normal density curve. The normal distribution originally received its name because many years ago, it was mistakenly held to be *the one* probability distribution underlying all continuous random variables.

To determine the mathematical expression for the *normal density function*, the procedure followed is different from heretofore. Specifically, a mathematical function whose graph is similar to the bell-shaped curve must be found. Having found such a function, one must modify it so as to make it meet the requirements for a probability density function. One such mathematical function whose graph has the appropriate shape is the exponential function:

$$g(x) = ke^{-1/2\left(\frac{x-\alpha}{\beta}\right)^2}.$$

Note that the function is symmetrical about a central value, α (because of the squared exponent) and that for positive values of k, the function is always nonnegative (another requirement of a probability density function). One primary requirement, which must be met by the function in order that it might serve as a density function, is that the integral of the function over all possible values of x must equal one. As in the case for the uniform distribution, this requirement can be met by finding a value for k which will cause the integral to sum to one; i.e., the following expression is solved for k:

$$\int_{-\infty}^{+\infty} k \times e^{-1/2\left(\frac{x-\alpha}{\beta}\right)^2} = 1.$$

The value of k for which this expression is true turns out (after some involved integration) to be

$$k = \frac{1}{\sqrt{2\pi}\,\beta}.$$

Therefore, the probability density function for the normal distribution is given by

$$f(x) = \frac{1}{\sqrt{2\pi}\,\beta} e^{-1/2\left(\frac{x-\alpha}{\beta}\right)^2}.$$

By a visual inspection of the plot of the normal density function, one can immediately see that the *point of symmetry*, or mean, occurs at the point $x = \alpha$, i.e., $\mu = \alpha$. Also, by some rather complicated integration, it can be shown that the *variance* for the normal distribution equals β^2, i.e., $\sigma^2 = \beta^2$. Therefore, the expression rewritten in terms of the familiar parameters μ and σ^2 is

Equation I-34
$$f(x) = \frac{1}{\sqrt{2\pi}\,\sigma} e^{-1/2\left(\frac{x-\mu}{\sigma}\right)^2},$$

from which it immediately follows that the cumulative distribution function is

Equation I-35
$$F(x) = P[X \le x] = \int_{-\infty}^{x} \frac{1}{\sqrt{2\pi}\,\sigma} e^{-1/2\left(\frac{x-\mu}{\sigma}\right)^2} dx.$$

As in any continuous distribution, probability statements are expressed as

$$P(x_1 \le X < x_2) = \int_{x_1}^{x_2} \frac{1}{\sqrt{2\pi}\,\sigma} e^{-1/2\left(\frac{x-\mu}{\sigma}\right)^2} dx.$$

In the case of the normal distribution, however, the density function cannot be readily integrated in order to find the cumulative distribution function or other desired probabilities. The problem presented by this difficulty is not serious, since the numerical value of a particular integral can be approximated to any desired degree of accuracy and tabulated for use. Some tables list values of $F(x) = \int_0^x f(x)\, dx$ for various values of x while others tabulate values of $\int_{-\infty}^x f(x)\, dx$. It is *not* necessary to tabulate values of the previous integrals for various values of μ and σ^2, since any normal distribution can be standardized in order to use tabulated integrals for the special case where $\mu = 0$ and $\sigma^2 = 1$. The standard symbol used to represent the normal distribution with mean μ and variance σ^2 is $N(\mu, \sigma^2)$. The standardized normal distribution then is denoted by $N(0,1)$. Let T be a normally distributed random variable having $\mu = 0$ and $\sigma^2 = 1$. Then

Equation I-36
$$f(t) = \frac{1}{\sqrt{2\pi}} e^{-\frac{1}{2}t^2},$$

and

Equation I-37
$$F(z) = \int_{-\infty}^{z} \frac{1}{\sqrt{2\pi}} e^{-\frac{1}{2}t^2}\, dt,$$

where z is a specific value of the random variable T.

This integral is the one sometimes tabulated for various values of z, representing

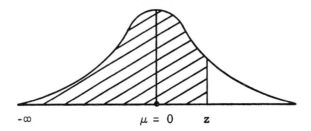

the area shaded under the standardized normal density function. In other tabulations, the integral is evaluated only from the mean up to the desired value of z. The results in

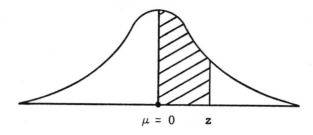

both cases are equivalent because the area under the normal density curve to the left of zero is always .5.

An excerpt from a standardized normal table of the former type follows:

$$F(x) = \frac{1}{\sqrt{2\pi}} \int_{-\infty}^{z} e^{-\frac{1}{2}t^2} \, dt;$$

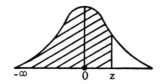

Standardized normal table

z	F(z)	z	F(z)	z	F(z)	z	F(z)
0.0	.500	0.8	.788	1.6	.945	2.4	.992
0.1	.540	0.9	.816	1.7	.955	2.5	.994
0.2	.579	1.0	.841	1.8	.964	2.6	.995
0.3	.618	1.1	.864	1.9	.971	2.7	.997
0.4	.655	1.2	.885	2.0	.977	2.8	.997
0.5	.691	1.3	.903	2.1	.982	2.9	.998
0.6	.726	1.4	.919	2.2	.986	3.0	.999
0.7	.758	1.5	.933	2.3	.989		

In order to use such tables to find probabilities for a given normal random variable X with mean μ and variance σ^2, it is necessary only to standardize this distribution by

Equation I-38
$$z = \frac{x - \mu}{\sigma}.$$

Then $dx = \sigma \, dz$, and as x goes from $-\infty$ to x, z goes from $-\infty$ to $(x - \mu)/\sigma$ so that

$$P(X \le x) = \int_{-\infty}^{x} \frac{1}{\sqrt{2\pi}\,\sigma} e^{-1/2 \left(\frac{x-\mu}{\sigma}\right)^2} dx$$

$$= \int_{-\infty}^{\frac{x-\mu}{\sigma}} \frac{1}{\sqrt{2\pi}} e^{-\frac{t^2}{2}} dt$$

$$= P\left(T \le \frac{x-\mu}{\sigma}\right).$$

It can be seen that z measures the distance from x to the mean, μ, in units of standard deviation.

As an example of normal probability calculations involving the use of the standardized normal tables consider the following:

Studies are being conducted concerning the amount of rainfall in Washington, D.C. Weather Bureau statistics indicate that for the previous five-year period the cumulative rainfall for April has been normally distributed with a mean of 10 inches and a variance of 4 inches. Based on these statistics, what is the probability of at least 15 inches of rainfall during the forthcoming month of April?

Let X be the total amount of rainfall in inches during the month of April. X is distributed $N(10,4)$. The problem is to find $P(X \ge 15)$.

$$z = \frac{x - \mu}{\sigma} = \frac{15 - 10}{2} = 2.5.$$

Then in terms of the standardized random variable T, the probability that the amount of rainfall will be greater than or equal to 2.5 standard deviation units above the mean rainfall is

$$P(X \geq 15) = P(T \geq 2.5)$$
$$= 1 - P(T \leq 2.5)$$
$$= 1 - P(-\infty < T \leq 2.5).$$

From the standardized normal table when $z = 2.5$,

$$F(z) = P(T \leq 2.5) = .994,$$

from which it follows that

$$P(T \geq 2.5) = 1 - .994 = .006.$$

The probability of more than 15 inches of rain during the forthcoming month of April then is .006.

It should be pointed out that the ordinate of the normal density function is greater than zero for *all* values of the random variable from minus infinity to plus infinity. One might reasonably question whether the distribution can be used to represent the distribution of inches of rainfall, which certainly cannot take on negative values, much less values approaching minus infinity. The answer lies in the fact that although the density function is defined for all values of x, the height of the curve is practically negligible for those values which are far removed from the mean. For example, 99.7 percent of the probability in a normal distribution is contained in an area enclosed by a range of three standard deviation units on either side of the mean. It is therefore safe to use this particular distribution, which has an infinite range, to approximate real-world distributions whose true ranges are finite.

I-24 STATISTICAL SAMPLING

The discussion in the last part of the previous section leads naturally to the consideration of the general subject of inferring broad generalizations from limited sample data. A good example of a generalization of this type is to be seen in the early paragraphs of Section I-23 when the notion of the relative frequency diagram was generalized so as to arrive at the smooth probability density curve.

Generalizations such as these are at the very heart of a well-known discipline devoted to the study and analysis of collected sample data. This discipline is referred to under the general heading of *statistics*. Although no effort will be made to undertake a study of this most interesting subject, it is worthwhile to consider briefly the close relationship between statistics and probability theory.

As an example, consider an inspector concerned with quality control of a production process, studying the thicknesses of washers turned out by an automatic machine. Suppose the manufacturer's specifications call for a washer thickness of x_0. The quality control inspector is therefore interested in knowing both the mean washer thickness which is actually being produced by the machine, and the amount of variance about this mean value. To determine these parameters, he might proceed by choosing a sampling of washers at random from the production line and measuring their thickness. The results could be plotted in the form of a relative frequency diagram and treated as a discrete probability distribution. In this manner, he would then be able to determine the mean value for *this particular sample* by use of Equation I-17, i.e.,

$$\bar{x} = \frac{1}{n} \sum_{\substack{\text{all } x_i \text{ of} \\ \text{sample}}} x_i$$

This expression is commonly referred to as the *sample* mean. The question which then arises is how certain can he be that the mean thickness of this particular sample is truly representative of the mean thickness of *all* the washers being produced by the machine. The degree of *confidence* one will have in the sample mean will depend, in no small measure, upon the number of measurements included in the sampling. In other words, the hypothesis that the sample mean is truly representative of the so-called *population* mean is subject to certain errors dependent upon the sample size. Statistical theory, among other things, can predict the various errors associated with hypotheses of this type for different values of sample size. These predictions also apply to sample variance and population variance. As a consequence, the inspector would then be in a position to make meaningful statements concerning sample size, taking into consideration the economics of sampling as well as the desired level of confidence in the findings.

This example was related solely for the purpose of giving the reader a very brief introduction to the subject of statistics. It can be seen from this that statistics may be viewed as the empirical counterpart to mathematical probability theory.

PROBLEMS

1. The probability density function may be defined over any domain. Here is a case in which the domain goes from zero to two. Consider the parabola $y = 2x - x^2$. If all the points enclosed between the parabola and the x-axis are equally likely, find the probability density function for the distribution of the distances of random points from the y-axis. First find the density function and then the cumulative distribution function. (Hint: let M and M' denote two straight lines parallel to the y-axis and cutting the x-axis at some points x and $x + dx$. Calculate the probability that a random point will fall between M and M'.)

2. Suppose a search vessel, at zero in the figure, is moving with constant velocity in the direction indicated by the arrow. The object searched for (life raft, enemy vessel, etc.) is likely to be anywhere on the ocean, and is assumed at rest for simplicity. A simplifying assumption is made (which is not a bad one for some cases) that if the object comes within a radius R of the vessel it will be discovered.

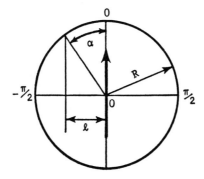

Relative to the search vessel, the ocean is moving along the parallel paths shown in the figure. The object will also move along one of these relative paths at some distance l from the searching vessel. It is not difficult to see that if the object is placed at random and if it is to be discovered, the value of l will occur at random between the limits $-R$ and R, and the approximate probability that the object, when seen, will be in the interval dl about l is given by $dl/2R$. This approach will produce a density function in terms of l.

    a. What is the probability that the object, if it is discovered, comes into view at a relative bearing α? (You must make a transformation to get the result as a function of α.)

    b. Verify that your result satisfies the conditions for a density function.

    c. Find the probability that the object will be discovered in the sector zero to 45 degrees.

    d. Show that restricting the lookouts to searching the forward quarter will only reduce the probability of sighting by 30 percent.

3. In Problem two, find the expected value and the variance of the distribution.

4. In single ship transits from Pearl to Auckland during World War II, there were 40 sinkings in 1,000 ship transits.

    a. What is the probability that a ship was sunk in one transit?

    b. Of 20 ships carrying strategic materials, three were sunk on these individual trips. Does this seem unlikely? What is the probability for this event?

    c. Calculate the probability that at most two ships would be sunk in the 20 transits of ships carrying strategic materials.

    d. What is the probability that any ship which enters this system will be available for the eleventh trip?

5. Consider a box of 200 fuses. It is known that the probability of a particular fuse being defective is .02.

    What is the probability that at least six fuses are defective? (Set up the problem but do not carry out the calculations. It will be seen later that a good approximation to this answer can be arrived at much more easily by means of the Poisson approximation.)

6. The probability of detection of a submarine by an ASW ship is a function of many variables, among which are *speed, depth, water temperature, condition of* ASW *ship's sonar* and *lateral distance*. Assume that two ASW ships are part of a screen and that a submarine attempts to penetrate between them somewhat closer to ship A than to ship B. Assume that A's probability of detection is .6 and that of B is .4, and that detection by A and detection by B are independent events. Find the probability that the submarine is detected.

7. Six destroyers are conducting an ECM search in a known submarine operating area. Each destroyer is monitoring a specific band of frequencies. There are no overlaps and no gaps in the coverage. Past experience indicates that it is equally likely that the submarine will transmit in any of the six range bands, but not in more than one band simultaneously.

    For problem purposes, assume that an individual destroyer's probability of detecting an emission made in its range band is one.

Define the following events:

(1) Event A: destroyers one, three or five detect a submarine emission.

(2) Event B: destroyers two, four or six detect a submarine emission.

(3) Event C: destroyers one, two, three or four detect a submarine emission.

(4) Event D: destroyers one, two, three, four or five detect a submarine emission.

a. Are the following independent? (Justify all answers mathematically.)
   (1) *A* and *B*?
   (2) *A* and *D*?
   (3) *A* and *C*?
   (4) *B* and *C*?
   (5) *B* and *D*?
   (6) *C* and *D*?

b. Answer Part a for the case where the destroyer's probability of detecting an emission made in its range band is not one but is one-half.

8. Consider a squadron of six submarines, four of which are nuclear and two are nonnuclear. The squadron has been ordered to provide two submarines for off-shore patrols over the Christmas holiday leave period. All of the submarines are fully capable of performing the mission. The decision narrows down to choosing two units to do an unpleasant job. The Squadron Commander decides to choose the two submarines by assigning numbers one through six to the submarines, drawing the numbers out of a hat without replacement, and sending the submarines whose numbers were drawn. Define *A* to be the event that exactly one nonnuclear submarine is sent. Define *B* to be the event that both nonnuclear submarines are sent.

a. Compute $P(A)$, $P(B)$, $P(A \cap B)$.
b. Are *A* and *B* independent events? Why?
c. Are *A* and *B* mutually exclusive events? Why?

9. Aboard a particular Polaris submarine, statistical records of many trials indicate that the probability of a successful missile launch is 3/5 and that the probability of two successful missile launches in a row is 2/5. Let *A* be the event that one launch is successful and *B* be the event that two successive launches are successful.

a. Are events *A* and *B* independent?
b. Justify your answer mathematically.

10. Find the probability that on successive rolls with a single die at least two aces will appear in succession by the end of the fifth roll. (This problem has a counterpart in the double-blip hypothesis found in radar detection theory.)

11. Solve Problem five using the Poisson approximation.

12. Write an expression for the probability of the union of four events, *A*, *B*, *C*, *D*, in terms of $P(A)$, $P(B)$, $P(C)$, $P(D)$, and the various intersections which may exist. Compare the simplicity of your expression with that of Equation I-7.

13. Let the random variable *X* denote the number of aces which appear when two dice are thrown.

   For every possible outcome, list the value of the random variable as in Section I-12.

14. Using the situation in Section I-14, but assuming that ships are as likely to transit the channel at one point as any other:

    a. Derive an expression for the probability density function.
    b. Compute the mean value of X.
    c. Compute the variance of X and the standard deviation.
    d. What common distribution fits this situation?
    e. Derive an expression for the cumulative distribution function.
    f. Compute the values of $F(250)$, $F(750)$, $F(-250)$ and $F(1250)$.

15. E and F are events which are subsets of the same sample space. If $P(E) = \frac{1}{3}$, $P(E|F) = \frac{1}{2}$ and $P(F|E) = \frac{1}{4}$, find:

    a. $P(F)$
    b. $P(E \cup F)$.

16. E and F are independent events and subsets of the same sample space. If $P(E) = \frac{1}{4}$ and $P(F) = \frac{1}{3}$, find:

    a. $P(E \cap F)$
    b. $P(E \cup F)$
    c. $P(E|F)$
    d. $P(F|E)$.

17. Three A-7s, A, B and C, are sent to bomb a certain target. Each plane is to drop one bomb. The probabilities of a plane's bomb hitting the target are $\frac{1}{2}$, $\frac{1}{3}$ and $\frac{1}{4}$ for planes A, B and C, respectively. Assuming independence, find the probability that:

    a. Bombs from all three of the planes hit the target.
    b. Bombs from exactly two of the planes hit the target.
    c. The target is hit at least once.
    d. The bomb from plane B hits the target, given that the bomb from plane A hits the target.

18. Two cards are dealt (without replacement) from an ordinary bridge deck. Find the probability that the:

    a. First card is *black*.
    b. Second card is *black*, given that the first one is *black*.
    c. Second card is *black*, given that the first card is *red*.
    d. Second card is *black*.

19. A man tosses a coin four times. Assuming that the events associated with each toss are independent, find the probability that:

    a. The tosses show alternately *heads* and *tails*.
    b. Exactly two of the tosses show *heads*.

20. An experiment consists of tossing a coin twice. Let X be the random variable whose value, after two tosses, is the number of *tails* that show on the two tosses.

    Find:
    a. $P(X = 0)$
    b. $P(X = 1)$
    c. $P(X = 2)$.

21. Given the following probability function:

$$p(x) = \begin{cases} \dfrac{x^2 + 7x + 1}{29}, & x = 0, 1, 2 \\ \\ 0, & \text{elsewhere.} \end{cases}$$

Find:
a. $P(X = 1)$
b. $P(X > 0)$.

22. Given the following density function:

$$f(x) = \begin{cases} 1/8, & 0 \le x \le 8 \\ 0, & \text{elsewhere.} \end{cases}$$

Find:
a. $P(3 \le X \le 5)$
b. $P(4 \le X \le 8)$
c. $P(4 \le X \le 5)$.

23. Given the following density function:

$$f(x) = \begin{cases} \dfrac{3x^2}{26}, & 1 \le x \le 3 \\ \\ 0, & \text{elsewhere.} \end{cases}$$

Find:
a. $F(x)$
b. $P(X < 2)$
c. $P(X > 2)$.

24. Given that X is a random variable with the following associated possibilities:

$$P(1) = \tfrac{1}{4}$$
$$P(2) = \tfrac{1}{2}$$
$$P(3) = \tfrac{1}{4}$$
$$P(X \ne 1,2,3) = 0.$$

Find:
a. $E(X)$
b. $E(X^2)$
c. $E(3X)$
d. Variance (X).

25. Given the following relationships:

$$E(X) = 2 \text{ and } E(X^2) = 7.$$

Find:
a. Variance (X)
b. $E(3X)$

   c. $E(3X + 1)$

   d. Variance $(3X + 1)$.

26. If X is a binomial random variable with $n = 4$ and $p = \frac{1}{3}$, find:

   a. $P(X = 3)$

   b. $P(X > 2)$

   c. $P(X > 0)$.

27. An ordinary die is thrown nine times. If the top face shows five or six spots, a success occurs. Find the probability of exactly three successes.

28. A coin is tossed five times. Find the probability that it shows heads:

   a. Twice.

   b. At least twice.

   c. More than twice.

29. If three ordinary dice are thrown simultaneously, the probability that the sum of the spots on the three dice is four is 1/72. If this experiment is repeated 144 times, find the approximate probability that the sum of the spots on the dice is four:

   a. One time.

   b. At least one time.

30. An ordinary deck of 52 cards is shuffled, and a card is removed from the deck and placed face down. A guess is made as to what card was removed, the results of the guess checked and the card replaced in the deck. Let this procedure be repeated 104 times.

   Find the probability of:

   a. Two correct guesses.

   b. At least two correct guesses.

31. Given: T is a standardized normal random variable. Find:

   a. $P(T < 1.20)$

   b. $P(T > 2.70)$

   c. $P(1.4 < T < 2.4)$

   d. $P(T > -1)$

   e. $P(-1.2 < T < -1.1)$

   f. $P(-.80 < T < .80)$

   g. $P(-.80 < T < 1.2)$.

32. Given: T is a standardized normal random variable. Find z so that each of the following probability statements is true:

   a. $P(T < z) = .964$

   b. $P(T > z) = .05$.

33. Given: X is $N(4,9)$, find:

   a. $P(X < 7)$

   b. $P(X > 2.5)$

   c. $P(-.5 < X < 4.3)$.

34. Suppose that the lifetime of electronic tubes is a normally distributed random variable. Suppose further that brand A has a lifetime X which is $N(30$ *hours*, 36 *hours*$^2)$, while brand B has a lifetime Y which is $N(34$ *hours*, 9 *hours*$^2)$. Of these two brands, which would you choose for use in an experimental aircraft with:

    a. 34 hours mission time?
    b. 40 hours mission time?

35. A claim is made by suppliers of a medical test for a certain disease:

> If you have that disease, the test will show a positive reaction 95 percent of the time;
>
> If you do not have that disease, the test will show a negative reaction 95 percent of the time.

Assume that 0.005 of a population as a whole have the disease, and that the claim is correct. Determine how significant the test is; i.e., if a person randomly chosen from the population gets a positive reaction, determine the new probability that he has the disease.

PROBLEM ANSWERS

(*Note: Some problem answers are not given.*)

Chapter One
No problems.

Chapter Two
2. a. 15 combinations of x and y b. 15 combinations of h_1 and h_2
   c. 25 combinations of r_1 and r_2 (therefore, there are $15 \times 15 \times 25 = 5{,}625$ ways)
4. (1) b   (2) d   (3) c   (4) c   (5) a   (6) d   (7) b   (8) a
6. a. $nk_1k_2(1 - s_2) - n_c - nk_1(1 - k_2)(1 - s_1)$ b. -4
   c. zero, -1.2
   d. Savings in lives of over five ship crews. More effective use of dollars elsewhere. Effect of the action on enemy's mode of operation, etc.
   e. 50 percent to over 53.4 percent.
   f. yes, i.e., 5 percent over what *time?*
7.

Search plan \ Sea state	Enemy tactic number one			Enemy tactic number two		
	0,1	2,3	4+	0,1	2,3	4+
1	.9	.4	.1	.5		
2	.7	.5	.4	.6	(etc.)	
3	.8	.7	.2	.3		
4	.5	.5	.5	.4		

Chapter Three
1. a. S2   b. S2   c. S2   d. at least 3/5
2. a. risk   b. S2
3. a. S2   b. S1   c. S2   d. S3
4. a.

		R1 Attack A	R2 Attack B
B1:	Defend A	0	-3
B2:	Defend B	-1	0

		R1 Attack A	R2 Attack B
B1:	Defend A	4	1
B2:	Defend B	3	4

   b. Number of units gained or number of units retained
   c. B2
5. a. (1) Z (2) W b. three dollars
6. a. saddle point; Blue $(1, 0, 0)$, Red $(0, 1, 0)$; $v = 0$
   b. saddle point; Blue $(0, 1, 0, 0)$, Red $(0, 1, 0)$; $v = -3$
   c. saddle point; Blue $(0, 0, 1, 0, 0)$, Red $(0, 0, 0, 1, 0)$; $v = 3$
7. a. Blue $(1/3, 2/3)$, Red $(1/3, 2/3)$; $v = 8/3$
   b. Blue $(6/13, 7/13)$, Red $(3/13, 10/13)$; $v = 70/13$
   c. Blue $(0, 2/5, 0, 0, 3/5)$, Red $(0, 0, 1/5, 0, 0, 4/5)$; $v = 22/5$
   d. Blue $(8/17, 9/17)$, Red $(10/17, 7/17)$; $v = 5/17$
   e. Blue $(6/13, 7/13)$, Red $(3/13, 10/13)$; $v = 3/26$
8. a. $S2$ b. $(1/4, 3/4)$ c. utilize a random device to yield Blue 1:1/4 the time, and Blue 2:3/4 the time
9. a.

		R1 2A, 0B	R2 1A, 1B	R3 0A, 2B
B1:	3A 0B	2	-1	-2
B2:	2A 1B	0	1	-3
B3:	1A 2B	-2	1	0
B4:	0A 3B	-1	0	2

   b. at least -1 with $B4$ c. at most $+1$ with $R2$ d. $-1 \leq v \leq 1$
11. yes; $v = -1/24$
12. yes; $v = 6\,3/4$
13. a. $R1$: attack lead (aircraft) on both attacks, unless lead (aircraft) is destroyed on first attack)

*R*2: attack lead on first attack and follower on second attack

*R*3: attack follower on first and lead on second

*R*4: attack follower on both attacks unless follower is destroyed on first attack

b.

	R1	R2	R3	R4
B1: Bomb in leader	.36	.6	.6	.72
B2: Bomb in follower	.72	.3	.3	.09

14. a. yes; $v = 2$ b. no; $v = 2$
15. a. no   b. yes ($R2$ eliminated)   c. no
16. a. up to .4; use $B2$ b. zero; use $B1$ c. up to .12; use optimal mixed.
    d. at least .3 if Red uses a mixed strategy while at least .9 if Red uses a pure strategy

Chapter Four

1. a.

n	g_n	p(n)	F(n)
1	.1	.1	.1
2	.2	.18	.28
3	.5	.36	.64
4	.4	.144	.784
5	.3	.0648	.849
6	.2	.0296	.878
7	0	0	.878

   b. .878   c. No, since $F(\infty) \neq 1$
2. a. $p(1) = 7/63$ $p(2) = 14/63$ $p(3) = 18/63$ $p(4) = 16/63$ $p(5) = 8/63$
   b. $F(1) = 7/63$ $F(2) = 21/63$ $F(3) = 39/63$ $F(4) = 55/63$ $F(5) = 1$
   c. yes   d. 3.06
3. a. $p(1) = .2$ b. Graph $F(1) = .2$
      $p(2) = .16$ $F(2) = .36$
      $p(3) = .128$ $F(3) = .488$
      $p(4) = .1024$ $F(4) = .5904$
      $p(5) = .0819$ $F(5) = .6723$
   c. .36
   d. It is compound probability involving no detection on the first $(n - 1)$ glimpses, then detection.
   e. .2   f. five
4. a. Detection of incoming enemy missiles before missile closes to a range of 100 N.mi.
   b. $F(n)$ c. $F(n) = .82$ for radar on slow
                    $F(n) = .77$ for radar on fast
                    Therefore, slow radar is apparently best.

5. a. g constant   b. D_2 and D_3 independent
   (1) no   no
   (2) yes   no
   (3) no   no
6. $1 - (1 - g)^{nN}$
9. a. .18   b. .08   c. 1.5   d. 10 minutes
10. $\pi/2$
11. a. 100 minutes   b. 160 minutes   c. .63
12. a. $\dfrac{40}{(2 - 10t)^3}$ b. .78

13. a. $r = 200 - 400t$ b. $\gamma(t) = \dfrac{1000}{200 - 400t}$ c. .83

   d. $\dfrac{1000}{200 - 400t} e^{-\int_0^t \frac{1000}{200 - 400t} dt}, \quad 0 \le t \le 1/2$ e. $\int_0^{0.5} t \cdot f(t)\, dt$

   $\qquad\qquad 0 \qquad\qquad\qquad , \quad$ otherwise
   f. $E(T^2) - [E(T)]^2$ g. 142.8 N.mi.
14. Device II is the better.
17. $\gamma(t)\, dt$
18. 2.5 to 3.5 Hz at 0.5 inch

Chapter Five
1. a. .786 foot   b. 1,200 watts   c. 16.7 pulses per scan
   d. 161.5 N.mi.   e. 49.1 square feet
2. a. 17.3 statute mi.   b. 26 N.mi.
   c. 3.9 minutes   d. 8.4 N.mi.
3. 2,870 feet (first reinforced zone), 8,600 feet (second reinforced zone), 14,350 feet (third reinforced zone)
4. a. 6.32 square yards   b. .245 watt
   c. 6.47×10^{-11} watt   d. 31.8 N.mi.
5. one (unity)
6. a. 250   b. 333
   c. No, the variable, x, varies too much from its mean value.
7. a. 30 scans per range interval
   b. (See table at top of p. 361.)
   c. .060   d. .062
8. a. .90   b. .904   c. .0006   d. .0294
   e. yes; $\ln(1 - .0294) = -.0298 \approx -.0294$
9. a. $g_{\Delta r_j} = p_0 \psi^3_{\Delta r_j}$ b. $g_{\Delta r_j} = p_0(\tfrac{5}{2})\psi^2_{\Delta r_j}(1 - \psi_{\Delta r_j})^3$
10. a. $N(1, 40) = 20$ b. $N(1, 0) = 20$ c. 20 N.mi.
11. $\overline{P}(0) = .748$ $\overline{P}(10) = .722$ $\overline{P}(30) = .559$ $\overline{P}(50) = .380$
    $\overline{P}(70) = .222$ $\overline{P}(100) = .078$
12. a. 135,000 yards   b. 2,940 feet   c. 1,784 yards
13. .81 watt
14. a. $J =$ zero tons $B = 2$ tons   b. .778
15. a. $G = 427$ pounds $W = 213$ pounds   b. 4/27
19. 3.76, 4.65, 5.89, 6.85, 7.52, 7.92, 8.05

7.b.

j	$\psi_{\Delta r_j}$	$\psi^2_{\Delta r_j}$	$\Sigma\psi^2_{\Delta r_j}$	F(m)
1	3/30	9/900	9/900	.02
2	6/30	36/900	45/900	.08
3	8/30	64/900	109/900	.20
4	19/30	361/900	470/900	.60
5	21/30	441/900	911/900	.84
6	16/30	256/900	1167/900	.90
7	15/30	225/900	1392/900	.94
8	10/30	100/900	1492/900	.94
9	8/30	64/900	1556/900	.96
10	0	0	1556/900	.96

Chapter Six

1. a. 14.14 knots   b. 135 degrees true   c. one hour
2. a. .6   b. .3   c. .83   d. 60 N.mi.
3. a. .53   b. same (.3)   c. .67   d. same (60 N.mi.)
4. a. 60 N.mi.   b. .5   c. 90 N.mi.   d. .75   e. .5   f. .92
5. a. .27   b. .47   c. higher
6. .622
7. a. .144   b. .856   c. .036   d. .324
8. a. $N(A \cap \bar{D}) = \dfrac{100r_0}{R_m} - \dfrac{100}{R_m} \displaystyle\int_0^{r_0} \bar{P}(x)\,dx$ b. $N(B \cap D) = \dfrac{100}{R_m} \displaystyle\int_{r_0}^{R_m} \bar{P}(x)\,dx$

Chapter Seven

1. a. .03   b. .54   c. .46   d. .45
2. a. .17   b. .42 (assuming each aircraft proceeds independently)
   c. 13
3. a. 3,000 N.mi.   b. .63   c. too low   d. one
4. $1 - e^{-\frac{WL}{A}}$
5. a. .26   b. 40 hours   c. 13.3 hours
6. a. (1) .8   (2) .68   (3) .64   (4) .68   (5) .8   (6) $.0016x^2 - .032x + .8$
   b. yes   c. .693, no   d. .8   e. .683
7. a. .528   b. .653   c. 19 N.mi.
8. .136, .038, .180, .646

Chapter Eight

1. a. 144 degrees 36 minutes   b. .1785 hour   c. 2.892 hours
   d. retiring   e. (1) increase number of aircraft

(2) sweep D' instead of D

(3) increase aircraft speed

2. a. two aircraft   b. 12.65 hours

3. 1.44 hours   b. advancing   c. four   d. no, NPP = 1.37 hours

   e. $S = 16$, $N = 5$, $n = 3$ (requires relief after $N = 3$)

   $S = 16$, $N = 3$, $n = 5$ (requires relief after $N = 2$)

   f. three

4. a. 16 N.mi.   b. four

   c. $S = 13$ N.mi., $M = 47.5$ N.mi., $a = 5$ degrees 26 minutes

   d. .984

5. a. detect and photograph shipping (with assigned probability of 90 percent)

   b. number of aircraft hours flown for a two-week period

   c. 22.85 N.mi.   d. 14   e. two   h. minimum of part b.

6. a. 30.47 N.mi.   b. two

   c.

	n	N	S	P(det)
1	2	4	30	.91
2	4	2	30	.91
3	3	3	26.7	.94

7. a. $2N\left[\dfrac{nSv}{v+u} - \dfrac{Du}{\sqrt{v^2-u}}\right] - \dfrac{nSv}{v+u}$

   b. $\dfrac{\left\{\left[2N\left(\dfrac{vnS}{u+v} - \dfrac{uD}{\sqrt{v^2-u^2}}\right) - \dfrac{vnS}{u+v}\right]^2 + D_2{}^2\right\}^{1/2}}{v}$

   c. 1/2 of part a

8. linear (from Figure 8-7)

9. a. $2\dfrac{R}{D} - \dfrac{R^2}{D^2}, 2\dfrac{R}{D}$

   b. Case 2

   c. Includes the possibility of stationing where range overlaps a boundary.

10. a. $\dfrac{2R_u T_{\mathrm{dp}} + \pi R^2}{Du\left[2\dfrac{R}{v} + T_{\mathrm{dp}}\right]}$

   b. .28

Chapter Nine

1. a. .667 × 10^{-8} dyne/centimeter-second

   b. .667 × 10^{-12} dyne/centimeter-second

   c. zero db   d. −40 db   e. 10^4 f. 40 db   g. 40 db   h. same

2. 76 db

3. a. pressure (depth)   b. yes, .01815 yard/second per yard of depth

4. a. a straight horizontal line   b. a downward refraction
   c. remain in layer   d. will be refracted downward

5. $R_h = \dfrac{2D}{\tan \theta}$

6. 21.8 degrees

7. range increases, $a_{5kc} = .369$ db/kiloyard
   $a_{10kc} = 1.042$ db/kiloyard

8. a. 75 percent   b. -5 db

9. a. 83 db   b. 13,500 yards   c. 28.66 db

10. a. 200 db   b. 245 db
    c. $r_{20kcs} \approx 7,000$ yards $r_{10kcs} \approx 31,500$ yards
    d. FOM, independent of sea conditions

Chapter Ten

1. a. 1,500 yards   b. 1,950 yards
2. a. zero   b. .4   c. utilize patrol station
3. a. 3,500 yards   b. .64
4. $\pm 7.7°$, $\pm 3.15°$, 0.
5. a. 1/5   b. 2/5   c. .336   d. .392
   e. differences in relative speed
6. 4.6000, 4.6015, 4.6030, 4.6330, 4.6345
7. a. 2.33 ESR   b. .72   c. .915
   e. (1) No, it should be moved out.
      (2) fire from outside
   f. Screen can be moved further out, and still keep some average probability of
      detection.

8. $\left[\dfrac{A}{K(\sigma - 1)}\right]^{1/\sigma}\left[\dfrac{E(\sigma - 1)}{A + (\sigma - 1)A}\right]$

Chapter Eleven

1. a. .32   b. .31   c. .45
2. a. .3   b. .49

3. a. $S = \dfrac{RK^2 - \rho \cos \phi \pm \sqrt{\rho^2 \cos^2 \phi - 2\rho RK^2 \cos \phi + R^2K^2 + \rho^2K^2 - \rho^2}}{K^2 - 1}$

   b. $R = \dfrac{\rho}{K}$

4. $\displaystyle\int_{\sigma}^{200} .01(1 - .005r) \int_{-\pi/4}^{\pi/4}\left[1 - e^{-\left\{\frac{.02(r^2 - \rho^2)}{2(r - \rho \cos \phi)}\right\}}\right]\dfrac{4}{2\pi} d\phi\, dr$

Chapter Twelve

1. a. $P_s = 1 - \left(1 - \dfrac{2R}{S}\right)^{tm}$ b. $P_s = 1 - \left(1 - \dfrac{30}{600}\right)^{20} = .642$ c. 11 mines

2. a. .72   b. 21, 26 mines   c. increased to nearly 100 percent

3. a. .415   b. .396   c. no

Chapter Thirteen

1. a. 11 hours   b. .091 failure per hour
3. a. $R(10) = .4$ b. chance type of failure
    $R(20) = .16$ c. .0921
    $R(30) = .064$ d. 10.9 hours
    $R(40) = .026$ e. Chance type of failures cannot be prevented by replacement.
    $R(50) = .01$
4. a. .558   b. .442   c. lower on board ship
5. a. .0164   b. .0082
    c. (1) .181   (2) .181   (3) .181   (4) .051   (5) .03
    d. .01   e. .01
7. a. wear-out   b. Bulb A: $\bar{X} = 75\ \sigma = 12$
                     Bulb B: $\bar{X} = 85\ \sigma = 10$
    c. Bulb B, since it has a longer mean life and a smaller standard deviation.
    d. No, since the standard deviations are so close.
8. b. $R(t) = \int_t^\infty \dfrac{1}{\sigma\sqrt{2\pi}} e^{-\frac{(t-\mu)^2}{2\sigma^2}}\, dt$

    d. $\lambda(t) = \dfrac{f(t)}{1 - F(t)}$

9. a. kt b. $f(t) = kte^{-kt^2/2}\ 0 \le t$
                 $f(t) = 0 \qquad\quad t < 0$

    c. $1/2\sqrt{\dfrac{2\pi}{k}}$

10. a. 14.8 minutes   b. .0675 failure per minute   c. .87
    d. $r_t = .0005$
       $r_p = .0001$
11. a. .096   b. .21   c. .261   d. .51
12. a. .90   b. two missiles   c. three missiles
13.

	R(1)	R(24)
Single radar	.92	.13
Single radar with improved failure rate	.96	.37
Two radars in redundancy	.99	.25

14. a. .53   b. .927; therefore, replace now.

15. a. $E(T) = \dfrac{1}{\lambda_A} + \dfrac{1}{\lambda_B} - \dfrac{1}{\lambda_A + \lambda_B}$ b. no

16. a. 200 barrels each 5 days   b. same

Chapter Fourteen
1. a. 327 type A, 982 type B b. 556.30 dollars
2. five type A, 10 type B b. .9983
3. zero type A, zero type B, nine type C
4. 18 model C per week
5. a. $L = 2.5$ b. $L \approx 11$ c. $L \to \infty$
11. 133.3 yards fore and aft, 140 yards either side

Appendix I
1. $f(x) = 3/4(2x - x^2)$, $0 \le x \le 2$
   $\quad = 0$,   elsewhere
   $F(x) = 1/4(3x^2 - x^3)$, $0 \le x \le 2$
   $\quad\quad = 0$, $x < 0$
   $\quad\quad = 1$, $x > 2$

2. a. $f(\alpha) = \dfrac{\cos \alpha}{2}$, $-\pi/2 \le \alpha \le \pi/2$

   $\quad\quad = 0$,   elsewhere
   is a probability density function since

   b. (1) $0 \le \dfrac{\cos \alpha}{2} \le 1$, $-\pi/2 \le \alpha \le \pi/2$

   (2) $\displaystyle\int_{-\pi/2}^{\pi/2} \dfrac{\cos \alpha}{2} = 1$

   c. P($D \mid 0 \le \alpha \le 45$ degrees) = .353
   d. P($D \mid -45$ degrees $\le \alpha \le 45$ degrees) = .706 which is less than a 30 percent reduction in probability.

3. a. $E(\alpha) = $ zero   b. $\text{Var}(\alpha) = \dfrac{\pi^2}{4} - 2$

4. a. .04   b. .0383   c. .956   d. .665

5. $\displaystyle\sum_{x=6}^{200} \binom{200}{x} (.02)^x (.98)^{200-x}$.

6. .76
7. a. (1) no   (2) no   (3) yes   (4) yes   (5) no   (6) no
   b. (1) no   (2) no   (3) no   (4) no   (5) no   (6) no
8. a. 8/15, 1/15, zero   b. no   c. yes
9. no
10. $751/7776 = .0966$
11. 215
12. $P(A) + P(B) + P(C) + P(D)$
    $-P(A \cap B) - P(A \cap C) - P(A \cap D) - P(B \cap C) - P(B \cap D)$
    $- P(C \cap D) + P(A \cap B \cap C) + P(A \cap B \cap D) + P(A \cap C \cap D)$
    $+ P(B \cap C \cap D) - P(A \cap B \cap C \cap D)$
13. Let zero denote an occurrence other than an ace

outcome	value of random variable x
$(0, 0)$	zero
$(0, 1)$	one
$(1, 0)$	one
$(1, 1)$	two

14. a. $f(x) = \dfrac{1}{1000}, \quad 0 \le x \le 1000$

   $= 0, \qquad$ elsewhere

   b. $E(x) = 500 \qquad$ c. $\sigma^2 = 83,400 \qquad \sigma = 295 \qquad$ d. rectangular

   e. $F(x) = \displaystyle\int_0^x \dfrac{1}{1000} \, dx = \dfrac{x}{1000}, \quad 0 \le x \le 1000$

   $\qquad = 0, \qquad\qquad x < 0$
   $\qquad = 1, \qquad\qquad x > 1000$

   f. $F(250) = .25 \qquad F(750) = .75 \qquad F(-250) = 0 \qquad F(1250) = 1$

15. a. 1/6   b. 5/12
16. a. 1/12   b. 1/2   c. 1/4   d. 1/3
17. a. 1/24   b. 1/4   c. 3/4   d. 1/3
18. a. 1/2   b. 25/51   c. 26/51   d. 1/2
19. a. 1/16   b. 3/8
20. a. 1/4   b. 1/2   c. 1/4
21. a. 9/29   b. 28/29
22. a. 1/4   b. 1/2   c. 1/8

23. a. $F(x) = \dfrac{x^3 - 1}{26}, \quad 1 \le x \le 3$

   $\qquad = 0, \qquad x < 1$
   $\qquad = 1, \qquad x > 3$

            b. 7/26   c. 19/26
24. a. two   b. 9/2   c. six   d. 1/2
25. a. three   b. six   c. seven   d. 27
26. a. 8/81   b. 1/9   c. 65/81
27. 0.273
28. a. 5/16   b. 13/16   c. 1/2
29. a. .2706   b. .8647
30. a. .2706   b. .5941
31. a. .885   b. .003   c. .073   d. .841   e. .021   f. .576
       g. .673
32. a. $z = 1.8$ b. $z = 1.64$
33. a. .841   b. .691   c. .4730
34. a. B b. A
35. .087

Index